Discourses on Immigration in Times of Economic Crisis: A Critical Perspective

Discourses on Immigration in Times of Economic Crisis: A Critical Perspective

Edited by

María Martínez Lirola

CAMBRIDGE SCHOLARS

PUBLISHING

Discourses on Immigration in Times of Economic Crisis:
A Critical Perspective,
Edited by María Martínez Lirola

This book first published 2013

Cambridge Scholars Publishing

12 Back Chapman Street, Newcastle upon Tyne, NE6 2XX, UK

British Library Cataloguing in Publication Data
A catalogue record for this book is available from the British Library

ISBN (10): 1-4438-4053-X, ISBN (13): 978-1-4438-4053-8

This book is peer-reviewed and places emphasis on theoretical and practical concerns in the discourses on immigration in times of economic crisis. The international advisory board is the following:

Advisory Board

TABLE OF CONTENTS

LIST OF ILLUSTRATIONS

LIST OF TABLES

FOREWORD

The press is generally regarded as a reliable source of information with the capacity to propagate ideologies, social conceptions and beliefs. In this regard, it seems evident that the social role of the press can by no means be underestimated: it can influence our knowledge, values and social codes through linguistic and other semiotic means, sometimes hidden under a euphemistic lexical disguise holding up a liberal and apparently respectful discourse.

The relationship between the press and society is a very complex one that requires careful conceptualisation so that it is possible to understand why texts in general and texts related to immigration in particular are created in the ways they are and not differently. The press offers access to all sorts of information and it also has the power to create or modify attitudes because each image and each linguistic component used to transmit a message is not predetermined or chosen at random. On the contrary, it is the result of a complex phenomena where the individual components may be selected systematically, reflecting the aims, purposes and motivations of the encoders/journalists.

The following book pays attention to the discursive and visual elements that are involved in reproducing ethnic and racial prejudices in contemporary press discourse. At present, the Western world is experiencing a period of economic crisis and there is no doubt that this affects the treatment of immigration, in which immigrants are usually represented as a "people-problem" and as a burden to society.

In this regard, the purpose of this book is to describe major aspects of discourse related to immigration in the present social context of economic crisis. More specifically, the main objectives of the book are the following:

- To approach the reality of immigration from diverse perspectives: discourse analysis, sociology, communication, anthropology, etc.
- To highlight the main aspects related to immigration in contemporary societies and in contemporary media discourse.
- To observe the ways in which the global economic crisis has affected the discourses on immigration.

- To analyse the main linguistic, visual and sociological characteristics of immigration in the press of different countries (Spain, United Kingdom, United States, Central Europe, etc.) in order to show to what extent the journalistic treatment of immigration contributes to racism and xenophobia within societies in general.
- To study the way in which female immigrants are represented in the press.
- To analyse political discourse related to immigration from a critical perspective.
- To answer the following research question: how are immigrants represented in the press? What is the purpose of the representation observed?
- To study the way in which journalists, as members of the main group, have power as well as how this power is involved in the process of drafting news on immigration.
- To make readers aware of the ways in which the texts on immigration are created and help readers to develop critical abilities in order to deconstruct the texts under analysis.

The main theoretical framework of this book is Critical Discourse Analysis (CDA) because it allows us to analyse texts from a critical perspective and thus to reveal forms of social inequality and discursive domination. This approach makes it possible to unmask unequal relationships, relationships of power and injustice in discourses related to immigration. Thus CDA allows the analysis of any social or political reality or problem. For this reason, it is also appropriate to analyse the discursive representation of immigration in the press within the present time of economic crisis and uncertainty.

Chapter 1, by María Martínez Lirola, analyses how the return of immigrants is portrayed in the press by paying attention to the visual and linguistic characteristics of the news items dealing with this topic in three newspapers: *El Mundo, Información,* and *Latino.* A comparison of how the return of immigrants is portrayed in the three newspapers will show that there are differences between the Spanish newspapers and *Latino*: immigrants' voices do not appear in the former, the photographs in the Spanish newspapers portray immigrants as idle, separated from Spanish people, etc. However, it is common to find immigrants' testimonies in *Latino,* together with photographs taken in their houses or in their countries of origin.

Chapter 2, by Jessica Retis, is part of a wider investigation that compares mainstream media representation of immigrant Latinas in the United States and Spain. This study seeks to remark the general trends based on previous investigations that took place in both countries. Incorporation of the transnational and genre perspectives helps us to understand the current status of women in the international immigration context of these two countries that are the main destinies of Latin American extra regional population flows. By analysing trends of diversity representation in the mainstream media, specifically in the portrayal of immigrants, the study seeks to examine which are the main topics in the news coverage and how these portraits are influencing public opinion. A comparison of how immigrant Latinas are portrayed in American and Spanish press will demonstrate that there are similarities in the representation of otherness: class, race and genre are, combined, constructing a triple discrimination in the public discourse.

Chapter 3, by Isabel Alonso Belmonte, Daniel Chornet Roses and Anne McCabe, has as its main purpose to identify and describe the ideological positions in user-generated online commentaries in the Spanish newspaper *El País*, and to shed light on the representations of immigrants within these ideological stances. With this purpose, the authors performed a critical discourse analysis of the 497 online comments that users posted at the end of a news article that reported a racist incident. The inductive analysis of the data yielded three ideological stances: (1) Some users acknowledged the incident published in the news article as racist; (2) some other users denied the incident as a racist one; and finally (3) some commentaries evidenced an unsettlingly ambivalent position vis-à-vis the incident. All three positions, but especially the Ambivalent ones and the Denials, operate within an ideological discursive formation of "whiteness" that articulates a particular type of racist discourse. These discursive practices, while generating ethnic (Spanish) group consensus, simultaneously discriminate black immigrants as burdens and problems to the Spanish economy in this time of crisis. Implications are discussed.

Taking Critical Discourse Analysis and Conceptual Metaphor Theory as theoretical paradigms, the main goal of chapter 4, by Eliecer Crespo Fernández, is to analyse the lexical elements used by journalists in order to characterize immigrants in the daily production of news and commentary. To this end, the author carries out a contrastive analysis of the X-phemistic (i.e. ortophemistic, euphemistic and dysphemistic) lexical units used to represent immigration and the figure of the immigrant in the current conservative Spanish and British electronic press, as X-phemism. Data have been drawn from two daily leading online newspapers: the Spanish

El Mundo and the British *The Daily Telegraph*, which are taken as representative examples of right-wing online press dealing with current political affairs and events in both countries.

Chapter 5, by Antonio M. Bañón Hernández, Samantha Requena Romero and María Eugenia González Cortés, makes an analysis of the discourses deeply rooted in the media in relation to migration processes and to immigrants to find whether the economic crisis has intensified the biased image offered of this collective in relation to information linked to health and education. To achieve this goal, a corpus of 50 pieces of news from newspapers, radio and television is analysed.

Chapter 6, by F. Javier García Castaños, Antonia Olmos Alcaraz and María Rubio Gómez, focuses on the way diversity is shown – in relation to foreign immigrant pupils at school – in public discourses (mass media, political and scholarly discourse). This chapter points out that these discourses are supporting an image of migratory phenomena at school that contribute to the differences between social groups. Firstly, there is a section which analyses the discourses that problematize the phenomenon of migration at school. Secondly, the chapter offers a reflection on the discourses that praise cultural diversity at school. Transversally in both parts the authors show the usual trend in identifying the concepts "*culture*" and "*nationality*", and the reductionist and essentialist consequences it has.

The objective of chapter 7, by Francisco Checa Olmos, Juan Carlos Checa Olmos and Ángeles Arjona Garrido is to understand the role played by political parties – through their party platforms – in shaping the migratory phenomenon and its related discourses. The authors analyze the messages put forward by the two main political parties of Spain (PSOE and PP) in the different general elections held in Spain between 2000 and 2011. Applying factorial analysis to the types of proposals written into each party platform, it is possible to understand the different electoral and ideological frameworks.

Chapter 8, by Jan Chovanec, analyses the discursive construction of immigrants and domestic minorities in news reports. It notes how the media represent immigrants and internal outsiders, such as the Roma, in opposition to the majority group. The dichotomy of contrasting the in-group and the out-group(s) is based on affective polarization, i.e. positive self-presentation and negative other-presentation, and is interpreted as a typical feature of intolerant and discriminatory discourse. Based on a series of news reports involving individuals from minority groups, the article documents how the Czech online media rely on underlying prejudices to cover crime-related events.

Chapter 9, by Nicolás Lorite, tries to answer the following question: How do the media affect how immigrants are integrated into the social and intercultural fabric of society in a time of financial crisis? To shed light on this question, this chapter adopts a multi-perspective, interdisciplinary approach, critically analyzing diverse data and examples collected by MIGRACOM. The results are particularly relevant in light of current, ongoing transformations in the media and society, especially since some countries, like Spain, have recently seen large numbers of immigrants. Given that much similar analysis is based on subjective judgments and ideological bias against the media, this paper's objective, scientific approach to the coverage of immigration and cultural diversity provides a key contribution to understanding how the media affect intercultural relationships.

Chapter 10, by Antolín Granados Martínez, F. Javier García Castaño, Nina Kressova, Lucía Chovancova and José Fernández Echeverría aims at providing some data and elements for analysis and consideration regarding institutional, judicial or other type of actions which clearly focus on constraining the emergence of ideologies and implementation of public policies built on specific behaviours, attitudes or rules that may provide the basis for social and/or cultural discrimination, especially against foreign persons or groups. Data analysis from opinion polls in Spain and other European countries show that there is a close relation between what the citizens think about immigration and immigrants, and their image in the media.

Chapter 11, by Gema Rubio Carbonero, aims at systematically analyzing Spanish political discourse on immigration between years 2010 and 2011. Thus, all the political speeches dealing with immigration in these two years produced in the Spanish parliament (*Pleno del Congreso de los Diputados*) by any political party are carefully studied in order to find out what attitudes and ideologies can be observed and, therefore are transmitted to Spanish population about immigration. The analysis shows that, as a result of the economic crisis, speeches on immigration are much less frequent and much less relevant that they used to be before the crisis started.

PROLOGUE

TEUN VAN DIJK
(POMPEU FABRA UNIVERSITY)

Racist ideology and attitudes are not innate but learned, and so are the social practices of discrimination based on them, together defining the social system of domination called 'racism'. Although some practices may be learned by experience, that is, by observation and participation, discriminatory practices presuppose shared social cognitions, such as prejudices, that can only be acquired, legitimated and socially reproduced by discourse. Hence the relevance of the study of text and talk as a crucial component in the study of the formation and reproduction of racism in society.

Some genres of discourse are more influential than others in the formation of shared ideologies and attitudes in society. Thus, most citizens have direct or indirect (via everyday conversations) access to public discourse of politicians, the mass media and education. The symbolic elites who control these forms of public discourse are therefore the primary definers of ethnic or racial prejudices and ideologies and responsible for their reproduction in society.

This present collection of articles edited by María Martínez Lirola presents evidence from Spain and some other countries that sustains this fundamental thesis about the role of public discourse in the reproduction of racism, especially by the mass media. Earlier research in many countries already had found that the mass media barely employ journalists from ethnic minorities, that reporting in a multi-ethnic society is hardly taught in journalism schools, and that news gathering routines selectively focus on information and opinions of elites sources of the 'white' ingroup, often ignoring expert minority voices. Together with widespread prejudices and stereotypes of dominant majority journalists, these conditions define the context that explains the systematic bias of news and opinion articles, programs and other discourses in the dominant mass media.

As also the papers in this volume show, this racist bias can be observed at all levels of text and talk, as predicted by the general principle of all ideological discourse, namely that positive information about ingroups is emphasized and negative information mitigated or ignored, whether the opposite is the case for information about outgroups: Negative information about *Them* tends to be emphasized and positive information ignored or mitigated.

If we apply this general ideological strategy to discourse we find at the level of topics or semantic macrostructures that negative topics about immigration and integration are dominant: *They* bring us problems, they are different and a threat to our borders, cities, neighborhoods, and labor market and do not want to adapt to *Our* language, religion or culture. Their contributions to our economy, culture and science are seldom acknowledged—beyond sport and entertainment. Stories on the many PhD candidates among the immigrants (and the problems of academic discrimination they face) do not fit the stereotype and hence are rare. On the other hand, stories on the *hijab* of some Muslim women may fill pages, because they confirm the stereotype of religious traditionalism and gender backwardness. On the other hand, *Our* prejudice, discrimination and racism are seldom explicit topics in dominant political, media or educational discourse—or attributed and limited to the Extreme Right (the outgroup within the ingroup), and never to Our own, mainstream institutions. On the contrary, *We* are modern, progressive and tolerant, whereas *They* are traditional, backward and intolerant. Thus, no dominant newspaper, on the left or at the right, will ever print a detailed story on racism in the press. Indeed, journalists carefully control and exclude the negative information about themselves—of course backed up or controlled by the media owners.

The same strategy may be observed in the use of metaphors (immigrants always arrive in *waves* and not simply by airplane), the lexicon (they are often called *illegal* if they don't get papers), quotations (their elite sources are little quoted), pictures (showing immigrants in stereotypical situations and occupations) and biased implications, presuppositions and person descriptions that locally detail the overall negative portrayal of immigrants and other minorities.

These and many other findings of earlier research are confirmed and further developed in the detailed studies in this important volume, bringing data—especially about Spain—that have hitherto not been known internationally and in English. María Martínez Lirola should be complimented for her efforts to invite major specialists on immigration discourse in Spain in one volume, which contributes to the critical study of public discourse as well as to our insight into immigration and racism.

The authors show how the discourse of politics and the media both express elite attitudes and ideologies on immigration as well as shape those of the public at large—which the elites in turn use as the 'democratic' legitimation of their own prejudices and policies. In other words, the elites, also in Spain—as well as in the UK, the USA and the Czech Republic—remain crucial part of the problem of racism, and as yet hardly part of the solution. Indeed, as shown elsewhere in Europe today, elite discourse in politics and the media increasingly yields to racist rhetoric portraying immigrants as a threat and as scapegoats of the economic crisis.

Teun A. van Dijk
Barcelona, June 2012

CHAPTER ONE

IMMIGRANTS GOING BACK HOME: AN ANALYSIS OF THE DISCURSIVE REPRESENTATION OF THE RETURN PLAN FOR IMMIGRANTS IN THREE SPANISH NEWSPAPERS

MARÍA MARTÍNEZ LIROLA
UNIVERSITY OF ALICANTE
UNIVERSITY OF SOUTH AFRICA (UNISA)

1. Introduction

This chapter intends to analyse the way the return of immigrants is portrayed in the press, in particular in three newspapers, two of which, *El Mundo* and *Información,* are published by Spaniards, and the third, *Latino,* by immigrants. *El Mundo* is one of the most popular newspapers in Spain and *Información* is the newspaper with the largest circulation in Alicante, the city with the third highest number of immigrants in Spain. *Latino* is the most popular newspaper among the Latin American community.

The way in which the return home of immigrants is portrayed has been studied in the social sciences (Conway and Potter, 2009; Christou, 2006; Long and Oxfeld, 2004) but specific attention has not been paid to its portrayal in the press. Therefore, this paper intends to explore this reality focusing on the linguistic and visual elements that create each item of news. In November 2008, the Spanish Government created a plan for the voluntary return of immigrants. This plan was intended to facilitate the return of immigrants who had lost their jobs as a result of the economic crisis. It allowed immigrants who wanted to return to their countries of origin to obtain 40% of the unemployment benefits they were entitled to before leaving Spain and the other 60% when they arrived home.

The decisions on how to portray the reality of migrations in the press show who communicates with whom and who has the power to present this reality in one way or another. In other words, the press has power over the population since it transmits facts and situations in the way it considers the most appropriate in order to achieve its objectives (to sell newspapers, to show that the main group in society -autochthonous population- is the one with the power, etc.) (Crespo and Martínez Lirola, 2012; Ferguson, 2007; Martínez Lirola, 2010; Moore, Gross and Threadgold, 2012).

Those who create multimodal texts on immigration belong to the majority group and they have the authority to present the items of news in one way instead of another in order to obtain a specific response from the reader. In Bañón's words (2002, 283): "The function of the media as transmitters of other discourses, as supporters of those discourses or as generators of discourses is crucial regarding the public treatment of immigration".[1]

This chapter will explore the relationships between the different linguistic and visual characteristics of the items of news analysed together with their meaning for and influence on the reader. The multimodal texts under analysis are produced and consumed in a socio-political context marked by an economic crisis in Spain. This, together with the fact that the news items published in the newspapers *Información* and *El Mundo* are produced by people belonging to the majority group (the Spanish population), implies that the return of immigrants is presented as positive for the immigrants concerned and as a very good measure taken by the Spanish Government, as the analysis will show. This contrasts with the news items in the newspaper *Latino*, produced by Latin American people. In other words, since it belongs to one of the minority groups, it shows the pros and cons of the return plan.

The chapter is organised as follows: section two deals with a description of the corpus of examples; section three concentrates on the presentation of the theoretical framework of this paper. Section four shows the main results of the analysis of multimodal texts dealing with immigrants' return in the three newspapers under study. The fifth section offers a comparison of the texts analysed in order to demonstrate that immigrants' return is presented differently in the newspaper produced by the Latino community. Section six concentrates on the discussion, where attention will be paid to the relationship between the media and racism. Finally, some conclusions are presented.

2. The Corpus of Examples

Three newspapers were selected for analysis in order to observe the discursive representation of the return of immigrants: *El Mundo*, one of the major newspapers in Spain, *Información*, the most widely read in Alicante, and *Latino*, the most popular newspaper among the Latino community in Alicante as well as in Madrid and Barcelona. These newspapers were selected because they are the most widely read in Alicante by both Spanish and Latin American people.

Data were collected daily from September 2008 to February 2011, that is, for two and a half years. As a result, 42 items of news dealing with immigrants' return were found in *Información,* and 49 in *El Mundo. Latino* has articles relating to the Latin community every day. Only copies of this newspaper from the beginning of June 2009 until February 2011 were analysed because no earlier editions were available in the virtual catalogue; only nine items of news dealt with immigrants' return.

Apart from paying attention to the main characteristics of visual grammar in the articles, it will also be seen that a positive image of return is created in the newspapers published by Spaniards. The above corpus was selected because the Spanish Government initiated a return plan in November 2008 in order to help unemployed immigrants to go back to their native countries and since then no studies on the portrayal of immigrants' return in the press have been done.

3. Theoretical Framework

The way ethnic attitudes are formulated in discourse has social repercussions because they show the relationship between the main group and the minority group and exhibit the social tendencies that carry power and dominance of one group over the other. In order to deconstruct how the items of news on immigrants' return are created, Critical Discourse Analysis (CDA) was chosen as the theoretical framework. CDA is concerned with power structures, inequality, and how discourse constructs the supremacy of white elites over minorities.

The intention of CDA as a perspective of analysis is to provide social criticism by observing structures of domination and inequality in society; it also observes how power is reproduced and maintained in any context (Fairclough, 1995; van Dijk, 1987, 1993, 2007, 2008; van Leeuwen, 2005, 2009). In order to do so, linguistics is applied in a domain of social, economic and political context, i.e., it studies the relationships between discourse and social power. In van Leeuwen's words (2009, 277):

> "Critical Discourse Analysis (CDA) is based on the idea that text and talk play a key role in maintaining and legitimizing inequality, injustice and oppression in society. It uses discourse analytical methods to show how this is done, but without restricting itself to one particular discourse analytical approach".

This quotation makes clear the suitability of CDA for studying immigration, a situation in which discrimination and unequal power relations can be clearly observed. CDA concentrates on text analysis in order to deconstruct the meanings included in each text and to understand the social context in which those texts are framed. In this sense, texts are understood as discourse with a social purpose and create their meaning through different linguistic and visual choices.

The fact that texts have more than one mode of communication - the linguistic (language) and the visual (photographs, diagrams, etc.) - makes it necessary to talk about multimodal communication. This is characterized by a combination of different semiotic resources to express meaning (Baldry and Thibault, 2006; Jewitt, 2009; Kress, 2003; Kress and van Leeuwen, 2001; Kress and van Leeuwen, 2006; O'Toole, 1994). Visual grammar (Kress and van Leeuwen, 2006) is a crucial theoretical framework for the analysis of multimodal texts. Their authors pay attention to 'information value', i.e., to the value the different elements of the composition have depending on where they are located; 'salience' concentrates on the most outstanding element of the composition, and finally 'framing' pays attention to the presence or absence of frames in the multimodal text indicating whether elements are connected or not.

For a multimodal text to be well created, first, the different elements that compose the text (verbal and non-verbal) should be complementary, i.e., images should be connected with the context that frames the text. Secondly, everything that is part of the multimodal text (vocabulary and structures used, type of letters, place in which the image appears, etc.) should contribute to the creation of the meaning of the text and, consequently, the combination of all the different visual and linguistic choices should influence the reader.

The way in which the meaning of these texts is decoded depends not only on what readers bring to the texts but also on what the authors put in them. In this sense, images are essential to persuade the reader to accept a particular image of immigrants. As Borchers (2002, 165) makes clear: "Like words, images are symbols that are building blocks of persuasive messages. Images communicate in ways that words cannot".

Analysing the way in which language and images are organized in the multimodal texts studied in this paper shows that these meanings are influenced by the socio-cultural context in which they are exchanged because their objective is to transmit a specific image of immigrants, which is normally based on presenting them as inferior to the rest of the population (Baldry and Thibault, 2006; Martínez Lirola, 2006, 2008; Reisigl and Wodak, 2001). These meanings are created when choosing between the different possibilities that language offers, which implies taking into consideration that language is always a semiotic process and that each choice has an influence in the creation of meaning (Halliday, 1978).

4. Results

4.1 General Description of Immigrants' Return in the Press

This section will concentrate on the main characteristics found in the multimodal texts dealing with the return of immigrants found in the corpus of examples in the three newspapers analysed.

Almost half of the news items in *El Mundo* (40.81%) and *Información* (45.23%) include a photograph. Photographs of immigrants appear in 18.75% of the articles in *El Mundo* and in 31.57% of those in *Información*. They appear as a group, not looking at the camera, idle and wearing dirty or casual clothes. Moreover, immigrants are portrayed and described as vulnerable and dependent. On the other hand, 26.31% of the articles analysed in *Información* and 68.75% of those in *El Mundo* include photographs of politicians, who are always well-dressed. In addition, members of NGOs appear in photographs in 6.25% of the articles in *El Mundo* and 15.78% of those in *Información*; they are clean and are wearing casual clothes. Moreover, in 26.31% of the articles in *Información* there are photographs of people at the airport or outside the INEM (National Institute of Employment) offices but it is not clear whether or not they are immigrants. The same occurs in 6.25% of the news items analysed in *El Mundo*.

Immigrants' names are never mentioned, i.e., their vision and experience of returning home is not taken into consideration. On the other hand, these newspapers pay attention to the number and nationality of people who have taken advantage of the return plan and highlight that Colombia, Ecuador and Argentina are the countries to which the greatest number of people are returning. These newspapers also highlight the amount of money that the Government is investing in the plan. The majority of the items of news on immigrants' return in these newspapers present the plan as something positive and only 7.1% criticise some of the aspects of this plan.

Latino's news items are concerned with the reality of Latin American immigrants in Spain: how they celebrate their feast days, information on the importance of education to improve their situation, what they do in their free time, sports, information on the laws affecting immigrants, etc. Although there are not many news items on the return plan, all of them cover the top part of the page or the whole page and all include photographs.

It is common to find the names and surnames of immigrants in the news items on return in *Latino*, i.e., they are based on the real stories of people who have been living and working in Spain and have decided to take advantage of the return plan. For this reason, these people know the plan well and their testimony is based on their personal experience.

The news items on return published in *Latino* concentrate on the experience of immigrants leaving Spain and when arriving in their countries of origin. *Latino* highlights that only 0.39% of immigrants have taken advantage of the return plan because to go back is expensive and because the situation in their countries of origin means finding a job is not easy. Moreover, *Latino* criticises the Government and the fact that there is no money to pay for the plane tickets. This implies that there is no money to help immigrants integrate in their counties of origin or to implement the process of returning home.

4.2 Text Analysis

The photograph in this news item (see figure 1-1) is small and appears on the right, the place where the most important information is found. The frame is not striking and new information appears on the right of the image, where the Minister is pictured. Corbacho appears in the foreground and appears to be concentrated on his speech as he is looking at the other politicians in Parliament but not at the camera. Only his head and shoulders appear in the photograph. The middle ground and the background situate the Minister in his context of situation: there is another politician sitting down in the middle ground but the figure is blurred and consequently cannot be properly distinguished; in the background there is the Parliament building, where there seems to be a door but it is also blurred.

elmundo.es

Portada > **España**

EL MINISTRO DE TRABAJO INCIDE EN SU CARÁCTER VOLUNTARIO

El Congreso avala el plan del Gobierno para favorecer el retorno de inmigrantes en paro

- **El decreto ha sido respaldado mayoritariamente por los grupos, excepto por el PP e IU**
- **Para el PP no resuelve 'los problemas, como la entrada masiva de los inmigrantes'**
- **Para IU es 'un mal mensaje' para los españoles e 'ingrato' para los inmigrantes**
- **Es aplicable en los 19 países con los que España tiene convenios en Seguridad Social**

Actualizado jueves 02/10/2008 12:14 (CET)

EFE

El ministro de Trabajo, Celestino Corbacho, interviene desde la tribuna del Congreso. (Foto: EFE)

MADRID.- El Congreso ha convalidado el Real Decreto del Gobierno sobre el **abono acumulado y de forma anticipada** de la prestación por desempleo a trabajadores no comunitarios que retornen voluntariamente a sus países de origen.

Durante la presentación de esta iniciativa en el Parlamento, el ministro de Trabajo e Inmigración, Celestino Corbacho, ha asegurado que se trata de una medida coherente con el ordenamiento jurídico, que no es improvisada y que pretende dotar al mercado laboral de **un instrumento para la gestión de los flujos migratorios.**

Corbacho ha recordado su **carácter voluntario** y ha insistido en que su objetivo "no es rechazar la presencia de desempleados extranjeros" en España. "Pueden quedarse en España con derecho a desempleo y buscar un nuevo trabajo o regresar a su país con el incentivo del cobro acumulado de esa prestación", ha explicado el ministro.

Corbacho ha defendido la extraordinaria y urgente necesidad de esta medida "por las dificultades de nuestra economía en un contexto de crisis de la economía mundial" y por el **elevado nivel de desempleo de este colectivo, con tasas del 16%.**

El decreto ha sido respaldado mayoritariamente por los grupos, **excepto por el PP e IU-ICV**, que no le han dado su voto afirmativo. Para el diputado del PP, Rafael Hernando, las medidas anunciadas por Gobierno se han quedado en un "mini decretín", que **no resuelve "los problemas, como la entrada masiva de los inmigrantes"**. Según Hernando, Corbacho habla mucho y hace poco y "se le va la fuerza por la boca" y "mientras sigue con los brazos cruzados, el desempleo sigue creciendo".

También ha mostrado su desacuerdo, Gaspar Llamazares de IU porque duda de su eficacia y conveniencia y ha calificado el decreto como una "legislación simbólica" y una "medida populista". "No es urgente, no es útil y **es un mal mensaje" para los españoles e**

"ingrato" para los ciudadanos de los países de origen de los trabajadores desempleados.

La diputada del PSOE Concepción Gutiérrez del Castillo ha destacado el carácter voluntario y ha opinado que es una oportunidad al inmigrante que se queda sin empleo. Desde CiU, Carles Campuzano ha prestado su apoyo a cualquier medida "que tienda a **aliviar a cualquier persona desempleada**" y ha opinado que el decreto del Gobierno "se topa con la realidad y actúa en consecuencia".

Emilio Olabarria, del PNV, ha dicho que "no sabe si es la mejor solución, pero **las razones que invoca son razonables**" y Olaia Fernández, del BNG, ha incidido en que debe ser una opción para los trabajadores desempleados, a los que debe ofrecerse "una buena información". Por su parte, Ana Oramas, de Coalición Canaria, ha opinado que la iniciativa del Gobierno es necesaria y le ha animado a que adopte otras medidas, como la de **favorecer la movilidad de los trabajadores entre comunidades**.

El Plan del Gobierno permitirá a los inmigrantes desempleados percibir la prestación en dos plazos: **el 40% en España, una vez reconocido el derecho, y el 60% en el país de origen**, transcurridos 30 días naturales desde el primer pago.

La medida está destinada a trabajadores desempleados de los 19 países con los que España tiene firmados **convenios bilaterales en materia de Seguridad Social**, pero deja abierta la opción de negociar con otros países interesados si garantizan cierta cobertura sanitaria y social.

Portada > **España**

elmundo.es

Figure 1-1. Text 1. Date: 2 October 2008. Newspaper: *El Mundo.*

Corbacho is wearing smart clothes: a navy blue jacket, a blue shirt and red and white tie. His hands rest on the papers where he has his written speech. There is a vector between his hands, the pieces of papers on the platform and the microphones, and another one from the microphones to his mouth as a way of emphasizing the importance of his speech on the return plan and that he as the Minister of Labour is the person who has promoted it.

The caption is: *El ministro de Trabajo, Celestino Corbacho, interviene desde la tribuna del Congreso* (The Minister of Labour, Celestino Corbacho, speaks in Parliament). This caption, together with the image already analysed gives importance to Corbacho's speech on the return plan. In this way it is highlighted that he is the person responsible for the return plan. Needless to say, he belongs to the white elite and as a politician is in a position of power.

The headline is: *El Congreso avala el plan del Gobierno para favorecer el retorno de inmigrantes en paro* (Parliament backs the Government's plan to foment the return of unemployed immigrants). Apart from using the word immigrants, which is normally associated with poverty, discrimination and other negative ideas, the headline highlights the fact that they do not have a job. This can be considered an example of dysphemism because it highlights some of their negative characteristics: being unemployed implies that they are idle, that they are not productive, that they do not have any money, that they could steal, etc.

The subheadlines are: - *El decreto ha sido respaldado mayoritariamente por los grupos, excepto por el PP e IU* (The decree has been backed by the majority of the groups except PP and IU).

- *Para el PP no resuelve 'los problemas, como la entrada masiva de los inmigrantes'* (For the PP (this measure) does not solve problems such as the massive arrival of immigrants).

- *Para IU es 'un mal mensaje' para los españoles e 'ingrato' para los inmigrantes* (For IU (this measure) sends out 'a bad message' for Spaniards and 'an unpleasant one' for immigrants).

- *Es aplicable en los 19 países con los que España tiene convenios en Seguridad Social* ((This measure) is applicable in the 19 countries with which Spain has social security agreements).

These subheadlines make explicit some of the reasons why two political parties have not lent their support to the return plan. The second subheadline has a very negative effect on readers because the arrival of immigrants is considered a problem instead of the right of any human being. Moreover, referring to this arrival as massive has the purpose of frightening readers since it seems that immigrants will take over all our territory. In this case, the subheadline aggravates the negative situation of immigrants.

Apart from the word immigrants, full of negative connotations, in the headline, subheadline and body of the article, there are other terms used in the article such as: *trabajadores no comunitarios* (workers who do not belong to the European Community), *desempleados extranjeros* (unemployed foreigners) and *trabajadores desempleados* (unemployed workers). They can be considered, at least in theory, more positive that the noun immigrants; these words are euphemistic because calling them workers implies that they are capable of earning money and doing a productive activity, even if they are unemployed at the moment. The use of the word foreigners is more neutral and means that immigrants could be assigned the same lexical label as other foreigners, say English residents in Spain, for instance, because the latter are not so closely associated with poverty and discrimination as are the majority of immigrants. These terms minimize the association of the word immigrants with poverty and illegality.

In addition, the noun phrase *inmigrantes desempleados* (unemployed immigrants) is also present in this news item and may be considered dysphemistic because apart from the negative connotations of the word immigrants, it is premodified by the adjective *desempleados* (unemployed), which implies that they are not active in society and therefore this adjective does not favour their social integration. Despite the use of euphemistic vocabulary to refer to immigrants who are out of work, the journalist tries to attract the reader's attention to the dramatic situation of unemployment among immigrants.

The image in the following news item (see figure 1-2) is medium sized and appears on the right side of the page, which is the place where the most important information is found. New information appears in the whole image, which can be considered the most important element of the multimodal text. The frame is not strong and there are just three people in the image. They are walking along the street and there is nothing of particular interest in the image so the attention is focused on these people. There is a person (it is not clear if it is a woman or a man) and a child in the foreground and a woman in the background. The child appears in the most prominent position since he is on the right. He faces the woman in the background, who is also on the right. The child is wearing white trousers and a black and yellow jacket. The person holding his hand is wearing blue jeans and also a blue shirt. The woman in the background is wearing a blue jacket and her trousers seem to be brown. The colours of their clothes are not very striking and their clothes are clean.

However, showing two people with their backs to the reader does not favour immigrants' integration in society; they seem to be ashamed of facing difficulties and having to take advantage of the return plan. They are portrayed as clearly separated from the readers because with their backs turned there is no possibility of interaction with the reader. In this case, readers assume an active role and it is obvious that they do not face the same situation as the immigrants in the photograph. Moreover, although the woman in the background is facing the reader, her face is blurred and cannot be properly distinguished. Therefore, we are not sure if she is looking nowhere or at the adult in the foreground, which does not favour interaction either.

elmundo.es

Portada > **Baleares**

A CAUSA DE LA CRISIS

Se duplican las peticiones de inmigrantes de retorno voluntario en un año

- **El programa ofrece ayudas económicas y burocráticas**
- **En lo que va de año han viajado de regreso 65 extranjeros residentes en Baleares**

Actualizado sábado 20/12/2008 12:50 (CET)

EFE

PALMA.- El programa de retorno voluntario de inmigrantes extracomunitarios que ofrece el departamento de Inclusión Social de Cruz Roja en Baleares ha recibido 319 solicitudes en lo que va de año, cifra que supone **un incremento del 111,25%**, más del doble, que las registradas en todo 2007.

Los inmigrantes son los más afectados por la crisis (Foto: Catí Cladera).

En concreto, este programa de ayuda a los inmigrantes que desean regresar voluntariamente a sus respectivos países de origen y carecen de recursos económicos para costearse el pago del pasaje, gestionó 151 solicitudes en 2007 en las islas, y hasta el 12 de noviembre de este año ha cursado 319 peticiones de once nacionalidades distintas.

En 2007 regresaron a sus países de origen gracias a este programa 19 personas que residían en Baleares, y en lo que va de 2008 ya han viajado de regreso 65, incremento que se sitúa en el 242%.

El aumento de solicitudes registrado en Baleares es superior al experimentado por este programa de Cruz Roja en el ámbito nacional.

En toda España Cruz Roja recibió 387 solicitudes de retorno voluntario en los tres primeros trimestres de 2007, y este año ha registrado 566 en el mismo período, cifras que implican un aumento del 46,25 por ciento. Hasta el 12 de noviembre, las peticiones en toda España han sumado 790, con un aumento del 104,1 por ciento.

El director autonómico de Inclusión Social de la organización, Marcelo Unamuno, ha destacado que **la población inmigrante "es tremendamente vulnerable en una situación de crisis económica**".

"Son los primeros que la padecen por la elevación de las tasas de desempleo, porque el estallido de la llamada 'burbuja inmobiliaria' y la consiguiente caída del sector de la construcción les ha afectado en mayor medida que al resto de la población", ha detallado.

Los datos del Ministerio de Trabajo corroboran las palabras de Unamuno, ya que si **la tasa de paro a nivel nacional ha aumentado en 2,4 puntos**, al pasar del 8 por ciento en el primer trimestre de 2007 al 10,4% en el mismo período de 2008; en el caso de los inmigrantes ha pasado del 12,3% al 17%, con un aumento de 4,7 puntos.

Según Unamuno, Cruz Roja estima que la demanda sea creciente en los próximos meses: "Prevemos que el próximo año este proyecto tendrá un incremento notable".

Por nacionalidades, **la mayoría de las solicitudes han sido de bolivianos, seguido de argentinos, brasileños y hondureños.**

Unamuno ha destacado sin embargo que en todo el ámbito nacional solo cuatro solicitudes, de las 790 totales, procedían de inmigrantes de alguna nacionalidad africana.

En su opinión, la razón es que "los inmigrantes del África subsahariana con el elemento visible de un proyecto migratorio familiar y **la presión que reciben para no regresar es muy superior** a la de aquellos para quienes la migración ha sido un proyecto personal".

El proyecto de retorno voluntario de Cruz Roja lo financia la Dirección General de Integración de los Inmigrantes del Ministerio de Trabajo e Inmigración y pueden acogerse a él los **extranjeros no comunitarios que acrediten haber residido en España durante al menos 6 meses.**

También se concede a inmigrantes rumanos y búlgaros "siempre que concurran circunstancias especies de vulnerabilidad como pueda ser la trata de blancas o el tráfico de personas", ha explicado Unamuno.

Cruz Roja se hace cargo de los gastos de documentación, viaje y alojamiento y manutención en el traslado si fuera necesaria, así como de otros gastos imprevistos y concede una **ayuda de viaje de 50 euros por persona**, así como otra para la **reinstalación en el país de origen de 400, hasta un máximo de 1.600 euros por familia.**

Portada > **Baleares**

elmundo.es © 2012 Unidad Editorial Internet, S.L.

Figure 1-2. Text 2. Date: 20 December 2008. Newspaper: *El Mundo.*

There are different vectors that connect the three people in the photograph. For example, there is one between the child's right hand, his left hand and the adult holding his hand. In this way, it is clear that there is a close relationship between the two. In addition, there are vectors between these two and the woman in the background because there is a vector between the heads of the two adults pictured; moreover, the shoulder of the person in the foreground is touching the shoulder of the woman in the background. These vectors have the purpose of joining the different participants as a way of pointing out that they are experiencing the same social situation and belong to the same group. The caption is: *Los inmigrantes son los más afectados por la crisis* (Immigrants are the most affected by the crisis). In this way, it is clear that immigrants are presented as a vulnerable group of people, especially in a situation of socio-economic crisis like the one experienced by Spain in recent years. This caption suggests that immigrants need help.

The headline is: *Se duplican las peticiones de inmigrantes de retorno voluntario en un año* (Immigrants' applications for voluntary return double in a year). Choosing the word immigrants establishes a division between the latter and the majority group because it has negative connotations as already mentioned. In the text they are referred to as immigrants and immigrant population, i.e., the journalist does not choose a more inclusive term such as foreigners.

The subheadlines are: *El programa ofrece ayudas económicas y burocráticas* (The program offers financial and bureaucratic aid), which emphasizes the idea that the program is created to help immigrants; therefore, they are placed in an inferior situation, dependent on the main group.

The second subheadline includes the number of immigrants who have taken advantage of the return plan in Baleares, one of the regions in Spain with the highest number of immigrants. In this way, it is highlighted that the return plan is working well since a large number of people have taken advantage of it: *En lo que va de año han viajado de regreso 65 extranjeros residentes en Baleares* (So far this year 65 foreigners living in Baleares have gone back to their native countries).

The headline, subheadlines, caption and photograph suggest the same idea of immigrants being in need of help and facing more problems than the majority group, Spanish citizens. Consequently, numbers are emphasized in this news item as a way of highlighting the increase in the number of immigrants without a job and, consequently, the increase in the number of applications to return home, especially among people from Bolivia, Argentina, Brazil and Honduras. Immigrants' voices are not present, there are just some statements pronounced by Marcelo Unamuno, the regional director of Social Inclusion in the NGO, the Red Cross (Cruz Roja), the organization most involved in offering information and financial aid to immigrants interested in going back to their countries of origin.

La Comunidad, tercera en alumnos extranjeros

Piden que los países de la UE garanticen el derecho a pedir asilo en Europa

El conflicto de Colombia, en el Casal Jaume I

Alicante es la quinta provincia en inmigrantes acogidos al plan de retorno voluntario

Desde noviembre, 238 inmigrantes de la provincia han cobrado el paro íntegro y han regresado a sus países

Para CC OO esta medida no es eficaz y pide una mejora de la protección social de los desempleados

Educación acuerda con el Gobierno de Rumanía la cesión de aulas para cursos de cultura rumana

La Consellería edita una guía para que los inmigrantes se inicien en el aprendizaje del valenciano

Nicaragua puede perder las ayudas de EE UU por no revisar el resultado electoral

Uribe eleva el pago por la liberación de un concejal

Bolivia podría llevar a Perú a un juicio internacional

Figure 1-3. Text 3. Date: Date: 9 June 2009. Newspaper *Información*.

This piece of news (figure 1-3) appears in the centre of the page, on the left part. It consists on three columns. There is a small photograph of Minister Corbacho in the middle. He looks serious and appears to be concentrating, with his hands together to reinforce his message. This picture is small and framed. The background is blurred and new information appears in the foreground, i.e., the Minister himself. The caption is The Minister of Work, Corbacho, i.e., there is no doubt about who the person represented is. As regards colours, he is wearing a blue shirt, a dark blue jacket and a red tie, i.e. his clothes are smart as in the previous photograph. The background of the image is blurred. The image is not the most salient element because of its small size and because its frame is small.

As was the case in the first text, there is a vector between the Minister's hands, his mouth and the subheading and heading. This vector is important because it seems to connect the image with the words in the heading, pointing out that they are said by the Minister: *Alicante es la quinta provincia en inmigrantes acogidos al plan de retorno voluntario* (Alicante is the fifth province in terms of immigrants who have followed the return plan). The subheading is the following: *Desde noviembre, 238 inmigrantes de la provincia han cobrado el paro íntegro y han regresado a sus países* (From November, 238 immigrants of the province have earned the total amount of the money from the dole and they have gone back to their countries).

Immigrants are referred to as *inmigrantes* in this multimodal text. They appear as passive: *inmigrantes acogidos al plan de retorno voluntario de trabajadores extranjeros* (immigrants protected by the voluntary return plan of foreign workers), *se habían acogido a esta opción 238 personas en Alicante* (238 people had been protected by this option in Alicante), *inmigrantes acogidos al plan* (immigrants protected by the plan), *extranjeros* (foreigners), *inmigrantes latinoamericanos* (Latin American immigrants).

The fact that the word immigrants is the one that appears in the heading, the subheading and in most of the examples in the written text does not contribute to offering a positive representation of the immigrants because this word conveys negative connotations linked to poverty, discrimination etc., as already mentioned in the previous text. For example, choosing the word *extranjeros* ('foreigners'), which occurs in the middle of the text, can be considered euphemistic because it is more neutral and does not imply the connotations of the word immigrants.

8 Latino — ACTUALIDAD NACIONAL — VIERNES 17 DE JULIO DE 2009

¿FUNCIONA EL RETORNO VOLUNTARIO? VOLVER A ESPAÑA NO SERÁ FÁCIL: LOS RESIDENTES TEMPORALES NECESITARÁN OFERTA LABORAL Y NO HAY TRÁMITE CLARO PARA PERMANENTES

La plata es segura, el regreso no

» Conversamos con dos personas que retornaron con el plan español

Redacción Latino

Una preocupación carcome a los interesados en regresar a su país cobrando las prestaciones por desempleo: ¿Y si me voy, quién me garantiza que allá me den la plata? ¿Dónde la pagan? ¿Es rápido? En realidad, son dos las inquietudes. La otra, más difícil de responder, gira alrededor del regreso: ¿Podré volver luego de los tres años?

Marta Cardona, una colombiana que regresó a su país a comienzos de este año, tiene su propia opinión. "Yo estoy muy satisfecha porque todo ha salido como me dijeron en Madrid, apunta. Una semana después de instalarse en Chinchiná (localidad del eje cafetero), Marta viajó al Consulado español en Bogotá. En una ventanilla especial para el retorno voluntario, entregó su NIE y el de su niño de 14 años. Veinte días más tarde recibió en su casa un cheque "nominativo" en dólares, por el 60% restante de su seguro de desempleo. "Cambiar ese cheque fue lo único complicado, pero el gerente de mi banco se averiguó el proceso y en poco tiempo ya tenía la plata en mi cuenta", cuenta Marta, que abrió un depósito bancario con el dinero. "De momento no tengo planes de regresar a España, aunque mi hijo dice que no ve la hora de que pasen los tres años para poder volver".

Fabiola Bautista todavía en Madrid cuando esperaba la confirmación de su vuelo de regreso a Ecuador.

¿Y EN ECUADOR?

La ecuatoriana Fabiola Bautista también regresó a su tierra con el Plan de Retorno del Gobierno español. Sin embargo, las cosas no le están saliendo como pensaba, a la enfermedad terminal de su esposo se suman las dificultades para arrancar un negocio propio que les permita salir adelante. "Estoy arrepentida de haberme venido, yo por mí me volvería mañana mismo a España porque aquí no hay trabajo". Su gran angustia es que el 60% de sus prestaciones, cuatro mil dólares que tardó tres meses en cobrar, luego de entregar su NIE en el Consulado español, ya se está acabando y una vez que la cuenta quede en cero no sabe qué va a pasar. "Me dijeron que pasados tres años puedo entrar tranquilamente a España porque yo tenía tarjeta permanente. Espero que el tiempo pase rápido para poderme ir de nuevo".

LOS QUE SE HAN IDO

- Las últimas cifras del Ministerio de Trabajo e Inmigración sobre el plan de retorno voluntario son de junio de 2009.
- 3.977 personas se han beneficiado del programa desde su puesta en funcionamiento en noviembre de 2008.
- Los ecuatorianos son los que más: 1.749 personas. Siguen Colombia (771), Argentina (364) y Perú (334).
- Por provincias, Madrid encabeza el listado con 807 solicitudes aprobadas, seguido de Barcelona con 461 y Murcia, 433.

NO SE TRATA SÓLO DE ESPERAR

El regreso a España no será tan fácil para los residentes temporales. Pasados los tres años de compromiso, los aspirantes tendrán que tramitar las "autorizaciones administrativas para vivir y trabajar en España", según indica la normativa del plan retorno. Es decir, se verán obligados a presentar una oferta de trabajo o ingresar en los cupos de contingente, como si vinieran por primera vez. Respecto a los residentes permanentes, la ley advierte que podrán recuperar su estatus mediante un "procedimiento simplificado que se establecerá reglamentariamente". Todavía no existe, así que habrá que esperar para ver si se puede volver a España tan fácilmente como dice el Gobierno.

RAZONES HUMANITARIAS DELEGACIÓN DE GOBIERNO REVOCA EXPULSIÓN PARA QUE SIGA CON TRATAMIENTO MÉDICO

Libre del CIE por sufrir cáncer

Andrés Restrepo > Latino/Madrid

Ni el cáncer ni la Ley de Extranjería han podido con Cristian Salazar. La batalla contra la enfermedad la comenzó este chileno en 2006, cuando le diagnosticaron un cáncer de testículos que se le extendió a los pulmones. Después de la dura quimioterapia y una operación, Cristian tuvo que seguir esquivando las redadas policiales mientras intentaba regularizar su situación en España y asistía a sesiones médicas de control.

La vida se le volvió a complicar la semana pasada cuando la Policía lo detuvo junto a su novia paraguaya, a la entrada del metro de Alcorcón, en una de esas "cacerías" de inmigrantes que el Gobierno asegura que ya no existen. De nada valieron sus cuatro años en España ni la cita médica que tenía que cumplir el jueves 16 de julio en el Hospital Ramón y Cajal. Al tener una orden de expulsión previa, lo subieron en la patrulla y lo condujeron ante un juez, que decretó su ingreso en el Centro de Internamiento de Extranjeros (CIE) de Aluche. María, su pareja y a la que Cristian llama "mi ángel", no fue detenida, al no pesar ninguna orden de expulsión previa. Con el susto todavía en el cuerpo, María llamó a Verónica, la tía de Cristian, a contarle que habían detenido al joven. Juntas buscaron la ayuda de Víctor Sáez, presidente de la Federación Estatal de Asociaciones de Inmigrantes y Refugiados en España (Ferine), quien inmediatamente envió una carta a la Delegación de Gobierno para solicitar la puesta en libertad del joven para que pudiera continuar con su tratamiento oncológico.

Cristian Salazar y su novia María quieren regularizar su situación en España.

Mientras, Cristian vivía los cinco días más largos de su vida en el CIE de Aluche. "Yo no era el único enfermo. Había un chico colombiano que se quebró la mano en un 'accidente' en el CIE. El médico sólo le recetó ibuprofeno para el dolor. También conocí personas portadoras de VIH que no reciben medicación", cuenta Cristian. "Yo ya había leído sobre los malos tratos en las 'cárceles de inmigrantes', pero otra cosa es vivirlo".

TERMINA LA ESPERA

Finalmente y tras la insistencia de Ferine y la diputada colombiana Yolanda Villavicencio, el martes 14 de julio la Delegación de Gobierno decidió revocar la orden de expulsión de Cristian Salazar y permitir su salida del CIE por "razones humanitarias". Una decisión que Víctor Sáez, no duda en calificar de "histórica". En cambio, dentro del centro de internamiento, Cristian no tenía tan claro que fuera a salir. "Mientras firmaba los papeles de la libertad, algunos policías me advertían que ya salía para el aeropuerto, porque el avión a Chile despegaba a las 16:00 horas". A pesar de la siniestra broma, Cristian recuperó la libertad en la tarde del martes y recibió otra buena noticia: la Delegación de Gobierno estudiaría su caso para concederle la residencia por circunstancias excepcionales. Una promesa que habrá que vigilar para que Cristian pueda seguir luchando contra el cáncer sin miedo a las redadas policiales.

"ALLÁ NADIE PUEDE PROTESTAR PORQUE HAY MIEDO"

Un colombiano busca justicia para sus hermanos asesinados

Alejandro no desvela su identidad por temor a las amenazas que está recibiendo.

La vida de Alejandro Sánchez (nombre ficticio) se parecía a la de cualquier inmigrante latinoamericano: llevaba siete años trabajando como camarero en Valencia para enviarle dinero a su familia. Hasta que un día el teléfono sonó para recordarle que venía de Colombia, un país donde todo el mundo tiene un familiar o amigo víctima de la violencia. En el caso de Alejandro las balas tocaron cerca. Los cadáveres de sus dos hermanos fueron encontrados flotando en un río cercano a Medellín. En menos de 24 horas y tras pedir plata prestada, Alejandro ya estaba en Colombia, poniéndose al frente del entierro, el dolor y las investigaciones criminales. ¿Investigaciones? "No hay un sólo acusado, ni siquiera un sospechoso. Nadie tiene la esperanza ni la voluntad de encontrar a los culpables y llevarlos ante la justicia", cuenta Alejandro, incrédulo. Ante su insistencia, un funcionario judicial le recomendó buscar el apoyo de una ONG europea para que presionara. Al regresar a España, consiguió una cita con Amnistía Internacional. En breve viajará a la sede central en Londres para buscar justicia para sus hermanos. "Porque creo que los inmigrantes colombianos no nos podemos quedar de brazos cruzados con lo que está sucediendo allá", puntualiza.

Figure 1-4. Text 4. Date: 17 July 2009. Newspaper: *Latino.*

The main characteristics of this text (figure 1-4) are the use of figures to indicate the number of immigrants who have followed the plan and the amount of money invested in them. In addition, in this case, we find the direct voice of the person responsible for Communication in the Trade Union, CCOO, pointing out the importance of creating measures to protect people who have no jobs.

This item of news takes up the top half of the page. The headline is in black and red: *La plata es segura, el regreso no* (The money is sure, the return is not). The headline highlights the fact that immigrants will receive their dole money but it is not so sure that they will be able to come back to Spain; the uncertainty of returning appears in red, which is the most important part of the message. This idea is emphasized in the line before the headline, in which we find a question in red and the answer in black: *¿Funciona el retorno voluntario? Volver a España no será fácil: los residentes temporales necesitarán oferta laboral y no hay trámite claro para permanentes* (Does the return plan work? Coming back to Spain will not be easy: temporary residents will need a job offer and there is no clear step to be taken by permanent residents). From the beginning of the article, it is clear that it evaluates the return plan. Moreover, the subheadline makes it clear that authentic testimonies will be offered to demonstrate the reality of the plan: *Conversamos con dos personas que regresaron con el plan español* (We talk to two people who went back under the Spanish plan).

This news item has six columns of written text and a medium sized picture illustrating it. The picture shows a woman sitting in her home in Madrid, when she was waiting to return to Ecuador. The background is clear, and therefore the woman can be clearly distinguished. The beige background (the sitting room) contrasts with the woman's black dress. The woman looks serious and concentrated on what she is reading and does not look at the camera. The fact that her dress is black, a dark and serious colour, also adds formality to the photograph. She appears on the right of the picture, the place of new information, and therefore she is given importance. The picture is framed and the most important element is the woman, who covers approximately one third of the photograph. There is a vector between her head, her arm and the book she is reading. The image can be considered the most important element of this multimodal text. There is no doubt that the woman portrayed is one of the persons who offers her testimony on the return plan in the written text because the caption gives us her name: *Fabiola Bautista todavía en Madrid cuando esperaba la confirmación de su vuelo de regreso a Ecuador* (Fabiola Bautista still in Madrid waiting for confirmation of her flight back to Ecuador).

This news item starts with some of the questions that worry immigrants who would like to return to their countries of origin: if I leave Spain how can I be sure that I will receive the unemployment benefits I am entitled to? Where do they pay them? Is it quick? They also doubt whether they will be able to come back to Spain after three years.

After these introductory questions, this article offers the testimony of Marta Cardona, a Colombian woman who is happy with the procedure she followed to return home and receive her Spanish unemployment benefits in Colombia. We find her voice: "*Yo estoy muy satisfecha porque todo ha salido como me dijeron en Madrid*" ("I am happy because everything worked out as they told me it would in Madrid").

In this case the person is happy to be back in her country of origin and she does not have any plans to come back to Spain: "*De momento no tengo planes de regresar a España, aunque mi hijo dice que no ve la hora de que pasen los tres años para volver*" ("At the moment I do not have any plans to go back to Spain although my son wants the three years to pass quickly so that he can go back").

On the other hand, this news item also offers the testimony of Fabiola Bautista, the woman from Ecuador who appears in the photograph. We can also hear her voice: "*Estoy arrepentida de haberme venido, yo por mí me volvería mañana mismo a España porque aquí no hay trabajo*" ("I regret having come back, if I could I would go back to Spain tomorrow because there is no work here"). She has spent almost all of the 60% of her unemployment benefits (almost 4000 dollars) which she received four months after arriving home and is waiting to return to Spain: "*Me dijeron que pasados tres años puedo entrar tranquilamente a España porque yo tenía tarjeta permanente. Espero que el tiempo pase rápido para poderme ir de Nuevo*" ("I was told that I can go back to Spain after three years since I had a permanent residence card. I hope the time goes by quickly so that I can go back to Spain again").

In the last column it points out that coming back to Spain will not be as easy as the Government says because people will need to have a job offer before they can apply to return. This contrasts with all the news items that appear in the Spanish newspapers viewing the return plan positively, in which going back to the country of origin and returning to Spain once the three years are up seems straightforward.

Moreover, in this news item the number of people who have taken advantage of the return plan from November 2008 to June 2009 is specified: 3977 people, mainly from Colombia, Argentina and Peru. It is also mentioned that Madrid, Barcelona and Murcia are the three Spanish provinces with the highest number of applications.

As in the example already commented, the following news item (see figure 1-5) also occupies the top half of the page. It is made up of two news items which consist of six columns. It is interesting to find a small photograph in the middle of the article with three immigrants pushing a trolley at the airport; the frame is not strong but placing it in the middle, after the headline, makes it the most salient element in the multimodal text.

ACTUALIDAD NACIONAL

Latino 9

SE AGOTARON LOS FONDOS ECONÓMICOS DEL MINISTERIO DE TRABAJO MUCHOS INMIGRANTES SE SIENTEN ENGAÑADOS: YA LES HABÍAN PROMETIDO EL BILLETE AÉREO

El Plan Retorno se queda sin dinero para pagar los pasajes

» Los que regresen tendrán que gastarse parte de su paro

PLANES DE RETORNO

LAS FOTOS DE EDU LEÓN HAN SERVIDO PARA PROBAR LOS CONTROLES A INMIGRANTES LLEVA DOS SEMANAS SIN SU HERRAMIENTA DE TRABAJO POR ORDEN DE UN JUEZ

Decomisan la cámara al fotógrafo de las redadas

ESTADOS UNIDOS ALERTA SOBRE RACISMO

Obama y la discriminación en España

Figure 1-5. Text 5. Date: 6 August 2010. Newspaper: *Latino.*

It can be deduced that the immigrants are flying to Latin America because the caption says that a one way ticket to Latin America costs more than seven hundred Euros (*Un tiquete solo de ida a Latinoamérica cuesta más de setecientos euros*). The three immigrants are walking and they look serious, they do not look at the camera but down at the trolleys with their luggage. The background is a section of the airport and the immigrants are clearly distinguishable. They appear on the right of the photograph, the area of new information, and therefore they are given importance. They are wearing clean clothes and their faces are not very expressive. The picture is framed and the most important elements are the three immigrants themselves. There are different vectors that join the three men represented: in their heads, in their hands, in the feet and in their trolleys. Joining them through vectors is a way of pointing out that they belong to the same group and that they are in the same situation.

The headline is in bigger letters and combines red and black in order to emphasize the information explained in the article. This news item explains the headline of this newspaper on page one: *Plan Retorno sin pasajes. Se acabó el dinero para pagar lo billetes aéreos de los inmigrantes que se acogen al programa de regreso voluntario; ahora tendrán que comprarlos con el primer pago del 40%"* (The return plan with no tickets. No money for flight tickets for immigrants taking advantage of the voluntary return plan. Now they must buy them with the first 40% of their unemployment benefits).

The headline of this news item is *El plan retorno se queda sin dinero para pagar los pasajes* (The return plan has no money to pay for flight tickets) and the subheadline is: *Los que regresen tendrán que gastarse parte de su paro* (Those who go back will have to spend part of their unemployment benefits). Consequently, they highlight the fact that immigrants willing to return home will have to pay for the air tickets themselves. This implies a criticism of the plan and that many immigrants feel deceived because they do not get a free ticket as they were told, as the line before the headline makes clear: *Se agotaron los fondos económicos del Ministerio de Trabajo. Muchos inmigrantes se sienten engañados: ya les habían prometido el billete aéreo* (Ministry of Labour funds exhausted. Many immigrants feel cheated: they were promised a ticket home).

The main characteristic of the written text is that immigrants' voices are present and they express their opinions about the return plan, which contrasts with the news items in the newspapers *Información* and *El Mundo*. The first part of the article starts by saying that Mónica González has decided to go back to Peru (*Mónica González ha decidido regresar a Perú*), *"Me voy", pensó cuando terminó su último contrato de trabajo* ("I'm going", she thought when her employment contract finished).

The voice of this woman appears in the article criticising the Government because when she asked about the return plan in the National Employment Institute (INEM), it was presented as being straightforward by the Government employee and then she realized that there was no money to pay for the air ticket home:

"Me dieron un listado con ocho asociaciones que me podían gestionar lo del billete. Arranqué a llamar: en la primera me dijeron que ya no tenían fondos, en la segunda igual y en la tercera ya perdí la paciencia "Aunque no me den el billete yo estoy decidida a irme, así me toque pagar a mí. Lo que me da rabia es que el Gobierno le diga mentiras a los inmigrantes: es un incumplimiento muy grave", subraya indignada" ("I was given a list of associations that could help me to get my flight ticket. I started phoning: In the first they said they didn't have any money left, in the second, they said the same, and with the third I lost my patience. Even though they won't give me a ticket, I have decided to leave so I'll have to pay for it myself. What makes me mad is that the Government lies to immigrants: that's a very serious breach of promise").

This article also offers the testimony of a Colombian woman, Luz Patricia Díaz, who has to leave Spain in 30 days because she is going to get 40% of the unemployment benefit she is entitled to next week: "*Yo ya estaba cobrando el paro hacía tres meses, o sea que tampoco es que me quede mucho*" ("I have been getting money from the dole for three months so there is not much left"). She intends to buy her flight ticket with this money. For this reason, she also criticises the Government and does not trust it: *"Me parece muy injusto, ya hasta me da desconfianza lo que pueda pasar con la otra parte de la plata"* ("It is very unfair and it even makes me have misgivings about what might happen with the other money").

This news item offers a contrast between reality – i.e., the fact that there is no money to pay for the air tickets of immigrants who want to go back to their countries – and the information that appears on the web of the Spanish Ministry of Labour. On this web page it still says: *podrá complementar el abono anticipado de la prestación con ayudas para el viaje a sus países de origen* (Financial help for the journey home may be available in addition to advanced payment of unemployment benefit). However, this news item also points out that when you ring the telephone number provided to obtain information about the return plan, you are told that nowadays no such additional help is being given for the return ticket ("*Eso sí, en el teléfono habilitado para información advierten que "actualmente no se están dando ayudas complementaria para el billete*".) This information has not appeared in the media, which contrasts with all the advertising given to the return plan when it was created to highlight that it was a good measure to favour immigrants' situation.

The article finishes with a very strong criticism of the Government: *Una estocada más para un plan que el presidente Zapatero presentó como una de sus medidas estrella contra la crisis económica* (Yet another blow to the plan presented by Zapatero as one of the main measures taken against the economic crisis). In addition, to the right of this news item, there is another short item on the return of immigrants. It also has a small photograph above it with the head of a woman looking very seriously at the camera saying "*Si estás pensando en regresar...Existen dos planes de retorno de inmigrantes*" ("If you are thinking about returning home there are two return plans for immigrants"). Information is provided about the return plan offered by the Ministry of Education and that offered by NGOs. There is interaction between this woman and readers because she looks directly at the camera.

5. Comparison of Texts

Although immigrants are the protagonists of the return plan, they do not appear in all the photographs in the articles on this subject in the newspapers *El Mundo* and *Información*; their voices appear in only 14.28% of the texts analysed. In most cases, we find the photographs of politicians. Immigrants are not referred to by their names. On the other hand, photographs of immigrants appear in all the news items on the return plan in the newspaper *Latino*. Moreover, immigrants appear with their names and surnames in *Latino*, which is not common at all in the other newspapers.

Most news items in *El Mundo* and *Información* see the return plan as something positive, whereas immigrants' voices in *Latino* (women and men) express their opinion about the return plan, they criticise the Government and the reality of the plan, and how it affects immigrants is contrasted with the information that appears on the web page of the Ministry of Labour. For example, *Información* highlights the amount of money the Government has invested in the return plan, which contrasts with the news items in *Latino* that say there is no money to pay for the one way tickets so that immigrants can go back to their countries of origin.

The position of the news items vary. In *Información*, most appear on the left and on the bottom half of the page, whereas in *Latino* the news items analysed cover the top half of the page. In addition, the news items in *El Mundo* and *Información* do not refer to the socio-economic situation of the immigrants' countries of origin, to which they are supposed to return and start a new life. On the contrary, *Latino* refers to the social situation of different Latin American countries and points out the difficulty of starting a new life there. In addition, *El Mundo* and *Información* talk about immigrants, whereas *Latino* not only talks about immigrants but also talks to immigrants, hears their voices, their opinions and their personal experiences of the return plan.

6. Discussion: Media and Racism

Immigrants are presented as stereotyped in the press because their main characteristics are reduced and simplified. This gives power to the majority group, i.e., the white elite. This process of stereotyping implies that the positive aspects of immigrants are silenced, for example, their cultural richness, their qualifications (a great number of immigrants have university degrees) and their importance for the economy of our country.

The discourse used by the media in the texts analysed can be considered 'elite racism' because there is a clear division between 'we' (the main group, white people) and 'they' (the minority group, immigrants) (van Dijk 2003, 2006, 2007, 2008). In addition, immigrants' voices are hardly ever heard (Alonso, McCabe and Chornet-Roses, 2010; Retis, 2006). However, 'elite racism' denies that it is racism and it is presented as being democratic and respectable.

Elite discourse represents the majority group in a positive way, whereas immigrants are represented negatively; moreover, this discourse points out that the measures to control immigrants benefit the main group (van Dijk, 2005, 28). The media audience are invited to establish a clear difference between whites and other ethnic groups, between 'citizens' and 'foreigners', and what predominates is the negative representation of immigrants, as Bañón (2007, 45) makes clear: "The non-positive valuation of immigrants has become the fundamental axiological framework for those who, from the political or socio-economic Spanish elites take part in the social debate on migratory processes".[2]

When paying attention to the characteristics of the different linguistic and visual choices that appear in the selected texts, readers are aware of the power of the press to influence knowledge, values and social relationships, in other words, it is observed that language and power coexist. Moreover, since journalists themselves belong to a society with prejudices, they create the items of news transmitting their own worldviews, prejudices or racist ideas (ter Wal, d'Haenens and Koeman, 2005, 938). For this reason, it is necessary for readers to assume an active role in the process of deconstructing the meaning of immigrants' reality presented by the press and question the credibility of the press discourse because, as in the case of elite discourses, they are considered true because they come from people with power.

7. Conclusions

The texts analysed show that there are two different discourses on return: on the one hand, the one transmitted by white elites (politicians, journalists, etc.), which highlight the positive aspects of the return plan; on the other hand, immigrants' discourse, which appears mainly in their newspapers. They criticize the Government and different immigrants describe the plan's reality with its positive and negative aspects.

The analysis done in this article points out that the media have power to modify or shape our attitudes because each image and each linguistic component is not chosen at random but, on the contrary, is motivated and created as a result of complex phenomena, capable of specifying meanings.

This implies that it is essential for readers to assume an active role in the process of observing how immigrants are represented and of interpreting the ideas and values associated with them in the multimodal texts analysed. Normally the press represents immigrants as "the others", as those that are not like us, the majority group, and that cannot be like us.

On the one hand, the two newspapers produced by Spanish people give power to the majority group since the return plan is presented as something positive, created by the Government to support immigrants in a vulnerable situation. However, immigrants' voices are not heard and their opinions of this plan are not taken into consideration, which gives power to elites. Moreover, the promotion of immigrants' return avoids referring to how they enrich our society by paying social security, sharing their culture and doing their job for years. On the other hand, *Latino* highlights immigrants' voices and makes visible immigrants' contribution to society since the news items found in this newspaper highlight the fact that immigrants enrich Spain through their work, by paying social security and through cultural exchange with people they come into contact with.

Choosing Critical Discourse Analysis and Visual Grammar as theoretical models offers the possibility of studying the texts paying attention to discursive forms of domination; in addition, they are appropriate frameworks because they are interdisciplinary since they give importance to the relationships between discourse and society, especially when they analyse the relationships of power, domination or inequality through the linguistic or visual characteristics of texts.

The return plan has not been a success because not as many immigrants as expected have taken advantage of it and because the Spanish Government designed it without taking into consideration the socio-economic situation in the countries of origin of the immigrants concerned. The plan's failure is a way of pointing out that the migratory politics of the Government needs to be improved. In addition, the plan does not take into consideration the personal and vital life projects of immigrants or the social networks they have created in Spain throughout the years; on top of this, the terrible situation in some of their countries of origin is disregarded.

Notes

1. The original quotation is: "La función de los medios de comunicación como transmisores de otros discursos, como apoyos a esos otros discursos o como generadores de discursos propios es determinante en lo que se refiere al tratamiento público de la inmigración" (Bañón, 2002, 283).
2. The original quotation is: "La valoración no positiva de los inmigrantes se ha convertido en el marco axiológico fundamental para todos los que, desde las élites políticas o socioeconómicas españolas, participan en el debate social sobre los procesos migratorios" (Bañón, 2007, 45).

Bibliography

Alonso Belmonte, Isabel, Anne McCabe and Daniel Chornet-Roses. 2010. "In their own words: The construction of the image of the immigrant in Peninsular Spanish broadsheets and freesheets". *Discourse and Communication* 4.3: 227-242.

Baldry, Anthony and Paul J. Thibault. 2006. *Multimodal Transcription and Text Analysis.* London: Equinox.

Bañón Hernández, Antonio Miguel. 2002. *Discurso e inmigración. Propuestas para el análisis de un debate social.* Murcia: Universidad de Murcia.

—. 2007. "El discurso periodístico a propósito del viaje de los inmigrantes pobres". In *Discursos sobre la inmigración en España. Los medios de comunicación, los parlamentos y las administraciones*, eds. Ricard Zapata-Barrer and Teun A. van Dijk, 45-67. Barcelona: Fundación CIDOB.

Borchers, Timothy A. 2002. *Persuasion in the Media Age.* Boston: Mc Graw Hill.

Christou, Anastasia. 2006. *Narratives of place, culture and identity: second-generation Greek-Americans return 'home'.* Amsterdam: Amsterdam University Press.

Conway, Dennis and Robert B. Potter. (eds.) 2009. *Return migration of the next generations.* Aldershot, UK and Burlington USA: Ashgate.

Crespo, Eliecer and María Martínez Lirola. 2012. "Lexical and visual choices in the representation of immigration in Spanish press". *Spanish in Context* 9.1: 27-57.

El Mundo (1 September 2008 to 28 February 2011).

Fairclough, Norman. 1995. *Media Discourse*. London: Arnold.

Ferguson, Robert. 2007. *Los medios bajo sospecha. Ideología y poder en los medios de comunicación*. Barcelona: Gedisa.

Halliday, Michael Alexander Kirkwood. 1978. *Language as Social Semiotic: The Social Interpretation of Language and Meaning.* London: Edward Arnold.

Información (1 September 2008 to 28 February 2011).

Jewitt, Carey (ed.) 2009. *The Routledge Handbook of Multimodal Analysis*. London: Routledge.

Kress, Gunther. 2003. *Literacy in the New Media Age.* London: Routledge.

Kress, Gunther and Theo van Leeuwen. 2001. *Multimodal Discourse: The Modes and Media of Contemporary Communication.* London: Arnold.

Kress, Gunther and Theo van Leeuwen, 2006. *Reading Images: The Grammar of Visual Design.* Second edition. London: Routledge Press.

Latino (1 June 2009 to 28 February 2011).

Long, Lynellyn D. and Ellen Oxfeld. (eds.) 2004. *Coming Home?: Refugees, migrants, and those who stayed behind.* Philadelphia: University of Pennsylvania Press.

Martínez Lirola, María 2006. "A Critical Analysis of the Image of Immigrants in Multimodal Texts". *Linguistics and the Human Sciences* 2.3: 377-397.

—. 2008. "Las relaciones entre las características lingüísticas y visuales de las noticias sobre inmigración en la prensa gratuita y su relación con la audiencia". *Discurso y Sociedad* 2 (4): 799-815.

Martínez Lirola, María (ed.) 2010. *Migraciones, discursos e ideologías en una sociedad globalizada. Claves para su mejor comprensión* Alicante: Instituto Alicantino de Cultura Juan Gil Albert.

Moore, Kerry, Bernhard Gross and Terry Threadgold (eds.) 2012. *Migrations and the Media.* New York: Peter Lang.

O'Toole, Michael. 1994. *The Language of Displayed Art.* London: Leicester University Press.

Reisigl, Michael and Ruth Wodak. 2001. *Discourse and Discrimination. Rhetorics of Racism and Antisemism.* London: Routledge.

Retis, Jessica. 2006. *Espacios mediáticos de la inmigración en Madrid: génesis y evolución.* Madrid: Observatorio de las Migraciones y la Convivencia Intercultural de la Ciudad de Madrid.

ter Wal, Jessika, Leen d'Haenens and Joyce Koeman. 2005 "(Re)presentation of Ethnicity in EU and Dutch domestic news: a quantitative analysis". *Media, Culture and Society* 27 (6): 937-950.

Van Dijk, Teun A. 1987. *Communicating Racism. Ethnic Prejudice in Thought and Talk.* London: Sage Publications.

—. 1993. *Elite Discourse and Racism.* London: Sage Publications.

—. 2000. "New(s) Racism: A Discourse Analytical Approach". In *Ethnic Minorities and the Media*, ed. Simon Cottle, 33-49. Philadelphia: Open University Press.

—. 2003. *Dominación étnica y racismo discursivo en España y América Latina.* Barcelona: Gedisa.

—. 2005. *Racism and discourse in Spain and Latin America.* Amsterdam and Philadelphia: John Benjamins.

—. 2006. "Discurso de las élites y racismo institucional". In *Medios de comunicación e inmigración,* ed. Manuel Lario Bastida, 16-34. Murcia: Convivir sin Racismo: CAM - Obra Social.

—. 2007. "Racismo y discurso en América Latina: una introducción". In *Racismo y discurso en América Latina,* coord. Teun A. van Dijk, 21-34. Barcelona: Gedisa.

—. 2008. "Reproducir el racismo: el rol de la prensa". In *La inmigración sale a la calle. Comunicación y discursos políticos sobre el discurso migratorio,* ed. Francisco Checa y Olmos, 19-49. Barcelona: Icaria.

Van Leeuwen, Theo. 2005. *Introducing Social Semiotics.* New York: Routledge.

—. 2009. "Critical Discourse Analysis". In *Discourse, of Course. An Overview of Research in Discourse Studies,* ed. Jan Renkema, 277-292. Amsterdam and Philadelphia: John Benjamins.

CHAPTER TWO

IMMIGRANT LATINA IMAGES IN MAINSTREAM MEDIA: CLASS, RACE AND GENDER IN PUBLIC DISCOURSE IN THE UNITED STATES AND SPAIN

JÉSSICA RETIS
CALIFORNIA STATE UNIVERSITY NORTHRIDGE

1. Introduction

A review of the literature on immigrant Latin American women in the United States and Spain reveals similar patterns. First, we see complex migration processes wherein women come to the fore: critical researchers have thus advocated the adoption of a gender perspective in order to approach the current situation of these groups of immigrants in a suitably comprehensive fashion. Second, these groups have a variety of origins, and come from diverse social, cultural, educational, and economic backgrounds: therefore critical authors are demanding more complex and nuanced approaches that are equal to the task of explaining the various opportunities and challenges of the migratory experience in the transnational life of Latin American immigrants. Third, it is claimed that journalistic discourse tends to homogenise the status of Latin American immigrant women in several respects: (a) it tends to ignore their presence in the discourse on immigration, (b) it tends to justify their subordinate position in the systems of social stratification, (c) it tends to generalise their position as poor and as victims.

This chapter compares and analyses sociodemographic patterns among Latin American immigrants in both the United States and Spain, in order to understand similarities and differences in their processes of displacement, arrival, and integration. This chapter will also explore general trends in the treatment of immigration in the countries that make up the Organisation for Economic Co-operation and Development (OECD), in order to understand the climate of opinion in which discourses on Latin American immigrant women are situated. The state of the art on the topic helps us to describe patterns of behaviour in the mainstream media and in news coverage of Latin American women in the United States and Spain. Based on these, this chapter proposes the adoption of a critical perspective to analyse the processes of production and dissemination of discriminatory and exclusionary discourses in terms of class, race and gender.

2. Latin American Immigrant Women in the US and Spain

During the last century, the number of nation-states quadrupled to almost two hundred, thus creating more borders to cross. Immigration policies became more restrictive, while, paradoxically, barriers to exchanging goods and capital flows decreased (United Nations 2009, 2).[1] In the last fifty years, the number of international immigrants has stayed constant and, among these, there are about thirty million without residence and work permits,[2] which excludes them from the welfare state, although they contribute to economic growth with their labour. To these figures must be added those who, although they are in their countries of origin, are part of the immigration experience: those who have benefited from the estimated $440 million in international remittances that circulated during 2010 (of which, $338 million was remitted to poor countries). Despite the worldwide economic crisis, the number of international immigrants has not changed noticeably. In 2010, there were 214 million international immigrants, comprising 3.1% of the global population and, of whom, 49% were women (International Organisation for Migrations (IOM, 2011).[3]

In this context, the case of Latin Americans is significant because there has been an increase in immigration flows from Latin America to the North, especially to countries like the United States and Spain, and because there has been a feminisation of these movements (Pedone, 2006; Martínez, 2011). These processes have resulted in a gradual transnationalisation of Latin American families. Studies of second and third generation immigrants prove that Latin America is growing abroad, concentrating its transnationality in the transborder circuits that flow through open channels of international capital flows but in the opposite direction, and with strategies of globalisation "from below" (Lewitt, 2009; Portes, Aparicio and Haller, 2009; Sassen, 2003; Smith and Guarnizo, 2006). Recent research has demanded a more comprehensive perspective because old and new challenges are merging: never before have immigration issues been so heavily discussed, yet at the same time they are being increasingly problematised, to such a degree that its very acceptance as a social process seems to be under threat (Martínez, 2011). This section outlines the increase and feminisation of Latin American migrations towards the United States and Spain.

The increasing demand for immigrant women to carry out the reproductive work of occidental societies reveals aspects of the international division of labour and shows the decanting of inequalities of class and race among women (Sole and Parella, 2005). The increased incidence of women in international migratory flows is reflected in the process of feminisation of the Latin American diaspora. The lifestyle of women in rich countries is made possible by the transference of tasks associated with women's traditional roles, such as taking care of children and housework, to women from poor countries in the context of global capitalism (Ehrenreich, Russell and Hochschild, 2003). The immigrant women transform the meaning, priorities, and shapes of organisation of motherhood in respect to the children that stay in their countries of origin; but they also reprocess their condition in the country where they are working and living, due to the social stratification of ethnicity, race, and class (Hondagneu-Sotelo and Avila, 1997).

With the inclusion of transnationalism in the literature on migration in the 1990s, we achieved a better understanding of the displacement, arrival, and settling processes of international immigrants (Smith and Guarnizo, 1998), promoting a breach with methodological nationalism and including the analysis of origin and destination conditions. Migrations do not involve a break with territorial roots but the configuration of a transnational social field through which the community of origin is transformed in the destination countries (Canales, 2011). Processes of economic globalisation necessitate that we reconsider the traditional way of observing national societies when they are converted into network societies (Castells, 2006), which have given rise to the deterritorialisation of social life, transforming its cultural dimensions (Appadurai, 2003).

In this context, the process of transnationalisation of Latin American immigrant women had passed unnoticed in the absence of an approach that allows promotion of policies according to their vulnerability (Sole, 2009; Martínez, 2006; Agrela, 2004; Oso, 2005; Stolke, 2004). The perspective of gender in sociological research on migration is vital due to its centrality in the formation of transnational families (Cortés, 2005; Pedone, 2006; Oso, 2009; Lewitt, 2001), and because they accentuate the disparities in the international distribution of the labour market (Sassen, 2003). Local, national, and international public policies have yet to understand the gender dimension of migration in the articulation of inclusive policies of integration (Nash, 2005b; Cortés, 2005; Martínez, 2003). More than thirty years after the convention for the elimination of all forms of discrimination against women in the world,[4] we still have more to do to advance in several areas: the discursive treatment of immigration, and of immigrant Latin American women in particular is one of those.

The era of the 1980s is known as the "Lost Decade" in Latin America, due to the economic crisis and the implementation of structural adjustment reforms in the region in compliance with the guidelines of the "Washington Consensus." These conditions led to a significant increase in the displacement of people outside of the region. In the United States, those years were known as "The Hispanic Decade." More than four million Latin Americans arrived in the United States during the 1980s; double the number of the previous decade and four times that of the 1960s (US Census, various years). In that era, the term "Hispanic" was incorporated in the census forms, and advertising discourse responded with ethnic marketing campaigns aimed at attracting the new potential consumers (Rodríguez, 2000; Dávila, 2001).

During the 1990s, international Latin American immigrations continued to grow. But it is in this last decade when, for the first time, the junction of Latin American migratory flows and second and third generations of Latin Americans born in the United States resulted in a significant effect: the major contribution to demographic growth was led by Latin Americans, comprising 34% of US population growth (Canales, 2011). This increase corresponds to the fertility rate among Hispanic women compared to non-Hispanic women (84 births per 1,000 Hispanic women, compared to 63 births per 1,000 non-Hispanic women), and in particular to that of first generation immigrant Hispanic women among whom the fertility rate is higher than that of US-born Hispanic women (96 per 1,000 Hispanic women compared to 73 per 1,000 non-Hispanic women) (Gonzales, 2008). According to the most recent census, taken in 2010, 58% of the population growth in the last decade is Hispanic: 50.5 million people, constituting 16.3% of the total population (US Census, 2010).[5]

The review of the key figures in terms of gender allows us to outline the demographic, socioeconomic, and educational development of Hispanic women in the United States. Almost half of Latin Americans residing in the US are women: 49.3% (Motel, 2012); a little over half of these women were born abroad (52%); and the majority of them came from recent migratory processes (57% had arrived since 1990) (Gonzales, 2008). A large proportion of these Hispanic women living in the United States are Mexicans (60%), followed by Central Americans (13.5%), Caribbean

(12.6%), and South Americans (11.6%) (Gonzales, 2008). Critical studies have pointed to the necessity of understanding their diversity of origins:

> "Call them Latinas, but you will be using a shortcut word for many different groups of women. Some are the descendants of settlers born in the Southwest when it was under Spanish rule, long before *Mayflower* brought the Pilgrims to New England. Some are Puerto Rican women (*Puertorriqueñas*) and women from other Caribbean and Latin American nations, thousands of whom arrived by ship in the early days of this century [...] Some Latinas come alone and others travel with husbands, fathers, children, friends, and family members. Some are educated and some, illiterate; some are old, some young; they represent a rainbow of colours, ideologies, and skills". (Garza, 2001, 11-12)

The average participation of Hispanic women in the workforce is similar to non-Hispanics (59% and 61% respectively). However, the wages of Hispanic women are significantly lower and they are at greater risk of becoming poor: one out of five Hispanics lives in poverty (Garza, 2001). Hispanic women are more likely than non-Hispanic women to be employed in blue-collar occupations such as building, grounds cleaning, and maintenance (10% versus 2%); food preparation and serving-related jobs (9% versus 6%); production (8% versus 4%); and personal care and service occupations (7% versus 5%). The occupations with a strong presence of Hispanic women are: farming, fishing, and forestry (42%); building, grounds cleaning, and maintenance (37%); production occupations (23%); food preparation and serving-related occupations (17%); construction and extraction occupations (16%); personal care and service occupations (14%); healthcare support occupations (13%). Not all Hispanic women have health insurance coverage: Hispanic women are nearly three times as likely as non-Hispanic women to be uninsured (36% versus 13%). The data are even more striking in the case of first generation immigrant Hispanic women, since almost half of them do not have medical insurance (47%), compared to 25% of Hispanics born in the United States.

To the vulnerability in the kind of occupation and in access to medical insurance is added adverse conditions in respect to education. A greater proportion of Hispanic women than non-Hispanic women have less than a High School diploma (36% compared to 10% respectively). The figure is higher in the case of Hispanic immigrant women (49% did not finish high school, compared to 24% of native Hispanics). In contrast, almost half of all native Hispanics (men and women) have some grade of college education (46%), compared to 24% of Hispanics born abroad (Gonzales, 2008). Language proficiency is a great obstacle to social advancement.

The majority of Hispanics born abroad acknowledge that they do not speak English well (73%); by contrast, the majority of those been born in the United States speak exclusively English at home (86%).

It is estimated that approximately twelve million undocumented immigrants live in the United States, of whom 4.1 million are women and 1.5 million are minors. Three-quarters of undocumented immigrants are Hispanics (76%). The majority is from Mexico (59%), followed by Central America (11%), South America (7%), and the Caribbean (4%). The transnational conditions of Hispanic families in the United States force them to live in vulnerability due to their migratory condition. Many homes are mixed status, for example, undocumented parents with American citizen children born in the United States (8.8 million people, according to the most recent data) (Passel, 2009). A recent survey shows that, although many Latin Americans are concerned about their immigration status (33%), they report that their main priorities are access to work (50%), education (49%), medical insurance (45%), and payment of taxes (34%). Almost two out of three Hispanics (59%) disapprove of how the Obama administration is handling deportations of undocumented immigrants, which has reached almost 400,000 cases, almost 30% more than the yearly average during the second term of President George Bush (López, González and Motel, 2012).

Changes in international labour relationships have consolidated the transnational condition of Latin Americans. Although emigration to the United States accounts for three-quarters of regional migrations and registers as part of a South–North migratory pattern, in recent decades new population flows have consolidated towards Europe, particularly Spain (Retis, 2009). During the 1980s, the flows, prominently from Peru and the Dominican Republic, begin to manifest the first migration movements due to economic factors. There is evidence of a gradual feminization of these groups, which is rooted in the incorporation of Spanish women in the labor market, increasing demand in Spain for childcare and care of the elderly.

The 1990s are known in Latin America as the "New Lost Decade" while in Spain they are known as the "Golden Decade" of Spanish investment in Latin America (Casilda, 2002). The end of the "Ecuadorian miracle," the agricultural and social crisis in Colombia, and the "Argentinean *corralito*" were correlated geopolitically with a labour market that opened its doors to a foreign workforce due to the modernisation process that was happening in Spain (Retis, 2006). In the demographic context, this conjunction is the setting for what at this time was called the era of "the preferred of the XXI century": Latin Americans burst into the non-European immigration context in preferential conditions in the public administration, in the business sector, and in the climate of opinion (Izquierdo, López and Martínez, 2002).

According to most recent data, out of the 2.6 million immigrants that have authorisation to live and work in Spain, 44 per cent are from Latin America (OPI 2011). The Colectivo IOE reports that by 1 January 2008, in Spain, there were 6 million immigrants (registered persons born in other countries), and 5.2 million foreigners (registered people with non-Spaniard citizenship), of whom 23.8% had irregular status (not counting European citizens registered without residency permits): overall the proportion of undocumented people in Spain was 13% (IOE 2008, 1). These numbers, although they are estimated, indicate that a great number of non-European immigrants are in a vulnerable situation. The recent policies of adjustment have also determined that irregular immigrants will be without the right to a health card (*tarjeta sanitaria*), meaning that there will be almost no access to free medical coverage.

The feminisation of Latin American migrations to Spain is higher than in flows to the United States (54% women versus 46% men) and it has become evident that women have progressed from accompanied migration or following their spouses, yet these forms of dependence are assumed in the majority of theoretical formulations regarding immigration (Martínez 2003, 8). At the end of 2011, the final count in Spain identified 1,190 thousand Latin Americans with residency permits, to which figure must be added naturalised immigrants and those without the proper documentation. More than half of all Latin American migrants in Spain are women.

The majority of Latin American women in Spain are in the economically active age range: most are 25 to 44 years old (57.27%); a lesser proportion are younger (8% are 20 through 24 years old) and mature women (8% are 45 to 49 years old). Little over a quarter of women had registered with Social Security as house employees (26%): the biggest group are represented by Ecuadorians (17.38%), Bolivians (12.4%), Colombians (11.82%), and Peruvians (6.04%). In regards to their administrative situation, more than half are in the national administration (66.5%), 4% are independent, and 4% work in farms. Out of the total number of Latin American working women registered with Social Security by the end of 2008, 30.23% were in Madrid, 23.19% in Cataluña, 8.67% in the Valencia Community, 7.11% in Andalucía, 4.71% in Murcia, 4.34% in Canarias, 3.22% in the Basque Country, 3.10% in Castilla and Leon, and 3% in Baleares (OPI, 2011).

A critical analysis by Colectivo IOE remarks that, although the estimates are based on the statistics of work permits, there are indications that the agency has a distorted image of the labour insertion of immigrant women in Spain because it does not take into consideration those who are registered with the communal administration, who may be working legally, but who do not feature in the statistics collected by the Ministry of Labour (IOE, 2001, 91). To sum up, what it is really evident is the input that foreign women are making to the recipient society:

> "The work of immigrated persons has facilitated at times the labour promotion of the native population. What stands out in this respect are the great numbers of foreign women (more than 300,000 according to the EPA) who leave their families in order to do reproductive work in Spaniards' houses, which allows native women to be incorporated into the paid labour market without substantial modification of the duties in their homes and facilitates the conciliation of work and family life". (IOE, 2008, 5-6; my translation)

The majority of studies of Latin American immigrant women in the United States and Spain have declared high grades of vulnerability in the migratory trajectory and in the settlement processes. Women start the journey outside their countries motivated by a diversity of structural, social, family-related, and individual reasons. What is more evident is their central position in the configuration of transnational families, and in the consolidation of patterns of care chains that allow the advancement of other women and their families. They are heads of households while family and economic relationships keep transforming around them. In addition, it is crucial to critically analyse the subordinate conditions in which they are incorporated into the labour market, and into the socio-cultural and political stratum of the countries of destination. In this sense, it is essential to analyse the central role of mainstream media to understand how Latin American immigrant women are perceived in the countries of destination.

Postcolonial perspectives (Said, 1993; Mignolo, 2003) allow us to understand how population flows follow capital flow, but in an opposite direction: in recent decades, Latin America became an exporter of an international labour force to northern countries. Upon their arrival, the majority of immigrants were incorporated into a social stratification process that places them in peripheral environments and disadvantageous positions in respect of social promotion and acquisition of full citizenship. In this context, the public discourse becomes central due to its influence in shaping public opinion on immigration and immigrants (Retis, 2006).

3. Discourses on Immigration and Latino Immigrants in the United States and Spain

The sixth report of the International Organisation for Migrations (OIM) focuses its analysis on the perception that several countries have regarding international immigration, because "in spite of the revolution in communications, there are many people who have inadequate information on the magnitude, the implications and the socioeconomic context of migration" (OIM, 2008, 8). The fact that the OIM dedicated its annual report to the treatment of immigration is evidence of the social significance that the topic has gained within public debate. In recent years, immigration has become a highly politicised issue and has been perceived in a negative way, despite the clear need for diversification of modern societies and economies.

> "International migration is likely to increase in scale and complexity due to growing demographic disparities, new global and political dynamics, technological revolutions and social networks, with profound impacts on the socio-economic and ethnic composition of societies. This will result in new policy challenges related to the successful integration of migrants into the host society, how they are perceived in their countries of origin and, more broadly, the way migration is experienced by the community at large. In this context, the image of migrants in their home and host societies acquires fundamental importance". (OIM, 2008, 8)

The OIM report notes the challenges we are facing in this era of globalisation and human mobility and calls for fundamental change in the ways immigration is communicated. To facilitate intercultural coexistence and to overcome the challenges of diversity, it is essential to have well-informed and clear debate in both the public and political arenas. The risk of maintaining the status quo is threefold:

> 1. Continued politicised debate will only serve to foster sectarian agendas, rather than promoting broader national, regional and international interests. One of the greatest challenges for those who seek to foster a rational debate is to prevent migration from being used as a platform for other political, social and economic issues.
>
> 2. Negative attitudes and reactive approaches are likely to continue to dominate over positive attitudes and proactive approaches.
>
> 3. Both integration and reintegration efforts will inevitably be undermined unless migrants themselves become active participants in the migration debate, rather than being the subject of debate. (OIM, 2011, 8-9)

To improve the mainstream media discourses of immigration it is essential to improve the participation of all the stakeholders, including policy makers, organisations, activists, and experts. This is a challenge for the political administration, the media corporations, and the immigrant communities. It is essential that public debate be opened up to participation of immigrants, who, to date, remain largely the subjects of public discourse. As this report points out, actual increases in migration flows or the extent to which perceived migration levels are considered to exceed "acceptable levels" often have a negative impact on public opinion. Some also attribute growing public anxiety and negativity about migration not only to migrant flow increases but also to the pace at which they occur (Papademetriou and Heuser, 2009).[6]

Apart from the pace of immigration growth, public opinion is influenced by disagreement over the formal status of those who migrate internationally, whether they are regular or irregular immigrants. Preferred levels of migration are thus not reduced to a simple question of numbers posed in isolation from questions related to the origin and status of the migrants. Through the analysis of several public opinion surveys, the OIM report shows that there has been a gradual decline in support for immigration in OECD countries, notably in the second half of the 1990s, suggesting that there may be a correlative relation with the increase in international immigrant flows (OIM, 2011).

In Spain, the public perception of Latin American immigrants deteriorated in the same years that immigrant flows from Latin America increased. Of particular note is the media treatment regarding the emergence of Latin Americans in the non-European immigration context (Retis, 2006). The OIM report remarks how important it is to remember that people of hosting countries often have false notions of the scale and nature of immigration and the policies that influence it. In other studies it has been demonstrated that reporters who cover news on immigration have a poor knowledge of the structural conditions of international migrations, and a weak understanding of social and cultural origins of Latin American immigrants (Retis, 2006).

The OIM report mentions a study conducted in eight international immigration recipient countries (Canada, France, Germany, Italy, Netherlands, Spain, UK, and US). The study found that respondents tended to significantly overestimate the size of the immigrant population. Interviewees were asked to choose from "too many," "a lot, but not too many," or "too few" immigrants in their countries as information about the current size of the immigrant population was given out. Other interviewees were not provided with this data. The former group was found to be less likely to say there were too many immigrants in the country (OIM, 2011, 8).

In the United States, the Gallup Polls have been measuring opinion regarding immigration since 1960. The most recent data demonstrates that a slight majority believes that immigration must decrease (58% in 2001, 51% in 2006, and 50% in 2009). An interesting result from the surveys is the notion that a slight majority considers that immigration is beneficial to the country (67% in 2006; 57% in 2010). OIM emphasises that Gallup's surveys indicate a more positive vision regarding immigrants versus results from other surveyors like Vision Critical/Angus Reid Public Opinion (OIM, 2011). In 2006, the Pew Hispanic Center reviewed a number of surveys and concluded that people appear divided between whether immigration overall was good for the country or not.

In other opinion polls, it has been confirmed that there is evidence of other opinions about several types of immigrant flows. In general, people tend to be more sympathetic to refugees than other kinds of immigrants. However, in countries that welcome a high number of refugees, the surveys verify that public opinion is more concerned about immigration consequences than in other countries:

> "It is unclear whether attitudes towards migration become more or less positive as the proportion of migrants within the total population increases and/or they come to be seen as an integral part of the community. In a World Values Survey, 214,628 persons were interviewed in 86 countries and asked if they would object to living next door to a migrant. There are, unsurprisingly, several high-migration countries where the percentages of objections are low (for example, Australia, New Zealand, Spain and Switzerland). However, there are also several countries with significantly high levels of migration where the proportion of the population objecting to a migrant living next door is high, especially in the Middle East and parts of Asia. This may be related to the relative newness of migration in those countries, as well as the specific migration dynamics in those regions. Clearly, however, there is no consistent correlation between the acceptance of migrants and the share of migrants in the national population". (OIM, 2011, 9)

What seems to be clear in the results of the several analysed interviews is that attitudes towards immigration are closely related to the availability of work in the recipient countries of foreign immigration. Respondents who support restrictions to immigration mainly relate them to employment or unemployment levels, availability of jobs, but also with the perception of immigrants taking jobs away from nationals or placing a strain on a country's resources. In Europe, 40% of respondents agree that immigrants greatly benefit their nations, but 52% disagree. The numbers vary depending on the country. In the Spanish case, for example, the figures are similar to the average in the European Union (40% support the concept); in the UK, there is a more positive perception (47%), but not as many as Finland (54%), Luxemburg (56%), or Sweden (79%). The OIM emphasises the importance of political and media discourses:

> "As migration has increasingly attracted media attention over the past decade, gaining saliency in political debates, it is important to consider the critical role the media play in both influencing and reflecting public opinion. Similarly, in terms of policy, the media have the ability to act as 'both an agenda setter and driver on immigration issues, and a mirror reflecting debates going on in public and policy circles' (Papademetriou and Heuser, 2009, 23). Accurate and balanced reporting is therefore a key role and responsibility of the media in partnership with relevant actors, particularly policymakers". (OIM, 2011, 24)

IOE points out that in Spain until 2000, when the proportion of undocumented immigrants was under 3%, the surveys showed an average of 10% of people answered in a xenophobic way. However, by the middle of the previous decade, the percentage increased to 30%, surpassing the ambivalent and getting close to the tolerant, yet still the largest group:

> "In the opinion of the "intolerant" people, the immigrants don't have a positive influence on Spanish society and coexist uneasily with them: they must be sent back to their countries or be selectively accepted only and on condition that they adapt to the native customs (cultural assimilation)". (Colectivo IOE, 2008, 7; my translation)

The analysis by IOE and OIM agreed that there is a correlation between the perception of immigration and respondents' education levels and economic status. OIM remarks that skilled working class members are the most negative. IOE declares the majority of xenophobic people are of low education and economic status levels, and thus they see the future with less optimism. Nonetheless, to clarify, qualitative studies take an open approach to exploring social discourse, allowing the attitudes of the native population in regards to immigration to be categorised into four basic positions: (a) Xenophobic rejection: mistrust of whoever does not share Spanish culture, and support for the closing of borders, repatriation of undocumented migrants, and jailing those who stay ("Spain for the Spaniards"); (b) Subordinate insertion: immigration is welcome if it benefits the native population's interest. Immigrants are accepted, but with the statute of subordinated citizenship ("The Spaniards are first"); (c)

Competitive integration: from the defence of the liberal-democratic state, it supports the plural Spain ("no first and second category people"); (d) Instituted projection: recognises immigrants as main characters of social life ("active democracy").

As remarked in other investigations, there is a scientific discourse that intends to describe, analyse, and predict the migratory experience. A greater number of researchers recognises its volatility, its changing nature and the impossibility of the maintenance of the arguments because numbers and data must be revaluated periodically. Academic researchers warn of the need for long-term analysis and comparative perspectives. The analysts of the legislative environment also warn of trends in immigration law and the fragile situation that immigrants are facing, which consistently marginalise them through restrictive legislation.

Progress in the studies of the analytic and critical postures to social behaviour have been echoed in academic publications, in professional conferences, in classrooms and in debate forums. However, this scientific discourse that attempts to understand immigrants does not seem to have had significant impact on the mainstream media discourse. Some researchers publish opinion pieces in newspapers, but their precepts do not seem to impact on the daily routines of news media coverage. This discrepancy between the scientific discourse and the dominant public discourse is especially reflected in the everyday information poured out in the mainstream media, and seems to be a spiral without end: the real nature of Latin American immigration is seen through a distorting glass that reveals only a few characteristics of some of its components, and this is the information that penetrates the public's opinion (Retis, 2006).

Teun van Dijk (1997) warns that the greater part of our social and political knowledge, and our beliefs about the world, comes from the dozens of pieces of information we read or listen to every day. It is likely there is no other discursive practice, aside from daily conversations, that is practiced more frequently and by more people than following the mainstream media news. In consequence, Latin American immigrants in Spain and the United States are known and recognised more through their presence in the media discourse than through daily coexistence. What is known about them derives from what appears in the news, articles, and interviews with politicians that take a position and have a tendency to problematise the presence of immigrants (Retis, 2006). In their analysis of how mainstream media portrayed the anti-immigration measures in the state of Arizona in 2010, Santa Ana and González de Bustamante claimed that:

> "These days the news media too often amplify the imagery of anti-immigrant demagogues; meanwhile news executives demonstrate no concerted strategy to moderate such anti-democratic discourse. They conveniently argue that they are only giving the public what it wants; read: what sells. So the public sphere, of which the news media is the most important institution, foments ignorance and fear". (Santa Ana and González de Bustamante, 2012, 278-279)

Latin American immigration is not a reality that can be contemplated simply by glancing opening the window, it is a social phenomenon collectively constructed, which has some non-typical characteristics. In other words, it doesn't constitute its nature, but it results in a symbolic construction that constitutes the "imagined immigrant" in a process of constituting a specific social figure with socio-political and cognitive resonance (Santamaría, 2002). In this symbolic construction of reality, the mainstream media discourse is the socio-cognitive gear of thinking and social sayings and, above all, the news press is the most coherent corpus. It is the constituted discourse that offers an inner coherence and a vision of the world formally structured: hence the task of newspaper as a marker of identity (Imbert, 1990). But it is also an ambivalent discourse in its referential pretension, as a pretended objective mirror of reality, and, in its function as mediator, it is also a strategic site of the constitution of social discourse. In this framework, the Latin American immigrant is represented as a symbolic actor, in a socio-cognitive ghetto created out of certain conventions (Santamaría, 2002; Retis, 2006).

Therefore, what is perceived of the reality of the Latin American immigrant is the image of a person that generates conflict and constitutes news value: hit men, exploited workers, prostitutes, drug dealers, "*illegals*," etc.[7] These pieces of information are represented in mainstream media out of context, in a more local approach and without delving deeply into the complexity of the phenomenon (Granados, 2002). Latin American immigration is a result of several factors at multiple levels but the intersection between local and global is rarely showcased in the news. The media tends to represent the negative side of immigration, ignoring information about the cultures and countries of origin, socio-historical causes that promote immigration, the relationship of co-dependency between pull/push immigration conditions, the global dimension of the immigration subject, information on personal and immediate matters to the immigrant, his/her fraudulent arrival, obstacles to his/her insertion into the host society, and the lived reality of the immigrant. All of the spatio-temporal and historic aspects of the immigrant's situation are reduced to a simple sensationalist anecdote of the newspaper headline (Granados, 2002).

4. Images of Hispanics / Latinas in the United States

Although there has been a growth of diversity in the demographic composition of the US, American newsrooms still have more to do in terms of incorporating journalists of ethnic and racial minorities. According to the American Society of News Editors (ASNE), there has been a constant decrease in minority representation in the newsroom. In the case of Latin Americans, the 2012 Census concluded that only 4% of the journalists are of Hispanic origin (1,650), which is 239 fewer than the year before and 448 fewer than in 2002. Out of the total of Hispanic journalists in newsrooms, 59% are men and 41% are women (ASNE, 2012). However, the majority of the population in US newsrooms are white (87% in total). Of the 35,584 white journalists that work in reporting and journalism, 64% of them are men and 36% are women. This unbalanced and unequal distribution explains in part why the US media tends to understand its audience as being led by middle-class white men (Weaver *et al.,* 2006).

As a consequence, the perception of "the others" in the mainstream media discourse tends to be represented in a distorted manner: members of a group that share certain ideologies are in favour of very general ideas, which constitute the base of specific beliefs about the world and are what guide their interpretations of events, aside from social practices (Wodak, 2003). Ideologies organise individuals and society in terms of polarisation: generally, the information regarding "us" in respect to "them" is incorporated. Van Dijk (1996) explains that the strategy of the ideological discourse is, in general, "To talk of our positive aspects" or "To talk of their negative aspects." The positive representation of the in-group and the negative representation of the out-group not only expose the conflict among the groups and contrast forms of interaction, but also condition how we talk of "us" and "the others." These four principles belong to what has been called the "ideological framework," which applies to all structures of discourse (Van Dijk, 1996, 21).

Media plays a very important role in the reproduction and dissemination of simplifications in terms of race, class, and gender. Thus some critical researchers discuss whether we are confronting the *mass media* or the *class media* when analysing the composition, structure, and behaviour of the mainstream media in United States (Wilson, Gutierrez and Chao, 2003). Several researchers point out that stereotypes allow the mental organisation of collective perceptions about other groups as different from the in-group or the reference group (Fiske and Taylor, 1991). In this sense, the images that have been constructed about Latin

Americans have contributed to consolidating stereotypes, which feed segregation or minority dominance, particularly revealed in fiction, where the new *alien* portrayal perception of the immigrant is shifting from neglect to resentment (Ramírez-Berg, 2002, 159). The metaphors or textual images reproduced in the public discourse about Mexicans and, by extension, Hispanics contribute to forming a window in which Americans frame their domestic worldview and their underlying political and social values (Santa Ana, 2002, 8).

Critical researchers state that the coverage of Latinos by the American press has been distorted and soaked in xenophobia, racism, ignorance, and social distance. As is the case for African Americans, the journalistic view of these groups perpetuates their exclusion and stereotyped images, and there is scarce participation of these groups in the mainstream media and hardly any opportunities to express or to input alternative points of view (Uriarte, 2003). Uriarte recalls that almost all American media have committed serious mistakes in their coverage of minorities, been immune due to its focus on extremely wider and immediate audiences. Among the paradigmatic cases is the coverage of the Zoot Suit Riots in 1943 or the events surrounding the demonstration against the Vietnam War in 1960, when Hispanics were considerably criminalised by press stereotypes. More recently, in 1982, during a campaign against undocumented immigration, Reagan approved the largest project of raids and deportations ever undertaken: *Operation Jobs*. During the four months of the events, the American press, which gathered information on their front pages, did not provide any context about the role of cheap labour in the United States. Reporters did not feature demographic information about work or labour conditions of the majority of underpaid workers who received below minimum wages. Coverage was not extended to the deportation process or to issues related to immigrant women involved in the events, and despite the engagement of a great number of researchers on these events, reporters did not mention any expert source (Uriarte, 2003, 43).

Generalisations about Hispanic youth as gang members and drug dealers criminalise the Hispanic group in general (Uriarte, 2003). In the coverage of the 1992 demonstrations, known as Los Angeles Civil Unrest or Los Angeles Riots, the media repeated the same mistakes. The reporters covered the events under the cloak of black/white conflict, when in fact, the neighbourhood where the incidents occurred was principally home to Hispanic and Afro-American people: "there have been few opportunities for Hispanics to report about them [the events of 1992] or to provide an alternative point of view. As a result, it has reinforced misunderstandings and stereotypical imagery. The social distance has raised blinders which obscure perception of Hispanics' contributions" (Uriarte, 2003, 44).

Quantitative studies conducted in the 1990s showed that the share of news concerning Hispanics decreased to 1% (National Council of La Raza, 1997): less than the Afro-American or Asiatic group (Entman and Rojecky, 2000). The most recent study by the National Association of Hispanic Journalists (NAHJ, 2006) showed that in the case of television, the representation margins decrease much more than in the written press. Only 0.83% of broadcast stories by ABC, CBS, and NBC in 2005 broached some topic regarding Hispanics. This low percentage is, paradoxically, an increase versus the previous year, when the average was 0.72%. The five most recurrent topics of these news stories were those related to national government (19%), crime (18.1%), human-interest issues (17%), immigration (14.3%), and sports (11.4%).

Events regarding immigration and crime are commonly represented in a negative sense in the news. A significant percentage of the featured stories lacked opinion diversity: 33.3% never mention any source, and from those that cited sources, one-third referred exclusively to a single one. NAHJ's report demonstrated that Hispanics are non-existent in those stories not related to Hispanics. In other words, they do not appear in the image of the general public represented by the media. One of the main findings of this report noted that despite an accelerated growth of the Hispanic population, the American media, still desensitised, does not present stories about the country's largest minority and, in respect to migratory issues, these topics are not presented from the perspective of Hispanic immigrants (NAHJ, 2006).

Hispanics tend to be made invisible in the mainstream media discourse and when they appear they are represented in a misinformed way and with a greater negative connotation than other ethnic minorities (National Council of La Raza, 1997). The analysis of the representation of Puerto Ricans in the New York Times and the New York Post found that three-quarters of the news was centred on conflict (*ibid*). In 1970, Wilson and Gutierrez (1985) stated that a major part of the news about Hispanics was around issues like youth in gangs, irregular immigration, or inter-racial violence.

American mainstream media tends to ignore the complex diversity of origins of the Hispanic communities. The terms "Hispanic," "Latino," or "Chicano" are used to represent a multitude of people (Del Olmo, 1985). The database exploration started for this ongoing research found other related topics, such as use of the terms, "aliens" or "illegal," which are terms commonly used in the news media discourse to talk about residents without administrative documentation. Alternative mass media and critics such as Colorlines (2011) plead for the exclusion of these terms from newsroom features; however, they continue to be accepted by the style book of Associated Press (Tenore, 2011).

In this context, Latin American immigrant women suffer triple invisibility in the media discourse: by class, race, and gender. Historically, Hispanic women have been represented by the American media through two antagonistic faces: extremely sensual and passionate, or as menial domestic helps (Wilson, Gutierrez and Chao, 2003). The second wave of feminist theories incorporated the concept of race, but it is within the third wave that more studies were produced about women of colour in the media, especially with respect to African Americans (Nerwick, 2000) or female journalists (Cropp, Frisbi and Mills, 2003; Cuklanz, 1995). Critical researchers such as Valdivia (2004) criticised these studies for approaching racial diversity in a binary sense – that is, black/white. In this schema, Latina/os, as well as other ethnic groups such as Asian Americans and Native Americans, among others, fell beyond the scope of public discussion and academic research:

> "As a result of the twin forces of institutional and marketing needs to construct, survey, and sell to an identifiable ethnic group as well as internal Latina/o community strategies to forge a pan-national, pan-ethnic political and cultural group from which to make demands on the state and other social institutions, we now have the category Latina/os, the cultural identity of Latinidad, the state of being or performing a Latina/o identity, and the formation of Latina/o Studies within the academy". (Valdivia, 2004, 108)

Valdivia takes up this reflection again years after remarking on the complexity of theorising the pan-ethnicity of Latinidad, which forces us to face the impurity of populations and cultures and the inability to keep the boundaries clean and static (Valdivia, 2010). In recent decades, the studies developed by Hispanic researchers have deconstructed the forms in which the dominant public discourse represents Hispanics and Latino immigrants. The works of Subervi-Velez (2005) and Vargas (2000) have demonstrated that Latinos have been underrepresented as sources and subjects of news and have been depicted as burdens for society in issues related to immigration, crime, and affirmative action. In this context, Latinas are almost invisible in the mainstream media, for several reasons ranging from their images being twisted, stereotyped, or simply being omitted. Consequently, the average attitude formed in the society is that of indifference, distrust, and mystification (Cortina, 2002). Empirical and historical approaches have demonstrated that Hispanic women have not been well represented, or they have been represented through distorted images (underrepresented/misrepresented) (Rodríguez, 1997). Moreover, when they appear, they are represented in a folk sense (Calafell and Delgado, 2004). Critical researchers such as Correa (2010) remark on the lack of studies about the coverage of Latinas in mainstream news media, making it a fertile ground for academic research.

5. The Discourse of Latin American Immigrant Women in Spain

As in the United States, several researchers in Spain have pleaded for the inclusion of gender perspectives to analyse the behaviour of our society in a critical manner. Dolores Juliano (2000) recalls that this perspective arrived relatively late to the studies of migratory movements in Spain. Her work has demonstrated that social visibility of immigrant men is highly superior to that of immigrant women, and recalls that incorporation of the gender variable does not mean simply providing data but changing the meaning of the data and rethinking the interpretative models. Gregorio (2006) reiterates that feminist perspectives, when interpreting the suitable act of categorising as an expression of power, propose the deconstruction of fixed categories assigned to the subjects. These critical perspectives allow the development of relevant strategies of analysis at the time we approach the subject of study.

Several investigations remarked on the structural and conjectural conditions of the migratory projects of Latin American women, and on racial and ethnic categories in relation to access to labour (Pedone, 2003; Herranz, 1998; Catarino and Oso, 2000). In her analysis of Ecuadorian immigrants in Spain, Pedone (2006) criticises the stigma of the adventurer immigrant man versus the immigrant woman who abandons her home, interpreting the collective ideal as one that overflows with emotional, familial and social relationships. Juliano (2000) reminds us that we would do better to name them as structural traveller women than accidental immigrants. Juliano also notes in a critical manner the need to rethink the way in which migrant women are incorporated into Spanish society when she remarks the double discrimination of the labour market by class and gender, which adds to discrimination by race, producing the ethnicisation of social reproduction: "what is interesting in regards to immigrant women, but also in regards to subaltern groups, is, in part, to critically analyse what *we* do with respect to *them* (how we see them, how we read them, which are our stereotypes, which paths we are providing them)" (Juliano, 2000, 389; my translation).

In Spain there has been great progress made in the critical analysis of media representation of non-European immigrants. However, the gender perspective has barely been touched upon. The pioneering studies of Mary Nash (2000, 2004) in this line have shown a series of guidelines in the representations of immigrant women in the Spanish press in the mid-1990s: the ethnocentric thinking of postcolonial symbols for immigrant women and men, and in specific way the androcentric thinking of a discourse of gender:

> "The news coverage of immigrant women does not reflect their actual weight in society, as the journalistic discourse generates a field of meanings from the silence that makes them invisible and creates a public opinion climate that minimises their presence and recognition. This discourse of invisibilisation affects a collective imagination on immigration that has very negative consequences, since it excludes women from a migration model based on a false male pattern. The perpetuation of a male model to form the popular approach of migration has led to a biased view that denies the current feminisation of migration. It may be an explanatory factor of the lack of gender-specific perspectives in articulating public policy of integration and, therefore, its ineffectiveness in certain situations". (Nash 2007, 59-60; my translation)

Nash found the existence of recurrent patterns between the dynamic of gender's power and the articulation of a collective experience of immigrant women as a cultural minority: "The prism of double otherness of gender and minority constitute a culturally prominent mechanism that denies a crucial role to women, conditioning them to collective projects and 'ethnicising' them in cultural terms" (Nash, 2007, 60; my translation). Pérez (2003) analysed news coverage of immigration during the first trimester of 2002 in the Basque Country and Navarre, and found that in three-quarters of the news coverage, women were invisible in text and photographs. The inclusion of women is the result of an exception process because it is wrongly assumed that immigrants tend to be male: "Women tend to appear mainly in the context related with the family and as victims of sexist values that are opposite to supposedly equalitarian values of the host society" (Pérez, 2003, 132). Pérez found that women are rarely shown as workers and when they are, they are portrayed in a paternalistic tone. In the representation of women working in domestic service the media discourse enhances their "kind" and "self-sacrificing" characters. Those who work in prostitution are seen as victims of human trafficking, and those who have married Spaniards are hyper-sexualised: immigrant women are seen as victims without migratory projects.

Reigada (2006) focused her analysis in three discursive strategies commonly utilised: (a) the construction of difference as an element of stigmatisation: it reflects in great measure how discourses of neo-assimilation, based in symbolic or cultural racism, have penetrated the mass media; this strategy of representation has contributed to expanding and legitimising the discourse of exclusion that understands cultural difference as an element of social conflict; (b) the victimisation of immigrant women which tends to consider them as passive, devoid of agency; (c) the discursive strategy which tends to objectify women, as in the case of immigrant women from East Europe hired to farm strawberries in Huelva, who are hyper-visualised because of their physical appearance: "while in the discourses about Muslim immigrant women, the journalist's eyes are attracted by the body (excessively) covered under the hijab (burka, veil or chador in other cases), in the discourses about Polish and Romanian immigrant working women, the eye stops at their semi-naked bodies. These aspects that are hyper-visualised through close-ups are, in that sense, opposite in each kind of representation" (Reigada, 2006, 12; my translation).

Aierbe (2008) examined the representation of immigrant women from March 2006 through November 2007, finding scarce representation of female figures in media framing of immigration. His study demonstrated that employment status is rarely mentioned (3.4% of the data). In case an immigrant women's occupation is mentioned, a major part of it refers to domestic service or to elderly care, or to situations related to prostitution. In contrast, information related to criminal activities against immigrant women reiterated information related to prostitution. The lack of representation of immigrant women as economic agents reiterates the image of an "auxiliary," "people that help us to take care of our elders and those whom seem to be doing us a favor" (Aierbe, 2008, 20; my translation). Agrela reminds us that the importance of institutional discourses resides in their position as dominant, through the utilisation of privileged channels for their dissemination, excluding alternative ways of thinking; and their legitimatisation, given their credibility gained as official objective theory: "both aspects give to institutional rhetoric a major capacity to define meanings from which practice is standardised" (Agrela, 2004, 32). State policies, far from being the product of rational objective analysis, are loaded with moral values and are an expression of relations of power within states and between them.

Mass media in Spain has reacted in consistent way with respect to the paths of political debate about immigration. The work of a variety of regional and national media observatories has been prolific, while there have been few initiatives instigated by professional journalism news media organisations. From various disciplines, as researchers of immigration, several of us have participated in workshops, seminars, and forums in undergraduate and graduate academic programs. In recent years, several manuals have been published, and initiatives and proposals for action have been forthcoming from academic as well as the administrative and associative sectors. All of these initiatives have been developed to help improve the coverage of diversity in the news discourses (Retis, 2008).

For several years now I have been working on the analysis of the representation of Latin American immigrants in the Spanish press (Retis, 2006). Through database explorations I found some events that have marked milestones in the forms of representation of Latin American immigrant women. The murder of Dominican Lucrecia Pérez in November 1992 put the image of a Latin American immigrant woman within the "problem of immigration" discourse, on the front page for the first time. With the case of Lucrecia Pérez, a female face was given to the phenomenon of population flows of Latin American household heads. The juncture of the debate about rising attitudes of racism in Spain was reproduced by the Spanish media during the days immediately following the event. During that time the mainstream media gathered concerns mainly from traditional sources. The debate, however, vanished from the media arena, making space once again for legal work framed in terms of the European "discomfort" discourse on immigration.

In January 2001 a train hit a truck carrying Ecuadorian workers in Lorca, Murcia. The Lorca case got an unusual amount of space in the Spanish mainstream media, including coverage of a survivor, Nancy, a 14-year-old young woman who had replaced her mother on that day in the picking of broccoli fields, who symbolised the extreme conditions of labour exploitation due to her status as an immigrant, female, and a minor. On 4 January 2001, the front covers of national newspapers coincided their headlines. The Lorca case turned out to be a milestone. It was the first time that Ecuadorians, the major group of Latinos in Spain, had been represented in the public discussions with such intensity. For the first time the Spanish media started to give an account of the increase in immigration flows from South America. It was the beginning of a new era in which Latin Americans started to occupy pages in the newspapers (Retis, 2006). A comparative discourse analysis demonstrated that at the turn of the millennium, the image of Colombian immigrant women was constructed mainly by frames related to delinquency, prostitution, and domestic violence conflicts. Discussion groups with Ecuadorian and Colombian immigrants reconfirmed their own perception: the mainstream media turned out to be a mirror in where not only Spaniards but also Latin

American immigrants represent themselves (Retis, 2006).

In January 2007, a fight between two teenage females, one Spaniard and one Mexican, led to a clash between their boyfriends, a young Dominican and a Bolivian in the city of Alcorcón, Madrid. This conflict triggered a series of confrontations between various youngsters in a confusion of nationalities that the Spanish press immediately reported as Latinos vs. Spaniards in several headlines throughout the following days. In the Alcorcón case, the figure of youth gang members was involved as part of a contemporary trend towards the overrepresentation of "moral panics" (Cohen, 2002). Media coverage of the events concentrated on the conjuncture of conditions, and the political debate among political representatives who utilised the debate on immigration conflicts as a card in partisan confrontations. The most immediate effect of this treatment was the projection of biased and partial views in public discourse, nurtured and fed by the media debate. In some cases, racist and xenophobic discussion received major media projection, reinforcing the tendency towards emotional treatment of news information, in this case related to fairness. This critical analysis demonstrated that women were rarely portrayed, and when they appeared at all they were minimised or portrayed as passive subjects or as followers of the contestants (Retis and García, 2009).

In October of the same year, aggression against an Ecuadorian girl by a young white Spanish man on a Barcelona train restarted a debate about racist attitudes and gender violence. In this case, Spanish newspapers covered the event in the social section. Eighteen uploads on YouTube generated hundreds of comments and, for the first time, online media and social networks started to take the lead in news information circulation. The analysis demonstrated that news coverage focused again on official sources, such as members of the police department and local administration. Journalists focused their attention on the attacker and his racist attitudes, even finding an excuse for his violent actions in the involvement of alcohol. The victimisation of the girl was evident in television's explicit treatment of images recorded on security cameras. Victimising and exclusionary discourses about Latin American immigrant women in mainstream media are more evident in the comparative analysis of news information and TV fiction series (Galán and Retis, 2010).

The Mugak observatory offers a useful tool for the analysis of daily newspapers. A search in this online database on topics such as immigration and immigrant women provides firm evidence: women are not represented in 48,188 of the 56,402 stories published between 2003 and 2010 . The sample further indicates that in cases in which they appear, only in 4,851 case they are portrayed as news subjects, whereas in 3,363 news stories, women are secondary news sources, appearing in the background. The invisibility of immigrant women in the media contrasts with the predominance of official sources. In the case of the sample, the sources of information mainly used are the representatives of the Ministry of the Interior, the police, the State government, courts, and regional and local administrations (a total of 2,341 news stories, compared to 723 in which minority people were mentioned). Linked to this invisibility in discourse is the minorities' poor access to public discourse, which reproduces dominant modes of discrimination in public debate (Bañón, 2002). In other words, the mainstream media barely portrays immigrant women. When the media does speak of them, it is essentially as secondary subjects of news information, and primarily in connection to issues related to law enforcement and immigration control policies. As a result, the most recurrent themes are events of crime against ethnic minorities and themes of religion, customs, employment status, hostility, discrimination, and racism.

6. Notes from an ongoing research

Throughout these pages I have traced trends in news coverage of Latin American women in United States and Spain. The review of secondary sources demonstrates gradual feminisation of these migration flows. It is essential to incorporate transnational and gender approaches to understand the complexities of the processes of displacement, arrival, and integration. As discussed in this chapter, most Latin American immigrant women have left their countries during the last two decades, which accounts for their recent settlement processes. Latin American women as heads of households transform their family and emotional relationships. In consequence, transnational motherhood is consolidated in transnational circuits across borders. Many Latin American immigrant women are incorporated into the processes of social stratification in their countries of destination, and in subordinate positions. Critical studies in both countries demonstrate the vulnerabilities of a large proportion of Latin American immigrant women and advocate a gender perspective for better understanding the complexities of their realities.

This chapter has also explored general trends in media coverage of international migration and its effects on the generation of public opinion. Critical studies call for better news coverage of immigration. They also argue for the need for a better understanding of the conditions of origin and destination. Comparative analysis showed that communication on immigration needs to be improved: public opinion in the countries of destination is not informed by a clear idea of its real dimensions, of the structural conditions of displacements, of their links to capital flows and to the international distribution of labour. It is essential to promote a better understanding of migration and the improvement of media coverage on the subject. This is a challenge for contemporary journalism and demands political willingness from all stakeholders involved in dominant public discourse.

This first contribution has tried to outline trends of media representation of Latin American women in two countries that have become the preferred destination of migratory movements. Deepening understanding of the sociodemographic context allows us to identify flows that occur simultaneously, in parallel fashion and, in some cases, circularly. Transnational and gender perspectives, and critical media theory, allow us to analyse and understand discourses of power, racism, and discrimination in the host societies. The sharing of recent studies on the treatment of diversity in Europe and the United States will facilitate the extrapolation of the conclusions and enrich the comparative analysis.

Notes

1. 740 million people move inside their own country, almost four times the number that move internationally. Out of the latter, only one-third moves from a poor country to a richer country (less than 70 million people). Unlike what is usually presented in the international media discourse, a great majority of international migrants move from an undeveloped country to an undeveloped country. According to this report, there is room for better policies of admittance and treatment of international immigrants.
2. Data varies from several reports. The UN Human Development Report of 2009 estimates that there are 50 million people living and working irregularly.
3. The Global Report of Migrations Worldwide in 2010 asserted that the crisis had five kinds of repercussions: (a) several thousand migrants lost employment, (b) the contingent of migrants did not decrease because many migrants chose not to return, (c) immigrants were affected by the crisis in the destination countries, (d) a direct effect of the crisis has been reduced irregular immigration currents, (e) despite a decrease in remittances, they remained constant, probably because returning migration was not as big as expected (IOM 2011, 60-61).
4. The Convention on the Elimination of All Forms of Discrimination against Women (CEDAW) is an international trade convention about human rights, dedicated exclusively to equality of gender. It was adopted on December 18, 1979 by the United Nations and usually described as the law project or program of women's rights. It has thirty articles, defines discrimination against women, and establishes an agenda for national action to end such discrimination.

5. Hispanics continue to concentrate in six states: Arizona, California, Colorado, Florida, Illinois, New Mexico, New Jersey, New York, and Texas. A new progression in geographic dispersion can be perceived: the states with greatest immigration growth in the last decade were South Carolina, Alabama, Tennessee, Kentucky, Arkansas, North Carolina, Maryland, Mississippi, and South Dakota (US Census 2010). Two-thirds of Latinos in the United States are Mexicans (32 million) and there are increasing numbers of Puerto Ricans (4.4 million), Salvadorans (1.73 million), Cubans (1.67 million), Dominicans (1.4 million), Guatemalans (1 million), Colombians (970,000), Hondurans (625,000), Ecuadorians (611,000), Peruvians (600,000), Nicaraguans (370,000), Argentineans and Venezuelans (230,000), and other Latin American groups (Motel 2012).
6. Cited by OIM 2008.
7. In comparative analysis of media discourse in both countries the term "illegal" related to issues of immigration. The discussion on the misuse of the term is outlined below.

Bibliography

Aierbe, Peio. 2008. "Representación de las mujeres trabajadoras inmigrantes en los medios de comunicación". In *Comunicación, empleo y mujer migrante*, coord. Antonio Bañón Hernández, 7-20. Madrid: Tercera Prensa

Agrela, Belén. 2004. "La acción social y las mujeres inmigrantes: ¿Hacia unos modelos de intervención?". *Portularia* 4: 31-42.

Calafell, Bernardette y Fernando Delgado. 2004. "Reading Latina/o Images: Interrogating Americanos". *Critical Studies in Media Communication* 21 (1): 1-21.

Canales, Alejandro. 2011. "Las profundas contribuciones de la migración latinoamericana a los Estados Unidos", In *Migración internacional en América Latina y el Caribe. Nuevas tendencias, nuevos enfoques*, ed. Jorge Martínez, 257-331. CEPAL: Santiago de Chile.

Catarino, Christine and Laura Oso. 2000. "La inmigración femenina en Madrid y Lisboa: hacia una etnización del servicio doméstico y de las empresas de limpieza". *Papers* 60: 183-207.

Casilda, Ramón. 2002. *La década dorada. Economía e inversiones españolas en América Latina 1990-2000*. Madrid: Ediciones de la Universidad de Alcalá.

Colectivo IOE. 2008. *Papeles de relaciones ecosociales y cambio global*, Madrid: CIP-Ecosocial, FUHEM, 103: 95-104.

—. 2001. *Mujer, Inmigración y trabajo*. Madrid: IMSERSO, Ministerio de trabajo y asuntos sociales.

Colorlines. 2011. Colorline's.com *Immigration Style Book*. Available: http://colorlines.com/droptheiword/resources/en/journalists.html# Last accessed on 30 March 2012.
Cortés, Patricia. 2005. Mujeres migrantes de América Latina y el Caribe: Derechos humanos, mitos y duras realidades. *Serie Población y Desarrollo* 61. Santiago de Chile: CELADE
Cortina, Guadalupe. 2002. "La política de la representación: la rebelión de las latinas en los *mass media*". *Arizona Journal of Hispanic Cultural Studies* 6: 115-127.
Correa, Teresa. 2010. "Framing Latinas: Hispanic Women through the lenses of Spanish-language and English-language news media". *Journalism* 11 (4): 425-443.
Cropp, Fritz, Cyntia Frisbi and Dean Mills. 2003. *Journalism Across Cultures*. Iowa: Iowa University Press.
Cuklanz, Lisa. 1995. "News Coverage of Ethnic and Gender Issues in the Big Dan's Rape Case". In *Feminism, Multiculturalism and the Media. Global Diversities*, ed. Angharad Valdivia, 145-162. Sage: Thousand Oaks.
Dávila, Arlene. 2001. *Latinos Inc. The Marketing and Making of a People*. Berkeley: University of California Press.
Del Olmo, Frank. 1985. *Latinos in the United States: A Resource Guide for Journalists*. Washington: NAHJ.
—. 2001. "The 'Latino Initiative' Reshapes the Los Angeles Times's Coverage". *Nieman Reports* 55 (2): 36-37.
Ehrenreich Barbara and Arlie Hoshschild. 2003. *Global Woman*, London: Granta Books.
Entman, Robert and Arnold Rojecki. 2000. *The Black Image in the White Mind: Media and Race in America*. Boulder: University of Chicago.
Galán, Elena and Jéssica Retis. Forthcoming. "Discursos en torno a la inmigración en España: Análisis comparado de la cobertura periodística y los programas de ficción", In *Al descubierto. El poder democrático de los medios*, coord. María García. Madrid: Fragua.
Garza, Hedda. 2001. *Latinas. Hispanic Women in the United States*. Albuquerque: University of New Mexico Press.
Gonzales, Felisa. 2008. *Hispanic Women in the United States*, 2007. Washington: Pew Hispanic Research Center.
Greco, Stephanie. 2006. *Media and Minorities. The Politics of Race in News and Entertainment*. Oxford: Rowman and Littlefield Publishers.
Gregorio, Carmen. 2006. "Contribuciones feministas a problemas epistemológicos de la disciplina antropológica: representación y

relaciones de poder". *Revista de Antropología Iberoamericana* 1 (1): 22-39.

Herranz, Yolanda. 1998. "La inmigración latinoamericana en distintos contextos de recepción". *Migraciones* 3: 31-52.

Hondagneu-Sotelo, Pierrette and Ernistine Avila. 1997. "'I'm Here, but I'm There' The Meanings of Latina Transnational Motherhood". *Gender & Society* 11 (5): 548-571.

International Organization for Migration (2008) *World Migration*. Ginebra: OIM.

Izquierdo, Antonio, Diego López Lera and Raquel Martínez. 2002. "Los preferidos del siglo XXI: la inmigración latinoamericana en España". In *La inmigración en España: contextos y alternativas,* eds. Francisco García and Carolina López, 237-289. Granada: Laboratorio de Estudios Interculturales.

Juliano, Dolores. 2000. "Mujeres estructuralmente viajeras: estereotipos y estrategias". *Papers* 60: 381-389.

—. 2002. "Los desafíos de la inmigración. Antropología, educación e interculturalidad". *Anuario de Psicología* 33 (4): 487-498.

Lewitt, Peggy. 2001. *The Transnational Villagers*, Berkeley: University of California Press.

Lewitt, Peggy. 2009. Routes and Roots: Understanding the Lives of the Second Generation Transnationally". *Journal of Ethnic and Migration Studies* 35 (7): 1225-1242.

López, Mark, Ana González and Seth Motel. 2012. *As Deportations Rise to Record Levels, Most Latinos Oppose Obama's Policy*. Washington: Pew Hispanic Center.

Martínez, Jorge (ed.). 2011. *Migración internacional en América Latina y el Caribe. Nuevas tendencias, nuevos enfoques*. CEPAL: Santiago de Chile.

—. 2003. "El mapa migratorio de America Latina y el Caribe". *Serie Población y Desarrollo,* 44. Santiago de Chile: CEPAL.

—. 2006. *América Latina y el Caribe: migración internacional, derechos humanos y desarrollo*. Santiago de Chile: CEPAL.

Mignolo, Walter. 2003. *Historias locales / Diseños globales. Colonialidad, conocimientos subalternos y pensamiento fronterizo*. Madrid: AKAL.

Motel, Seth. 2012. *Statistical Portrait of Hispanics in the United States, 2010*. Washington: Pew Hispanic Center.

Nash, Mary. 2000. "Construcción social de la mujer extranjera". In *Mujeres y migración en el Mediterráneo occidental*, dir. María Angeles Roque, 275-290. Barcelona: Icaria.

—. 2004. *Mujeres en el mundo. Historia, retos y movimientos*. Madrid: Alianza.

—. 2005a. *Inmigrantes en nuestro espejo. Inmigración y discurso periodístico en la prensa española*. Barcelona: Icaria.

—. 2005b. "La doble alteridad en la comunidad imaginada de las mujeres inmigrantes". In *Inmigración, género y espacios urbanos. Los retos de la diversidad*, eds. Mary Nash, Nuria Benach and Rosa Tello, 17-32. Barcelona: Bellaterra Ediciones.

—. 2007. "Repensar las representaciones mediáticas de las mujeres inmigrantes". *Cuaderns de la Mediterraneia* 7: 59-62.

National Association of Hispanic Journalists. 2006. *The Brownout Report 2006. The Portrayal of Latinos and Latino Issues on Network Television News*. Washington: NAHJ.

National Council of La Raza. 1997. "Out of the Picture: Hispanics in the Media". In *Latin Looks. Images of Latinas and Latinos in the U.S. Media*, ed. Clara Rodríguez, 21-35. Boulder: Westview Review.

Nerwik, Pamela. 2000. *Within the Veil. Black Journalists, White Media*, New York: New York University Press.

Observatorio Permanente de la Inmigración (OPI). 2011. *Extranjeros residentes en España*. Madrid: Ministerio de Empleo y Seguridad Social.

Organización Internacional para las Migraciones. 2011. *Informe sobre las migraciones en el mundo*, Ginebra: OIM.

Oso, Laura. 2005. "Las jefas de hogar en un contexto migratorio: modelos y rupturas". In *Mujeres en el camino: en fenómeno de la inmigración femenina en España*, coord. Francisco Checa, 85-104. Madrid: Icaria.

—. 2009. "Familia, empresa y movilidad ocupacional: mujeres latinoamericanas en España". *Melanges de la Casa de Velázquez* 39: 75-96.

Passel, Jeffrey. 2009. *A Portrait of Unauthorized immigrants in the United States*. Washington: Pew Research Cencer.

Passel, Jeffrey, Cohn D'Vera and Mark López. 2011. *Census 2010: 50 Million Latinos. Hispanic Account for More than Half of Nation's Growth in Past Decade*. Washington: Pew Research Center.

Pedone, Claudia. 2003. "Las relaciones de género en las familias ecuatorians dentro del contexto migratorio internacional hacia el Estado español. *Treballs de la Societat Catalana de Geografía* 56: 709-106.

—. 2006. *Estrategias migratorias y poder: tú siempre jalas a los tuyos*. Quito: Abya-Yala.

Pérez, Clara. 2003. "Género y discurso sobre la inmigración en la prensa." *Análisis de prensa 2002*: 123-174.

—. 2005. "Las inmigrantes en la prensa: víctimas sin proyecto migratorio". *Mugak,* 24. http://revista.mugak.eu/articulos/show/260 Last accessed on 31 May 2012.

Portes, Alejandro, Rosa Aparicio and William Haller. 2009. "La segunda generación en Madrid, un estudio longitudinal". *ARI* 67: 1-10.

Ramírez-Berg, Charles. 2002. *Latino Images in Film: Stereotypes, Subversion and Resistance.* Austin: University of Texas Press.

Reigada, Alicia. 2004. "Barreras culturales y barreras de género: la construcción de la otredad a través de la prensa". Paper presented at Forum Universal de las Cultures, Barcelona. 9 May- 16 September 2004.

—. 2006. "Pensar la(s) diferencia(s) desde la comunicación: inmigración femenina y discursos sociales". Paper presented at IX Congress Ibercom. Sevilla. Universidad de Sevilla. 15-18 November 2006.

Retis, Jéssica. 2006. *El discurso público sobre la inmigración latinoamericana en España. Análisis de la construcción de las imágenes de los inmigrantes latinoamericanos en la prensa de referencia*. Unpublished PhD thesis. Madrid: Instituto Universitario de Investigación Ortega y Gasset - Universidad Complutense de Madrid.

—. 2008. *Espacios mediáticos de las migraciones en Madrid: Génesis y evolución.* Observatorio de las Migraciones y la Convivencia Intercultural de la Ciudad de Madrid: Madrid.

—. 2009. "Derechos humanos de las mujeres inmigrantes latinoamericanas en el reciente cine documental de Estados Unidos: Maid in America y Maid in L.A". Paper presented at International Association of Mass Communication Research Conference, México. 21- 24 July 2009.

Retis, Jéssica and Paola García. 2009. "Imágenes mediáticas de los jóvenes latinoamericanos en la prensa europea: la construcción mediatica de los pánicos morales". Paper presented at 53 Congreso Internacional de Americanistas. México. 19 -24 July 2009.

Retis, Jéssica and Elena Galán. 2010. "Qué nos siguen contando sobre la inmigración en España: Análisis comparado de los recientes discursos en la ficción televisiva y la prensa de referencia". Paper presented at Congreso Internacional AE-IC Málaga *2010 Comunicación y desarrollo en la era* digital*.* University of Málaga, 3-5 February 2010.

Rodríguez, Clara. 1997. *Latin Looks. Images of Latinas and Latinos in the U.S. Media*. Boulder: Westview Review.

—. 2000. *Changing Race. Latinos, the Census, and the History of Ethnicity in the United States*. New York: New York University Press.

Santa Ana, Otto. 2002. *Brown Tide Rising: Metaphors of Latinos in Contemporary American Public Discourse*. Austin: University of Texas Press.

Santa Ana, Otto and Celeste González de Bustamante. 2012. "Can America Learn to Think Globally? We Don't at Our Own Risk". In *Arizona Firestorm. Global Immigration Realities, National Media, and Provincial Politics*, eds. Santa Ana, Otto and González de Bustamente, Celeste, 277-289. Lanham: Rowman & Littlefield Publishers.

Sassen, Saskia. 2003. *Contrageografías de la globalización. Género y ciudadanía en los circuitos transfronterizos*. Madrid: Traficante de sueños.

Smith, Michael and Luis Guarnizo. 2006. *Transnationalism from below*, New Jersey: Transaction Publishers.

Solé, Carlota. (dir.). 2008. *Las trayectorias sociales de las mujeres inmigrantes no comunitarias en España, Estudios e Investigaciones*. Madrid: Ministerio de Igualdad. Instituto de la Mujer.

Solé, Carlota and Sonia Parella. 2005. "Discursos sobre la "maternidad transnacional de las mujeres de origen latinoamericano residentes en Barcelona". *Mobilitiés au féminin, Tanger.* http://lames.mmsh.univ-aix.fr/Papers/ParellaSole_ES.pdf. Last accessed on May 31 2012.

Tenore, Mallary. 2011. "Despite criticism, AP Stylebook dictates that journalists use 'ilegal immigrant', Poynter, available: http://www.poynter.org/latest-news/top-stories/152290/despite-criticism-ap-stylebook-dictates-that-journalists-use-illegal-immigrant/ Last accessed on 30 January 2012.

United Nations. 2009. *State of World Population*. New York: UNPFA.

United States Census Bureau. Various years. Available: www.census.gov. Last accessed on 30 January 2012.

Uriarte, Mercedes. 2003. "A problematic Press Latinos and the News". In *Journalism Across Cultures*, eds. Fritz Cropp, Cynthia Frisby and Dean Mills, 39-63. Iowa: Iowa State Press.

Wilson, Clint, Félix Gutiérrez and Lena Chao. 2003. *Racism, Sexism and the Media*. Sage: Thousand Oaks.

Wilson, Clint and Félix Gutiérrez. 1985. *Minorities and Media*. Sage: Beverly Hills.

CHAPTER THREE

IDEOLOGICAL STANCES IN INTERNET USERS' DISCURSIVE CONSTRUCTION OF IMMIGRATION, RACE, AND RACISM: AN ONLINE NEWSPAPER CASE STUDY

ISABEL ALONSO BELMONTE
UNIVERSIDAD AUTÓNOMA DE MADRID
DANIEL CHORNET
SAINT LOUIS UNIVERSITY (MADRID CAMPUS)
ANNE MCCABE
SAINT LOUIS UNIVERSITY (MADRID CAMPUS)

1. Introduction

In today's society, the Internet has augmented and enhanced the ways in which citizens can partake in a form of public political conversation that in the past was partly relegated to the private sphere of human activity (Landert and Jucker, 2011). The development of new media has allowed for a relative democratization of viewpoints (Castells, 2001) on topics of paramount importance for the citizens of a nation, such as immigration and race. One way in which the Internet allows citizens to speak up on controversial topics is through the creation of spaces for user commentary in newspapers or discussion forums (Goss, 2007; Del-Teso-Craviotto, 2009). However, democratic online discussion does not always foster a civic ideal (Dahlgren, 2005).

In light of the opportunities that the Internet provides for civic participation in conversation, and by expanding on previous work in Peninsular Spanish written journalism (Alonso Belmonte, McCabe, and Chornet-Roses, 2010; Alonso Belmonte, Chornet, and McCabe, forthcoming), we monitored the online version of the broadsheet newspaper

El País, the most widely-circulated daily newspaper in Spain, for a period of one year, with a sensitivity towards identifying news articles about immigration, race, and racism during the current socioeconomic context in our country.

After a decade of economic growth in which Spain's immigrant population swelled from 2% of the total to 12%, the economic recession brought about 20% unemployment, almost twice the average for the euro zone. One outcome of this dire socio-economic panorama was newspapers' discursive practices of scapegoating immigrants (Alonso Belmonte, McCabe, and Chornet-Roses, 2010), which exacerbated the already tense Spaniard-immigrant relationships. Indeed, we noticed that articles that reported on immigrants, and in particular those that used the word *negro* (black) and *racismo* (racism), and other related terms, resulted in a plethora of readers' comments. Thus we chose one of these articles titled *Aquí no pasan negros. Queremos mantener un rollito español* (No blacks allowed. We want to keep a Spanish thing going)[1] to conduct an exploratory case study on the discursive positioning of the commenters towards the notions of immigration, race and racism. This article, which appeared for several hours on the front page of the online newspaper version on February 1st 2010, reports that Black Africans and Black Latinos find some nightclubs closed to them in Torrejón de Ardoz. Torrejón is a Madrid suburb with a high percentage of immigrant population. It is run by the Spanish conservative party (Partido Popular, or PP) since 2007. People commented on this piece of news for at least 2 days. More than 500 comments were posted in the online response forum.

In this study we performed an in-depth critical discourse analysis (CDA) of the readers' interactions surrounding the topics of immigration, race, and racism by determining how the article's readers position themselves discursively in relation to the facts reported by *El País*. We believe a CDA opens a window onto the racial ideological frames in Spanish society. The kind of comments that users post in newspapers have the added value of resembling a naturally occurring conversation, at times unfolding synchronically, and at others asynchronously.

As we will show, the results of our investigation reveal that online users who posted comments in these news articles in *El País* are steeped in the same ideological positions that render immigrants as racial beings who are a burden for the economy. Furthermore, the analyses evidence how users speak within the frame of a dominant ideology of whiteness, from which the concept of "white" and "white race" are strategically kept invisible and unquestioned (Nakayama and Krizek, 1995). Within this frame, users appear as relatively intolerant of immigration and racial issues through mainly denials of racism.

2. Theoretical Framework

Traditional racism—as cases of overt and blatant discriminative behaviors justified on a person's skin color—is still alive in today's society. But nowadays, we also encounter racism as a "multi-dimensional reality in which race, ethnicity, culture and immigrant status come together" (Martínez, 2004, 111). Racism has transmogrified into a layered phenomenon characterized by a marked elusiveness, though with the same hegemonic power (Wachtel, 1999). It takes on different shapes and functions that keep changing as our world becomes more globalized (McConahay, 1986). For example, Fekete (2001) coined the term "xeno-racism", which separates the white European from the immigrants; van Dijk (2005) speaks of "ethnicism", and Kauth (2001) refers to "classism". Espelt and Javaloy (1997, 5) argue that modern racism is grounded in the premises that "racism is bad," and that "discrimination is a thing of the past". In other words, the elusive and toxic nature of today's notion of racism is its potential to be denied as such.

The type of scholarship that carefully investigates racist discourse in the media is abundant (for Spanish media, see van Dijk 2005, 2007; Bañón, 2002; Lorite, 2006, 2007; Martínez Lirola, 2008, 2010; *inter alios*). We do not intend to provide here a comprehensive review of the literature, but rather to articulate the theoretical and methodological foundations for a critical discourse analysis (Fairclough, 1995). There are four theoretical concepts that guide our study: ideology, media, discursive practices, and racism. Understanding the relationship among these four concepts is crucial to expose how dominant groups in society function discursively to perpetuate their existence in positions of privilege. Van Dijk (2007, 60) posits that ethnic dominant systems have two main components: "social cognition (prejudice, racist ideologies) … and social practices (discrimination, exclusion, etc.)". He argues that to engage in racist practices, there has to be a set of cognitions consistent with racial discrimination, and to become equipped with those, there has to be exposure to racist discourses, "which are themselves prominent social practices of the system of racial domination". In other words, racist discursive practices are discriminatory actions and simultaneously constitutive of racist cognitions.

Racist discursive practices can take several forms and functions. Van Dijk (1993, 2005) identifies "denials of racism" as a pervasive rhetorical strategy that functions to present its users in a positive light while enhancing and protecting their public face. Discursively, these tactics "play down, trivialize or mitigate the seriousness, extent or consequences of one's negative actions [...]" (van Dijk, 1993, 180); and socially,

> "[...] they express in-group allegiances and white group solidarity, they defend us against them, that is, against minorities and other anti-racists. They mark social boundaries and reaffirm social and ethnic identities, and self-attribute moral superiority to their own group" (van Dijk, 1993, 181).

In other words, denials strengthen majority group cohesiveness thus widening the social fault line with the "other." According to van Dijk (1993, 181), denials "manufacture ethnic consensus, and indirectly contribute to the legitimation of white group dominance, that is, to the reproduction of racism". Other scholars, for example, Espelt and Javaloy (1997, 1) refer to similar strategies which they describe as "contradictions", such as: "I'm not a racist but I don't want a gypsy family living in my apartment building".

Scholars in the United States have carved a theoretical space from which to debunk racist discourses in society (Foster, 2009; Hill, 2008; McIntosh, 2002; Nakayama and Krizek, 1995). They have started by naming and exposing an invisible but powerful ideology of whiteness through which "whites" legitimate each other. Conceptually, whiteness is similar to van Dijk's (1993) "manufactured ethnic consensus" and functions to perpetuate an unwitting privilege that excludes whites, at the most basic level, from the systematic discrimination that African Americans experience in the U.S., and Latin American immigrants in Europe. Nakayama and Krizek speak of whiteness as a kind of strategic rhetoric, that is, a discursive practice, or "discursive formation" in Foucault's (1972) terms. Discursive formations are premises upon which social actors make sense of the world; they are the cultural lenses through which social reality becomes normative. As McIntosh (2002, 98) posits, "whites are taught to think of their lives as morally neutral, normative, and average", or simply that they have been learned not to think of their racial identity as a "white privilege." One of the most basic white privileges is a white person's positioning in denying that these privileges, together with racism, exist.

Although racism in Spanish media has been widely investigated, there is a dearth of studies that take into account Spaniards racial identity as "white" as the starting point to understand race relations with ethnic minority groups, namely immigrants. In this case study, we believe that the U.S.-based concept of "whiteness" can be a fruitful starting point to understand Spaniards' ideological stance on issues of race, immigration, and racism in user-generated online discourse, during the economic crisis. Thus the research questions that guide our study are as follows:

RQ_1: What are the newspaper's online posters' ideological stances in relation to issues of racism in user-generated online discourse?

RQ_2: How are immigrants represented within these racial ideologies?

3. *Aquí no pasan negros*: the News in Context

Torrejón de Ardóz is a dormitory town located 20 km east of Madrid capital. It is part of a large industrial zone, *the Corredor del Henares*. This municipality is widely known in Spain because in the 1950s, under Franco's regime, a US Air Force Base was established there to protect NATO's southern flank. During decades, the town lived an intercultural and apparently peaceful experience until US soldiers abandoned the city in 1992. Traditionally run by left wing parties (*Partido Socialista Obrero Español*, or PSOE) for 27 years, during the period of Spanish economic growth, Torrejón's population kept growing, basically due to immigration. In 2010, the year in which the article under analysis was written, Torrejón had a total population of 120.559 inhabitants, of which 20.5% were immigrants.[2] Unfortunately, their integration in the town was only a partial success. Some immigrants settled in ghetto neighborhoods like San José. Progressively, the increasing number of immigrants in Torrejón and their access to local public education and health care services—often perceived as competing with locals—became a major concern for the local Spanish population. This was determinant for the Spanish conservative party (PP) to win the municipal elections in 2007. The new local government implemented some controversial policies, such as keeping some immigrants off municipal registers of residents, which guarantee access to free health and education.[3]

In this socioeconomic context, the article under analysis reports the cases of Andy, a black Nigerian, and Gilbert and Wilson, two Dominicans, who are not allowed into some nightclubs reportedly because of their race. According to *El País*, the nightclubs mentioned in the article are run by the local PP party elected authorities or by their relatives. According to Spanish law[4], a public bar can only refuse entry based on inappropriate or violent behavior and it is strictly forbidden to limit access to clients "[...] in an arbitrary or discriminatory way, or place the user in a position of inferiority, helplessness or unfairness" (Article 24, 2).

4. Data and Methodology

To investigate how online commenters write about racial issues in the context of *El País*, we performed a computer-assisted qualitative data analysis using Altas.ti 6.0. We saved and analyzed the 497 commentaries that were posted following the online news article.[5] Many of these comments showed indignation and concern about racist acts of this sort in Spain; others defended the owners' right to restrict entrance to some clients over others based on different criteria; others expressed ambivalence towards the situation.

As for the methodology, we performed the analysis of the writers' stances following the constant comparison method (Glaser and Strauss, 1967). We immersed ourselves in the data first to get a holistic understanding, and then we continued to code the first case of opinion. We interpreted it and gave it a descriptive label as close as possible to the participants' words. Then we coded the second instance of opinion and compared it to the first one to assess whether they were similar or different. If different, we then gave it a different descriptive code. Through an inductive analysis of all the posts we identified four broad ideological stances: Acknowledgement [of discrimination based on race], Denial [of discrimination based on race], Ambivalence [towards discrimination based on race] and Uncertainty [unknown position towards discrimination based on race]. The Acknowledgement category was identified from the following cases: a) when the writer admits implicitly or explicitly that there is a case of discrimination in the fact reported; b) when the writer admits implicitly or explicitly that there is racism in Spain:

> (post no. 256) *Racismo puro y duro. (Hard core racism).*

Contrarily, the Denial category emerged from comments that rejected the incident reported by *El País* as a case of racism:

> (post no. 190) *No es racismo. Es reservar el derecho de admisión y basta, lo cual es absolutamente legal. El que quiera ver racismo en esto tiene un problema serio.* (This is not racism. It is reserving the right of admission and that's it, which is absolutely legal. Whoever wants to see racism in this has a serious problem).

The Ambivalent category was applied to those posts in which opposing opinions (both admission and denial of racial discrimination) were presented:

> (post no. 481) *A mí me parece fatal que no dejen entrar a alguien a un sitio por su color de piel o su procedencia, pero también tengo que decir que por lo que me han dicho (aunque yo no lo sé) en Torrejón hay también bares en los que ponen cartelitos de "Blancos no" y demás.* (I think it's terrible that they wouldn't let someone in a place because of the color of their skin or origin, but I also have to say that from what I've been told (although I don't know) in Torrejón there are also bars with signs that say "No Whites").

And finally, when the writers' opinions were not at all clear in terms of their discursive stance with respect to issues of race and discrimination, we identified them as Uncertain:

> (post no. 373) *A TODOS INMIGRANTES SE PP Y DERECHA QUIER LUCHA VAMOSXAAAAAAAAAAAAAAAAAAAAAAAAAAA)*[6] (To all immigrants of PP and right want fight let's goxaaaaaaaaaaaaaaaaaaaaa).

As for the consistency of the coding, we divided the corpus into 3 overlapping sections respectively for each author to analyze. Subsequently, in a joint meeting, we recoded parts of the data set to check the consistency of our interpretive efforts from the initial analyses. Finally, we made adjustments accordingly that resulted in identifying three types of discursive stance in terms of a continuum of opinion, with clear Acknowledgements and clear Denials on either end, and Ambivalent comments in the middle. Given the difficulties of determining the position of the writers in the uncertain cases, we decided to leave them aside. We also left out of this paper a large number of quotes which function to criticize, challenge, question or support other commenters' views about unrelated issues to discrimination (i.e. spelling and bad grammar, political views, criticism for posting behavior such as perceived boasting, etc.).We now turn to the results.

5. Results

Although a frequency count of the different positionings would have not been significant given the case study nature of the present investigation, a perfunctory count hinted at a higher number of Acknowledgements versus a slightly fewer number of Denials. However, the shock value which Denials of racism cause in the present age of over-celebration of diversity, together with the worrying inconclusiveness emerging from most Ambivalent cases, made these two discourse stances stand out as newsworthy from the rest of commentaries. For presentation purposes, findings are reported under the following subsections: Acknowledgements, Denials and Ambivalent posts.

5.1. Acknowledgements: forms and functions

The analysis of the participants' Acknowledgments of the news article as instances of racism allows us to identify four different rhetorical configurations:

[Acknowledgement] + [Rejection]
[Acknowledgement] + [Reaction]
[Acknowledgement] + [Causes] + [Consequences]
[Acknowledgement] + [Follow up actions]

The Acknowledgment of racial discrimination is not explicitly stated in every post labeled in this category, but its rejection, the explanation of its causes and consequences, and the posters' call for action implicitly acknowledge that the event indeed was an instance of racism. Comments which simply admit the inherent racism of the reported incident in a direct and clear way are few, such as:

(443) *España es escandalosamente racista.* (Spain is scandalously racist).

At times, the posters do their acknowledgement indirectly, for example, through the use of rhetorical strategies such as irony to further augment the force of their acknowledgment:

(393) *Y sigue habiendo quien sostiene que "España no es racista".* (And there are still those who hold the view that "Spain is not racist").

5.1.1. Rejections and Reactions to Racism

Rejections are straightforward patterns through which the posters decry racial discrimination. The following two examples emphatically condemn racism and make an appeal to human nature and harmonious coexistence through the use of capital letters or specific set phrases:

(291) *¡NO AL RACISMO NI A LA DISCRIMINACIÓN! ¡SÍ A LAS PERSONAS!" (NO TO RACISM AND TO DISCRIMINATION! YES TO PEOPLE!).*
(438) *¡¡Abajo todo tipo de racismo que encharca los afanes de una mejor convivencia sobre esta minúscula arenilla espacial que vaga sin rumbo por*

el espacio desconocido...(Down with all types of racism that spoil desires for an improved coexistence on this tiny bit of spatial dirt that wanders without direction through unknown space).

As for reactions, writers frequently acknowledge racial discrimination through emotional retorts that express shame, sympathy, regret and disgust:

(2) *La noticia es lamentable, y lo peor es que no sorprende a nadie. Querer ver intenciones políticas de tres al cuarto es patético de tu parte. Discriminación por el color de la piel?!?! no estamos un poco mayorcitos para seguir midiendo el valor de la gente por ... un poco más o menos de melanina???? una vergüenza para esos locales, para ese pueblo, y para toda la raza humana. Yo al menos siento una mezcla de asco y tristeza al ver noticias así de lamentables.* (The news is lamentable, and the worst is that it comes as a surprise to no one. Wanting to see petty political intentions is pathetic on your part. Discrimination because of skin color?!?! aren't we a little old to keep measuring people's worth by…a little more or less melanin???? a shame for those places, for that town, and for the whole human race. I at least feel a mix of revulsion and sadness upon seeing such lamentable news).

We also identified cases of more rational reactions to racial discrimination. For example, some commenters consider racism to be an incomprehensible attitude in the 21st century:

(52) *Estamos en el siglo 21, no los años 30.* (We are in the 21st century, not in the 30s).

Other posts blame the Spanish Conservative Party (PP) politicians for the facts reported in *El País*:

(437) *Lo que pasa es que sus dueños son concejales del PP, el partido nazi que gobierna en Torrejón. Seguro que no reciben ni una sanción. Hatajo de sinvergüenzas.* (What happens is that the club owners are councilmen for the PP, the Nazi party that governs Torrejón. For sure they will not be fined. Bunch of crooks).

Altogether, these posts denounce and reject the news article as racist through a series of appeals to humanity, reason, revulsion, and politics. The next section illustrates other warrants for the Acknowledgment of racism.

5.1.2. Causes and Consequences of Racism

In the discussion threads analyzed, people's general ignorance and their lack of principles and values are pointed out as other reasons behind racism and xenophobia:

> (191) *El racismo, la xenofobia, la homofobia o el clasismo no son más que manifestaciones de la estupidez y de la estulticia humana más que de la razón.* (Racism, xenophobia, homophobia or classism are just manifestations of stupidity and of human foolishness rather than of reason).

> (449) *Ahora bien... creo que la Xenofobia se gesta en el seno de la familia sin principios ni valores.* (Now...I think that Xenophobia is conceived in the bosom of the family which has no principles or values).

More specifically, writers believe racism is rising in Spain due to the Spaniards' lack of knowledge about history, about their own past as colonizers, and about their recent past experience as immigrants themselves:

> (41) [...] *El mundo está lleno de ignorantes que nunca han salido de su casa y que olvidan que millones de españoles fueron acogidos durante muchos años cuando aquí se pasaba hambre.* (The world is full of ignorant people who have never left their home and who forget that millions of Spaniards were well received for years when here there were times of hunger).

Other writers believe Spaniards have an "inferiority complex," probably developed during the period when they were immigrants, which would explain the existence of racist beliefs and racism in Spain:

> (101) *Joer Asombroso, después de considerarnos que los españoles eran los negros en nuestra suiza, fíjate ahora van de blancos jejejejejeje.* (Geez Surprising, after we consider that Spaniards were the blacks in our switzerland, notice now they consider themselves white hahahahaha).

> (224) *Lo que hacen a nosotros no es más que la forma de desquitarse de cómo tratan a los españoles en el resto de Europa (dígase Alemania, Inglaterra, Francia, Bélgica, etc.)* (What they are doing to us is nothing more than a way of getting even for the way Spaniards are treated in the rest of Europe (read Germany, England, France, Belgium, etc.).

As for the effects that racial discrimination has in Spanish society, some writers explain that Spaniards' treatment of immigrants as second class citizens will hinder their future adaptation and integration into Spanish society:

> (8) *Pero ahora ya lo vemos todo normal, luego nos quejaremos cuando no haya integración y adaptación de los inmigrantes...pero como lo va a ver si los tratamos como ciudadanos de segunda.* (While now we see it all as normal, later we will complain when there is no integration and adaption of immigrants…but how can there be if we treat them like second class citizens).

All these posts indirectly repudiate the news article as racist via a series of reasonings that invoke history, ignorance and poor treatment of immigrants in Spain. The next section illustrates some comments that go beyond rejections and explanations and on to a call for action.

5.1.3. A Call for Action

Finally, some other posts call for action and ask individuals and/or NGOs to report cases of discrimination to the police:

> (6) *Si en una discoteca no te dejan entrar por ser blanco, DENUNCIA, al igual que si es por ser negro, en España la discriminación por cuestiones de raza está penada y prohibida por la Constitución.* (If you are not allowed into a club because of being white, REPORT IT, the same as if it were because of being black, in Spain discrimination due to questions of race is penalized and prohibited by the Constitution).

Some commenters also expect that authorities would sanction these clubs economically or with the closure of their premises:

> (294) *Para cuándo un acompañante no periodista, sino policía, juez, o lo que haga falta para meter un buen puro a estos señores?? A ver si nos vamos acostumbrando ya, que ya va siendo hora, a que exista gente de distintas nacionalidades o razas, y todos con los mismos derechos.* (When will we see a companion who is not a journalist, but a police officer, judge, or whatever it takes to really give it to these people? Let's see if we can start getting used to it already, as it's about time, that there are people of different nationalities or races, and all of them have the same rights).

> (186) *Puesto que vivimos en un país democrático, las discriminaciones en general y ésta en particular, que atenta contra la integridad de las personas por razones de raza o color de piel, deberían ser suficientes para cerrar los locales que las aplican. Simplemente vergonzoso.... este país cada vez lo es más.* (Given that we live in a democratic country,

discrimination in general, and this case in particular, that threaten the integrity of people based on race or skin color, should be enough to close down the places that do it. Simply shameful…this country is becoming more and more so).

Finally, some writers suggest that xenophobic people should travel, and get an education to correct their myopic beliefs about race and racism:

(454) *ESTÁ CLARO QUE HACE FALTA ALGÚN TIPO DE ENSEÑANZA EN LOS COLEGIOS, PARA CONTARLE A LOS NIÑOS, COMENZANDO POR LOS MÁS PEQUEÑITOS, EL RESPETO POR LA DIVERSIDAD DE RAZA, RELIGION ETC... ES MUY URGENTE.* (IT IS CLEAR THAT SOME TYPE OF TEACHING IS NEEDED IN SCHOOLS, TO EXPLAIN TO CHILDREN, STARTING WITH THE SMALLEST, RESPECT FOR DIVERSITY OF RACE, RELIGION, ETC…THIS IS VERY URGENT).

In these comments, acknowledging racial discrimination is not enough, and they call for action to counter racism. The following section features a set of comments that construct an opposite stance to the one described in this part of our analysis.

5.2. Denials: Forms and Functions

The analysis of the online comments which deny the news article as an instance of racism yielded the following salient rhetorical pattern:

[Denial] + [Explanation] + [Remark]

As happens with Acknowledgments, Denials are not usually present in the posts, at least explicitly. As for the Remarks, they only appear in a few instances with which posters try to augment the strength of their Denials (e.g. 223 *...todos los negocios tienen su clientela y el que monte uno para negros..........tendrá muchísimos impagados!!)* (…all businesses have their clientele and whoever establishes one for blacks…will have a lot of debtors!!). Among the three rhetorical components, the Explanation is the only one always present in the comments. Explanations function as the warrants for the Denials of racism, and they take 3 different forms: (1) Law-based explanations; (2) scapegoating; and (3) ideological explanations. These types of explanations generally appear separately across comments and in some cases, participants invoke several of them together but as we will show, they function interrelatedly to construct an overall discursive positioning that denies the racist nature of the incident reported in the news article to which they respond.

5.2.1. Law-Based Explanations

This pattern emerged from writer's claims that invoke "the right to refuse entry" to flesh out why the event reported in the article was not an instance of racism. The arguments posited are varied but the gist of them is that clubs that refuse entry to a black person are not racist:

> (352) *Veamos, por ser negro es inmoral no dejar pasar, pero ¿Y por ser pobre? ¿y por ser feo?¿o por llevar calcetines blancos?¿Es lógico no dejarte pasar por ser poco moderno o demasiado, poco pijo o demasiado y no lo es por ser negro, latino, rumano o español? O existe el derecho de admisión o no existe y tampoco nos tenemos que ofender. Son recintos con derecho de admisión y ya está. Otra cosa es que debiera o no existir ese derecho por parte de los clubs, pero si existe pues cada uno que vaya donde le dejen pasar y que no se empeñe en entrar donde no quieren dejarle entrar.* (Let's see, because of being black it is immoral to not let someone in, but, And if you are poor? and if you are ugly? or if you wear white socks? Is it logical to not let someone in because of not being fashionable enough, or because of being too fashionable, not preppie enough or too much so, and it isn't because of being black, latin, Rumanian or Spanish? Either the right to refuse entry exists or it doesn't and we can't take offense. They are spaces with right to refuse entry and that's that. Another thing is whether or not clubs should hold that right, but it does exist so everyone should go where they let them in and they shouldn't try to get in where they don't want to let them in).

In other words, these posters argue that if a club can discriminate based on features such as clothing for instance, then they should be allowed to discriminate on the basis of race. Furthermore, as a way to justify that these clubs are not racist, they affirm that this law is applied to everybody, white people included:

> (296) *No sé a quien le sorprende eso, pero los locales de ocio se han caracterizado siempre por seleccionar el ambiente y no tiene nada que ver con la raza. Yo tengo 40 años, soy bien blanquito y en según qué locales de Barcelona (que es donde vivo) cuando ni existía la inmigración ya te ponían pegas o te pedían las inexistentes invitaciones (un día en uno no pude acceder por no llevar camisa teniendo en mi poder la tarjeta VIP del local, si un portero te dice no, mejor no discutir). Lo mejor es no discutir y irte con tu dinero a otra parte, allá cada cual con su negocio.* (I don't know who is surprised by this, but leisure clubs have always been

characterized by choosing the atmosphere and that has nothing to do with race. I am 40 years old, I am very white and in certain clubs in Barcelona (which is where I live) when racism didn't even exist they already made it difficult, or they asked for non-existent invitations (one day in one I couldn't get in because of not wearing a shirt having with me the VIP card of the place, if a bouncer tells you no, it's best not to argue). It's best not to argue and take your money somewhere else, to each his own with their business).

The solution to deal with these clubs' elitism is to avoid them, these people claim. As is evident from these comments, participants misinterpret the law by assuming that discrimination of this type is legal, even when it is grounded in race.

5.2.2. Scapegoating

The most salient pattern of scapegoating emerged from writer's claims to justify minority racial discrimination with instances of majority racial discrimination. In the following illustration a law-based explanation is juxtaposed with a scapegoating strategy:

(303) *Estoy harto de ver este tipo de noticias y ver q si racismo, xenofobia.... joder, esq si yo q soy blanco intento entrar en un garito y me dicen q no puedo entrar porq es fiesta privada (q es lo mas tipico) o por mis ropas o por cualquier otra cosa, yo no tengo ninguna razon para quejarme, ahora bien si yo fuera negro podria decir perfectamnte q es porq son racistas. Si se quiere la igualdad, q se deje de achacar todo al racismo. Ademas yo he intentado tb entrar en alguna discoteca d torrejon q es de negros y no me han dejado entrar ¿ a eso como le llamamos ?? ...asi no vamos a ningun lao.* (I'm sick of seeing this type of news and seeing racism, xenophobia…shit, if I who am white try to get into a place and they say that I can't because it is a private party (which is most typical) or because of my clothes or any other thing, I have no reason to complain, now if I were black I could say perfectly that it is because they are racist. If what is wanted is equality, then it shouldn't all be blamed on racism. Besides I have tried to get into some club in Torrejón that is run by blacks and they haven't let me in. What do we call that??...this way we won't get anywhere).

The goal of this comment is to highlight that people use the "race card" too often and that that hinders the establishment of equality. This poster denies that the news article is a racist incident because it happens to everybody (be it a black or a white person), but only blacks are entitled to call it racism. The Denial is further augmented by blaming minority groups as the perpetrators of similar discriminative actions against whites. Finally, a pervasive premise emerged from this type of posts that seems to run across the entire data set: "white Spanish people feel as equally underprivileged as black people." This theme, from the viewpoint of these allegedly white individuals, seems to be a solid reason to deny that racism exists and void the need for its public exposure in news outlets.

Another frequent strategy employed to justify the application of the right to refuse entry on the basis of race is attributing violent traits to racial minorities and immigrants, as in the following post:

> (210) *Pues a lo mejor cuando uno se entera de que el 75% de los delitos graves en España los comete ese 12% de la población que llamamos inmigrantes (datos del Sindicato de Prisiones), y calculando entonces que su tasa de criminalidad es un 625% mayor que la de los españoles, prefiere uno evitar posibles problemas en su negocio haciendo caso de la estadística.* (Well maybe when one learns that 75% of serious crime in Spain is carried out by that 12% of the population that we call immigrants (data from the Prison Union), and calculating then that their rate of criminality is 625% higher than that of Spaniards, one prefers to avoid possible problems in one's business paying attention to the statistic).

This post adds another warrant to racially profile immigrants and prevent their entry in clubs and other businesses. According to the explanations illustrated so far, the right to refuse entry, as these online posters mistakenly understand it, is not only a "right" but there are statistics that further support its application.

In addition to blaming immigrants as the source of crime, they are also singled out as the ones exhausting the welfare state resources, and thus rendered a burden for the Spanish society:

> (154) *A muchos españoles se les queda la misma cara que a Andy y Wilson cuando van a pedir ayudas sociales para guardería, comedor escolar, vivienda o subsidio familiar y les dicen que todas las plazas las han llenado ya los inmigrantes ilegales.* (Many Spaniards have the same expression as Andy and Wilson when they seek social aid for day care, school lunches, housing or family subsidies and they are told that all of the positions have been taken by illegal immigrants).

The plight of the immigrant no longer prevails; according to these comments, it is now "the plight of the Spaniard." They complain that the Spaniards' prerogative, as citizens, has been displaced by the immigrants' plight. As the following comment argues, this type of news article is generating unwarranted hype during this time of crisis:

(323) ESTIMADOS SRES. DEJENME DECIRLES MI HUMILDE OPINION, NO CREO QUE NINGUN LOCAL DE ESPAÑA, SEA DEL MUNICIPIO QUE SEA ACTUE DE ESTA MANERA, PERO AUN ASÍ OPINO QUE LA GENTE EN GENERAL SOMOS UNOS HIPOCRITAS. ME EXPLICO. A TODOS NOS MOLESTA CUANDO NOS ENTERAMOS DE QUE UN HIJO DE UN IMIGRANTE OBTIENE MAS PUNTOS=MAS POSIBILIDADES PARA ENTRAR EN UN COLEGIO PUBLICO Y NOSOTROS TENEMOS QUE LLEVAR A LOS NUESTROS A UNO PRIVADO, CUANDO LES VEMOS QUE APENAS Y SI ACASO HAN COTIZADO A LA SEGURIDAD SOCIAL Y LES ATIENDEN EN URGENCIAS ANTES QUE A NOSOTROS, QUE NUESTRO PRIMO, AMIGO O TIO ESTA EN EL PARO CASI SIN SUBSIDIO Y QUE UN EXTRANJERO ESTA OCUPANDO EL PUESTO QUE NUESTRO FAMILIAR PODRÍA ESTAR OCUPANDO,SI POSIBLEMENTE POR MENOS DINERO, PERO SI NO SE PRESTASEN A HACERLO NOSOSTROS NO TENDRÍAMOS QUE COBRAR MENOS, O CUANDO CON TODO EL MORRO TE DICEN QUE HAN DEJADO DE IR A TRABAJAR PARA QUE SE LES DESPIDA Y ASI PODER COBRAR EL PARO, O CUANDO VIENEN DE UN PAIS EXTRANJERO Y "PRETENDEN" QUE NOSOSTROS NOS ADAPTEMOS A SUS COSTUMBRE Y LEYES Y NO ELLOS A LAS NUESTRAS (EJEMP. SRA. TESTIFICANDO CON BURCA), ETC. ETC. SRES. DEJEMOS DE RASCARNOS LAS VESTIDURAS Y NO ESCANDALIZARNOS POR ALGO QUE POR FALTA DE GANAS NO HACEMS O DECIMOS LOS DEMAS A LAS CLARAS, SINCERAMENTE CREO QUE ESTE PAIS TIENE PROBLEMAS MUCHO MAYORES QUE EL PREOCUPARNOS DE SI EN UN LOCAL DEJAN O NO ENTRAR A ALGUIEN, POR QUE NO HABLAN EN "EL PAIS" DE LA CRISIS Y DE LA GENTE QUE NO TIENE PARA COMER, ETC. (DEAR SIR, LET ME TELL YOU MY HUMBLE OPINION, I DON'T BELIEVE THAT ANY PLACE IN SPAIN, IN WHATEVER TOWN, ACTS THIS WAY, BUT EVEN IF THEY DID I THINK THAT PEOPLE IN GENERAL WE ARE HYPOCRITICAL. I EXPLAIN. ALL OF US ARE UPSET WHEN WE FIND OUT THAT THE CHILD OF AN IMMIGRANT GETS MORE POINTS = MORE POSSIBILITIES OF GETTING INTO A STATE SCHOOL AND WE HAVE TO TAKE OURS TO A PRIVATE ONE, WHEN WE SEE THAT THEY HAVE HARDLY PAID INTO THE SOCIAL SECURITY SYSTEM AND THEY RECEIVE ATTENTION IN URGENT CARE BEFORE WE DO, THAT OUR COUSIN, FRIEND OR UNCLE IS UNEMPLOYED WITH HARDLY ANY COMPENSATION AND THAT A FOREIGNER IS TAKING THE POSITION THAT OUR FAMILY MEMBER COULD HAVE TAKEN, YES POSSIBLY FOR LESS MONEY, BUT IF THEY DIDN'T AGREE TO DO THAT WE WOULDN'T HAVE TO EARN LESS, OR WHEN WITH TOTAL CHEEKINESS THEY TELL YOU THAT THEY'VE STOPPED GOING TO WORK IN ORDER TO GET FIRED TO RECEIVE

UNEMPLOYMENT BENEFITS, OR WHEN THEY COME FROM A FOREIGN COUNTRY AND "EXPECT" THAT WE SHOULD ADAPT TO THEIR CUSTOMS AND LAWS AND NOT THEY TO OURS (E.G. WOMEN TESTIFIES WITH BURKA), ETC. ETC. SIRS, LET'S STOP ACTING SO SURPRISED AND SCANDALIZED BY SOMETHING THAT BECAUSE OF LACK OF WILL WE DON'T DO OR SAY CLEARLY, SINCERELY I BELIEVE THAT THIS COUNTRY HAS FAR GREATER PROBLEMS THAN WORRYING ABOUT WHETHER A CLUB LETS SOMEONE IN OR NOT, WHY DOESN'T "EL PAIS" TALK ABOUT THE CRISIS OF THOSE PEOPLE WHO DO NOT HAVE ANYTHING TO EAT, ETC.).

The writer of this comment indicates that refusing the right of entry to an immigrant is unimportant and that Spaniards should be concerned about more pressing issues such as the current economic crisis. These types of explanations construct a well-wrought discourse that emphasizes the paucity of resources for and the discrimination against Spaniards, thus rendering them as—or even more—vulnerable and exposed than immigrants.

5.2.3. Ideological Explanations

For some citizens, articles of this sort are just a smoke screen to bury the economic difficulties and the curtailing of social rights that Spain is undergoing:

(354) *Vale ya de cortinas de humo!!! Ya estamos acostumbrados día tras día a oír de un amigo o conocido al que han despedido. También nos hemos acostumbrado a escuchar cada día en las noticias que nos están recortando los derechos sociales...y mantenemos todos una posición muy cómoda...seguimos aguantando...el descontento social está creciendo, cada vez la situación es más insostenible..y a que se dedican ustedes??a hacer un reportaje de investigación sobre un tema ya conocido por todos. A mí personalmente no me han dejado entrar en locales por ir con personas que llevaban el pelo largo...es eso RACISMO???? POR FAVOR DEJENSE DE TANTO PARTIDISMO POLÍTICO Y HABLEN DE LO REALMENTE IMPORTANTE!! Yo siendo de ideas de izquierdas me avergüenzo de la aberración de realidad social que está creando este gobierno... (Enough red herrings! We are used day after day to hearing of a friend or acquaintance who has been fired. We are also used to hearing every day in the news that our social rights are being curtailed...and we all are in a comfortable position...we continue to put up with it...social discontent is growing, the situation is becoming more and more unsustainable...and what do you do? a report of an investigation of a topic*

> *everyone knows about. Personally I have not been allowed into clubs because of being accompanied by people with long hair…is that RACISM???? PLEASE STOP ALL OF THIS POLITICAL PARTISANSHIP AND SPEAK OF WHAT IS REALLY IMPORTANT!! Myself being of leftist ideas am ashamed of the social reality that this government is creating….).*

In sum, like many others have argued, this poster emphasizes the double plight of Spaniards' current status: on the one hand, "we have all been discriminated against for many reasons (for having long hair, for wearing tennis shoes and the like) and it has never been blown out of proportion like it has in this case" and on the other one, "our government is trying to avert the citizens' attention from important matters."

5.3. Ambivalent posts: Forms and Functions

As explained in section four, we coded a number of posts as Ambivalent, as they seemed to be expressing contradictory views on discrimination in which an Acknowledgement and a Denial of racism come together. Within this ideological positioning, two different rhetorical patterns emerged:

[Acknowledgment-Rejection of Racism] + [Denial-Scapegoating] + [Assessment] or [Call for Action]
[Acknowledgment-Rejection of Racism] + [Denial-Law-based explanation] + [Racism = Media Attention]

These rhetorical patterns illustrate the clash of competing opinions that discursively outline the struggle-riddled socio-cultural milieu in Spanish society at present.

5.3.1. Rejecting Racism while Scapegoating the "Other"

Some of the online posters rejected racist practices but simultaneously blamed "others"—other immigrant club owners—for engaging in similar practices:

> (422) *Me parece mal que no dejen entrar a alguien por ese tipo de razones racistas, pero ellos pueden dejar pasar a quien les plazca a su local privado.* (I think it's bad that someone is not allowed in due to these types of racist reasons, but they can let in whoever they want in their private club).

The use of the adversative discourse marker "but" juxtaposes two conflicting and simultaneous opinions about the issue. The rejection of racist practices coupled with an attempt at justifying them by indicating that "Others" do it too constructs an ambivalent stance for these participants.

This same pattern recurred in other posts with the only difference being that the scapegoating strategy blamed immigrants for being violent:

> (321) *Yo tengo amigos de Torrejón que votan al PP y en el fondo apoyan esto. Me pregunto si debo tener este tipo de amigos. Me caen bien, me parecen buena gente, pero cuando hablan de este tema, tengo que hacer un gran esfuerzo de tolerancia con su intolerancia para seguir aceptándolos como amigos. Pero por otro lado nos encontramos con las visiones sectarias de algunos colectivos que acogemos, la violencia de algunos caribeños, el fanatismo de algunos árabes, la delincuencia de algunos del este. Me pregunto qué actitudes generan cuáles.* (I have friends in Torrejón who vote for the PP, and deep down they are in favor of this. I wonder if I should have this kind of friends. I like them, they seem like nice people, but when they talk about this topic, it takes a lot of effort to be tolerant of their intolerance to keep accepting them as friends. But on the other hand we find the sectarian images of some of the collectives who we take in, the violence of some of the Caribbeans, the fanatical nature of some Arabs, the delinquency of some from the eastern countries. I ask myself which attitudes cause which).

Again, these writers seem to position themselves against racist practices, but their subsequent contributions, almost always prefaced with the adversative discourse marker "but," clash with their initial attempts at presenting themselves as tolerant and sensitive individuals.

Other speakers, still from this ambivalent positioning, write about the complexity of the issue.

> (454) *Ejem, ejem. Este tema es mucho más serio y complicado como para tratarlo con este articulito. Yo he vivido y he visto en Torrejón de Ardoz, hace ya años (7, tal vez más) bares en barrios con población mayoritariamente negra con carteles de "prohibida la entrada a blancos". No justifico ningún tipo de discriminación, sólo quiero comentar que el tema viene de lejos y es complejo, por favor trátenlo con más seriedad!!* (Ahem, ahem. This topic is much more serious and complicated than can be treated in this little article. I have lived in and seen in Torrejón de Ardoz, for some years (7, perhaps more) bars in mainly black neighborhoods with signs that say "no entry for whites". I do not justify any type of discrimination, I only want to comment that the topic is very old and is complex, please treat it with greater seriousness!!).

At the beginning of the post, by adding the diminutive suffix (*-ito*) to *artículo* [news article], in a pejorative way, and with his final comment, this participant emphasizes the complexity of the issue that might require a lengthier coverage than just a news article. Nonetheless, this assessment of the complexity of the issue comes after having established an ambivalent stance by rejecting discrimination as unjustifiable, and simultaneously blaming the black population in Torrejón for engaging in racial discrimination too. In this case, the contrast of opinions was not marked with a discourse marker, but with the simple juxtaposition of both competing thought units separated by a comma in the last two lines.

A final variation of the ambivalent stance suggests that those who are discriminated against should do something about it and about the crime issue among their collective:

> (404) *Esto se lleva haciendo muchos años en torrejón, pero también a la inversa con locales de gente de color [...]... es muy triste, todas estas situaciones solo generen guetos, inadaptación social y xenofobia. Bastante lamentable que los extranjeros de color todavía siguen diciendo que son americanos de la base para que los intenten respetar más y dejar de ser ciudadanos de segunda. Deberían luchar más por sus derechos pero también por mejorar el abrumador índice de delincuencia que tienen en Torrejón.* (This has been going on a long time in Torrejón, but also in reverse in the bars of people of color [...]...it's very sad, all of these situations only bring about ghettos, lack of social adaptation, and xenophobia. It's sad enough that the foreigners of color still say that they are Americans from the airbase in order to gain more respect and not be considered second-class citizens. They should fight more for their rights but also to stop the incredible rate of crime that they have in Torrejón).

This comment illustrates the same ambivalent rhetorical structure as the previous ones: "I condemn racism, 'but' they do it too." As a conclusion, the writer urges these immigrants, who pose as members of the US airforce base, to avoid racial discrimination, and to fight for their rights and to try lower the criminality rate within their ethnic group in Torrejón. The last petition functions again to indirectly blame this immigrant group as the perpetrators of crime.

5.3.2. Rejecting Racism while Explaining it

In this last pattern, writers decry the news article as racist but then justify it with the application of club's right to refuse entry to their premises:

(383) *Está claro que es un caso de racismo injustificable, pero que conste que yo soy español, vivo en Sevilla y estoy harto de escuchar en la puerta de lo bares de copas que para entrar al local hace falta invitación, media vuelta y a no volver nunca, sin embargo parece que eso no tiene mucho eco ya que no eres africano, sudamericano, rumano o gitano.* (It's clear that this is a case of unjustified racism, but for the record I am Spanish, I live in Seville, and I am sick of hearing at the door of bars that to get into the place an invitation is needed, turn around and never return, however, it seems that does not get much attention, because you're not African, South American, Rumanian or Gypsy).

This comment is similar to "303" in the denial section, insofar as they share the same goal: To highlight the "real" plight of the Spaniard. This writer rejects racism as unjustifiable, but then retorts that club owners' application of their right to refuse entry to Spaniards is not "newsworthy," of report in the media. The premise that emerges from this pattern, though a fallacious one, is: "Spaniards are discriminated against when they are not allowed entry to clubs, but our predicament is not as important as the plight of minority ethnic groups."

We believe that the ambivalence of these comments that illustrate denials and acknowledgments of racial discrimination are symptomatic of an important socio-cultural struggle, augmented by the rampant economic crisis, within which citizens have to cope with not only the transformations of their societies into "global multicultural villages," but the concomitant realization of their own racial identities as white human beings.

5.4. Summary

Overall, the three discursive positionings that we have analyzed map out the ideological terrain of the individuals who participated in the public debate that ensued after the publication online of the news article in question. Table 3-1 summarizes the main rhetorical patterns identified in the analysis:

Table 3-1. Rhetorical forms and functions.

Rhetorical Forms & Functions	
Acknowledgments	(1) [Acknowledgement] + [Rejection] (2) [Acknowledgement] + [Reaction] (3) [Acknowledgement] + [Causes] + [Consequences] (4) [Acknowledgement] + [Follow up actions]
Denials	(1) [Denial] + [Law-based Explanation] + [Remark] (2) [Denial] + [Ideological Explanation] + [Remark] (3) [Denial] + [Scapegoating Explanation] + [Remark]
Ambivalent posts	(1) [Acknowledgment-Rejection of Racism] + [Denial-Scapegoating] + [Assessment] or [Call for Action] (2) [Acknowledgment-Rejection of Racism] + [Denial-Law-based explanation] + [Racism = Media Attention]

We elaborate on the implications of writers ideological stances in the following section.

6. Discussion and Conclusion

The goal of this case study was to identify and describe the ideological stances in user-composed online commentary in *El País*, and to expose the representations of immigrants within these ideological positions. Given the dearth of studies that investigate user-generated discourse in online newspapers (Goss, 2007; Cook, 2011), we decided to conduct a case study, as opposed to increase the breadth (different types of newspapers) and depth (the amount of data until saturation) of the data. The case study methodology zooms in on a specific event thus augmenting the intensity of the descriptive and interpretive effort, at the expense of other criteria such as the generalizability of the results (Blatter, 2008). Despite this deficiency – and other important ones, such as for example, the difficulty of knowing the national origin of the online posters –, we believe that concentrating our efforts on a snapshot of what one can encounter in the Internet has allowed us to capture ideological patterns of meaning that can be of great importance to understand race relations in Spain, and in particular, as they play out during the current economic crisis. Further research should strive to compare reader-generated comments in online newspapers across different titles and different types.

Our analyses showcase three main ideological stances throughout the discussion threads that ensued after the publication online of a news article reporting a racist incident in Torrejón de Ardoz, a suburb of Madrid. Some online users of the newspaper acknowledged the reported event as racist and rejected it; some others denied that it was a case of racism; and finally others expressed ambivalent opinions that simultaneously acknowledged and denied the racist nature of the event. These three racial stances were warranted in a series of explanations and justifications that revealed how these writers represented black people and immigrants during this period of economic recession. Overall, the Acknowledgements point at Spaniards' lack of values and principles, their lack of knowledge about their own history and a certain inferiority complex as the main reasons for racial discrimination. On their part, the Denial and Ambivalent stances sketch out the contours of an image of the immigrant (black or not) as a burden to the Spanish economy; as the ones who deplete the welfare state resources; as violent social actors; and as "privileged" individuals who overplay the race card to stimulate the public's sympathy and pity.

In the analysis of the justifications of these ideological positions—particularly, of Denials and Ambivalent stances—we identified, using Fairclough's (1995) term, a powerful ideological-discursive formation: "a strategic rhetoric of whiteness" (Nakayama and Krizek, 1995). In other words, a way of speaking about racial issues grounded in a series of premises about whiteness. The most important feature of this discursive formation is its ideological nature, that is, its invisibility and its deniability if it ever becomes visible. Nakayama and Krizek (1995, 296) explain that the definition of "white" is not avowed in a top-down fashion, but its power resides in how "it is constituted in everyday discourse and reinscribes its position on the social landscape". The mundane everyday life is difficult to capture, "it escapes and belongs to insignificance, and the insignificant is without truth, without reality, without secret, but perhaps also the site of all possible signification" (Blanchot, 1987, as quoted in Nakayama and Krizek, 1995, 296). Accordingly, what makes the notion of whiteness an elusive concept is its constitution in the everyday discursive moments of life. This trait is key to the perpetuation of this ideology and thus the privileging of white writers, as some posts allowed us to infer.

It is only from this rhetoric of whiteness that commenters online were entitled to argue that their discrimination as white people was comparable to discrimination of blacks. As van Dijk (2005, 4) explicates, this argument is fallacious in as much as

> "[...] white people in white societies are not systematically discriminated against for being white. What happens to all of us occasionally, and for personal or ad hoc reasons, happens to black and other minority people in Europe and the Americas every day, systematically, and only for just one reason: for being black or otherwise different".

Ultimately, this ideological-discursive formation of whiteness furnishes some of the white online users who are steeped in it with a set of social cognitions and rhetorical strategies to turn around what others identified as "the plight of the immigrant" (Alonso Belmonte, McCabe, and Chornet-Roses, 2010) and transform it into "the plight of the (white) Spaniard." We argue that the online posters' representations of immigrants as burdens for the economy and the concomitant self-victimization of alleged Spaniards, as it was evidenced in their Denials, frame a new form of racism that, as van Dijk (1993) explains, functions to protect oneself from accusations of being racist and at the same time keeps widening the social breach that separates "us" from "the Other." We hypothesize here that the dire economic recession which Spain is undergoing generated a series of circumstances that led these online participants to articulate a communal identity or "ethnic consensus" (van Dijk, 1993) throughout their online comments. Such articulation strengthened the self-victimization of the white Spaniard. Borrowing from Goss' (2007, 368) application of Ellul's sociological propaganda to his analysis of reader-composed comments in the online blog *The Nation*, we similarly posit that "the participatory and unrehearsed format of the threads enact horizontal diffusion in which citizens encircle and nudge each other toward consensus, without filters or direct cues from the leaders". In other words, their privilege as white social actors gets articulated and rearticulated publicly in their prosaic discourse through the expression of beliefs that used to be relegated to the private sphere.

This form of racism, we argue, can be equated in our case study with Del-Teso-Craviotto's (2009) use of the concept of xeno-racism. Del-Teso-Craviotto (2009, 573) explains that this concept is becoming more prevalent in Europe and is no longer based on racial features as much as it is on "economic inequalities between the rich Europeans and the poor Other". As Sivanandan elaborates, this form of racism even applies to immigrants who are white; "it is racism in substance, but xeno in form" (as cited in Del-Teso-Craviotto, 2009, 573). Although the two immigrants in the news article incident are black, the participants' comments also referred to Latin American immigrants (not necessarily black) in their ideological positionings. In this sense, xeno-racism is a more suitable term for our study because discrimination is grounded either in physically visible racial traits or on simple "differences." This form of racism is a powerful one in that it never misses in its task of otherizing, be it in terms of race or be it in terms any kind of difference.

Despite the three different stances that we identified throughout the data set, participants coalesced towards homogeneity of opinion. On the one hand, a group of participants coalesced into denying the incident reported as a case of racism, but the fallacious warrants of these denials rendered these commenters as racist. And, on the other hand, another group of participants acknowledged that the incident was a racist one. Either way, both of these stances together do nothing but reveal the existence of a xeno-racist reality in this online medium. Such a xeno-racist set of beliefs delineates and reinforces the contours of an ideologic discursive formation of whiteness.

Acknowledgements

The authors would like to thank Dr. Brian Goss for his constructive commentaries of an earlier version of this chapter.

Notes

1. Available at: http://www.elpais.com/articulo/madrid/pasan/negros/Queremos/mantener/rollito/espanol/elpepiespmad/20100201elpmad_2/Tes#EnlaceComentarios.
2. Source: Ministry of Immigration of the Madrid Regional Government.
3. Sources: http://elpais.com/diario/2010/01/24/madrid/1264335854_850215.html and http://elpais.com/diario/2007/06/03/madrid/1180869855_850215.html
4. Source:http://noticias.juridicas.com/base_datos/CCAA/ma-l17-1997.t3.html#a24
5. While more commentaries were posted online, a number of them were censored by *El País* and either not published or removed.
6. Capital letters, abbreviations and misspellings in all the posts which illustrate this chapter are original.

Bibliography

Alonso Belmonte, Isabel, Daniel Chornet and Anne McCabe. Forthcoming. "Burden or Benefit? The Press Representation of Immigrant Workers during the Spanish Economic Recession". In *Discourse and Crisis,* eds. Zuraidah Mohd Don and Antoon de Rycker. Amsterdam and Philadelphia: John Benjamins.

Alonso Belmonte, Isabel, Anne McCabe and Daniel Chornet-Roses. 2010. "In their Own Words: The Construction of the Image of the Immigrant in Peninsular Spanish Broadsheets and Freesheets". *Discourse and Communication* 4.3: 227-242.

Bañón, Antonio Miguel. 2002. "Racism and Cultural Diversity in the Spanish Media". In *Racism and Cultural Diversity in the Media: An Overview of Research and Examples of Good Practice in the EU Member States, 1995–2000,* ed. Jessika ter Wal, 173–202. Vienna: EUMC.

Blatter, Joachim K. 2008. "Case Study". In *The SAGE Encyclopedia of Qualitative Research Methods*, ed. Lisa M. Given, vol. 1 and 2, 17-68. Thousand Oaks, CA: Sage Publications, Inc.

Castells, Manuel. 2001. *The Internet Galaxy: Reflections on the Internet, Business, and Society*. Oxford: Oxford University Press.

Cook, Mariam. 2011. *"guardian.co.uk: online participation, 'agonism' and 'mutualisation'"*. MSc in Communication. Electronic Thesis, London School of Economics, London. http://www2.lse.ac.uk/media@lse/research/mediaWorkingPapers/MScDissertationSeries/2010/Cook.pdf Last accessed on 17 May 2012.

Dahlgren, Peter. 2005. "The Internet, public spheres, and political communication: Dispersion and deliberation". *Political Communication* 22 (2): 147-162.

Del-Teso-Craviotto, Marisol. 2009. "Racism and xenophobia in immigrants' discourse: the case of Argentines in Spain". *Discourse and Society* 20 (5): 571-592.

Espelt, Esteve and Federico Javaloy. 1997. "El racismo moderno". http://www.ciudadredonda.org/spip/IMG/pdf/El_racismo_moderno.pdf. Last accessed on 17 May 2012.

Fairclough, Norman. 1995. *Critical Discourse Analysis: The Critical Study of Language*. London: Longman.

Fekete, Liz. 2001. "The Emergence of Xeno-racism". *Race and Class* 43 (2): 23-40.

Foster, John D. 2009. "Defending whiteness indirectly: a synthetic approach to race discourse analysis". *Discourse and Society* 20 (6): 685-703.

Foucault, Michel. 1972. *The Archeology of Knowledge and the Discourse on Language*. New York, NY: Pantheon Books.

Glaser, Barney G. and Anselm L. Strauss. 1967. *The Discovery of Grounded Theory: Strategies for Qualitative Research*. New York: Aldine De Gruyter.

Goss, Brian M. 2007. "ONLINE "LOONEY TUNES": An analysis of reader-composed comment threads in The Nation". *Journalism Studies* 8 (3): 365-381.

Hill, Jane H. 2008. *The Everyday Language of White Racism*. Malden, MA: Wiley-Blackwell.

Kauth, Ángel Rodríguez. 2001. "El racismo del miedo y el miedo al racismo". *Revista de Psicologia Social* 16: 371-381.

Landert, Daniela, and Andreas H. Jucker. 2011. "Private and public in mass media communication: From letters to the editor to online commentaries". *Journal of Pragmatics* 43 (5): 1422-1434.

Lorite, Nicolás. 2006. *Tratamiento informativo de la inmigración en España 2005*. Madrid: Ministerio de Asuntos Sociales.

—. 2007. *Tratamiento informativo de la inmigración en España 2006*. Madrid: Ministerio de Asuntos Sociales.

Martínez, Elisabeth. 2004. "Seeing more than black and white". In *Race, Class, and Gender: An Anthology*, eds. Margaret L. Andersen and Patricia Hill Collins, 111-117. Belmont, CA: Wadsworth/Thomson Learning.

Martínez Lirola, María (ed.) (ed.) 2008. *Inmigración, discurso y medios de comunicación*. Alicante: Instituto Alicantino de Cultura Juan Gil Albert.

—. 2010. *Migraciones, discursos e ideologías en una sociedad globalizada. Claves para su mejor comprensión*. Alicante: Instituto Alicantino de Cultura Juan Gil Albert.

McConahay, John. 1986. "Modern racism, ambivalence, and the modern racism scale". In *Prejudice, Discrimination, and Racism*, eds. John Dovidio and Samuel L. Gaertner, 91-126. San Diego, CA: Academic Press.

McIntosh, Peggy. 2002. "White privilege: Unpacking the invisible knapsack". In *White Privilege: Essential Readings on the Other Side of Racism*, ed. Paula S. Rothenberg, 97-101. New York, NY: Worth Publishers.

Nakayama, Thomas K., and Robert L. Krizek. 1995. "Whiteness: A strategic rhetoric". *Quarterly Journal of Speech* 81 (3): 291-309.

van Dijk, Teun. 1993. *Elite Discourse and Racism*. Thousand Oaks, CA: Sage Publications, Inc.

—. 2005. *Racism and Discourse in Spain and Latin America*. Amsterdam and Philadelphia: John Benjamins.

—. 2007. "Racism and the press in Spain". In *Discurso periodístico y procesos migratorios*, ed. Antonio Bañón Hernández, 27-80. Donostia: Gakoa Liburuak.

Wachtel, Paul L. 1999. *Race in the Mind of America*. New York, NY: Routledge.

CHAPTER FOUR

THE TREATMENT OF IMMIGRANTS IN THE CURRENT SPANISH AND BRITISH RIGHT-WING PRESS: A CROSS-LINGUISTIC STUDY

ELIECER CRESPO-FERNÁNDEZ
UNIVERSITY OF CASTILLA-LA MANCHA

1. Introductory remarks

The increase in the influx of immigrants[1] into Western European countries in the last two decades has triggered nationwide immigration debates and led to manifestations of resentment, racism and xenophobia. As a consequence of the economic crisis and the high rate of unemployment in the European Union, in traditional recipient countries like United Kingdom, Germany or France attitudes towards immigrants have hardened. Together with this, it is worth noting that countries that have seen relatively low levels of immigration until recently, such as Spain, have developed into popular destinations for immigrants in the last few years. To those that enter the country legally, we must add the mass of undocumented immigrants, who constitute the most vulnerable individuals. According to Moore and Miller (cited in Bilger and Van Liempt, 2009, 1), the so-called "illegal" immigrants "lack the ability to make personal choices, to make personal decisions, to maintain independence and to self-determine". Immigrants, and above all, irregular immigrants constitute a social group which is obviously subject to discrimination and social stigma.

The association between immigration and crime, marginality and poverty makes immigrants easy targets for every sort of intolerance and violence, and for considering them as a burden on society because they invade "our" territory, increase unemployment rates, reduce economic growth and threaten our welfare system. In this regard, it is not surprising that immigration has become an emotionally charged social and political issue, a matter of vital importance for public opinion sparking debate within the recipient countries.

The economic and social impact of immigration on the host societies is reflected, as one might expect, in the media. Indeed, immigration has become one of the most passionately contested issues in the media, whose power and influence on society should by no means be underestimated. One should not forget that the media are able to make a specific image of immigrants credible and ultimately shape public opinion concerning immigration. Among the mass media, the press is generally regarded as the most reliable source of information and the one with the greatest capacity to propagate ideologies and social conceptions in the daily production of news and commentary.

In this regard, it seems necessary to gain an insight into the verbal elements used by the press in the representation of immigrants. More precisely, the main goal of this chapter is to analyse the lexical elements used by journalists in order to characterize immigrants in the daily production of news and commentary. To this end, I will carry out a contrastive analysis of the X-phemistic (i.e. ortophemistic, euphemistic and dysphemistic) lexical units used to represent immigration and the figure of the immigrant in a sample of current conservative Spanish and British electronic press, as X-phemism – we should not forget – constitutes a very effective persuasive element at the journalist's disposal to orientate the reader in a manipulative way. To this end, taking Critical Discourse Analysis and Conceptual Metaphor Theory as theoretical paradigms, I will analyse the X-phemistic lexical items used to deal with immigration in a sample of Spanish and British centre-right press. More specifically, I will analyse the news items concerning immigration found in the online newspapers *El Mundo* and *The Daily Telegraph* published from January to March 2012.

The journalistic treatment of immigration has been the focus of a considerable number of scholarly studies. In the Spanish press, apart from my own contributions to the subject (Crespo-Fernández, 2008 and 2010), and Sabés Turmo's (2010) study in a corpus of electronic press, Martínez Lirola (2009) and Crespo-Fernández and Martínez Lirola (2012) analysed how lexical and visual elements combine in the press to characterize immigrants. As far as the analysis of immigration-related issues in the British press is concerned, Gabrielatos and Baker (2008) and KhosraviNik (2009), among others, have approached this subject through corpus-driven studies. Of particular interest is the analysis of the role of metaphor in political communication on immigration carried out by Charteris-Black (2006). Despite these studies, the linguistic analysis of immigration-related news items that I will carry out here would appear to be justified, since, to the best of my knowledge, there is no cross-linguistic study so far devoted to investigate the way in which two right-wing newspapers published in different countries deal with immigration.

This chapter is structured as follows. After briefly dealing with the corpus data and considering the theoretical paradigms on which this study relies, I will analyse how the X-phemistic lexical devices encountered in the Spanish and British news items of my corpus deal with the issue of immigration. To this end, I will divide the analysis into two parts, one devoted to the X-phemistic references to irregular immigrants and the other dealing with the lexical labels encountered in the corpus to refer to the immigrants that reside legally in the host countries. I will then offer the results of the comparison between both subcorpora of news items analyzed. The conclusions and the final remarks obtained from the contrastive analysis will bring this study to an end.

2. Corpus Data and Methods

As stated above, the data for the analysis was collected from the daily online newspapers *El Mundo* (Madrid, hereafter EM) and *The Daily Telegraph* (London, hereafter TDT) published over a three-month period, from January to March 2012. The data from the Spanish subcorpus consists of 57 news items concerning immigration and the English subcorpus does not differ significantly from the Spanish one: it consists of 44 news items. In an attempt to minimize variables, when compiling the data for the analysis, the selection of the newspapers for this study was limited by certain parameters: they are regarded as *serious newspapers*;[2] they are representative examples of *centre-right*, online press dealing with current political affairs and events; both are leading electronic newspapers in Spain and UK which are aimed at a spectrum of conservative readers; and both belong to the same year and the same month.

The choice for conservative press was not at random: I decided that it was interesting to study how the controversial issue of immigration was dealt with in conservative newspapers, centre-right in political orientation, like *EM* and *TDT*, which are supposed to hold critical views on the issue of immigration. Other newspapers that have more radical right-wing attitudes on immigration in both countries, like *The Daily Mail* or *La Razón*, for example, have not been considered, as these newspapers do not reach such a wide spectrum of readers. It is my contention here that this right-wing position towards immigration should be reflected in X-phemistic lexical devices which tend to provoke, whether consciously or not, discriminatory attitudes towards immigrants.

When selecting the news items, the topic of immigration was the main criterion. It must be noted that direct quotations of politicians' speeches have been left out, as my main purpose here is not to analyse politicians' discourse, but rather the journalistic treatment of immigration issues in the production of news and commentary.

As for the methods employed, I searched the newspapers for items of news related to immigration. Once selected, I analysed the different lexical devices used by journalists and commentators to deal with the issue of immigration and characterize the figure of the immigrant, paying special attention to persuasive X-phemistic language. Regarding figurative language, I identified metaphorical expressions in the corpus and saw what conceptual metaphors underlie them following the framework of Conceptual Metaphor Theory. Then, I considered what emotions and feelings the metaphors try to evoke.

I should make it clear that the study presented here can make no claim to being complete or exhaustive. Indeed, the limited scope of the present essay, the logical space limitations and, above all, the number of newspapers that constitute my corpus do not allow me to reach valid conclusions in quantitative terms. My analysis is therefore mainly qualitative, following the tradition of critical discourse analysts, who have usually relied on small data samples, as Hakam (2009, 36) notes. Despite this, I believe that the sample of 101 news items analysed offers significant results regarding the representation of immigrants in both the Spanish and British conservative press.

3. X-phemism and verbal manipulation

In the process of social legitimization that serious-minded newspapers carry out, at the linguistic level X-phemism constitutes a very effective persuasive element at the journalist's disposal to portray immigrants and orientate the reader in a manipulative way. Journalists resort either to *ortophemism* (i.e. the axiologically neutral term), *euphemism* (i.e. the semantic or formal process thanks to which the taboo is stripped of its most explicit or obscene overtones) or to *dysphemism* (i.e. the process whereby the most pejorative traits of the taboo are highlighted with an offensive aim to the addressee or to the concept itself). Though to resort to the explicit advocacy of dysphemism is not very common in the serious press on which this study is based, euphemism is not trustworthy in all cases. Euphemism is frequently used in the press to refer to immigrants in a socially acceptable way, avoiding responsibility for what is said and the idea hidden behind the words. Indeed, euphemism is a strategic device of politically correct (PC) language[3], very common in public discourse or official language to implicitly transmit an idea without departing too far from the appearance of objectivity and, what is more important, without damaging the speaker's public image or *face*, as Goffman (1967) put it.[4] Through euphemistic labels journalists try to make the negative appear positive or at least tolerable and avoid responsibility for the idea hidden behind the words.

Granted that the connotative value of lexical units is much more significant than their purely denotative value, to opt for one of these semantic resources constitutes an indirect expression of implicit values and affective meaning. In this regard, euphemism and dysphemism can be considered as antithetical resources of *referent manipulation*[5] in the social use of language, and useful devices in the condescending and preventive discourses on immigration, as Bañón Hernández (2002) has demonstrated. After all, rather than being instruments of exposition of ideas, euphemism and dysphemism are persuasive devices used to carry out ideological and social control depending on the journalist's intention and the interests of the owner of the newspaper. From this it can be deduced that language is far from being powerless; it actually moulds perception, culture and attitudes and does not merely mirror social reality, which is quite important in hegemonic struggles and very useful for ruling groups.

4. Theoretical frameworks

I will rely on Critical Discourse Analysis as main theoretical framework used in the analysis of the lexical elements present in the immigration-related texts of the corpus. Critical Discourse Analysis takes social reality as its reference; to be more precise, it focuses on the manifestations of conflict, dominance and discrimination in relation to textual structures and contextual clues. Following this approach, I consider language as social behaviour and related to social structure. In this sense, language is understood as a social activity that is developed through the different functions it performs and through the structures used to perform these functions. Consequently, language may be regarded as both social practice and a mode of social action insofar as it is capable of expressing meanings in different sociocultural contexts. In this way, language has potential behaviour, i.e., it determines the behaviour that speakers or writers of a particular language can perform, and it is a social event having a direct influence on the context in which it is used.

According to Van Dijk (2000), Critical Discourse Analysis is overtly biased insofar as it is clearly on the side of the dominated groups; it is therefore especially suited to the study of immigration, an issue so prone to discrimination and unequal power relations. Within this framework, I find the "social-theoretical" sense of discourse developed by Fairclough (1992) especially useful for my purpose here. Fairclough offers a three-dimensional concept of discourse, i.e., discourse as a piece of text, discourse as an instance of discursive practice and discourse as an instance of social practice: "My three-dimensional approach enables relationships between discursive and social change to be assessed, and detailed properties of texts to be related systematically to social properties of discursive events as instances of social practice" (1992, 8). In this sense, Fairclough's socially – and linguistically – oriented view of discourse allows us to relate the linguistic elements found in pieces of news to social values and ideologies concerning immigration.

As discourse is manifested in the linguistic form of a 'text' in the conception postulated by Fairclough (1992, 71), I will consider here the pieces of news as goal-oriented texts with a social purpose. From this perspective, the news items can be viewed as instances of functional language, i.e., language that is doing some job in some context (Halliday, 1985, 10), insofar as the verbal devices perform a particular function in their context; to be more precise, the journalistic texts can be said to be socially oriented, and their social purpose is likely to be deciphered by exploring their observable elements and patterns.

Granted that certain values are given priority in the metaphorical structuring of concepts (Lakoff and Johnson, 1980, 10), the filter of metaphorical conceptualization through which reality is presented provides us with a partial understanding of the concept, masking or revealing particular aspects of the topic being dealt with. This process makes conceptual metaphors readily accessible for X-phemistic reference and provides significant information concerning the way in which a given topic (immigration, in this case) is actually transmitted, perceived and understood.

Given that metaphor is vital to persuasion and verbal abuse, I will also rely on the frame of Conceptual Metaphor Theory, as defined initially by Lakoff and Johnson (1980) and developed by later works, most notably Lakoff and Turner (1989) and Lakoff (1993), to gain an insight into the figurative language encountered in the corpus. It is not my purpose here to analyze in depth the well known model of Conceptual Metaphor Theory.

Suffice it to say that this approach claims that metaphor is a device with the capacity to structure our conceptual system, providing, at the same time, a particular understanding of the world and a way to make sense of our experience. From this standpoint, metaphor is defined as "a cross-domain mapping in the conceptual system" (Lakoff, 1993, 203), that is, a mapping or set of conceptual correspondences from a source domain (i.e., the realm of the physical or more concrete reality) to a target domain (i.e., the concept we want to delimit and reify). Through this correspondence between the linguistic content of metaphors (i.e., the source domain) and what they describe (i.e., the target domain), metaphors stand as a means of creating, organizing and understanding reality.

In what follows, I will analyse how textual elements are used in the representation of immigration and immigrants in the news items used as corpus data.

5. Data Analysis

5.1 On irregular immigrants

The lexical references to immigrants without legal documents are basically euphemistic in the Spanish subcorpus. A considerable number of phrases aim at veiling the illegal status of the undocumented immigrants. This is the case of *ciudadanos extranjeros insuficientemente documentados* 'insufficiently documented foreign citizens'. Consider the quotation that follows:

(1) *En cuanto al resto de centros (de inmigración), un total de nueve en España, solicita que se proceda a su cierre progresivo y sustitución por otros equipamientos que salvaguarden la salud, la libertad y la dignidad de los ciudadanos extranjeros insuficientemente documentados.*[6] (EM, 18 January) (As for the rest of the (immigration) centers, nine in total in Spain, he demands their progressive closure and their substitution for other facilities that safeguard the health, the freedom and the dignity of the insufficiently documented foreign citizens).

In the text in italics we find various euphemistic labels like *ciudadanos extranjeros* 'foreign citizens', whereby immigrants without legal documents are lexically treated as other foreigners who are not associated with the poor living conditions and the marginality of the so-called irregular immigrants whatsoever; and the downtoning adverb *insuficientemente* 'insufficiently' in the adjectival phrase 'insufficiently documented' which avoids an overtly pejorative term like *indocumentado* 'undocumented'.

The noun *extranjero* appears in the headline in (2) to refer to the detention centers irregular immigrants are sent to. These centers are in turn euphemistically labelled as *centros de extranjeros* 'centers for foreigners':

(2) *La Policía se limitará a labores de seguridad en los centros de extranjeros.* (EM, 31 January) (The Police will only carry out surveillance activities in the centers for foreigners).

In the same vein, in the following quotation the euphemistic periphrasis *no tener su situación administrativa regularizada* ('not to have regularized their administrative situation') tends to disguise the illegal status of those immigrants without legal documents:

(3) *Diversas entidades, colectivos y organizaciones ciudadanas de Barcelona han pedido el cierre del centro de la Zona Franca y de todos los CIE de España por considerar que* ***no se puede privar de libertad a nadie por no tener su situación administrativa regularizada*** (in bold in the original). (EM, 17 January) (Various organizations, groups and citizen organizations from Barcelona have demanded the closure of the center of Zona Franca and of all the CIE (i.e, detention centers) in Spain considering you cannot detain anyone for not having regularized their administrative situation).

In citations (1) and (3) above, the journalists consider that recipient countries should preserve the freedom and health of immigrants, who should be treated with dignity regardless of the fact that they may lack legal documents. In fact, by resorting to emotionally loaded words such as *libertad* 'freedom', *dignidad* 'dignity' or *salud* 'health', the fact that the immigrants lack a residence permit becomes a matter of lesser importance. Immigrants without legal documents are treated as human beings, regardless of the fact that they may be living illegally in the country. This is the reason why the noun *personas* 'people' acquires a clear euphemistic sense in a considerable number of news items in the corpus to avoid a pejorative term like *illegal* in reference to immigrants lacking a residence permit. This noun appears as part of the noun phrase *personas immigrantes* 'immigrant people', what demonstrates that the term *immigrant* itself is not totally far from being a "safe" term to refer to undocumented immigrants. *Personas* is also part of euphemistic periphrases like "personas llegadas a las costas de Granada" 'people who have reached the coast of Granada', "personas llegadas a nuestro país" 'people who have arrived in our country' or "personas extracomunitarias" 'non-European people'.

In this line of empathy with irregular immigrants, I have detected other euphemistic labels to refer to immigrants lacking a residence permit which are characteristic of the Spanish press. One of them is *irregular*, an adjective which is constantly applied to the phenomenon of immigration in phrases like *inmigración irregular* 'irregular immigration' or *entradas irregulares* 'irregular entries' and is also used to represent the figure of the immigrant in phrases like *inmigrante irregular* 'irregular immigrant', *immigrantes en situación irregular* 'immigrants in an irregular situation' or *ciudadanos irregulares* 'irregular citizens' in the following quotation:

(4) *Hemos denunciado la política de traslado y puesta en libertad de ciudadanos irregulares que durante años se ha ido practicando en la ciudad de Barcelona.* (EM, 13 January) (We have denounced the policy of transfer and release of irregular citizens that has taken place for years in Barcelona).

One of the most common labels used to refer to illegal immigrants in both formal and informal contexts is *sin papeles* 'without legal documents'. This lexical label does not necessarily transmit a negative image of the immigrants being referred to; rather, it is used in texts which clearly support immigration:

(5) *Ofensiva política y social contra los centros de retención de 'sin papeles'. Los definen como "agujeros negros" o "espacios de impunidad" donde se vulneran derechos de los 'sin papeles'.* (EM, 17 January) (Political and social offensive against the detention centers for immigrants without documents. They are defined as "black holes" or "areas of impunity" where the rights of the immigrants without documents are violated).

Quotations (4) and (5) provide evidence for the fact that the journalist is clearly aware of the hard living conditions of undocumented immigrants, who are crowded together in detention centers and treated as if they were criminals, which is unfair. In cases like these, in which immigrants are regarded as victims, the empathy of the journalist is strategic and encourages a positive response on the part of the reader (Van Dijk, 2003, 107). By doing so, the fact that the immigrants are illegal and lack a residence permit becomes a matter of lesser importance. However, it is worthy of note that by using a lexical label like *sin papeles* in (5), the journalist reduces the immigrant to his or her administrative situation, whether consciously or not, and by doing so, the immigrant's condition as a human being is indirectly devaluated. This is a clear example of a lexical label which, though not used with an offensive purpose, indirectly transmits a negative image of the immigrant.

Other lexical references to irregular immigration are overtly pejorative in reference to immigrants lacking documents. Indeed, through the adjective *ilegal* 'illegal' the illegal status of those undocumented immigrants is highlighted and, needless to say, the effect is clearly offensive, as happens in the quotation that follows:

(6) *La llegada de inmigrantes ilegales a las costas españolas en 2011 (5.443 personas) aumentó casi un 50% respecto a 2010, cuando se contabilizaron 3.562.* (EM, 2 February) (The arrival of illegal immigrants to the coasts of Spain in 2011 (5,443 people) increased by almost 50% compared to 2010, when there were 3,562).

By considering irregular immigrants as illegal, the journalist is portraying them as problematic, dangerous and associated with illegal activities. As commented elsewhere (Crespo-Fernández, 2010, 279-280), from a semantic point of view, this adjective is intrinsically dysphemistic. In fact, through this metonymic term, the administrative situation of the person stands for the person itself. This implies a semantic impossibility: the person is not illegal, but his or her administrative situation is. This violation of the semantic laws supposes a way to stigmatize the immigrant without documents, who is automatically associated to illegal activities in the belief that law breaking is in the nature of the immigrant. Besides, the use of the term *illegal* to qualify immigrants implies a generalization which is obviously unfair. Besides, this association of ideas could also be seen as a violation of the Maxim of Quality, whereby language users are supposed not to say what they believe to be false or that for which they lack enough evidence (Grice, 1975, 46).[7] It goes without saying that the journalist lacks enough evidence for this generalization. The term *illegal* is the source of a considerable number of lexical labels to represent immigrants like the above commented *inmigrante ilegal* or *estancia ilegal* 'illegal stay'. While not so overtly offensive, in periphrases like "personas que cruzan ilegalmente la frontera" 'people who cross the border illegally' or "inmigrantes que entran ilegalmente" 'immigrants who enter illegally', the idea of illegality is still present:

(7) *Se duplican las cifras de los inmigrantes que entran ilegalmente en Ceuta.* (EM, 26 January) (The number of immigrants entering illegally in Ceuta has doubled).

The pejorative reference to those immigrants without legal documents abounds in the British subcorpus, especially through the use of the same adjective *illegal*. The presence of this dysphemistic adjective is particularly striking in headlines and subheadings. After all, we should not forget that headlines and subheadings, together with captions, are the most eye-catching, attention-grabbing elements in a news item. The following headline aims at denouncing, through a specific case, the burden on the economy of the country caused by irregular immigration:

(8) More than 100 staff used to escort 35 *illegal* immigrants. (TDT, 26 January)

The adjective *illegal* also appears in the subheading that follows. Its dysphemistic strength is reinforced by the presence of the participle *caught*, which implies that immigrants were acting illegally when they were trying to enter Britain and had necessarily to be stopped for the security of the country:

(9) Border staff have been instructed to stop fingerprinting *illegal* immigrants *caught* trying to enter Britain via the Channel Tunnel. (TDT, 8 January)

The dysphemistic quality of *caught* is linked to the context in which the verb is used. After all, as Allan and Burridge (2006, 51) argue, mitigation or offence ultimately depend on the context in which the word is used, and thus the euphemistic or dysphemistic quality of a word can never be considered as an intrinsic quality of the word regardless of context. Indeed, given the presence of the adjective *illegal*, the pejorative power of *caught* is contextually consistent in quotation (9): those involved in illegal activities must be caught and detained.

The pejorative reference to irregular immigrants also appears through another overtly dysphemistic noun, *clandestino* and its English equivalent *clandestine*, which appears in both the Spanish and British subcorpora:

(10) *Las expulsiones de clandestinos se incrementaron un 17,5% hasta un nivel récord de 32.195, lo que supone 5.000 más del objetivo que el propio Ejecutivo se había fijado inicialmente.* (EM, 10 January) (The expulsions of *clandestines* increased by 17,5% to a record level of 32,195, which is 5,000 more than the objective than the Government itself had initially set).

(11) So-called "*clandestines*" caught at the border have been fingerprinted and handed over to police since 2006. (TDT, 8 January)

As happens with the term *illegal* commented above, the dysphemistic term *clandestino / clandestine* reinforces the stereotypical association between immigration and criminality. In fact, the definition of the term given in the OED2 ("Secret, private, concealed; usually in a bad sense, implying craft or deception; underhand, surreptitious") does little to create a positive image of immigrants; rather it portrays them as a potential threat to the host society, as individuals who have broken the law even before entering the country and therefore are not to be trusted.[8] Furthermore, by using *clandestine* as a noun to refer to irregular immigrants in (10) and (11), the pejorative traits of the concept are highlighted to a greater extent than by employing non-nuclear terms within the phrase like the adverb *illegally* in (7) or the adjective *illegal* in (8) and (9). The dysphemistic power of the noun *clandestine* is indeed stronger than when it functions as an adjective in phrases like "inmigración clandestina" 'clandestine immigration' or "de manera clandestina" 'clandestinely'.

The same is true for the term *indocumentado* ('undocumented'), which is used in the Spanish subcorpus both as an adjective in the noun phrase *foráneos indocumentados* 'undocumented foreigners' (EM, 14 March) and as a noun: *los indocumentados indios* 'the undocumented Indians' (EM, 11 January). We should not forget that by using a dysphemistic term as noun, the negative quality denoted by the noun in question is given special prominence, as happens in (10) and (11). In these quotations, the use of quotes and the expression "so-called" is simply a strategy, motivated by conventions of tact and politeness, on the part of the journalist to avoid responsibility for what is said. In fact, it seems that the journalist in these two quotations does not dare to take full responsibility for the utterance and tries to preserve, through these mitigating techniques, his or her public image.

Having dealt with the lexical references to immigrants lacking documents, I will move on now to analyse the X-phemistic lexical labels used in the corpus to refer to those immigrants residing legally in the host countries.

5.2 On "legal" immigrants

Many of the euphemistic lexical labels used to refer to those immigrants who lack a residence permit seen in 5.1. are also employed to refer to those who are residing legally in the host country or to those whose immigration status is unknown. The most common one is the polysemic term *extranjero* and its equivalent *foreigner* in the subcorpus of British press. In the same vein, other lexical labels tend to emphasize the foreign origin of immigrants. For instance, *foráneos* 'foreigners', *personas extracomunitarias* 'non-European people' or *colectivo extranjero* 'foreign group' in the Spanish subcorpus and noun phrases like *foreign-born people* or *foreign staff* in the British press consulted. These lexical labels are deliberately ambiguous in order to avoid any specific reference to the origin of immigrants. And this is precisely where its euphemistic nature lies. Consider the following quotations:

(12) *De 2000,* ***cuando el INE contabilizó 923.879 extranjeros*** (in bold in the original)*, a 2010, este colectivo se incrementó en la astronómica cifra de 4.823.855 personas*. (EM, 13 January) (From 2000, when the INE (i.e. National Statistics Institute) counted 923,879 foreigners, to 2010, this group increased by the astronomical number of 4,823,855 people).

(13) 30,000 *foreign workers* entered UK under transfer schemes.
Business have told the Government not to cut the number of *foreign staff* coming to the UK via company transfers or risk damaging economic growth. (TDT, 28 February)

The euphemistic term *extranjeros* 'foreigners' in (12) and the noun phrases *foreign workers* and *foreign staff* in (13) should be, at least in theory, positive for the image of the immigrants. The same happens with euphemistic periphrases like "migrants from outside the EU that arrive in UK" in (14):

(14) A Briton is "displaced" from the labour market for every four extra *people from outside the EU that arrive in the UK*, the Migration Advisory Committee (Mac) concluded. (TDT, 10 January)

In the three previous quotations, the journalist resorts to euphemistic lexical alternatives that portray immigrants, first and foremost, as foreigners. The euphemistic force of the items in italics lies in their intentional and deliberate ambiguity (Chamizo Domínguez, 2005). Such ambiguity leaves a door open to a more favourable interpretation, as commented on in Text 1, and leads the reader to explore beyond the literal meaning and arrive at the connotations hidden behind the lexical items employed by the journalist. In fact, neither *extranjero* / *foreigner* nor "people from outside the EU that arrive in UK" present certain semantic traits that the word *immigrant* is associated with (poverty, illegality, marginality, discrimination, etc.), as not all foreigners residing in UK have the same living conditions as immigrants.

However, the reader should not be misled by the presence of apparently inoffensive euphemistic lexical labels. In (12), (13) and (14) the image of immigration transmitted by the journalist is not actually positive; rather, the idea that is implicitly transmitted is too harsh to put it plainly: immigration is a problem for the host countries, such a serious problem that immigrants take jobs away from British citizens, as indicated in (14). In these quotations, the belief that immigration is problematic and a burden on the host societies is given the appearance of objectivity through figures.

This leads me to reflect on the use of figures and percentages in the discourse of immigration. The use of figures and percentages in immigration-related news items is not at random; rather, it serves the purpose of giving credibility to the idea of immigration as something chaotic and out of control, which makes the problem appear more serious. Take the following quotation:

(15) *En 2010 se censaron 561 inmigrantes, mientras que en 2009 fueron 339 personas las que entraron en España.* (EM, 26 January) (In 2010 the census counted 561 immigrants, whereas 339 people entered Spain in 2009).

Despite the euphemistic reference to irregular immigrants *personas* 'people', the journalist tends to aggravate the problem of immigration by making reference to the increasing number of immigrants that have reached the Spanish territory. To this end, in (12) the journalist resorts to the hyperbolic adjective *astronómica* 'astronomical', which considerably upgrades the magnitude of the problem being dealt with. Similarly, in the headline and subheading below the euphemistic alternatives to immigrants *passengers* and *people* do not attempt to favour their integration into British society whatsoever. What is highlighted is the number of immigrants (repeated at the beginning of the headline and the subheading) that have reached British territory without border checks:

(16) 500,000 *passengers* allowed to enter Britain on Eurostar without border checks.
500,000 *people* were allowed to enter Britain on the Eurostar without being checked against a warning index between 2007 and 2011, it emerged today. (TDT, 20 February)

However, one should bear in mind that the use of figures does not objectively reflect the real state of affairs; rather, it builds the belief of a massive and uncontrolled arrival of immigrants that must be stopped and controlled at all costs for the sake of social stability.

In the British press consulted, the presence of "alarm words" (cf. Van Dijk 2005, 117-118) is worthy of note. Alarm words constitute an effective means of persuading the readership into considering immigration system a disaster insofar as it is seen as something chaotic and dangerous to the citizens and a burden on the economy of the host countries. In fact, in the following quotation, alarm words like *mess* (reinforced by the presence of the intensifying adjective *complete*) and *wave* contribute to building an image of immigration as a serious problem not only for the economy of the country but also for the security of its citizens:

(17) Labour left our immigration system in a *complete mess* [...]. Other countries erected temporary barriers to immediate migration. Britain did not – and saw a *wave* of people come here to find work. (TDT, 19 January)

Alarm words are sometimes more explicit and shocking to the reader. In the following news item, it is significant that the journalist puts in the same sentence the words *migrant* and *beheaded* in the headline. Emotionally loaded verbs like *attacked* and explicit references like "sawing off his head" add a tragic tone to the news item:

(18) Violent past of *migrant* worker who *beheaded* victim. [...] He *attacked* the former public schoolboy with a cheese knife, *sawing off his head*. (TDT, 20 March)

In cases like these, the journalist resorts to the explicit advocacy of dysphemism in the form of emotionally loaded and intemperate language which does not leave the readers indifferent.[9] The use of explicit terms of violence without any verbal mitigation in a news item whose headline refers explicitly to an immigrant effectively contributes to building a sense of fear in the reader, to be precise fear of criminal attack. The same happens in such a shocking headline as the one that follows:

(19) Jailed for life: Czech *murderer* who committed *string of sex attacks*. (TDT, 28 January)

In the last two quotations, it seems evident that fear is very useful to persuade the reader on the potential threat of immigrants. After all, we should not forget that those who are afraid are more sensitive and likely to be convinced.

Of particular interest is the use of the metaphorical (and alarm) word *wave* in (17). Metaphor plays a crucial role in the representation of immigration issues, given the wide range of conflicting representations of immigrants and immigration issues in public discourse, as Charteris-Black (2006, 4) points out. There is a fruitful line of cognitive research regarding the rhetoric potential of metaphor to deal with social issues like racism or immigration along the lines of the well-known model of Conceptual Metaphor Theory in different cultures and societies (cf. Santamaría, 2002; O'Brien, 2003; Chateris-Black, 2006; Semino, 2008, among others). Following this cognitive model, *wave* is included in the conceptual metaphor IMMIGRATION IS A NATURAL DISASTER. The metaphors that evoke natural phenomena base their dysphemistic capacity on the association between the target domain (immigration in this case) and a dangerous and wild nature as source domain, which leads to the consideration of immigration as something irrational and chaotic, as a threat which should be avoided at all costs for the sake of the survival of the host societies (cf. Crespo-Fernández, 2008, 53-54). More precisely, the term *wave* is related to the image of an excessive flow of water (cf. Charteris-Black, 2006, 570-572; Semino, 2008, 89-96), which provides the raw material for attacking immigration. Though water metaphorical items like *wave* and *tide* are conventional in talking about immigration, as Semino (2008, 89) points out, this conceptualization does keep its dysphemistic force intact; indeed, this water metaphor makes us believe that immigration will devastate the host societies as it is – the same as uncontrolled water – an irrational and dangerous natural phenomenon. Besides, what this conceptual equation implicitly transmits is a disastrous loss of control over immigration, as Van der Vilke (2003) demonstrated in the discourse of French political right in immigration-related parliamentary debates.

I have detected other water-related metaphorical items to target the issue of immigration. One of them is *presión* (and its equivalent in the British subcorpus *pressure*). This term provides evidence for the existence of the underlying metaphor THE NATION IS A CONTAINER whereby the country is conceptualized as a container which is made up of three parts, namely an exterior, an interior and a boundary (i.e. the political borders). That this is so can be gathered from Chilton: "The spatial-containment schema grounds the conceptualization of one's country as a closed container that can be sealed or penetrated" (2004, 118). The movement of people across borders that immigration supposes, as Charteris-Black (2006, 576) argues, tends to weaken this container because it leads to social change and loss of control and security. In fact, a massive arrival of immigrants implies a pressure from the interior of the container which may eventually perforate its boundary. Take the quotations that follow:

(20) *La Unión Europea ha aprobado este jueves impulsar un plan de solidaridad para los países que, como le ocurre ahora a Grecia, sufren una alta presión de inmigración y solicitantes de asilo.* (EM, 8 March) (The European Union approved this Thursday a plan to promote solidarity for countries that, like Greece, suffer a *high pressure* of immigration and asylum seekers).

(21) This is expected to increase *pressure* on immigration judges amid growing concerns over how criminals are exploiting human rights laws. (TDT, 11 February)

The use of the term *presión* / *pressure* above leads to the symbolic representation of immigration as an uncontrollable body of water which threatens social cohesion and security, as an invasion from an external agent which human beings cannot control and, precisely for this reason, is dangerous and harmful to the nation.

The term *inflow* has the same conceptual basis. As happens with *pressure* in (20) and (21), this term conceptualizes immigrants as a fluid that can perforate the boundary of the container that represents the nation at a conceptual level:

(22) While the *inflow* of students will be restricted, the Government will also focus on ensuring they leave at the end of their visas. (TDT, 11 February)

In the three examples above the metaphor brings focus to the water destructive qualities, associating immigration to a destructive force and immigrants to an uncontrollable body of water that harms the country and its citizens. In this conceptualization that equates water to immigration, certain values are given priority. Indeed, the filter of metaphorical conceptualization through which the target domain of immigration is presented provides the reader with a partial understanding of the concept, ignoring the fact that water slowly drains and leaves fertile soil while highlighting its destructive qualities, as pointed out by O'Brien (2003).[10]

Another metaphorical item detected in the corpus belongs to the dysphemistic conceptualization IMMIGRATION IS A DISEASE or, as O'Brien (2003, 38) puts it, IMMIGRANTS AS DISEASED ORGANISM. Here the nature of the source domain makes it evident that immigration (and not only irregular immigration) is seen in a very negative light. In fact, as Knowless and Moon (2006: 161) point out, "we conceptualize malice and resentment in terms of poison and destruction (poisonous, venomous, toxic, etc.)". This is the case of the following headline:

(23) Multiculturalism has left Britain with a *toxic* legacy. (TDT, 12 February)

The idea that is transmitted here through the adjective *toxic* is that even the so-called legal immigrants are evil by nature and their presence is likely to have an evil influence on the host societies. The dysphemistic basis lies on the implicit association between immigrants and an infectious disease, which leads to considering them as potentially life threatening. The notion behind the disease metaphor is that, as Cunningham-Parmeter (2011, 1568) argues, immigrants are believed to contaminate the social body just as infectious diseases threaten our health. Besides, this dysphemistic metaphor implicitly reinforces the idea that immigrants are spreading dangerous diseases typical of less developed countries. Therefore, immigrants pose a serious threat to locals staying nearby and make them be afraid that immigrants will carry infectious disease into their families.[11] As O'Brien claims, "stigmatized environments serve to make the metaphorical real, and thus solidify the use of disease metaphors as an apt means of portraying the group in question" (2003, 38). Through this metaphor fear plays again a crucial role in the rejection of immigrants, as they are feared as carriers of diseases against which we have no antidote.

The last dysphemistic lexical device observed in the corpus is the conceptual metonymy[12] THE EFFECTS OF IMMIGRATION STAND FOR IMMIGRATION. Consider the case that follows:

(24) Ministers asked the committee to recommend an increase in the current threshold – equivalent to £13,700 a year before tax – which would prevent the entry of *those who could be considered a burden on taxpayers*. (TDT, 24 March)

The periphrasis highlighted in italics explicitly focuses on the negative effects of immigration for the economy of the country. The message is clear: the immigrant is no longer a person, but a burden. The dysphemistic basis of this conceptual equation lies on the fact that immigrants are singled out as economic threats and therefore dehumanized, which makes the reader rejects them.

6. Results and Discussion

The findings obtained from the analysis reveal that immigrants are portrayed in ways which differ significantly in the Spanish and British subcorpora of right-wing online press. The following figure shows the differences between the Spanish and the British press as far as the X-phemistic lexical representation of immigrants is concerned:

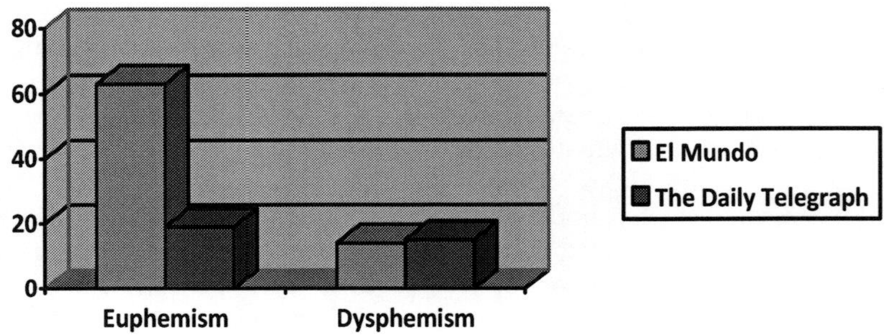

Figure 4-1. The X-phemistic treatment of immigration in the corpus.

The first noticeable quality is that the presence of euphemism is much more relevant in the Spanish subcorpus than in the British one. Indeed, I have detected 63 euphemistic items to represent the figure of the immigrant in the Spanish press, whereas in the British press I have only found 19 immigration-related euphemistic labels. This difference is more evident if we consider the number of euphemistic substitutes per news item: 1,1 in EM and 0,43 in TDT.

However, the type of euphemistic substitutes used in both subcorpora does not differ significantly: the most common euphemistic labels are based on the fact that immigrants come from abroad: *extranjero* both as a noun ('foreigner') and as an adjective ('foreign') in noun phrases like *residente extranjero* ('foreign resident'), *ciudadano extranjero* ('foreign citizen'), *colectivo extranjero* ('foreign group') and in the periphrases "ciudadanos extranjeros insuficientemente documentados" ('insufficiently documented foreign citizens') or "extranjeros que quieren mejorar su calidad de vida" ('foreigners who want to improve their quality of life'). Similarly, in the British press most of the euphemistic items detected are based on the same notion of the immigrant as someone coming from outside the UK: the noun *foreigner*, the adjective *foreign* (*foreign-born people*, *foreign staff* or *foreign workers*) and other lexical labels like *newcomers*, *born overseas*, *people arriving from outside the EU* or *those from outside the EU*. The greater presence of euphemism in the Spanish subcorpus can be partly explained insofar as the ortophemistic term *inmigrante* 'immigrant' is used to refer euphemistically to the so-called "illegal" immigrants on 14 occasions, whereas in the British press, the dysphemistic alternative is preferred to refer to those lacking a work permit.

Not always does the use of euphemistic labels truly benefit the integration of immigrants in society; rather euphemism is, on too many occasions, a useful device to transmit prejudices against immigration in a socially acceptable way. Actually, despite the presence of euphemism, the number of news items that offer a negative view of immigrants is more relevant than those which present a non-negative view, even in the Spanish subcorpus, in which euphemism abounds. The negative representation of immigrants is especially noteworthy in the British press, in which the percentage of positive representations of immigrants is extremely low (around 20% out of the total of news items), whereas in the Spanish press this percentage of negative representations tends to 50%. This significant difference between both samples is graphically shown below:

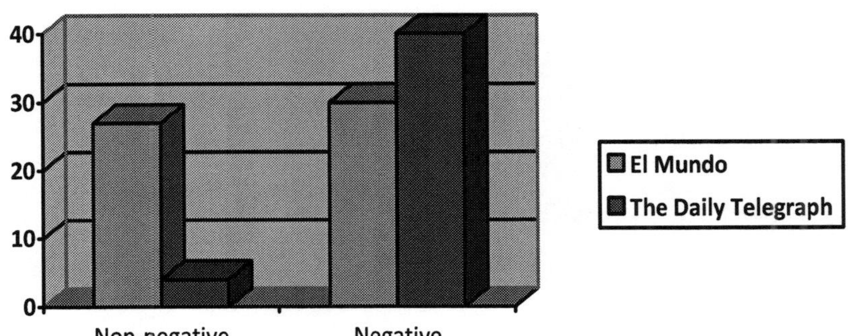

Figure 4-2. Non-negative and negative representations of immigrants.

Whereas euphemism is more relevant in quantitative terms in the Spanish subcorpus, dysphemism is slightly more common in the British one: 0,2 dysphemistic items found in EM per news item versus 0,34 in TDT. Here the nature of the verbal elements used for a dysphemistic purpose does not differ in a significant way either: in the samples of both countries, the adjective *ilegal* / *illegal* is the most common way to refer disparagingly to undocumented immigrants lacking documents (with 4 and

7 occurrences respectively). The greater presence of dysphemism in the British subcorpus also derives from the important role that figurative language plays in verbal abuse: the conceptualization IMMIGRATION IS A NATURAL DISASTER is the source of four dysphemistic items in TDT (*wave*, *inflow*, *pressure* and *tide*) whereas it is responsible for two pejorative labels in EM (*flujos migratorios* 'migratory flows' and *presión* 'pressure'). In the subcorpus of British press, journalists resort to another metaphor like IMMIGRATION IS A DISEASE, in which the adjective *toxic* is included.

Though beyond the scope of this paper, I will briefly consider two indexes which are highly significant of the position of the newspaper towards immigration. One of them is the association between immigration and crime. In the British press consulted, immigrants are associated with illegality in almost half of the news items that constitute the corpus: in 21 out of the 44 immigration-related news items there are references to different types of criminal activity such as drug dealing, sexual assault, theft, organized crime, murder, terrorism, etc. By contrast, the presence of illegality is much less significant in the Spanish subcorpus: there are only five references to criminal activities (illegal prostitution, terrorism, forgery, drug dealing and theft), which only makes 0,08 references per news item. The use of figures and percentages is also worth considering. They are more commonly used in the British subcorpus: in 14 news items figures are used to give credibility to the idea of immigration as a burden on the host society, whereas they only appear in five items of news in the Spanish corpus.

7. Conclusions and Final Remarks

The hypothesis that I proposed to argue for in this piece of research was that the right-wing position towards immigration should be reflected in lexical X-phemistic items which tend to provoke discriminatory attitudes towards immigrants. The analysis carried out reveals that different lexical units and patterns found in the news items consulted can be argued to serve this role.

Evidence from the corpus suggests that in most of the samples of Spanish and British right-wing press consulted, immigrants are represented in negative, or, to say the least, non-positive terms and phrases. This is especially the case in the British press, in which the percentage of news items in which immigrants are represented positively is very low. However, the treatment of immigration in the Spanish subcorpus is, in general terms, less damaging to the immigrant community. This is deduced from the following findings:

- Euphemism is much more relevant in quantitative terms in the Spanish subcorpus than in the British one, especially in the representation of irregular immigrants. By contrast, the number of dysphemistic labels is smaller in the Spanish press.
- Neutral or ortophemistic terms like *inmigrante* 'immigrant' are employed to refer to undocumented immigrants in the Spanish press, whereas British journalists and commentators opt for the explicit advocacy of dysphemistic terms like *clandestine* or *illegal*. In this respect, it must be noted that the repeated use of the adjective *illegal* in the British subcorpus unavoidably triggers readers' inclinations to associate them with criminals.
- The few cases of positive representations of immigrants appear in the samples of Spanish press. In these cases, immigrants are regarded as victims, which encourages a positive response on the part of readers.
- There are two main areas of dysphemistic metaphors to portray immigrants – especially the so-called "illegal" immigrants – in negative light: metaphors of natural disaster and container metaphors. These conceptual metaphors, which can be argued to be powerful ideological devices, occur more frequently in the British subcorpus. Significantly enough, there is a total absence of positive metaphors for immigrants in the corpus, a finding which is common across research on the discursive representation of immigration.
- The British journalist resorts to the explicit advocacy of dysphemism in the form of emotionally loaded and intemperate language, i.e. explicit terms of violence or alarm words, which contributes to building the image of the immigrant as a potential threat to the citizens and causes the readers to fear immigrants. This exploitation of fear as a means of ideological control is not present in the samples of Spanish press consulted.

It is worthy of note that, despite the high frequency of euphemism in the Spanish subcorpus, most of the euphemistic units detected do not necessarily transmit a positive image of immigrants. The same is true for the British subcorpus. In fact, many of the euphemistic labels that refer to immigrants are examples of politically correct (PC) language; that is, they are merely instruments at the journalists' disposal to implicitly transmit an idea too harsh to put it plainly: immigrants constitute a potential threat to social order and a burden on the economy of the country. Hence the high percentage of news items that transmit a negative image of immigrants despite the presence of euphemism.

In line with the negative view of immigration held by the British press, figures occur more frequently in *The Daily Telegraph* than in *El Mundo* in order to give credibility to an image of immigration as something chaotic and out of control. In addition, in the British newspaper the connection between immigration and criminal behaviour is so overwhelming that it clearly supports the social exclusion of immigrants. After all, the association between immigration and crime has traditionally been a center point of anti-immigrant discourse.

In sum, the cross-linguistic study carried out here reveals that immigrants are portrayed in too much negative light in the conservative online press. In fact, X-phemistic references to immigrants betray a series of ideological codes and values that considerably damage the image of immigrants, what is particularly evident in the British press, in which word choice contributes in a decisive way to give credibility to the image of the immigrant as a potential threat to the host societies at a social, personal and economic level. From this we can conclude that in the British right-wing press, whether consciously or not, immigrants are depicted as targets of public outrage and almost systematically derogated and criminalized, which does not happen, at least not so overtly, in the Spanish online press.

Notes

1. In this study, I understand by immigrants people belonging to an ethnic minority coming from poor countries, stigmatized and tending to social exclusion.
2. I understand by *serious newspapers* those focused on serious journalism dealing with current political affairs and events. Also known as "the quality press", serious-minded newspapers are in contrast with less serious newspapers (i.e. "the popular press") which generally deal more with subjects such as celebrities or sports.
3. Burridge (2004, 206) defines PC language as "conformity to current beliefs about correctness in language and behaviour with regard to policies on sexism, racism, ageism, etc."
4. The notion of *face* (Goffman, 1967) is related to the self-image that the participants in a communicative act claim for themselves. The use of mitigating strategies responds to the speaker's need to soften potential social conflicts derived from his assertions which may alter his or her prestige, preserving thus the speaker's positive face. See the seminal work by Brown and Levinson (1987) for a full account of the positive and negative dimensions of face.

5. *Referent manipulation* is the process whereby the language user presents the taboo concept in a particular way, either softening its less acceptable aspects or, on the contrary, intensifying them. The referent does not undergo any alteration in itself, though it is manipulated by the speaker or writer, and the result of this manipulation is what the receiver notices (for a full description of this process, see Crespo-Fernández, 2007).
6. Hereafter the terms and expressions I want to highlight in the quotations proposed as examples will appear in italics.
7. See Danziger (2010) for a fine-tuned study of Grice's Maxim of Quality and its cultural implications.
8. As I demonstrated in a previous study concerning the lexical treatment of irregular immigrants in the Spanish press (Crespo-Fernández, 2010, 281), the term *clandestine* is commonly used in texts which, at least in theory, are not intended to be offensive towards irregular immigrants. In fact, in the daily local newspaper *La Verdad de Alicante*, I detected cases in which the word *clandestinos* 'clandestines' was used in news items which aimed at denouncing the hard living conditions of immigrants in Spain.
9. As shown by Van Dijk more than twenty years ago, in the journalistic representation of ethnic minority groups, British headlines generally appeared rather aggressive: "Even routine political and social relationships and minor conflicts are often expressed with words from the aggression and violence registers, or with military metaphors" (1991, 56). Unfortunately, judging from news items like (18) and (19), the situation has not really improved.
10. The same applies to the conceptual metaphor IMMIGRANTS ARE ILLEGAL ALIENS. This metaphor, as Cunningham-Parmeter (2011, 1556) argues, highlights the criminal characteristics of some immigrants, while ignoring the obvious fact that most immigrants are legal residents in the United States.
11. That this idea is present in current discourse concerning immigration in Britain can be gathered from the online version of BBC news, in which a news item from the year 2006 entitled, significantly enough, "Migrants carry disease burden" considered the relationship between immigration and disease as follows: "Migrants make up about 70% of TB, HIV and malaria cases in England, Wales and Northern Ireland, a report has found".
12. Metonymy coexists and interacts with metaphor in the conceptualization of abstract concepts like immigration. Indeed, a considerable number of metaphors have a metonymic basis, as I have recently demonstrated in a corpus of death-related figurative language (Crespo-Fernández, 2011).

Bibliography

Allan, Keith and Kate Burridge. 2006. *Forbidden Words: Taboo and the Censoring of Language*. Cambridge: Cambridge University Press.

Bañón Hernández, Antonio. 2002. *Discurso e inmigración. Propuestas para el análisis de un debate social*. Almería: Universidad de Almería.

Bilger, Veronika and Ilse Van Liempt. 2009. "Introduction". In *The Ethics of Migration Research Methodology. Dealing with Vulnerable Immigrants*, ed. Ilse Van Liempt and Veronika Bilger, 1-24. Eastbourne: Sussex Academic Press.

Brown, Penelope and Stephen Levinson. 1987. *Politeness. Some Universals in Language Usage*. Cambridge: Cambridge University Press.

Burridge, Kate. 2004. *Blooming English*. Cambridge: Cambridge University Press.

Chamizo Domínguez, Pedro J. 2005. "Some theses on euphemisms and dysphemisms". *Studia Anglica Resoviensia* 25: 9-16.

Chateris-Black, Jonathan. 2006. "Britain as a container: immigration metaphors in the 2005 election campaign". *Discourse & Society* 17.5: 563-581.

Chilton, Paul. 2004. *Analysing Political Discourse*. London and New York: Routledge.

Crespo-Fernández, Eliecer. 2007. *El eufemismo y el disfemismo. Procesos de manipulación del tabú en el lenguaje literario inglés*. Alicante: Universidad.

—. 2008. "El lenguaje de la inmigración. Atenuación y ofensa verbal en la prensa alicantina". In *Inmigración, discurso y medios de comunicación*, ed. María Martínez Lirola, 45-64. Alicante: Juan Gil Albert.

—. 2010. "Eufemismo y disfemismo léxico en la designación del inmigrante 'sin papeles'". *Bulletin of Hispanic Studies* 87.3: 273-289.

—. 2011. "Euphemistic conceptual metaphors in epitaphs from Highgate Cemetery". *Review of Cognitive Linguistics* 9.1: 198-226.

Crespo-Fernández, Eliecer and María Martínez Lirola. 2012. "Lexical and visual choices in the representation of immigrants in the Spanish press". *Spanish in Context* 9.1: 27-57.

Cunningham-Parmeter, Keith. 2011. "Alien language: Immigration metaphors and the jurisprudence of otherness". *Fordham Law Rev.* 79: 1545-1598.

Danziger, Eve. 2010. "On trying and lying: cultural configurations of Grice's Maxim of Quality". *Intercultural Pragmatics* 7.2: 199-219.

El Mundo. "Immigración" (1 January to 31 March 2012). http://ariadna.elmundo.es/buscador/archivo.html?q=inmigración&t=1&s=1. Last accessed on 31 March 2012.

Fairclough, Norman. 1992. *Discourse and Social Change*. Oxford: Blackwell.

Gabrielatos, Costas and Peter Baker. 2008. "Fleeing, sneaking, flooding: A corpus analysis of discursive constructions of refugees and asylum seekers in the UK Press 1996-2005". *Journal of English Linguistics* 36.1: 5-38.

Goffman, Erving. 1967. *Interaction Ritual: Essays on Face-to-Face Communication*. New York: DoubleDay.

Grice, H. Paul. 1975. "Logic and Conversation". In *Syntax and Semantics: Speech Acts*, ed. Peter Cole and Jerry L. Morgan, 41-58. New York: Academic Press.

Hakam, Jamila. 2009. "The cartoons controversy. A critical discourse analysis of English-Language Arab newspaper discourse". *Discourse & Society* 20: 33-75.

Halliday, M.A.K. 1985. *Language, Context, and Text: Aspects of Language in a Social-Semiotic Perspective*. Oxford: Oxford University Press.

KhosraviNik, Majid. 2009. "The representation of refugees, asylum seekers and immigrants in British newspapers during the Balkan conflict (1999) and the British general election (2005)". *Discourse and Society* 20.4: 477-498.

Knowless, Murray and Rosamund Moon. 2006. *Introducing Metaphor*. Abingdon: Routledge.

Lakoff, George. 1993 (1979). "The Contemporary Theory of Metaphor." In *Metaphor and Thought* (2nd ed.), ed. Andrew Ortony, 202-251. Cambridge: Cambridge University Press.

Lakoff, George and Mark Johnson. 1980. *Metaphors We Live By*. Chicago: The University of Chicago Press.

Lakoff, George and Mark Turner. 1989. *More than Cool Reason. A Field Guide to Poetic Metaphor*. Chicago: The Chicago University Press.

Martínez Lirola, María. 2009. "Immigration news in the free press". *Brno Studies in English* 35.1: 63-76.

O'Brien, Gerald V. 2003. "Indigestible food, conquering hordes, and waste materials: Metaphors of immigrants and the early immigration restriction debate in the United States". *Metaphor & Symbol* 18.1: 33-47.

OED2: *Oxford English Dictionary* 1992 (1989) 2nd ed. on CD-ROM. Oxford: Oxford University Press.

Sabés Turmo, Fernando. 2010. "Analysis of the journalistic treatment given to the migration phenomenon in www.elPaís.com". *Revista Latina de Comunicación Social* 65: 30-44. http://www.revistalatinacs.org/10/art/881_UAB/03_SabesEng.html. Last accessed on 24 January 2012.

Santamaría, Enrique. 2002. *La incógnita del extraño. Una aproximación a la significación sociológica de la "inmigración comunitaria"*. Barcelona: Anthropos.

Semino, Elena. 2008. *Metaphor in Discourse.* Cambridge: Cambridge University Press.

The Daily Telegraph. "Immigration News" (1 January to 31 March 2012). http://www.telegraph.co.uk/news/uknews/immigration/. Last accessed on 31 March 2012.

Van der Vilke, Ineke. 2003. "Right-wing parliamentary discourse on immigration in France". *Discourse & Society* 14.3: 309-348.

Van Dijk, Teun. 1991. *Racism and the Press*. New York and London: Routledge.

—. 2000. "New(s) Racism: A discourse analytical approach". In *Ethnic Minorities and the Media*, ed. Simon Cottle, 33-49. Philadelphia: Open University Press.

—. 2003. *Ideología y Discurso*. Barcelona: Ariel.

—. 2005. *Racism and Discourse in Spain and Latin America*. Amsterdam and Philadelphia: John Benjamins.

CHAPTER FIVE

HEALTH, IMMIGRATION AND THE WELFARE STATE IN TIMES OF CRISIS: A CRITICAL DISCOURSE ANALYSIS

ANTONIO M. BAÑÓN HERNÁNDEZ
UNIVERSITY OF ALMERÍA (CYSOC)[1]
SAMANTHA REQUENA ROMERO
UNIVERSITY OF ALMERÍA (CYSOC)
Mª EUGENIA GONZÁLEZ CORTÉS
UNIVERSITY OF MÁLAGA

1. Introduction[2]

On 5 April 2011, approximately a year ago, *Diario Médico*, one of the most influential means of spreading scientific knowledge in Spain, included an opinion article written by its editor-in-chief, Carmen Fernández, entitled "Indicios de xenofobia en salas de espera" ("Evidences of xenophobia in waiting rooms"). The article ended this way:

> "The impression that foreign people have more rights than the autochthonous ones, especially in health, it is on the up and up". "They are attended the first ones", "with them, doctors are not in a hurry", "they always finish loaded with prescriptions", " you have to fight to be able to go to rehabilitation and for them everything is just nothing", "for the slightest little thing they get sick leave [...]." These and other similar comments can be heard in any waiting room. The sector does not seem to be worried by it (it is an inconvenient and politically incorrect matter) but let the citizenship acknowledge the cuts in the budgets of health [...]" (Diario Médico, 2011, 2)[3].

In April 2012, immigrated people have gained particular attention due to Mariano Rajoy's government and his decision to cut immigrants' free access to the health service. It is not only necessary to be registered; now the process is more complex. Curiously, this social debate has been associated with another one that has a different profile: "health tourism".

It is reasonable to wonder about the educational or miseducational function of the mass media in relation to these kinds of results. In the *Annual Report Andalucía and Immigration 2010* it was indicated the following:

> "A second highlighted fact consists in a certain progressive erosion of the citizen's help for the integration of the immigrant population into the receiving society. This tendency affects not only the opinions with respect to the political participation of the immigrated people but also those of the rights to regroup their relatives and of their inclusion into the main welfare policies (education and health)" (*Annual Report Andalucía and Immigration 2010,* 2011, 131)[4].

Moreno and Bruquetas, for their part, claim in *Inmigración y Estado del Bienestar en España* (*Immigration and Social Welfare State in Spain*):

> "Although the favourable attitude towards immigrants is still a majority, the native population tends to think, with a high frequency, that immigrants compete against the natives to get their jobs and their social benefits (health, school places, housing help, public assistance) [...] The perception that the immigrant population is favoured with the provision of social benefits provokes in large native sectors a communitarian reaction and/or nationalist of "those who live here first [...]" (Moreno and Bruquetas 2011, 9)[5].

These kinds of perceptions and attitudes are occasionally expressed through generalised anecdotes, as we will comment on later. In the book *Opiniones y actitudes de la población andaluza ante la inmigración (III): Más allá del discurso funcionalista (Opinions and Attitudes of the Andalusian Population on Immigration (III): beyond the Functionalist Discourse)*, Rinken and Pérez (2011, 53) reproduced some of the testimonies about a tendency of immigrants to miss their turns while waiting in health centres.

2. Health and immigration in the media before the crisis

When we examine the representation of the migratory processes in the media from a discursive point of view, health is not one of the first topics to come up. Antolín Granados (2006, 62)[6] explains:

"About the immigrant's conditions of living in Spain with relation to job, housing, education and health, the headlines that cover them represent just a small number. Therefore, it is not the number that draws the attention in this kind of news, but the little attention that newspapers give to a series of circumstances that due to its importance in the life of any collective of citizens usually covers a major relevance in the information when it is about Spanish people".

In fact, Granados' work offers truly revealing figures taken from a corpus of news items compiled between 1 June 2006 and 30 September 2006 in the national newspapers: *El País, El Mundo, ABC* and *La Vanguardia*. The author looked for articles dealing with health and found seven pieces of news in *El País* (1% of the total), six in *El Mundo* (0.8%), five in *ABC* (1%) and three in *La Vanguardia* (0.8%). Clara Pérez found a similar shortage of news items on this topic in her work about immigration, gender and mass media (2003, 83), as did Escobar in an examination of Almería's press (1998).

Manuel Moreno, for his part, in the analysis done about the same headlines during the 15 days of the March electoral campaign in 2004, declares:

"It is surprising that the only reference to health in "Immigration and vaccination" (*La Vanguardia*, 4th March) is produced in the sense of fear of the imported illnesses. Despite the fact that situations like the ones referred by the piece of news already mentioned (in relation to the necessity of preventing four imported illnesses: poliomyelitis, measles, rubella, and hepatitis B, active in the different countries where immigrants came from) take place in specific contexts, immigrated people are, in general terms, healthy people and acquire above all what the microbiologists Margarita Barquero and Mercedes Subirats (*Diario Médico*, 21st November 2003) call "pathologies of destination", meaning those related to their condition of migrant people. I also think that in the health circle there is a certain obsession for the search of the exotic case in relation to the migrant people" (Moreno, 2006, 223)[7].

However, health and illness are transverse elements in the social debate about immigration in the way they are represented by mass media. In this sense, we could mention three lines of work: a) the analysis of the representation of immigrated people or of the migratory processes including health topics (in a broader sense) as a nuclear element or as a secondary element in this representation; b) the use by the media (including "ethnic media", produced by a group of immigrated people) as an element of health formation and prevention of illnesses addressed to people who are not aware of the health system dynamics in our country on some occasions due to problems with the language; and c) the reception of Spanish media in the origin countries and the interpretation made of the messages that appear on them (especially on television and on the Internet) connecting, for example, quality of life and the welfare state with health and health services access. In this chapter, we choose the first line of investigation.

Given that health is a topic given surprisingly little attention in headlines or informative preferential spaces, we are sometimes obliged to move from the analysis of headlines to a more detailed analysis of the textual developments of the different informative genres and subgenres and to the observation of what we could call 'the second informative level'. In other words, discussions of health in relation to immigration primarily exist as a particular concealed social debate in the mass media.

In 2006, studying the discursive association between immigration and terrorism, we already stated the following:

> "Cross-cutting is nowadays the most important feature of immigration from a thematic viewpoint; it is difficult not to find references to it on every thematic context: economy, health, art, security, etc. The "thematic extension" of immigration has always been a claim for those who have defended a less stigmatised discourse with respect to immigration. However, the truth is that this relocation has also some risks: the maintenance of a hidden debate equally discriminatory and preventive in many occasions" (Bañón, 2006, 273)[8].

Discriminatory and prejudiced discourse regarding immigrants, in fact, has had a very solid base in communicative strategies in which health and the health system have had a prominent place. If we had to approach the topic, we would highlight a very useful macrostrategy when dealing with immigrants that combines two well-known processes: association and generalisation. Both processes affect *Others* (immigrants) and *Us* (people native to the area). Following Teun A. van Dijk's (1998, 267) ideological square, in which a prejudiced sight tends on the one hand to emphasise the negative and lessen the positive of the out-group and, on the other hand, to intensify the positive and lessen the negative of the in-group, we could adapt this idea to the main topic of this work and say that immigrated people are associated with notions such as 'hazard for the community' (for infection, unhygienic habits, or because, supposedly, they are a threat to public health) and 'high use of the welfare state' (they abuse the health service, contributing very little economically but using the service a great deal).

On the other hand, native people are represented in an indulgent way, associating them with behaviors that show compassion, generosity, patience and solidarity toward the immigrants. In the second phase, positive characteristics as well as negative ones are generalised to cover the highest possible number of people belonging to *Us* or *Them*, respectively.

Studies on the discourse of immigration, not only in the media but also in daily conversation, have already mentioned some of the questions posed in the previous paragraph. We can cite, in this sense, *Prejudice in Discourse,* the pioneer work by Teun A. van Dijk; the said book was translated into Spanish in 2011. On page 128, for example, he mentions as one of the most frequent topics when talking about foreign people the idea that they abuse the Spanish National Health Service.

This idea of immigrants having unhealthy habits comes out (2011, 136, 178, 183, 247) in different ways and on different occasions. These examples tend to be anecdotes or one-time experiences, but speakers incorporate them into their mental models of immigrants in general.

In our earlier work about spoken discourse in relation to immigration in Almería, we discussed the popular preconceptions that immigrants brought *muchas enfermedades* ('too many illnesses') (Bañón, 1997, 113) or that those who came should not *seguir con las drogas* ('continue with drugs') (1997, 119). The debate about whether media reproduce the social discourse (that includes expressions like the previous ones) may have a simple answer: there is a mutual influence between society discourse and mass media discourse, but mass media logically have more protagonism.

We also find the topic of health in this idea of media discourse on immigration. In *Nuevas reflexiones sobre la representación periodística de los inmigrantes* (*New Reflections about the journalistic representation of immigrants*), we included a heading entitled "About Health, Illness and the Discriminatory Representation of Immigration" (Bañón, 2003). Here, we analysed the frequent association between minority ethnic groups or immigrants and contagious illnesses such as HIV since the 1980s.

In the 21st century this association is still being prioritized in the press with letters to the editor in which this attitude becomes apparent (*La Razón*, 3rd August, 2002), or creating, deliberately or not, negative connections when placing opposed pieces of news such as "*El Gobierno minimiza el riesgo de ofensiva marroquí contra España*" ("The Government minimises the Moroccan offensive risk against Spain") on the one hand, and "*Los inmigrantes son el mayor grupo de riesgo ante la tuberculosis*" ("Immigrant people are the major group at risk of getting tuberculosis") (*La Voz de Almería*, 4 April 2002), on the other. Another similar example from the same year occurred on page 25 of the 10 August issue of *La Razón*, which consisted of two pieces of news. The first referred to a sit-in of immigrants at the University Pablo de Olavide in Seville and was entitled "*La rectora de Sevilla pide investigar a las ONGs que apoyaron el encierro*" ("Seville's vice-chancellor asks to investigate NGOs that supported the sit-in"). At the same level, in the second headline appeared: "*Alerta médica en dos condados de Florida por la propagación del virus del Nilo*" ("Medical alert in two Florida counties due to the propagation of the West Nile virus").

Social elite develops a discourse around immigration based on not positive evaluation. This type of valuation promotes prejudices towards immigrants (Bañón, 2002, 38-49). Actually, this valuation conceals, in many occasions, a clearly negative look. On the 19 August, 2000, *La Verdad* published "*Extreman la limpieza en las zonas de descanso de las autovías frecuentadas por magrebíes*" ("Maximize the cleaning of the rest areas in the motorways frequently used by Maghribian people"). The subheadline said: "*El objetivo es prevenir que la fiebre aftosa, una enfermedad de origen animal, se extienda por la Región*" ("The objective is to prevent foot-and-mouth disease, with animal origin from spreading through the Region"). Actually, this valuation conceals, in many occasions, a clearly negative look.

The wording of this headline establishes associations between Maghribian people and dirtiness, contagious illnesses and illnesses with animal origin. In reality, there is little evidence linking the arrival of immigrants with the appearance of illnesses (Martín, 2008, 5).

The same allusions happened years ago in regard to the purpose of the welfare estate and the use that immigrants make of it. An entire page of *La Verdad*'s editorial section was devoted to a news item titled "*Los inmigrantes copan los paritorios*" ("Immigrants fill labour rooms"). The editor referred to the birth of two children from immigrant families in the last New Year's Eve. This headline seems inappropriate given the context and the use of the hyperbolic word '*copar*' ('fill'). The same exaggeration happens in the case of abortion.

Finally, in this selection of brief examples from the press, we would like to comment on the cases in which an association is drawn between immigration and crimes against public health. For instance, on 20 July 2001, the editorial department of *La Razón* elaborated a chronicle about an immigrant sit-in, at the University Pablo de Olavide in Seville. The title chosen was "*Huelga de hambre a la desesperada de los 250 inmigrantes encerrados en Sevilla*" ("Hunger strike as a desperate measure of the 250 immigrants enclosed in Seville"). At the same level, on the right, another headline said, "*El 80 por ciento de los jóvenes españoles cree que las drogas deben ser ilegales*" ("80 per cent of Spanish young people think drugs should be illegal"). The choice of the word '*ilegal*' ('illegal') could not have been innocent, although we are conscious of how difficult it is to analyse the intention of these headlines, especially in the case of editors whose headline choices are limited by print space.

Television is no exception. In our analysis of a piece on *España Directo* (*Live Spain*), TVE, about immigration, we found references to overcrowding, unhealthiness, lack of hygiene, and so on to be common in the journalistic text and also in the witnesses' statements (Bañón, 2007, 221).

Audiovisual mass media "*disponen de muchos mecanismos para influir en nuestras elecciones espontáneas sin que seamos conscientes de ello*" ("have many mechanisms at their disposal to influence our spontaneous elections without being conscious") (Aznar, 2002, 59). It is possible that the root of the problem is "*el gran analfabetismo audiovisual del que se aprovechan las televisiones*" ("the high audiovisual illiteracy from which televisions take advantage") (Aznar, 2002, 70). It has been highlighted, on some occasions, that television is an example of mass media with a more sensationalist profile than, for example, newspapers (Igartua *et al.*, 2005a, 117; Igartua *et al.*, 2005b). Because health is an easy topic to treat in a sensationalist manner, it is easy to expect that this sensationalism will only increase when linked to immigration, another topic given a sensationalist treatment. Articles on topics such as the arrival of open boats also show frequent health concerns, although at a second level (Igartua, Muñiz and Cheng, 2005b, 159). See this extract from *Antena 3*:

> "The wave of illegal people has also arrived to the Peninsula. This open boat approached Motril with 32 Sub-Saharan people this morning, all of them in good health. A total of 370 illegal immigrants have reached our coasts during the whole weekend" (*Antena 3*, 11/11/2007. Quoted in Albert *et al.*, 2010, 59)[9].

In the journalistic discourse it is more difficult to find positive associations in relation to health and social welfare, like those referring to immigrated women and women's agency in the care of the elderly in Spain, as Peio Aierbe underlined (2008, 20).

Therefore, we cannot fall into the same trap that we are denouncing and say that all mass media or all journalists offer a preventive, even discriminatory treatment of immigrants. Professionals have also shown a critical and constructive capacity and an interest in generating discussion about the treatment that media provide of the migratory processes (Tomás, 2006, 246; Pérez, 2006, 274).

3. Spain in crisis 2011: Analysis of an audiovisual corpus

This paper uses a corpus taken from the Project for Excellence *Discursos de extranjería en los medios de comunicación audiovisuales andaluces: la construcción discursiva y visual de la nueva Andalucía* (*Immigration matters discourses in Andalusian audiovisual mass media: the discursive and visual construction of the new Andalucía*) (P10-TIC-6517). As described at the beginning of this chapter, we want to determine how often television in Andalucía gives information on health topics related, in one way or another, to immigrants and how this information is presented. Specifically, we have consulted 137 informative unities, *Canal Sur News* from April to July 2011, and we have centred our search not only on the presence of pieces of news that focus their attention on medical and health matters as main topics, but also on incidental references to hospitals, medical attention, crimes against public health, etc. as secondary topics.

We have found 25 articles that discuss these topics. This might seem like a very low number if we consider the important role that health questions have in people's lives, but on the other hand, this number coincides with the tendency shown by the conclusions of the scholars mentioned before. More surprising is the fact that only one out of these 25 articles actually focuses on a health topic. It is about a boy from Cameroon who came to Seville to have an operation because he suffered from hydrocephalus. The table below summarizes these 25 pieces of news.

Table 5-1. Identification of informative units and summary sentence

UNIT 1. Detención de dos personas acusadas de tener encerradas a tres mujeres. (Arrest of two persons accused of kidnapping and locking up three women) 14.04.11
UNIT 2. Un narcotraficante colombiano es detenido (A Colombian drug trafficker is arrested). 19.04.11
UNIT 3. Informe sobre actitudes hacia los inmigrantes (Report on attitudes towards immigrants). 04.05.11.
UNIT 4. Interceptado un camión que transportaba hachís (A truck carrying hashish is intercepted). 05.05.2011
UNIT 5. Rescate a inmigrantes en la isla de Lampedusa (Rescue of 500 immigrants on the island of Lampedusa). 08.05.11500
UNIT 6. Salvamento Marítimo rescata a 37 inmigrantes en la costa de Granada (Marine Salvage rescues 37 immigrants off the coast of Granada). 22.05.11

UNIT 7. Dos pateras llegan al puerto de Motril (Two open boats at the Port of Motril). 23.05.11
UNIT 8. Rescate de dos pateras en aguas de Almería (Rescue of two open boats off the coast of Almeria). 25.05.11
UNIT 9. 20 inmigrantes rescatados de una patera en el sureste de Cabo de Gata (20 immigrants rescued from an open boat in the southeast of Cabo de Gata). 28.05.11
UNIT 10. Encuentran el cadáver de una mujer en una planta de residuos en Granada (A woman's corpse is found at a sewage plant in Granada). 28.05.11
UNIT 11. Presentan el dispositivo Paso del Estrecho (The device Crossing the Straits is presented). 30.05.11
UNIT 12. Incautados 790 kilos de hachís en cartones de leche (790 kilos of hashish seized in milk cartons). 03.06.11
UNIT 13. Salvamento marítimo rescata a 39 inmigrantes de origen subsahariano (Salvage rescues 39 immigrants of sub-Saharan origin). 15.06.11
UNIT 14. Niño camerunés intervenido con éxito de hidrocefalia en Sevilla (Cameroonian child with hydrocephalus successfully operated on in Seville). 15.06.11
UNIT 15. Observatorio Europeo de Gerontoinmigración (Gerontoimmigration European Observatory). 17.06.11
UNIT 16. Una joven sueca muerta y otra herida por un marroquí en Fuengirola (A Swedish girl is killed and another wounded by a Moroccan in Fuengirola). 18.06.11
UNIT 17. La Policía Nacional ha desarticulado un punto de venta de drogas (The National Police break up a drug outlet). 22.06.11
UNIT 18. Joven marroquí ahogado al salvar la vida a dos niños (Moroccan boy drowned in saving the lives of two children). 28.06.11
UNIT 19. Detenido el patrón de una patera en aguas próximas a la isla de Alborán (An open boat in waters near the island of Alboran is stopped). 03.07.11
UNIT 20. Se cumple un año de la entrada en vigor de la nueva ley que regula el aborto (First anniversary of the enforcing of a new law regulating abortion). 05.07.11
UNIT 21. Salvamento Marítimo ha rescatado a 50 inmigrantes subsaharianos (Marine Salvage has rescued 50 African immigrants). 07.07.11
UNIT 22. A salvo 67 personas que intentaban llegar a la costa de Granada (Sixty-seven people reached the coast of Granada safely). 12.07.11
UNIT 23. Un joven muerto y otro herido, rescatados en alta mar (A young man dead and another wounded, rescued at sea). 25.07.11
UNIT 24. Huyendo de la miseria. 94 personas de origen subsahariano llegan al puerto de Motril (Fleeing poverty, 94 people from Sub-Sahara reach the port of Motril). 24.07.11
UNIT 25. Encuentro con niños saharauis (Meeting with Sahrawi children). 25.07.11

A quick look at these headlines can give a clue about the contexts in which topics related to health tend to appear. In the first place, we have to underline those pieces of news about the arrival of people in open boats and ships, and in which the main interest is centred on the health attention given to the recently arrived, especially if there are pregnant women and children among them. Eleven articles in total—44% of the occurrences of the topic we are dealing with in this article—are related to open boats and to the social and health assistance received.

These articles included a number of archetypical expressions: "*aunque algunos han tenido que recibir atención médica*" ("although some of them had the necessity of receiving medical attention") (unit 5); "*fueron atendidos por voluntarios de Cruz Roja que les dispensaron los primeros cuidados sanitarios*" ("they were attended by Red Cross Volunteers who gave them the first health-care") (unit 6), "*todos se encuentran en buen estado de salud*" ("all are in good health") (unit 7), "*fueron atendidos por voluntarios de la Cruz Roja*" ("they were attended by Red Cross Volunteers" (unit 8), "*se encuentran en buen estado de salud*" ("they are in good health") (unit 9), "*tuvieron que ser atendidos y trasladados al Hospital Santa Ana*" ("they had to be attended and transferred to Hospital Santa Ana's Hospital") (unit 13), "*Cruz Roja las trasladó al hospital comarcal para pasar una revisión médica*" ("the Red Cross transferred them to a regional hospital to get a medical checkup") (unit 19), "*el pequeño ha sido trasladado al Hospital Torrecárdenas, igual que una de las cuatro mujeres que navegaban*" ("the children have been transferred to Torrecardenas Hospital as well as one of the women who was sailing with them") (unit 21), "*la mujer ha pasado un reconocimiento médico rutinario al llegar*" ("the woman has had a routine medical examination on arrival") (unit 22), "*ingresó en el Hospital Carlos Haya y esta mañana ha recibido el alta médica*" ("he/she was admitted in Carlos Haya's Hospital and this morning discharged from hospital") (unit 23) and "*a excepción de tres mujeres que estaban en avanzado estado de gestación y que continúan ingresadas en el hospital comarcal de Motril*" ("except for three women who were in advanced pregnancy and continue admitted to district hospital in Motril") (unit 24).

Another group is formed by pieces of news related to crimes against public health (such as drug-dealing) or violent acts (assaults and murders) in which immigrants participate as aggressor or victim. In five of them, the informative frame develops around matters related to drugs. Health appears in phrases such as the following: "*y que además de obligarlas a mantener relaciones sexuales también las forzaba a traficar con droga*" ("and that did not only force them to have sexual relations but also into drug trafficking") (unit 1); "*su cuñado es el hijo de Leónidas Vargas, un conocido narcotraficante que en el año 2009 fue asesinado en el hospital 12 de octubre*" ("his brother in law is the son of Leonidas Vargas, a known drug dealer who in 2009 was killed in the hospital on 12 October") (unit 2); "*han interceptado un camión que transportaba una tonelada de hachís*"("have intercepted a truck carrying a ton of hashish") (unit 4); "*la Guardia Civil ha desmantelado una red dedicada al tráfico de drogas*" ("the Civil Guard has dismantled a network dedicated to drug trafficking"); "*los detenidos importaban supuestamente la droga desde Marruecos a España*" ("detainees allegedly imported drugs from Morocco to Spain") (unit 12); and "*la Policía Nacional ha desarticulado un punto de almacenamiento, distribución y venta de anabolizantes, medicamentos falsificados y drogas tóxicas en Málaga y Marbella*" ("the National Police have broken up a storage and distribution ring of anabolic steroids, counterfeit drugs and toxic drugs in Malaga and Marbella") (unit 17).

This group of news could be related to another block, that of violent acts: the body of a woman '*con rasgos latinoamericanos*' ('with Latin-American features') found in a residues plant and that "*se encuentra en el Instituto de Medicina Legal de Granada*" ("is located in the Institute of Legal Medicine of Granada") (unit 10), or the murder of a Swedish woman at the hands of a Moroccan man who also wounded another woman later "*atendida en el Hospital Costa del Sol de diferentes cortes producidos por arma blanca*" ("treated at the Hospital Costa del Sol from different knife cuts") (unit 16).

The last group is formed by news with topics that appeared only once, such as the following: a report on attitudes towards immigrants, in which immigrants are perceived as "*como causantes de la degradación en sanidad y en educación*" ("the cause of health and education degradation") (unit 3); a piece of news about the device set off for Crossing the Strait, that includes "*voluntarios de la Cruz Roja*" ("Red Cross volunteers") and "*servicios médicos*" ("medical services") (unit 11); the information referenced before about the Cameroonian child who suffered from hydrocephalus and who had an operation in Seville (unit 14); the presentation in the University of Málaga of the Gerontoimmigration European Observatory activities, "*un fenómeno creciente que implica una serie de necesidades sociosanitarias que el país de destino tiene que cubrir*" ("a growing phenomenon that involves a series of social needs that the country of destination has to cover") (unit 15), in which the Observatory director is quoted in this article as saying, "*Ya hay una directiva europea que ahora hay que trasponer, que no soluciona, no soluciona totalmente, pero trata de contribuir a equilibrar esta sanidad transfonteriza*" ("There is already a European directive which must now be transposed, that does not help, does not completely solve, but tries to help balance this cross border healthcare") (unit 15); the sad death of a Moroccan person who tried to save the lives of two drowning children: "*las asistencias sanitarias, sólo pudieron certificar su fallecimiento*" ("health workers could only certify his death") (unit 18); an assessment of the Abortion Act on the first anniversary of its enforcement through a report by the Association of Clinics for the Termination of Pregnancy, which stated that the number of abortions has decreased since 2008, "*pero no por la entrada en vigor de la ley sino porque ha disminuido el número de mujeres inmigrantes*" ("not by the entry into force of the law but because it has reduced the number of immigrant women") (unit 20); and, finally, the presence of Sahrawi children taken in by families in Andalucía who take advantage of their visit to "*someterse a revisiones médicas periódicas*" ("undergo periodic medical examinations") (unit 25).

Despite the fact that the immigration process presupposes certain effects at social, political, economic, and cultural levels, those pieces of news about matters related to immigrants are still located in the same sections as the ones that traditionally found a place in accident and crime reports and society. However, it is important to bear in mind that in audiovisual news programs the structure in sections is more diffuse or abstract and is far from the reality observed, as opposed to print media, which visibly divide the different sections.

With respect to the immigrants' presence as interviewed subjects, we find a low participation of them (as well as of native people) in the extracts we are analysing. Only one piece includes a quote from an immigrant, but it is of high significance. It is the piece of news published on 15 July about the Cameroonian boy who had an operation in Seville for hydrocephalus.

The images show not only the declarations of a health professional and expert in the matter but also of his great-grandmother, who is grateful for the help and alludes to new technologies. The selected passage is positive and therefore less interesting; in it, the old woman from Cameroon refers to the possibilities offered by the Internet, allowing the boy's mother to observe the development of this process from the family's origin country. In this case, the country of origin is thus detached from the topics of poverty and backwardness.

The duration of news ranged from 44 to 80 seconds, which is a logical timing in the audiovisual format of a television news bulletin where there is no space for reflection or analysis and only the headlines are left. The majority of them include images of support, beyond the entrance that the presenter makes, and this part of the analysis shows the evolution in the representation of the migratory phenomenon.

We can definitely observe an informative view in which the economic crisis does not appear explicitly mentioned (only in unit 3), and only one occasion where the suggested topic is health tourism (when dealing with the Gerontoimmigration Observatory in unit 15). In the rest of the examples, the health problems of immigrated people are associated on a high percentage with the attention received when they arrive in open boats or after conflicts. On the other hand, Spain is still represented as a supportive country that offers health care to those who need it, especially in news items about children.

Due to the reduced space available in this work, we cannot deeply analyse the group of 25 pieces of news. We have made a selection of three. The chosen news items are transcribed below and later discussed in more detail.

Table 5-2. Transcriptions

Unidad (Unit) 3. 04.05.11
Los inmigrantes asentados en España aportan más al Estado de bienestar de lo que reciben, una realidad que dista de la percepción mayoritaria. Es una de las conclusiones de un informe que destaca que la crisis económica ha aumentado el rechazo social hacia los inmigrantes que precisamente han sido los más castigados por el desempleo. La concentración de población extranjera en barrios y municipios aumenta en estas zonas, ese rechazo de los ciudadanos autóctonos que perciben a los inmigrantes como los causantes de la degradación en la sanidad y en la educación. Un desajuste que según el estudio deben corregir las administraciones con más servicios. (The immigrants settled in Spain contribute more to the welfare state than they receive, a reality that is far from the prevailing perception. This is one of the conclusions of a report that highlighted the economic crisis that has increased the social rejection of immigrants who have been hit the hardest by unemployment. As the concentration of foreign populations in districts and municipalities in these areas increases, so does the rejection of native citizens who perceive immigrants as the cause of degradation in health and education. According to the study, this imbalance should be corrected by administrations with more services).

Unidad (Unit) 14. 15.06.11
Les contamos ahora la historia de Evan Loic, un niño de Camerún de diecisiete meses, que ha sido intervenido con éxito de hidrocefalia. Ha sido en la clínica Sagrado Corazón de Sevilla, gracias al *Proyecto Timún* y a la *Sociedad Cooperativa Pro años*. (Maribel Fatou, redacción) Tiene tan sólo diecisiete meses de edad y ha superado con éxito la operación de neurocirugía que se le ha practicado el pasado 24 de mayo. (En créditos: Francisco Trujillo Madroñal, jefe de servicio de neurología UPS): "Dentro de la cabeza se le administra por ese reservorio que regula la presión de salida y va directamente el peritoneo donde se reabsorbe". Tras la exitosa operación su cerebro se ha reducido hasta dos centímetros en su perímetro. En Camerún la hidrocefalia afecta a uno de cada quinientos niños. Es una enfermedad mal vista por la sociedad. Su bisabuela no encuentra las palabras adecuadas para mostrar su enorme agradecimiento. (Bisabuela, traducción al español): "La madre está muy contenta. Sigue los avances por Internet y por la foto". Evan deberá regresar a Sevilla para completar sus revisiones. Con Evan son ya sesenta los niños que han sido intervenidos en esta clínica sevillana. (Now we tell the story of Evan Loic, a child of seventeen months born in Cameroon, who has undergone a successful operation for hydrocephalus. It was in the clinic Sagrado Corazón, Seville, thanks to the Project Timun and the Cooperative Society Pro years (Maribel Fatou writes). He is only seventeen months old and has successfully passed the neurosurgical operation practiced on 24 May. (In credits: Francisco Trujillo Madroñal, head of neurology UPS): "Inside the head is given by the reservoir that regulates the output pressure and goes directly to the peritoneum where it is reabsorbed". After the successful operation, his brain has shrunk to two inches in circumference. In Cameroon, hydrocephalus affects one in five hundred children. It is a stigmatised disease in this region. His grandmother could not find the right words to show her great gratitude. (Great-grandmother, Spanish translation): "The mother is very happy. She follows the progress on the Internet and through images". Evan will return to Seville to complete his checkups. Including Evan, 60 children have undergone surgery at this clinic).

Unidad (Unit) 20. 05.07.11
Solo entre el 4 y 5% de las menores que abortan lo hacen sin el conocimiento de sus padres. Es una de las conclusiones de la Asociación de clínicas para la interrupción voluntaria del embarazo que se ha conocido hoy cuando se cumple un año de la entrada en vigor de la nueva ley que regula el aborto. En su informe, además, señala que Andalucía es la única comunidad que garantiza una asistencia pública transparente y equitativa. El informe de esta asociación dice más: señala que el número de abortos ha descendido desde 2008 pero no por la entrada en vigor de la ley sino porque ha disminuido el número de mujeres inmigrantes. Sobre la polémica del aborto de menores sin el conocimiento de sus padres la realidad es que solo se ha producido en un 5% de los casos. La asociación de clínicas alerta sobre la diferencia de aplicación de la ley en las distintas comunidades. En algunas como La Rioja y Navarra la mujer tiene que abandonar su comunidad para abortar. Andalucía la cita como la única región que garantiza un modelo público transparente y equitativo. En este aniversario de la ley la organización 'Derecho a vivir', que mantiene un campamento en la Puerta del Sol, está recogiendo firmas para que se derogue la ley. (Only between 4 and 5% of minors who have abortions do so without the knowledge of their parents. It is one of the conclusions of the Association of Clinics for Voluntary Abortion that has become known today on the first anniversary of the new law regulating abortion. This report also pointed out that Andalucía is the only community that ensures transparent and equitable public assistance in this issue. The association's report also indicates that the number of abortions has declined since 2008, not because of the law but because the number of immigrant women has decreased. On the controversy of abortion for minors without their parents' knowledge, the reality is that it has only occurred in 5% of the cases. The association of clinics also reported on the difference in law enforcement in different communities. In some communities like La Rioja and Navarra, women must leave their communities to receive abortions. Andalucía is cited as the only region that ensures a fair and transparent public model. On this anniversary of the law, the organization 'Right to Live', which maintains a camp in Puerta del Sol, is collecting signatures to repeal the law).

3.1 Selection of Audiovisual units of information: Critical approach

Unit 3. This piece of news makes reference to a subsidized study by *Obra Social 'La Caixa'* out of which it is understood that the great benefactor of immigrants' contribution is the Estate General Administration. The study, whose results were published in May 2011, explains that it is not about the fact that immigrants are using the social services more than native people, but that the increase of the population provokes an increase in demand, which logically goes together with an increase in the use of the public services. The inclusion of this piece of news denotes an interest in separating two of the most deeply entrenched ideas in this collective thought, as a result of the connection between immigration and social policies, especially between education and the degradation of health.

The language used puts a special emphasis on the "social rejection" suffered by the part of the population, especially immigrants, that is "punished" by unemployment. However, this piece of news leans on images which are more sensitive to negative criticism; in this way, for example, although it refers to immigrants in a broader sense, the people on screen are characterized by their phenotypic features (Moroccan, blacks, Latinos with indigenous features, etc.). It is also important to highlight that when talking about their labour situation the story turns to a Kleenex seller immigrant in the street, reinforcing the stereotype of immigrants performing low-class functions in a submerged economy. This image contrasts with that of two employees in white coats: the first in an old '*Instituto Nacional de Empleo*' ('National Employment Office') (opposite an unemployed immigrant), the second in a clinic. Both cases correspond to native women

Unit 14. The piece of news about the baby from Cameroon who had a successful operation on Hydrocephalus in Seville repeats the idea of the solidarity of Andalucía with those countries that lack good health infrastructures. The description of the number of children who have received surgeries at the clinic—sixty—and the explicit gratitude to the organizations "*Proyecto Timoun and Sociedad Cooperativa Pro años*" ("Timoun Project and the Cooperative Society Pro years") that made the surgery possible add to this a positive outlook. The first shots of the baby and his great-grandmother and the references to his country of origin balance an audiovisual discourse in which Spanish medical professionals are also the main protagonists.

Unit 20. "*El informe de esta asociación dice más, señala que el número de abortos ha descendido desde 2008 pero no por la entrada en vigor de la ley, sino porque ha disminuido el número de mujeres inmigrantes*" ("The report of this association says more: it indicates that the number of abortions has declined since 2008, not by the law but because the number of immigrant women has been reduced") says the voice-over. The structure "*pero no* [...] *sino porque*" ("but not [...] but because") is clearly intensifying, as it corresponds to one of the uses of the contrastive sense; the same can be stated about "*dice más*" ("says more"). These kinds of argumentative notes directly associate abortion with immigration, despite the fact that birth rate has remained stable in Spain over the last years, thanks to immigrated couples. *El País* titled a similar piece of news like this: "*Los inmigrantes que no nacen*" ("Unborn immigrants"). (*El País*, 15.12.2002, pg. 32), and its subheadline said, "*La interrupción del embarazo ha aumentado especialmente entre las extranjeras residentes en España, según algunas clínicas privadas*" ("Termination of pregnancies has increased especially among foreign residents in Spain, as some private clinics state"). The article begins this way:

> "The National Statistics Institute stated this week that immigrant mothers have tripled, in the last six years, their contribution to the number of births in Spain, so that eight of every hundred babies have foreign mothers. However, terminations of pregnancy cases have also increased among immigrant women, according to private clinics that have begun to study these cases. Although the Ministry of Health does not collect the nationality of those who undergo an abortion, some clinics are beginning to do so concerned about the increase in customers from abroad."[10]

The strategic position of the linking word '*sin embargo*' ('however'), again meaning contrast, or the '*preocupación*' ('concern') of some clinics addresses the reading indirectly to the presupposition that immigrant women should not receive abortions, because abortions may damage the maintenance of the birth rate, one of the positive associations related to immigrants. These interventions carry an economic cost, too. Moreover, although in certain areas it is true that the rate of abortions is higher among immigrant women, there is never any reference to the reasons why this can happen, such as the relationship between the socioeconomic status of families and the use of contraceptives (Malmusi and Pérez 2009, 64-66).

As far as images are concerned, none of immigrant women could be identified. However, social and health professionals do appear, as well as medical-care areas and instruments.

4. Spain in crisis 2012: Cuts in health and its representation in readers' comments

The implicit discourse about health care costs derived from attention to immigrants in Spain has become explicit in 2012 as the current economic crisis becomes more dramatic. The Spanish government's announcement that they were going to make budget cuts in health spending has made clear the discriminatory discourses towards immigrants, and the argument that they take advantage of the welfare state has gained strength, aided also by the official political discourse in which this argument has been stated without any hesitation.

On 20 April 2012, Spanish Health Minister Ana Mato announced before the Council of Ministers eight measures to reduce investment in health by 7,000 million euros.

1. Reform in the Immigration Law to prevent "illegal" access to health care.
2. Control of "health tourism" by modifying a European directive.
3. Medicament copayment based on income.
4. Homogeneous portfolio of services in all the autonomous communities.
5. Centralized purchasing platform for drugs and technology.
6. Promotion of generic drugs.
7. Suitability of the packaging of medications to treatments.
8. Human resources to facilitate the mobility of professionals within health services.

Among these measures, as we see, it was indicated that there would be a reform of the Immigration Law to demand new requirements for immigrants to have access to the health card. This measure would save 500 million euros. One of the arguments that the minister gave to justify this decision was the fact that some immigrants, she declared, brought their families to make an improper use of the Spanish Health system.

Similarly, she talked of another emergency measure: the adoption of European legislation to control what she called "health tourism", preventing the transfer to Spain of EU foreigners for the sole purpose of being treated by our health system. This care was estimated to be 917 million euros a year.

These were two different measures, aimed at different groups. However, the explicit reference to the presence of immigrants' relatives to receive health care provided an argumentative approach to the concept of "health tourism". The risk was that the two concepts were confused and that immigrants with limited financial resources or their families were conceived as "health tourists". We cannot agree with the possibility that the information was presented this way intentionally, aware of the reactions that might arise from many immigrant groups.

Here is the headline, the subheadline and the first sentences of an article that the newspaper *Público* published after the press conference in which cuts were reported:

Headline: "*El Gobierno endurecerá el padrón a inmigrantes para limitar el acceso a la Sanidad*" ("The Government will harden immigrants register to limit access to healthcare").

Subheadline: "*El ministerio de Sanidad modificará la Ley de Extranjería para evitar el "turismo sanitario" y ahorrar así 1.500 millones de euros*"("The Ministry of Health will modify the Immigration Law to prevent "health tourism", thereby saving 1,500 million euros").

Beginning: "*El Consejo de Ministros ha aprobado hoy un Real Decreto-Ley con el que el Gobierno pretende ahorrar más de 7.000 millones de euros en gasto sanitario. Para lograrlo, el Gobierno modificará la Ley de Extranjería. Endurecerá los requisitos del padrón a los inmigrantes en aras de "poner coto" al denominado "turismo sanitario", que en 2009 hizo perder a España 917 millones de euros después de atender a 700,000 extranjeros*" ("The Cabinet approved today a Royal Decree-Law with which the Government aims to save over 7,000 million in health spending. To achieve this, the Government will amend the Immigrant Law. It will toughen the requirements of registration for immigrants in order to "put a stop" to the so-called "health tourism", which in 2009 Spain lose 917 million euros after attending 700,000 foreigners").

As seen, the confusion of the two measures is clear and readers can easily associate health tourism with the reform of the immigration law and, therefore, with immigrants who have little or nothing to do with EU foreigners who travel in order to be attended free of charge by the Spanish health system. The figures are also presented in a confusing way.

The newspaper *El País*, meanwhile, published on its digital edition another story with the following headline: "*El Gobierno niega la atención sanitaria a los inmigrantes en situación irregular*" ("The government denies health care to illegal immigrants"). The article began this way:

"La ministra de Sanidad, Ana Mato, ha anunciado una reforma de la ley de extranjería para impedir que los 'ilegales' accedan a la atención sanitaria. "El padrón no les bastará. Necesitarán las residencia fiscal", ha dicho la ministra. En aclaraciones posteriores concretó más las propuestas, destinadas a evitar 'abusos'".
("Health Minister Ana Mato has announced a reform of the Immigration Law to prevent the 'illegal' access to health care. 'The registration will not be enough. Tax residence will also be needed,' said the minister. In subsequent declarations she specified the proposals were designed to prevent 'abuses'").

The idea is to return to the situation prior to the Immigration Law when illegal immigrants were allowed access to a health insurance card with registration as the only requirement. Until then, only children, pregnant women and emergencies were treated at the national health system. Now it is going back to that situation. Mato quantifies the savings at 500 million euros.

The Minister also explained that countries require reciprocity, so that the provision of the health care system will only be given to foreign countries that reciprocate this provision. With that and a higher control of the care received by foreign residents, the government expects to save another 971 million, according to the minister.

The measure is part of the package of measures announced on Wednesday and approved today by Royal Decree Law on the Council of Ministers, which the government says will save over 7,000 million euros. The reform also includes the control of the so-called "health tourism" by the inclusion of a European guideline that prohibits foreign people from travelling to receive health care only.

Contrary to what was published in *Público*, there is a clear difference between the measure related to immigrants and that passed in relation to the behavior of EU foreigners. However, the figures do not show this difference clearly, as the 971 million of spending on health tourism appears to be associated with the other measures. We also see the permanence of the adjectival noun '*ilegales*' ('illegal') in the journalistic discourse despite the many opposing recommendations that have been offered in recent years.

These headlines clearly show that the topic emphasized is the change to the Immigration law, even though this measure is not the most substantial in terms of spending supposedly saved. From the speaker's viewpoint, then, we could talk about a special interest in drawing attention to this decision by the Government, which in principle would be valued as a form of discrimination or lack of solidarity, changing the situation over recent years.

However, because the communication process is not limited only to the production of the message but also to its interpretation, it is possible that this attempt to issue a complaint will portray the spending produced by undocumented immigrants as one of the fundamental reasons for the gap in our country's health expenditures.

In this sense, the observations in the comments from readers of the digital versions of newspapers give us clues to the phases of interpreting the information. We have consulted the comment sections for the piece of news published in *Público* and in *El País* following the day of its publication (April 21). In the first case, we found 148 comments on the first article and 470 on the second. We found that most of these 618 contributions from readers were about the measure related to immigrants and only secondly about "health tourism". Far behind were references to the other six measures announced by Ana Mato. Naturally, we found signs of support for the measures and demonstrations against. We preferred to focus on the latter to analyse the argumentative techniques used in these cases and which directly refer to the health care system.

Here are 20 examples from *El País*:

Table 5-3. Examples from *El País*

Nº	Commentaries
1	Aparte sentimentalismos y actos más o menos políticamente correctos, un cierto control sobre el gasto asistencial a personas extrañas al sistema no está demás. (Apart from sentimentality and more or less politically correct acts, some control over health care spending to strange people outside the system causes no harm).
2	De acuerdo con la medida, puesto que ningún sistema es sostenible si no se tiene una base firme de contribución y además España no se encuentra actualmente en una situación que permita realizar obras de caridad. (I agree with the measure, since no system is sustainable without a firm basis of contribution, and Spain is not currently in a situation that allows charities).
3	No me parece mal. No tengo nada contra los extranjeros que vienen a trabajar, pero a todos aquellos que vienen a vivir de las ayudas y a aprovecharse del sistema creo que se les debería haber cortado el grifo mucho antes. (I do not dislike the measure. I have nothing against foreigners coming to work, but to all those who come to live and take advantage of the support given by the system, I think it should have been cut long before).
4	Mucho han tardado en hacerlo, y lo que siento es que el PSOE no hubiera tomado las medidas oportunas, en su momento. No hay un sistema de Seguridad Social como el nuestro, gratuito y universal, en ningún pais, ni de Europa ni fuera de ella; pero es obvio, que los abusos han corroído los cimientos del sistema y hay que cortar por lo sano, o ir preparando la Visa oro. (They have taken a long time to do it and I feel that PSOE had not taken appropriate measures in due course. There is no Social Security system like ours, free and universal, in any country or in Europe or outside, but it is obvious that the abuses have eroded the foundations of the system and must take drastic action, or go preparing the gold Visa).
5	Aquí solo caben los que han trabajado y cotizado como los españoles, los demás, los que quieren vivir de la sopa boba, los delincuentes y aprovechados del sistema, que se vayan. (Here only fit those who have worked and paid contributions as the Spanish, the others, those who want to scrounge any other's meals, criminals and those who take advantage of the system have to leave the country).

6	Pero que no emigren para ocasionar gastos a otras culturas y buscando el desarrollo de los demás. (They must not migrate to cause costs to other cultures seeking the development of others).
7	Esta medida está encaminada a que la gente regularice su situación, y cotize y pague impuestos. La tarjeta sanitaria es el vehículo para obligarles a ello. Por supuesto que la gente relativamente joven que ha inmigrado no tiene tiempo ni para ponerse malo, no colapsan ahora la sanidad. Pero la colapsarían llegado el día que sean jubilados porque no han pagado lo que les corresponde en su etapa activa. Yo al menos así entiendo la nueva regulación. (This measure is aimed for people to regularize their situation paying contributions and pay taxes. The health card is the vehicle to force it. Of course, relatively young people who have immigrated have no time to be ill, and do not collapse the health system. But they would destroy it when they retire if they have not paid their taxes in their active stage. Well, this is the way I understand the new regulations).
8	La sanidad española para los españoles que cotizan. Los españoles primero. (The Spanish health system is for the Spanish who pay their contributions. Spanish people first).
9	Esta no es la noticia, la noticia es como pueden darle sanidad a unas personas que jamás han contribuido un centavo en impuestos. INCREIBLE, POR ESO ESTAN COMO ESTAN. (This is not the news; the news is how you can offer the health system to people who have never paid a penny in taxes. AMAZING, THAT'S WHY THE SITUATION IS LIKE THIS).
10	No podemos pagarles la sanidad a quien no ha contribuido nunca.... Es muy razonable que pusieran un periodo de cadencia o algo así. Porque estamos pagando entre todos, la sanidad no solo del inmigrante, también de sus hijos, mujer, suegros..... Esto no hay bolsillo que lo soporte.. ¿ Todavia no se han dado cuenta???? Si quiere la izquierda "solidaria" que haga un fondo con SU dinero y haga como Cáritas.... Pero no con el dinero de nuestros impuestos. (We cannot offer health care to those who have never contributed to the social security... It is reasonable to establish a probation period or something like this. Why are we paying for the health not only of immigrants but also their children, wife, parents in law… There is not enough money to support it... Haven't you realized?? If the "supportive" left wants, they should create funds with THEIR money and do like Caritas do.... But not with our tax money).
11	Las medicinas hay que pagarlas porque gratis no hay nada. Tal vez una solución sea a los jubilados cobrarles 30 o 40 euros cada mes y asi poder darles a los inmigrantes irregulares las medicinas gratis. Si queremos ser generosos habrá que sacar el dinero de algún sitio. (Medicines must be paid because nothing is free. Perhaps one solution is to charge retirees 30 or 40 euros per month in order to be able to give illegal immigrants free drugs. If we are generous we will have to take the money from somewhere).

12	Este país no puede convertirse en los servicios sociales de los alrededores, porque simplemente no sería factible. (This country cannot become the social service department of the vicinity, because it would just not be feasible).
13	El otro dia en Hospital Virgen Macarena Sevilla estube con mi padre en urgencias y habia mas sudamericanos que españoles en urgencias. (The other day in the Hospital Virgin Macarena, Seville, I was with my father in the emergency room and there were more South Americans than Spanish in the emergency).
14	Ya es hora que alguien ponga orden en la SS, somos los mas generosos con todo el mundo,pero nosotros los Españoles a pagar los medicamentos,para que todo el mundo venga a curarse aqui por el morro, ?ya esta bien gracias PP si quitas todo esto¿ (It is time for someone to put order in the SS, we are the most generous with everyone, but we, Spanish people, pay for the medicine of everyone for them to come and get healed for free? it is enough, thanks PP if you remove all this¿).
15	que muchos inmigrantes no quieren regularizarse, porque todo lo que pillan es para mandarlo a sus paises, y aprovecharse de nuestros servicios gratis. (that many immigrants do not want to be regularized, because they all get to send back to their countries, and take advantage of our free services).
16	Me parece bien, a los irregulares y a algunos regulares que solo se la den a los buenos. Los malos y regulares a Melilla. (It sounds good, the irregular and regular, only give to the good ones. The bad and regular to Melilla).
17	Si, hay que darles la tarjeta sanitaria, que es lo primero que hay que ponerles entre los dientes nada más entrar ilegalmente en España. Además, si no tienen trabajo, hay que darles un piso, una paga de integracion, reagrupacion familiar, educacion y libros gratis, pensiones no contributivas a los mayores que vengan a España, vales de comida, luz, agua y gas gratis.... todo lo necesario para que su estancia sea todo lo agradable que debe ser. (Yes, we must give them the health card, which is the first thing to put in their teeth when you enter Spain illegally. Furthermore, if they haven't got a job, an apartment must be given to them as well as an integration payment, family reunification, education and free books, non-contributory pensions to the elderly who come to Spain, food vouchers, electricity, water and free gas ... everything you need to make your stay as pleasant as it should be).
18	Yo llevo pagando 40 años y la poca pasta que queda es para mi pensión, no para regalarla a los primeros que llegan, por la cara. (I have been paying for 40 years and the little money remaining is for my pension , we cannot give away to the first people who come, for nothing).

19	Hay muchísimos extranjeros accediendo a pensiones no CONTRIBUTIVAS, además de la sanidad y medicación completamente gratis. Por lo general son gente mayor, y que por arraigo familiar están en España. Mucha gente, una vez conseguida su pensión, vuelven a su país de origen, y a vivir con NUESTROS IMPUESTOS. POR FAVOR MAS CONTROL. (There are many foreigners accessing NON-CONTRIBUTORY pensions in addition to the health and completely free. In general they are usually older people whose family roots are in Spain. A lot of people, once they have gained their pension, return to their country of origin, and live with OUR TAXES. PLEASE, MORE CONTROL).
20	La mejor noticia que he oído desde hace días. (The best news I have heard for days).

The positive evaluation of the measure is presented in a clear way, as seen in messages 4 and 16: "*Mucho han tardado*"/"*Me parece bien*" ("They have taken a long time"/ "It sounds good") or number 20's much more direct "*La mejor noticia que he oído desde hace días*" ("The best news I have heard for days"), or with less strong forms, as shown in message 3, "*No me parece mal*" ("I do not dislike").

The important thing, in any case, is the set of arguments that appear to support this positive assessment. These arguments (or pseudo-arguments) are established a few times in relation to '*Nosotros*' ('Us') and others in relation to '*Ellos*' ('Them').

In the first case, it is recalled that in the current situation "we cannot" meet the needs of immigrants because "our system" has exceeded the possible extent, "*no hay bolsillo que lo soporte*" ("there is no money to support it") (10), and we cannot do '*obras de caridad*' ('charity') (2) for those who "*quieren vivir de la sopa boba*" ("want to scrounge any other's meals") (5). We cannot '*regalar*' ('give away') the fruit of our efforts (18).

In addition, we cannot be more generous than other countries and do what those others do not (4) and we particularly cannot become, as written in message 12, "*los servicios sociales de los alrededores*" ("the social services department in the vicinity") (this hyperbole has a high profitability in this kind of message; it can also be seen in messages 17 and 19). On this last point, our generosity could be seen as naive (11 and 14). Some people refer to immigration as a process that causes only "*gastos a otras culturas*" ("expenses to other cultures") (6). The transfer of generic messages of racist discourse ("*Los españoles primero*") ("Spanish first") to the specific area of health is also listed among the examples reproduced (8).

They, the immigrants, cannot receive health care because they have not economically contributed to maintain their tax status in the welfare state they are enjoying (2, 9 and 10). In message 1, they are called "*personas extrañas al sistema*" ("strangers to the system"). In some cases, it is even stated that "many" do not want to register with Social Security to avoid paying these taxes (15) and that this measure would "*obligarles a ello*" ("force them to it") (7). Nothing is said about the fact that it is not only their responsibility to become regularized if they are working; their employers share this responsibility. Furthermore, the commenters generalize immigrants to be responsible for the possibility of the present collapse of the health care system (emergencies are often the most frequently mentioned service: message 13) or its collapse in the future (7). In other words, they abuse the services we offer (4) or that they and their families take advantage of these services (3 and 10). The messages also establish typologies which are not based on strictly administrative terms but also on behavioural terms. This happens in message 16, when talking about good, bad and regular immigrants, suggesting that only the former should be allowed to have the health card. In addition, the adjective '*regular*' ('regular') is used with a double sense, administrative and evaluative, increasing the confusion.

Finally, we would like to draw attention to the messages that compare the groups of "irregular" immigrants with other groups of people with low incomes (retirees) in order to demonstrate that the effort made by Spain to help immigrants is not possible.

5. Conclusions

As usual, the representation of immigrants in health-related news is scarce. Its absence on the agenda of mass media becomes even more obvious when compared with the presence of health information relating to the Spanish population.

In the audiovisual corpus analysed, we see that health does not appear in discourses as main topic but as a secondary issue, especially in those news items about the arrival of immigrants, who are primarily attended by the Marine Salvage (*Salvamento Marítimo*) and members of the Red Cross (*Cruz Roja*) or Civil Guard (*Guardia Civil*). Such cases tend to refer to the health status of the new arrivals through prototypical expressions (already mentioned) that explain whether the immigrants needed transfer to a hospital.

As a positive note, we would like to mention that, despite the lack of attention being paid to this issue and the fact that its treatment is conditioned by a paternalistic discourse with a supportive tone, there are communication professionals who emphasize the need to combat the myths and stereotypes that erroneously link immigrants with a higher rate of health risks or with an improper use of the Spanish public health system.

In addition, when the relationship between health and immigration does appear in the media as relevant news, the result is not usually positive for the image of immigrants—even less if that appearance is related to the uses of the health system in times of crisis. At those times, overlapped fears and prejudices reappear stronger than ever, as we have seen in the news from *El País* and *Público*, as well as in the comments made to them by readers.

Notes

1. CYSOC: Centro de Investigación en Comunicación y Sociedad de la Universidad de Almería (Centre of Research in Communication and Society, University of Almería).
2. The analysis will be related to two research projects we are carrying out at the moment, 'Health and Migration in Andalucía' and an Excellence Research Project entitled 'Immigration discourses in the Andalusian Audiovisual Media', both subsidised by the Junta de Andalucía (Spain).
3. The original quotation is: "La impresión de que los foráneos tienen más derechos que los autóctonos, especialmente en sanidad, va a más. "Entran los primeros", "con ellos no tienen prisa", "siempre salen cargados de recetas", "tú tienes que pelearte para poder ir a rehabilitación y para ellos todo es poco", "a la mínima les dan la baja [...]." Estos y otros comentarios similares se pueden oír en cualquier sala de espera. El sector no parece preocupado por ello (es un asunto incómodo y políticamente incorrecto) pero dejen que la ciudadanía empiece a notar los tijeretazos en los presupuestos de salud [...] (Diario Médico, 2011, 2)".
4. The original quotation is: "Un segundo hallazgo destacado consiste en cierta erosión progresiva del apoyo ciudadano a la integración de la población inmigrante en la sociedad de acogida, tendencia que afecta a las posturas respecto de la participación política de los inmigrados, del derecho de reagrupar a sus familiares y también de su inclusión en las principales políticas del bienestar (educación y sanidad)" (Annual Report Andalucía and Immigration 2010, 2011, 131).
5. The original quotation is: "Aunque la actitud favorable hacia los inmigrantes sigue siendo mayoritaria, la población autóctona tiende a opinar, con una frecuencia cada vez mayor, que los inmigrantes compiten con la población autóctona por los puestos de trabajo y las prestaciones sociales (sanidad, plazas escolares, ayudas a la vivienda, asistencia pública) [...]. La percepción de que la población inmigrante es favorecida en la provisión de recursos públicos provoca en amplios sectores autóctonos una reacción de corte comunitarista y/o nacionalista de «primero los de casa» [...]" (Moreno and Bruquetas, 2011, 9).

6. The original quotation is: "Sobre las condiciones de vida del inmigrante en España en lo relativo al trabajo, la vivienda, la educación y la salud, los titulares que las cubren representan sólo un pequeño número. No es por tanto la importancia de su número lo que llama la atención en este tipo de noticias sino la poca atención que los periódicos le prestan a un conjunto de circunstancias que, por su relevancia en la vida de cualquier colectivo de ciudadanos, suelen ocupar una parte muy significativa de la información cuando se trata de la población española" (Granados, 2006, 62).
7. The original quotation is: "Es curioso que la única referencia a la salud «Inmigración y vacunación» (*La Vanguardia*, 4 de marzo), se produzca en el sentido del miedo a las patologías de importación. A pesar de que situaciones como las que refiere la noticia citada (se refiere a la necesidad de prevenir cuatro enfermedades de importación: poliomielitis, sarampión, rubéola y hepatitis B, activas en diferentes países de procedencia de los inmigrantes) se dan en determinados contextos, los inmigrados son, por lo general, gente sana y adquieren sobre todo lo que las microbiólogas Margarita Baquero y Mercedes Subirats (*Diario Médico*, 21 de noviembre de 2003) llaman la *patología del destino,* es decir, las de su condición de migrantes. Creo también que en el medio sanitario existe una cierta obsesión por la búsqueda del caso exótico en relación a los migrantes" (Moreno, 2006, 223).
8. The original quotation is: "La transversalidad es al día de hoy la característica más importante de la inmigración desde el punto de vista temático; es difícil no encontrar referencias a la misma en cualesquiera contextos temáticos: economía, salud, arte, seguridad, etc. La *deslocalización temática* de la inmigración ha sido siempre un reclamo de quienes han defendido un discurso menos estigmatizado con respecto a la inmigración. Ahora bien, lo cierto es que esa deslocalización también tiene sus riesgos: el mantenimiento de un debate oculto en muchas ocasiones igualmente discriminatorio y preventivo" (Bañón, 2006, 273).
9. The original quotation is: "La avalancha de sin papeles también ha llegado a la península. Este cayuco se aproximaba a Motril con 32 subsaharianos esta mañana, todos en buen estado de salud. Un total de 370 inmigrantes ilegales han llegado a nuestras costas en todo el fin de semana". [Antena 3, 11/11/2007. Citado en Albert *et al.* (2010, 59)].
10. The original quotation is: "El Instituto Nacional de Estadística señalaba esta semana que las madres inmigrantes han triplicado en los últimos seis años su aportación al número de nacimientos en España, de tal forma que ocho de cada cien bebés tienen madre extranjera. Sin embargo, también han aumentado los casos de interrupción de embarazo entre las inmigrantes, según apuntan desde las clínicas privadas que han comenzado a estudiar estos casos. Aunque el Ministerio de Sanidad no recoge la nacionalidad de quienes se someten a un aborto, desde algunas clínicas están comenzando a hacerlo, preocupadas por el aumento de clientes de procedencia extranjera".

Bibliography

Aierbe, Peio. 2008. "Representación de las mujeres trabajadores inmigrantes en los medios de comunicación". In *Comunicación, empleo y mujer inmigrante,* edited by Antonio Miguel Bañón, 7-20. Donostia: Gakoa.

Albert, Mª Carmen, Eva Espinar and Mª Isabel Hernández. 2010. "Los inmigrantes como amenaza. Procesos migratorios en la televisión española". *Convergencia. Revista de Ciencias Sociales* 53: 49-68.

Annual Report Andalucía and Immigration 2010. 2011. Sevilla: Dirección General de Coordinación de Políticas Migratorias, Consejería de Empleo, Junta de Andalucía.

Aznar, Hugo. 2002. "Naturaleza de la comunicación audiovisual: Todo por la audiencia". In *Ética de la comunicación y de la información,* eds. José Ángel Agejas and José F. Serrano, 55-74. Barcelona: Ariel.

Bañón, Antonio Miguel. 1997. "La representación discriminatoria de los inmigrantes africanos en el discurso oral". *Discurso. Teoría y análisis,* 21/22: 103-132.

—. 2002. *Discurso e inmigración. Propuestas para el análisis de un debate social.* Murcia: Servicio de Publicaciones de la Universidad de Murcia.

—. 2003. "Nuevas reflexiones sobre la representación periodística de los inmigrantes". In *Comunicación, cultura y migración,* eds. Fernando Contreras, Rafael González and Francisco Sierra, 55-73. Sevilla: Consejería de Gobernación de la Junta de Andalucía.

—. 2006. "La asociación discursiva de terrorismo e inmigración. Un ejemplo de incomunicación intercultural". *Comunicación. Revista Internacional de Comunicación Audiovisual y Literatura* 4: 259-277.

—. 2007. "El simulacro y su aplicación al análisis crítico del discurso". In *Comunicación y simulacro,* ed. Jesús Baca, 213-231. Sevilla: ArCiBel.

Escobar, Pedro. 1998. "La exclusión social de la inmigración africana. Un análisis de la prensa diaria almeriense (1990-1994)". In *Africanos en la orilla,* ed. Francisco Checa, 235-270. Barcelona: Icaria.

Granados, Antolín. 2006. "Medios de comunicación, opinión y diversidad (social y cultural). Reflexiones en torno al fenómeno migratorio". In *Medios de comunicación e inmigración,* ed. Manuel Lario, 59-83. CAM. Murcia: Convivir Sin Racismo.

Igartua, Juan José, Carlos Muñiz and Lifen Cheng. 2005a. "La inmigración en la prensa española. Aportaciones empíricas y metodológicas desde la teoría del encuadre noticioso". *Migraciones* 17: 143-181.

—. 2005b. "La imagen de la inmigración en la prensa y la televisión. Aproximaciones empíricas desde la teoría del framing". In *Psicología política, cultura, inmigración y comunicación social,* ed. José Manuel Sabucedo, José Romay and Ana López-Cortón, 239-246. Madrid: Biblioteca Nueva.

Malmusi, Davide and Gloria Pérez. 2009. "Aborto legal en mujeres inmigrantes en un entorno urbano". *Gaceta Sanitaria* 23.1: 64-66.

Martín, Inma. 2008. "Tratamiento informativo de las minorías étnicas en los medios españoles. Una cuestión de responsabilidad social". *Comunicación e ciudadanía* 6: 1-19.

Moreno, Manuel. 2006. "Imagen y discursos sobre la inmigración: la campaña electoral del 14 de marzo de 2004 en los medios de comunicación escritos". *Revista de Dialectología y Tradiciones Populares* 61: 211-227.

Moreno, Francisco Javier and María Bruquetas. 2011. *Inmigración y Estado de bienestar en España*. Barcelona: Obra Social 'La Caixa'.

Observatorio Permanente Andaluz de las Migraciones. 2011. *Informe Anual Andalucía e Inmigración*. Sevilla: Consejería de Empleo.

Pérez, Clara. 2003. "Género y discursos sobre la inmigración en la prensa. Análisis de prensa". *Inmigración, racismo y xenofobia* 4: 67-119.

Pérez, Javier. 2006. "El discurso de los medios. Hacia un enfoque positivo de la inmigración". In *Medios de comunicación e inmigración*, ed. Manuel Lario, 273-285. Murcia: CAM, Convivir Sin Racismo.

Rinken, Sebastián and Manuel Pérez. 2011. *Opiniones y actitudes de la población andaluza ante la inmigración (III): Más allá del discurso funcionalista*. Sevilla: Consejería de Empleo.

Tomás, Juan. 2006. "Las diversas caras de la inmigración en los medios informativos". In *Medios de comunicación e inmigración,* ed. Manuel Lario, 237-251. Murcia: CAM, Convivir Sin Racismo.

Van Dijk, Teun A. 1984. *Prejudice in discourse.* Amsterdam and Philadelphia: John Benjamins.

—. 1998. *Ideology. A multidisciplinary approach*. London: Sage.

CHAPTER SIX

BETWEEN ENRICHING DIVERSITY AND SEGREGATING DIFFERENCE: CONTRADICTING DISCOURSES ON THE PRESENCE OF FOREIGN STUDENTS IN THE EDUCATION SYSTEM[1]

F. JAVIER GARCÍA CASTAÑO, ANTONIA OLMOS ALCARAZ AND MARIA RUBIO GÓMEZ
MIGRATIONS INSTITUTE, UNIVERSITY OF GRANADA

1. Introduction

Since the presence of foreign immigrant students started to be detected in Spanish schools, this phenomenon has been mainly addressed in terms of *diversity* (García García, 1996; García Castaño, *et al.*, 1999; Terrén Lalana, 2007). In other words, even if schools in Spain were widely diverse before immigrant students arrived, it is from that moment that – media, political and social– debate on diversity surfaced in the country. This suggests that some diversities are more obvious than others; or better said, some are intentionally made more obvious and given more media coverage than others.

But what do we understand by diversity? We are biologically[2] and culturally diverse, but, when we talk about "*cultural diversity*", we mean the "variety or multiple forms of human social structures, belief systems and strategies of adaptation to situations prevailing in different parts of the world" (Rodríguez and Schnell, 2007, 60). This leads us to question the very concept of culture when analysing diversity, since we tend to forget to what extent this is partly an adaptation mechanism with a dynamic and process-related nature. This article intends to analyse, in particular, the way diversity is exposed in the mass media,[3] as we have observed that the way images are presented there contribute to the creation of differences between the various groups.

We have also observed that diversity is mainly understood as *diversity of nationalities*, which translates into *cultural diversity* (as if each nationality had a corresponding culture). This is why nationalities are used to address diversity[4]. But, how is diversity understood? Sometimes it is seen as a positive characteristic and sometimes as a handicap that some students have, or as a source of problems for the whole school. More importantly, what consequences does this understanding of diversity bring to the development of social relations between "autochthones" and "foreigners"?

For the uninformed eye, this would imply a contradiction in itself since, on the one hand, this "new" diversity at school is praised due to the presence of "many cultures" but on the other, the presence of "immigrant students" is seen as a problem because they "disrupt" the global progress of each school. True, these two arguments do not always go hand in hand or are presented by the same people, in the same contexts, but they do represent a paradoxical way of portraying schools. Far from understanding them as contradictory discourses, we see these ideas as contrasting approaches to build difference, putting the sense of belonging as a frontier, and essentializing it by means of culture-based identification processes. In other words, they consider identity and culture as synonyms.

These questions will be developed in the following lines. The first part will include the analysis of discourse that regards the phenomenon of diversity as a problem; and the second part, the discourse that eulogizes cultural diversity. Transversally throughout our analysis, we will point out the constant association between the concepts of "*culture*" and "*nationality*", and the reductionist and essentialist consequences that such association brings.

2. Upsetting Diversity: the Image of Immigrant Students as a Problem

When we begin analysing the image of foreign students as a source of diversity in the press, the first idea that emerges is that diversity, *their* diversity is understood as *difference, inequality, inferiority*. In fact, they are portrayed and perceived, in some way as, "worse than –and inferior to – our children".

If we observe the headlines of national newspapers thoroughly, we realize that school failure, decline in academic level, emergence of school ghettos, increasing complication of teachers' work, rise in education expenditure and escalation of classroom violence are the most common topics regarding immigrant students. This information is only related to school issues and such problems are directly connected to their arrival to "our classrooms". In fact when Spanish newspapers mention foreign immigrants at school, they mainly show figures of increase and comment on the incorporation process or "late enrolment" of these students, in order to highlight consequential segregation; or they even cover events related to the use of the Islamic headscarf –therefore Islam– as a controversial issue at school.

Concerning "immigration figures", we frequently read about the negative consequences caused by the *large* presence of immigrant students in Spanish society. The first relevant aspect of this discursive logic is the emphasis put on the growing percentage of students and how this poses a threat from several points of view. In other words, we witness the alarmist discourse about the migratory phenomenon that so many researchers have pointed out (Granados Martínez, 1998; Santamaría, 2002; Bañón, 2002, 2006; Márquez Lepe, 2006; García Castaño and Olmos Alcaraz, 2010), but now related to the school environment in particular. We find headlines such as the following:

> *La inmigración desborda la escuela pública. Sindicatos y padres denuncian la falta de previsión y presupuesto ante el desembarco de extranjeros.* (Public Schools Inundated with Immigration. Unions and parents claim lack of provision and budget facing the immigration of foreigners) (*El País*, 29/09/2003).
> *Los estudiantes extranjeros se quintuplican en 10 años.* (Fivefold Increase in Foreign Students in Ten Years) (*El Mundo* 18/10/2002).
> *Nuevo récord de inmigrantes* (New Record Figures of Immigrants) (*El Mundo*, 08/10/2007).

As we see, when mentioning school-related figures, there is an evident use of alarmist language that contributes to viewing this phenomenon as a social problem. "Excessive growth", "relentless increase", "surge", "inundation", "landing", "record of immigrants in Spanish schools", are some examples of this kind of language. Also, the figures used, in most cases, are not real because what they show is the visibility process based on statistics and not the school enrolment process which has taken place for longer, although unequally throughout the country, during the last twenty years[5].

It is also interesting to observe problems associated with this professed *alarming increase* of the foreign immigrant population in Spanish schools. In this regard, the mass media analysis mainly underlines two ideas: decline in academic level, allegedly caused by the arrival of immigrants; and deterioration of cohabitation supposedly provoked by them. Both issues are often explained by what is known as *tolerance threshold*[6] towards diversity. The following are some examples:

> *El fenómeno de la inmigración está cambiando la realidad de la escuela. Su integración en las aulas crea problemas nuevos, que afectan tanto a la convivencia como al nivel educativo.* (Schools changed by Immigration Phenomenon. Immigrants' integration in classrooms creates new problems, affecting both coexistence and academic level) (*El Mundo*, 21/09/2003).
> *El Defensor del Pueblo llegó a la conclusión de que los conflictos en los centros se incrementan cuando el porcentaje de alumnos inmigrantes supera el 35%.* (Ombudsman concludes Conflicts at Schools increase when Immigrant Students exceed 35%) (*El Mundo,* 23/02/2004).

The foregoing headlines imply that these problems exist because there are many foreign immigrant students. This rhetoric which supports the existence of conflicting episodes with quantity-related reasons maintains that coexistence is deteriorating –in short– because, "they are here". They seek a scapegoat to justify situations of intolerance that have more to do with *us* than with *them*, since, "there is no proven statistical evidence correlating a certain percentage of immigrants and the emergence of tensions or conflicts" (Santamaría, 2002, 173). However, the opposite case, "strong prejudice and hostility towards communities that are scarcely present amongst the population, as is the case of anti-Semitism in Spain" (Calvo Buezas, 1995, in Santamaría, 2002, 173) has actually been confirmed. We believe, thus, that this rhetoric is a product of preconceptions and stereotypes and not of verifiable evidence. This is confirmed by the variable and arbitrary character of this "tolerance threshold" to which different percentages are assigned. Also acknowledging such an argument would be accepting that all societies are xenophobic by nature and that racism is innate to all human beings and not a learned behaviour (Stolke, 1992; Van Dijk, 1999, 2003).

But how is this information represented? We have mentioned some phrases or expressions frequently used for this purpose, but we cannot forget mentioning the images used to illustrate articles about "immigration figures at school". Some say photonewspaperism conveys a literal, real and "fully objective" message. Nevertheless this is only a façade (Barthes, 1982) because this alleged objectivity is fraught with connotations and signification processes, applied according to the photographer's, at first, and subsequently the editor's and news writers' intentions. This is why, when newspapers publish certain images related to foreign students in classrooms and their increase in numbers and such images are recurrent in time, a new effect and connotation-signification are created.

Out of the various images found we are especially interested in those we call "racialized" images, since they make emphasis mainly on phenotypic differences. This is clearly evidenced in one of the foregoing examples, especially when we consider the headline and the photo that illustrates it. See Figure 6-1.

EL PAÍS, lunes 29 de septiembre de 2003 SOCIEDAD / 33

Educación **LA ESCOLARIZACIÓN DE LOS INMIGRANTES.** Este curso ha aumentado por primera vez en 15 años el número de alumnos gracias a la inmigración. Hay 400.000 estudiantes, hijos de extranjeros, 100.000 más que el curso pasado. Ésta es la radiografía de la situación en España y de cómo se aborda en ocho comunidades autónomas

La inmigración desborda la escuela pública

Sindicatos y padres denuncian la falta de previsión y presupuesto ante el desembarco de extranjeros

Alumnos de un colegio de Madrid el pasado 15 de septiembre, al inicio del presente curso académico.

Figure 6-1. Foreign students and public school. Date: 29 September 2003. Newspaper: *El País*.

The picture chosen by the newspaper to illustrate this supposed overcrowding of public schools with immigrant students shows a group of children lined-up. First in line –not by chance– we find a little girl with very specific phenotypic characteristics (darker skin, black-curly hair, dark eyes, etc.). We do not understand how this image can illustrate an, "increase in immigrant students at public schools", as stated in the headline. We do not know how this point can be illustrated.[7]

However by constantly and continuously presenting the picture of a black child as an advertisement for news related to immigration at school, in other words, by associating image and text, newspapers harmfully portray some communities as exotic ones. Also they identify and/or reduce the immigration phenomenon to other elements linked with ethnification of some diversities. These image-related courses of conduct and strategies correspond to what Stuart Hall calls, "The Spectacle of the other" (2010), as they respond to some representation practices used by the media to establish stereotypical differences.

As we have just seen, the association of text and photograph add a new connotation to the whole news article. Barthes (1982) considers that the text "illustrates" (burdens with *culture*) the image by introducing new meanings (connotations) which, due to the photographic analogy-objectivity (denotation), are considered as an "echo of the natural denotation", or a naturalization process of cultural elements. In other words, text and image are different structures and in consequence one cannot duplicate the other. What it does is to give certain connotation. In other words, it explains and emphasises a given aspect contained in the picture creating a new meaning or even contradicts that image to balance connotation (*ibid*). The conjunction of the foregoing photo and text creates what we have identified as "racialization" or "exotization". This connotation comes and is founded on a tradition, history and social construction that we comprehend as "natural" due to the "objective"-analogical charge that photos have as witnesses of real facts.

We can also highlight some articles in which newspapers decide not to show any image, because they touch sensitive issues such as "arrival" of foreign immigrant students who are *overcrowding* schools. However, they design the front page layout in a way that some headlines are associated to a completely unrelated image. This is the case in Figure 6-2.

18

ESPAÑA

Los estudiantes extranjeros se quintuplican en 10 años

▸ 20.000 escolares inmigrantes están en situación irregular, según CCOO ▸ Educación prevé que este curso se matriculen 280.000 extranjeros

Figure 6-2. Increase of foreign school students. Date: 18 October 2002. Newspaper: *El Mundo*.

The headline mentions a fivefold increase in the number of foreign students during the last years. However, the image next to it shows two people who have just arrived in Spain in a *patera* or *cayuco* (name given to small boats often used for immigration). This is the image of a specific type of immigration, which is not the most frequent, but the toughest and most striking one to the eyes of readers. In fact this image corresponds to another piece of news, but they are displayed in a way that immigrants wrapped in blankets are shown next to the education-related headline, while the headline corresponding to the image "*Archivo para 'ilegales'*" ("File for Illegal Immigrants") is shown in smaller caption and at the end of the page. This way of juxtaposing ideas ends up generating new connotations that make people think that the number of foreigners in general –not only students– may be increasing and a very specific type of immigrants.

These associations are not casual. As we mentioned before, editors and news writers have a precise intention when they give each page a given structure. Depending on where and how the words are displayed, they have a different effect and connotation. Paradoxically, as the image shows a closest look, it seems more neutral, due to the "objectivity" attributed to images; however, they really have the opposite effect: a greater connotation and modification of meaning (Barthes, 1982). The various texts and images displayed on newspaper pages convey messages, but their arrangement, as a whole, convey another message, a different one. For example, Figure 3, below, shows this information construction logic, relating shocking photographs with unrelated education topics.

The element that call our attention on the front page –besides the newspaper name– is a big photograph related to one piece of news placed dangerously close to a headline with four columns referring to a different piece of news.

First analysing the front page photo, we find an overhead view of a group of lifeless, dark-skinned people, heaped inside a receptacle defined by two, almost vertical wood laths which confine and contain the jumbled corpses. We read a headline located above the picture *"Cataluña segrega a los niños africanos fuera de la red escolar"* (African Children excluded from the Education System in Catalonia). It refers not only to an increasing number of students, but also a measure applied in Catalonia to manage this "increase": the "Welcome to School Spaces". This headline, which is the most important in the front page, is given a very clear connotation due to its (small) separation from the picture. What do they want to evoke with this image-headline combination?: pity? paternalism? guilt? unrest? fear? Maybe what they mean is that "African" corpses are separated and heaped up on that boat as African children outside the Education System in Catalonia; or maybe they want to show the shocking image of the way these children come to the country. We really do not know. It seems as if the aim of this kind of arrangements were no more than feeding people's morbid curiosity, and obtaining an economic profit with it, of course.

EL PAÍS

www.elpais.com

EL PERIÓDICO GLOBAL EN ESPAÑOL

El estrés de parar de trabajar

Renace la ciudad perdida de Sechín

Nuevos cronistas de América

Cataluña segregará a los niños africanos fuera de la red escolar

Generalitat y ayuntamientos decidirán qué menores serán discriminados

La inflación escala al 5% por el petróleo y la huelga de transportes

La tormenta de la estanflación asoma en la economía española

Martinsa Fadesa se desploma tras incumplir con su préstamo

LA MUERTE VIAJA A DIARIO HACIA ESPAÑA EN PATERA

Figure 6-3. "Segregation" of African students. Date: 12 July 2009. Newspaper: *El País.*

The second issue brought up by the media is foreign immigrant students' enrolment and incorporation to the education system related to school overcrowding and segregation. This sort of news is usually, but not exclusively, published every year in September –or near the beginning of the school year– with headlines as the following:

> *Los inspectores advierten que se están creando guetos de alumnos inmigrantes.* (Inspectors Warn about Creation of Immigrant Students Ghetto) (*La Vanguardia,* 19/10/2001).
> *Desbordados por la matrícula tardía. La falta de plazas provoca que 300 niños se queden en la calle el primer día de clase.* (Overwhelmed by Late

Enrolment. 300 children left out on their first day for lack of school places) (*El País*, 29/09/2003).
La segregación escolar. El reto de frenar la proliferación de escuelas gueto. (School Segregation. The challenge: hindering proliferation of school ghettoes) (*El Mundo*, 10/06/2007).

It is evident that the language chosen to describe foreign immigrant students' enrolment process is fraught with alarmism: public schools overcrowding, school segregation, ghettoes are frequently mentioned. It is worth clarifying, in this regard, that identifying immigrant students' concentration with school ghettoes – defined as schools with poor education and high conflictive levels – apart from being hasty, is simplistic and reductionist. We agree with Silvia Carrasco (2008) when she argues that concentration is not always equal to segregation or ghettoization, the same as "dispersion" or distribution does not necessarily mean integration. This is a very complex process where other aspects must be taken into consideration.[8]

Some issues should be taken into account before asserting that an education centre has ghettoization characteristics. First, as Anyon (2005) and Carrasco (2008) explain, we need to analyse the relationship between that specific centre and the institutions, that is, if there is a situation of economic or professional disregard. Second, we need to see whether teachers and families trust the integrating and emancipating capacity of school, considering the inequalities implied by students' socio-cultural characteristics. Third, ghetto schools are deeply isolated from society, that is to say, they are not related to any other institution from the same context whatsoever. Considering the aforesaid elements, the percentage of foreign immigrant students is not a determining factor to declare an education centre as ghetto.

Nevertheless, something that contributes to schools ghettoization, as Zirotti (1998) states, is public acknowledgement of problematic centres; i.e. talking about "ghetto schools", "integration centres", "compensatory education centres", "problem schools". The reason, according to the author, is that this makes those schools more prone to receive children from the most marginal families only, as well as incite other students to flee.

Therefore, linking concentration with poorer education quality and higher conflict levels is a clear stereotyped and preconceived reasoning that does not lead to achieve equality and maintain social cohesion (Olmos Alcaraz, 2009), but a way to further polarize the education system. Unfortunately, analysed newspapers are encouraging this idea when the sole important conclusion they reach, regarding this issue, is that the gap between public and private (subsidized and non-subsidized) schools is larger due to the "increasing number of immigrant students".

Once more, students with different phenotypic characteristics are shown in images illustrating concentration and segregation discourses (see Figure 6-4).

SOCIEDAD / 36

Educación LA ESCOLARIZACIÓN DE LOS INMIGRANTES

CATALUÑA

Desbordados por la matrícula tardía

La falta de plazas provoca que 300 niños se queden en la calle el primer día de clase

CANARIAS

La escuela de las 121 nacionalidades

Primer día de clase en el colegio Pla Ametllet de Banyoles (Girona).

Figure 6-4. Foreign students and late enrolment. Date: 29 September 2003. Newspaper: *El País*.

Judging by the picture corresponding to this headline, the newspaper intends to show a group of black children at the school entrance, although this is not characteristic of most schools in Spain. There is a clear intention of linking, once again, migration with a specific group of people, offering a reductionist and biased view which is profitable in terms of business –as it represents something exotic, different and distant.

This is the same rhetoric for most news articles that dwell on students' concentration, although the underlying "phobias" may change. Another example is the –excessive– use of images showing Muslim women with headscarves to illustrate news related to foreign students' concentration in specific locations and schools. A flood of pictures show mothers –sometimes their daughters too– wearing this garment while taking their children to school. See Figure 6-5, below:

SOCIEDAD

Los inspectores de enseñanza advierten que se están creando guetos de alumnos inmigrantes

EDUCACIÓN

▪ La Associació d'Inspectors d'Ensenyament de Catalunya considera que un compromiso de todos los agentes sociales sería más eficaz que las normas

Figure 6-5. School ghettoes and immigrant students. Date: 19 October 2001. Newspaper: *La Vanguardia.*

Apparently, all students regarded by the media as protagonists of school concentration and segregation processes are Muslim, and all Muslim people wear this specific piece of clothing. We need to de-construct this media-promoted image, and corresponding stereotype, that suggests Muslims are responsible for the emergence of ghetto-schools in Spain. Firstly, we must understand that the native population is as or even more responsible for this phenomenon (if it exists; we have expressed our reservations about it), since, as we said, there is a *flight* of some students to private (subsidized or non-subsidized) schools. Secondly, foreign immigrant population in Spain is widely diverse in origin, religious practices and ethnic characteristics.

Then why is the Islamic headscarf repeatedly shown in a variety of shapes, colours and users, and associated to immigration at schools? We understand that they choose the most controversial symbols to the public opinion since they are the most aesthetically noticeable; exotic for Spaniards or demonized by society in general. As a consequence, Muslim students are blamed for all diseases that threaten education today: Islam is responsible... in this case, for school ghettoes. The story of association of public and private schools with foreign students and Islamic headscarf is repeated in Figure 6-6.

Sociedad

Ana Pastor

La hora de la escuela pública

El Govern reforma el acceso a los centros para que la privada acoja a más inmigrantes

Figure 6-6. Public schools, private schools and foreign students. Date: 7 February 2004. Newspaper: *La Vanguardia.*

This discursive construction works as base to address the following and last topic that is frequently seen in the media concerning the creation of an image that regards diversity as *something that generates discomfort:* the Islamic headscarf and Islam in general[9]. This issue appears in two different ways: as subject of news, addressing the controversial use of the headscarf (teenage girls who use a headscarf at schools where it is not allowed), or, as a cross-sectional topic, in many other news that dwell on immigration and education in general, but which are illustrated with symbols related to Islam.

Let us consider the first case where Islamic headscarf is explicitly mentioned in news articles. We have already said that wearing an Islamic headscarf in Spanish schools is not a social issue, contrary to other European countries, where the use of this garment is banned by law[10]. This has been a source of controversy for both the affected community and other social actors; yet confrontation cases that have reached the media have been given excessive coverage.

The most controversial episodes occurred in Madrid in 2002, in Girona in 2007 and again in Madrid in 2010. Below, we find some examples of headlines published in relation to those events, specifically, in the case of Madrid 2002 by *El Mundo*:

> *El padre de una niña marroquí pide un colegio público para que su hija pueda llevar chador.* (Moroccan Father Demands Public School to Let his Daughter Use Headscarf) (*El Mundo,* 15/02/2002).

Educación y el PSOE se oponen al uso del chador en las escuelas por considerarlo discriminatorio. (Education and PSOE Object to Wearing Headscarf as it is Considered Discriminatory) (*El Mundo*, 16/02/2002).
"*Mi hija tiene que llevar el velo*" ("My Daughter must Wear the Headscarf") (*El Mundo*, 16/02/2002).
La Comunidad de Madrid autoriza a Fátima a ir ya mañana con chador al colegio. (Community of Madrid Authorizes Fatima to Attend School with Headscarf Tomorrow) (*El Mundo,* 17/02/2002).
El ministro Aparicio lo compara con la ablación. (Minister Aparicio Compares it with Genital Mutilation) (*El Mundo,* 17/02/2002).
Los colegios públicos en Madrid, desbordados por la inmigración. (Public Schools in Madrid Overflowing with Immigrants) (*El Mundo,* 18/02/2002).
Los alumnos reciben a Fátima con aplausos y los padres piden su pase al centro concertado. (Fatima Received with Applause from Classmates While Parents Demand her Enrolment in Private Subsidized School) (*El Mundo,* 19/02/2002).
El ejemplo de tolerancia de los compañeros de Fátima (An Example of Tolerance from Fatima's Classmates) (*El Mundo*, 19/02/2002).
La intolerancia de un padre marroquí. (Intolerance From a Moroccan Father) (*El Mundo,* 20/02/2002).
Un marroquí se niega a enviar a 6 de sus hijos al colegio que les asignaron por ser católico (Moroccan Father Refuses to Send His 6 Children to Assigned Catholic School) (*El Mundo*, 20/02/2002).

Although we did not collect every headline published by this newspaper during that period, we can get a pretty clear idea of the message they convey: the headscarf is a symbol of female discrimination; the headscarf is always imposed by Muslim men on Muslim women; however, we –the Spanish society– are very permissive and tolerant when allowing its use, keeping in mind that, "our schools are overflowing with immigrants", and that using a headscarf, "can be compared to other cultural practices such as genital mutilation". What is the newspaper trying to achieve with such a news sequence? Once more, the answer is their goal to relate immigration, in general, with immigration of people who practice the Muslim faith, in particular. Also, in this case, they try to reinforce the idea that this "invasion" can lead us to loosen *our* democratic standards, since, compared to *us,* this part of the population is basically portrayed as intolerant and authoritarian.

The second group of news articles worth highlighting –due to its frequency– is the one using Islamic symbols to illustrate non-religious content. These are news articles that address the issue of foreign immigrant students' incorporation and presence in Spanish classrooms, in general, but which are illustrated with photos and images showing individuals from immigrant population with some specific characteristics. Some examples are presented below.

The headline "36% of Students Reject Immigration" (*El Periódico,* 23/01/2003) is illustrated with a picture of a mother wearing a headscarf and pushing her baby-trolley; this image also includes several graphs to support figures and trends (see Figure 6-7). We wonder, then, what kind of immigration are we rejecting if the pictures show a woman with an Islamic headscarf? The answer is evident.

Figure 6-7. Islam, schools and immigration (I). Date: 23 January 2003. Newspaper: *El Periódico*.

The following example is even more surprising. The headline states "Integration Fails at School", due to the creation of ghettoes (*La Vanguardia,* 16/05/2008); and the picture shows a girl wearing a headscarf from behind (see Figure 6-8).

Tendencias

La integración fracasa en la escuela

El Síndic denuncia que la Administración no actúa de forma efectiva para evitar guetos

En primaria hay más concentración de escolares inmigrantes que en secundaria

Las diferencias se dan más entre los propios centros públicos que con los concertados

El Síndic advierte que se prima la elección de centro antes que el principio de equidad

Sant Feliu: en vías de solución

Figure 6-8. Islam, school and immigration (II). Date: 16 May 2008. Newspaper: *La Vanguardia.*

What can we understand from this? Maybe girls who wear headscarf are not integrated? Or maybe ghettoes are mainly composed by girls who wear headscarves? Moreover, why are headscarves so controversial? We ignore the answer, but it is certain that this way of presenting facts gives priority to some connotations and to the detriment of others. In consequence, as stated before, diversity is represented as *difference, inequality* and *inferiority*.

This is the way foreign immigrant students are portrayed in the media. In fact, if we go through news articles, we can find statements such as, "the arrival of immigrants slows down class pace"·(*El País*, 24/02/2002); "this situation is detrimental for the education quality, to say the least" (*El Mundo*, 18/10/2002); "30% of parents consider the presence of immigrants makes academic level poorer" (*El País*, 17/02/2003); "average academic success drops with the arrival of immigrants" (*La Vanguardia*, 15/11/2005); "bad distribution of immigrant population affects all children learning" (*El País*, 27/05/2006); or even, they sarcastically affirm the following: "Schools are already multicultural. The presence of 133,000 immigrant students worsens school deficit" (*La Vanguardia*, 09/09/2007). We find numerous examples similar to the previous ones maybe because one of the objectives of the media is creating controversy through the news. This is undoubtedly achieved by giving priority to that kind of declarations and not to others, less subjective or more positive ones.

Before concluding this section, we would like to show that the use of different building rhetoric is not exclusive to the mass media. In previous works we have thoroughly analysed political and academic discourse on the subject (Olmos Alcaraz, 2009, 2010). In this regard, both politicians and teachers regard immigration at school as a threat to the quality standards of the Spanish education system. This can be evidenced in the following statement:

> INFORMANT: yes, we've got compensation education plans [...]. 40 schools of this province are participating in those plans, they have been authorized, and intervention with foreign students is the most important part of the plan. Why? Because what is diverse, different in most schools in our province, is the presence of foreign students; foreign students who show compensation characteristics (Education Administration Official, 2004).

And considering immigration as a threat to normalized coexistence at school, we find the following:

> INFORMANT: [...] those students cause many problems in every sense, they have all kinds of problems, socio-cultural disadvantage; they belong to families who aren't supportive with their schoolwork; there is absenteeism [...]. They become what some call destructive students; that is to say, angry, indeed very angry children. In theory all deficiencies are summed up; but the thing is that there's nothing these children can do. They receive tough discipline and that's it. I mean, I'm not saying "poor children" because they are impossible! But often, even if they are given opportunities, they don't use them well (Primary education teacher, 2005).

These are statements that demonize and stigmatize foreign immigrant students as a whole through a rhetoric that highlights differences and not similarities between *them* and *us*.

Once we know how foreign immigrant students' diversity is frequently seen we should ask ourselves the following question: when is academic quality really made poorer? This seems to be the most worrying issue for all social agents analysed. Although this question would need a deeper, studied and holistic explanation this rhetoric maintains that the quality of education becomes poorer when it is democratized, in other words, when everyone is included. This is a pretty elitist reasoning –to say the least– rooted on a verifiable trend, as we have seen, of changing national students from public to subsidized –do not forget, with public funds– private schools. These discursive trends and practices are strengthening even more this image of otherness: an image that puts the *other* as a threat.

2. Eulogizing a Diverse World: Foreign Immigrant Students who Enrich *us*

Yet, there is another way of understanding diversity that we cannot leave out. Saying that migration, when linked to the education system, is regarded as threatening, prejudicial and harmful for the host society in every single discourse analysed is manipulating reality. Therefore, our intention is to consider cultural diversity in positive terms, as an *enriching* situation for *our society*.

Some advantages specifically pointed out as a consequence of having diverse schools are that they let *our children* know, "other cultures", avoid closure of some schools and make generational turnover possible. These are arguments gathered from the analysed newspapers, but also, sketched from politicians' and teachers' words.

However, the extent to which this idea is penetrating public opinion, better said, ordinary people, is unknown to us. In fact, we believe this is not the opinion of those parents who rather take their children to subsidized private schools than to public ones. When we see this kind of rhetoric of enriching cultural and ethnic diversity, we cannot avoid thinking that "enriching" is not the best term since we have always been diverse. That is what culture means: organizing capacity among diversity (Díaz de Rada, 2010; García García, 1996; García Castaño, 1996; García Castaño, *et al.*, 1999; Wallace, 1972). This is not reflected in the discourse analysed. On the contrary, it is seen as a great novelty nowadays.

Let us analyse the way these *advantages* or positive aspects of diversity are reflected in the press. First, we notice that all those news articles covering specific experiences in schools where there are immigrant students (see Figure 6-9) highlight cohabitation and coexistence of students with different nationalities or origins. They talk about cultural exchange that makes possible a general knowledge of everyone's traditional food, customs, language and folklore (see Figure 6-10).

Undoubtedly, the intention of these news articles is pointing out positive aspects of diversity. However, we notice an over-identification or association of some characteristics that we could call cultural ones (language, customs, lifestyles…) with specific nationalities, for example students are identified as Moroccans, Ecuadorians, Chinese, Rumanians, etc. in order to know how many of them speak Arabic, Spanish, Mandarin Chinese or Romanian. But, do all Moroccans speak classic Arabic or Darija? No. In fact, many of them speak dialects or other languages such as Berber. Some of them were born here, and they speak Spanish, Catalan or Valencian. There is a strong inclination to associate nationalities with a specific language and, therefore, a culture. These kinds of mechanisms and logic of thought are the first step towards essentialization of cultures. This outlines a racist and xenophobic discourse that is not based on biological grounds anymore, but exclusively on cultural ones. Moreover, as reflected in the previous figure, we often find that this *enriching diversity* is illustrated with photographs showing children who are phenotypically different compared to the majority. This fosters the image of foreign immigrant students as deeply different, exotic and distant from *us*.

4 / COMUNIDAD VALENCIANA

HACIA UNA ESCUELA MULTICULTURAL

La educación no tiene nacionalidades

Escolares de varios países cuentan cómo viven su aprendizaje en colegios de Alicante y Benimámet

Figure 6-9. Enriching (nationality) diversity (I). Date: 3 March 2002. Newspaper: *El País* (Valencian Community).

Cosas de la vida GRAN BARCELONA

el Periódico

HISTORIAS DE BARCELONA

Fin de curso en el cole de Babel

Una mezcla de folklore mundial despidió a los alumnos de 25 países de la escuela Cervantes

Más de 15 lenguas

Figure 6-10. Enriching (language) diversity (II). Date: 19 June 2004. Newspaper: *El Periódico*.

In this context, we often read the phrase, "colours at school". "We have children of every colour, here", said a teacher as a joyful, uninhibited and pleasant way of talking about multiculturalism at that school (see Figure 6-11).

TENDENCIAS

El IES Pau Claris de Barcelona, con un 99% de inmigración, es un ejemplo de multiculturalidad que convive sin problemas

Colores en la escuela

Figure 6-11. Enriching (colour) diversity (III). Date: 15 October 2007. Newspaper: *La Vanguardia.*

Again, we believe this contributes –even with no obscure intention– to the essentialization of cultural differences. This type of rhetoric contributes to the identification of culture with biology, (understood as skin colour), and multiculturalism with "race" diversity, which easily leads to think that "race"[11] and culture are something *natural* that defines and is carried by each person from birth to death. Nothing is further from reality since *cultures*, as we said, are the way human beings organize themselves among diversity; and, as such, they change, they are transformed, merged and reconstructed in time and space.

Finally, as in the case of perception of diversity as *something upsetting,* there are similarities between the message found in news articles and the ideas expressed by school officials and politicians when it comes to viewing diversity as an *enriching* element. When our politicians express that diversity is good, they do it in a *utilitarian* or *functional* way. In other words, diversity of immigrant students in Spanish schools is extolled, yet emphasising on economic, social and cultural advantages that their presence implies for *us,* the autochthonous population:

> "[...] a phenomenon that is not strange for any of us, and which, undoubtedly contributes to the economic, social and cultural development

of our people and Autonomous Community" (Andalusian Parliament, 2006).

Andalusia is being economically, socially and culturally benefited by those Andalusian men and women who were not born here, who have a different skin colour from yours and mine, and other Gods – or, at least, they are called differently (Andalusian Parliament, 2006).

"[...] this is an important phenomenon to build a socially and economically richer society." (Andalusian Parliament, 2006).

Moreover, the way these prerogatives are presented leads us to think that they are used to convince citizens that "immigration is not that bad", and not an example of objective elements that compose the migration phenomenon. After almost ten years of exhaustively analysing Parliamentary sessions addressing immigration topics, especially in relation to education, we can assert that such advantages are part of a "politically correct discourse" that disappears when there is political confrontation between parliamentary groups. When confrontation emerges, all virtues of diversity brought by immigration become social problems. The politically correct discourse turns into a threatening one, with clear allusion to what immigration means for the rest of the world: crime. This was exemplified in the previous section.

3. Conclusions

Being an immigrant student today is almost an automatic synonym of requiring compensatory education, among other negative classifications. But if we analyse the previous statement we realize that many of us and our children are immigrants (in today's globalized society we often move to another city, region or country; and that is what being an immigrant means, moving from one place to another).

We know, however, some migrations produce deeper effects than others when establishing otherness relations. While some will always be Spaniards (returning migrants, emigrants' children who migrate to Spain), some others will always be immigrants, and they will be referred to as "second" or "third" generation. This is something that is totally mistaken for being vague in demographic terms, as well as pejorative. "Second generation" immigrants, who share classroom with our children, are considered "second-class students". They seem to be marked by what Goffman calls *stigma:* something composed by a series of discrediting attributes which seem to be inherited (Goffman, 2001), but which are simply culturally-signified social constructions strongly influenced by the mass media.

As social scientists, but also as citizens, we must continuously question the existence and reproduction of this normal and regular *social problematization*. In the case of the construction of the idea of immigrant students as a threat and social problem, we need to know what is said and contrast it with what is done in consequence, since "the meaning we give to things is relevant to our behaviour" (Cristoffanini, 2003, 3). If we perceive and signify migration at schools as a problem, we will behave towards immigrant students in accordance.

The rhetoric analysed (mass media, political and teachers' discourse) continues to open up rifts, yet denying them or considering them as natural. It is only *natural* for foreign immigrant students to be concentrated in some schools even if we all pay taxes, because, as it is *natural,* it is unavoidable. It is them who prefer *being with their own people* and it is them who create ghettoes –note the sarcasm in our statements.

True, we have observed two contrasting messages regarding this issue: *enriching* vs. *upsetting diversity*. Regardless of the differences between both ideas, they keep portraying immigrants in terms of difference and radical oddness against the autochthonous society. In other words, by saying, "school colours" are enriching to all of us, we are also reproducing the idea that (colour, phenotypical) difference is important – since it affects school functioning in some way. This idea seems dangerous, to say the least.

The possibilities to open up those rifts are countless. Part of the solution for this "problem" would be educating to foster a change in attitude among the autochthonous population (teachers, newspaper writers or even politicians and officials). However, this idea has not been clearly or slightly mentioned during more than ten years of study and analysis of the discourse. We cannot continue blaming diversity for the problems affecting schools since this kind of thinking is superficial, misconceived and even racist.

Notes

1. This work was carried out as part of the Science, Technology and Innovation Department of the Government of Andalusia Excellence Project entitled "Multiculturalism and Integration of Immigrant Foreign Population in Schools of Andalusia" (P06-HUM2380) and Spanish Ministry of Education and Science R&DI project entitled "Integration of Students called 'Immigrants': School Success/Failure and Family/School Relations" (SEJ2007-67155/SOCI). We thank both institutions for funding our research. Also, this text is part of a more

exhaustive work developed by Antonia Olmos Alcaraz in her doctoral thesis: "Foreign Immigrant Population and the Construction of Difference; Discourse of Otherness in Andalusian Education System", presented at University of Granada in 2009 and directed by F. Javier García Castaño.

2. By saying "biologically diverse" we do not support what is commonly known as "race" –nothing further than that– as the definition of "races" introduced in the late 19th century is scientifically unclear and socially prejudicial. Needless to say that, according to the latest discoveries on human genome, differences between members of a group identified as "race" are more profound than those between members of different "races".

3. We have analysed press releases regarding the migratory phenomenon in relation with education in five national newspapers (*ABC, El País, El Mundo, La Vanguardia* and *El Periódico)* for a period of eight years (2000-2008). Also, we base our analysis on ethnographic fieldwork carried out in Andalusian primary and secondary schools included in the project and on speeches addressing questions related to migration and education given in the Andalusian Parliament during sessions held between 2000 and 2009 (all of this compiled in the doctoral thesis written by Antonia Olmos, 2009).

4. Many policies designed and implemented to manage diversity at schools in our country are based on statistics that count students according to their country of birth or nationality because flow (migratory movements), as such, is difficult to quantify, record or measure. This obviously leads to many mistakes because immigration is often addressed using data provided by the immigration department.

5. Notice that, according to statistics regarding non-university education published by the Ministry of Education on its web page (http://www.educacion.es), the highest percentage of foreign students at schools was reached on late 2000s, when there were nearly ten foreigners for every hundred students. It is true that in some areas, such as La Rioja, Madrid, Catalonia or Balearic Islands, percentages are considerably higher (between 130 and 160 foreigners for every thousand students), but in other locations the proportion is thirty immigrant students for every thousand. So can the presence of five foreign students in a classroom of thirty, i.e. 15%, be truly considered as a "threat", "inundation" or "invasion"? We have our doubts.

6. The expression "tolerance threshold" is originated from the application of ethological parameters in some animal species to human social life. This fits perfectly with arguments introduced from what is known as *new racism* (Stolke, 1994; Fernández Enguita, Gaete and Terrén, 2008), suggesting that when a minority exceeds a given quantitative limit (tolerance threshold) the territorial imperative operates, which means defence of the territory against intruders.

7. Even if over 20% of foreign students has African origins, we cannot admit that this origin is linked to dark skin, except in the case of biased and stereotyped representations. Moreover, if that 20% of "Africans" is important, it is not more important than 28% Europeans, or 38% South Americans. Dark skin is not the most important feature among immigrant students, yet diversity shown in this photograph is focused on skin colour, or better said, the absence of colour (the figures quoted are taken from the Ministry of Education web page, for 2009-2010.

For the dates we have referred to (school year 2003-2004) "Africans" only accounted for 18% of foreign students and South "Americans" for 46%, so this picture is not representative of the situation).
8. The fact that "concentration" should not be used as a synonym of "segregation" or "ghettoization" does not mean there is no concentration of foreign population at school. In fact, when we look at schooling figures for Obligatory Secondary Education, we realize that more than 60% of students are enrolled in public schools. Unlike the previous figure, 80% of foreign students attend public schools. This percentage has been relatively constant during the last two decades. Nonetheless, these figures also need to be nuanced depending on the region and moment of observation of this phenomenon (see García Castaño and Rubio Gómez, 2012).
9. There already exist some insights and academic analysis regarding the use of the Islamic headscarf at school and other public spaces, which go beyond opinions published in the mass media. See Tourneau (1997), Antón Valero (2004), Labaca Zabala (2008), Llorent Bedmar (2009) and Ramírez (2011), among others.
10. This is the case of France, where in 2004 a national law was passed banning the use of the Muslim headscarf and other visible religious symbols.
11. As they have been conceived, even in scientific spheres at some point, and as they are still understood outside the academic world.

Bibliography

Antón Valero, José Antonio. 2004. "La discusión sobre el velo y la capacidad de la escuela por el debate cultural". *Revista MUGAK* 26, s/p.

Anyon, Jean. 2005. *Ghetto schooling: a political economy of urban education reform.* New York: Teachers College Press.

Bañón Hernádez, Antonio Miguel. 2002. *Discurso e inmigración. Propuesta para el análisis de un debate social.* Murcia: Universidad de Murcia.

Bañón Hernádez, Antonio Miguel. 2006. "La asociación discursiva de terrorismo e inmigración. Un ejemplo de incomunicación intercultural". *Comunicación. Revista Internacional de Comunicación Audiovisual y Literatura* 4: 259-277.

Barthes, Roland. 1982. *El mensaje fotográfico. Lo obvio y lo obtuso.* Barcelona: Paidós.

Carrasco Pons, Silvia. 2008. "Segregació escolar i immigració: repensant plantejaments i alternatives". *Revista Nous Horitzons* [Monogràfic Immigració i societat catalana] 190: 1-11.

Cristoffanini, Pablo Rolando. 2003. La representación de los Otros como estrategia de construcción simbólica. http://www.sprog.aau.dk/discurso/pablo_final_maj03.pdf.

Last accessed on 24 February 2012.
Díaz de Rada, Ángel. 2010. *Cultura, antropología y otras tonterías.* Madrid: Editorial Trotta.
Hall, Stuart. 2011. "El espectáculo del Otro". In *Textos de Antropología Contemporánea*, comp. Francisco Cruces Villalobos and Beatriz Pérez Galán, 75-94. Madrid: UNED.
Fernández Enguita, Mariano, José Manuel Gaete and Eduardo Terrén. 2008. "¿Fronteras en las aulas? Contacto transcultural y endogamia en las interacciones del alumnado". *Revista de Educación* 345: 157-181.
García Castaño, Francisco Javier. 1996. "Sobre algunas intenciones del concepto antropológico de cultura". In *Las prácticas culturales en el aula: metodologías y evaluación*, ed. José Luis Gallego, 13-32. Granada: Centro de Profesores de Granada.
García Castaño, Francisco Javier, Rafael Pulido Moyano and Ángel Montes del Castillo. 1999. "La educación intercultural y el concepto de cultura". In *Lecturas para educación intercultural*, ed. Francisco Javier García Castaño and Antolín Granados Martínez, 47-80. Madrid: Trotta.
García Castaño, Francisco Javier and Antonia Olmos Alcaraz. 2010. "La promoción de la plena integración de los extranjeros por parte de las administraciones públicas: ¿hacia una protección legal para la construcción de una sociedad multicultural?". In *Protección jurídico-social de los trabajadores extranjeros*, dir. José Luís Monereo, 111-177. Granada: Comares.
García Castaño, Francisco Javier and María Rubio Gómez. In press. "Juntos pero no revueltos: procesos de concentración escolar del alumnado extranjero en determinados centros educativos".
García García, José Luis. 1996. "Sobre el significado y las consecuencias de la diversidad cultural". Paper presented in the summer course: Diversidad cultural, exclusión social e interculturalismo, de la Universidad Internacional de Andalucía. Baeza: UIA.
Goffman, Erving. 2001. *Estigma. La identidad deteriorada.* Buenos Aires: Amorrortou.
Granados Martínez, Antolín. 1998. *La imagen del inmigrante extranjero en la prensa española: ABC, Diario 16, El Mundo, El País (1985-1992).* Unpublished PhD thesis. Granada: Universidad de Granada.
Labaca Zabala, María Lourdes. 2008. "La prohibición del velo islámico en los centros educativos de Francia: límite al principio de laicidad de la República". *Cartapacio de Derecho* 15: s/p.
Llorent Bedmar, Vicente. 2009. "Utilización de signos religiosos en los centros escolares de Alemania y Reino Unido: el velo islámico". *Educación XXI: Revista de la Facultad de Educación* 12: 97-121.

Márquez Lepe, Esther. 2006. *La gestión política de la diversidad cultural en España: análisis de los discursos parlamentarios sobre inmigración.* Unpublished PhD thesis. Granada: Universidad de Granada.

Olmos Alcaraz, Antonia. 2009. *La población inmigrante extranjera y la construcción de la diferencia. Discursos de alteridad en el sistema educativo andaluz.* Unpublished PhD thesis. Granada: Universidad de Granada.

—. 2010. "Construcción discursiva del alumno inmigrante extranjero en Andalucía: el otro en nuestras escuelas". *Revista de Educación* 353: 469-493.

Ramírez, Ángeles. 2011. *La trampa del velo.* Madrid: La Catarata.

Rodríguez, Nadia and Bettina Schell. 2007. *Diccionario de migraciones: del concepto a la palabra.* Madrid: Adeire.

Santamaría, Enrique. 2002. *La incógnita del extraño. Una aproximación a la significación sociológica de la "inmigración no comunitaria".* Barcelona: Anthropos.

Stolcke, Verena. 1992. "¿Es el sexo para el género como la raza para la etnicidad?". *Mientras Tanto* 48: 87-111.

—. 1994. "Europa: nuevas fronteras, nuevas retóricas de exclusión". In *Extranjeros en el paraíso,* comp. Alicia Sánchez and Graciela Malgesini, 235-266. Barcelona: Virus.

Terrén, Eduardo. 2007. "Inmigración, diversidad cultural y globalización". In *Educación e Inmigración: nuevos retos para España en una perspectiva comparada,* ed. Miquel Ángel Alegre and Joan Subirats, 261-274. Madrid: CIS.

Tourneau, Dominique. 1997. L´islam et une remise en cause de la laïcité à partir du port du hidjab dans l´école publique en France. *Revue Juridique* 5: 11-29.

Van Dijk, Teun. A. 1999. *Ideología. Una aproximación multidisciplinaria.* Barcelona: Gedisa.

—. 2003. *Racismo y discurso de las élites.* Barcelona: Gedisa.

Wallace, Anthony. 1972. *Cultura y Personalidad.* Buenos Aires: Paidós.

Zirotti, Jean Pierre. 1998. *Currículum intercultural y educación nacional en Francia.* Barcelona: Pomares-Corredo.

CHAPTER SEVEN

IMMIGRATION AND POLITICAL DISCOURSE IN SPAIN: THE EXAMPLE OF PARTY PLATFORMS

FRANCISCO CHECA OLMOS,
JUAN CARLOS CHECA OLMOS
AND ÁNGELES ARJONA GARRIDO
CEMYRI (CENTRO DE ESTUDIO DE LAS MIGRACIONES Y LAS RELACIONES INTERCULTURALES – CENTER FOR THE STUDY OF MIGRATIONS AND INTERCULTURAL RELATIONS) UNIVERSITY OF ALMERÍA

1. Introduction

The presence of foreigners in Spain – calculated at 5,730,667, or 12.2% of the total population – has surpassed that of other European countries with an immigrant tradition, such as France and Germany. The size of the phenomenon is unprecedented, with the influx of foreigners rising 318% in the period 2001-2011.

Nevertheless, the truly important aspect is not the quantity of persons but the challenges posed, particularly in the integration process (Zapata, 2004). Immigration in Spain has become a highly-debated issue in the public opinion and in the political agenda. For example, in the different national polls that have measured opinions and attitudes toward immigration over the years, results are seen to be increasingly negative (Cea D'Ancona, 2005, 2009). So much so that in the past decade, in all measurements taken by the Spanish Center for Sociological Research, immigration has placed between the first and fourth most important problem for Spaniards, along with unemployment, terrorism and housing, reaching its highest point at moments of mass immigrant legalization

(2001 and 2005). These were moments when immigration was given the label of "social emergency", equating it to other matters of social alarm such as drugs, delinquency, etc. Such social perceptions and cognitions have undoubtedly given rise to discriminatory attitudes and behaviors, hostility and even violence[1].

This process is not the product merely of population increase, since politicians and the media contribute to the scenario through targeted, substantiated discourse. On the one hand there is the "numbers game" (exaggerated figures, out of context), and on the other hand is the insistence on how immigration threatens work stability, national-cultural identity and public safety. In other words, the reality of immigration is subject to interpretation and portrayal, according to the interests of social and political agents.

The objective of this paper is to understand the role played by political parties – through their party platforms – in shaping the migratory phenomenon. In this way we continue the thread within international literature that was initiated by Simon and Lynch (1999) and furthered by Bauer *et al.* (2000) and Lahav (2004), in Spain by Celaya (1997), Checa, Arjona and Checa (2002) and Zapata (2009), among others.

To do this, we analyze the messages put forward by the two main political parties of Spain (PSOE and PP) through their party platforms in the different general elections held in Spain between 2000 and 2011.

We have chosen the discourse and messages of political parties because they fulfill certain basic ideological functions that are conveyed to the rest of society. It is expected of political parties, particularly those that are in office, first, that they "organize public opinion and communicate demands to the center of power and government decision", and second, for the party followers, that they "articulate the concept and meaning of the general community" (La Palombara and Weiner, 1996, 3).

As with any social phenomenon, the most prominent players in transforming immigration into a social problem were the media and the politicians, the latter through the ideas expressed in their party platform. This was our first reason for choosing to examine the role of party platforms. It has been shown from *Agenda-Setting Theory* that perception of social affairs is conditioned, in large part, by this contribution (Dearing and Rogers, 1996; Scheufele, 2000). This *framing* is related to two basic operations, selecting and emphasizing expressions and images to attribute a viewpoint, a perspective or a certain angle to information. As understood by Valkenburg, Semetko and de Vreese (1999, 550), "a media frame is a particular way in which journalists and politicians compose a news story to optimize audience accessibility".

Secondly, any party platform represents a way of addressing the social reality within which it was developed. It is a *model*, an ultimate objective, a target for society, drawn up and debated within the context of the political party; thus, it is a proposal for government. In short, it is a commitment that, if the elections are won, will become a social contract.

Finally, we chose general elections because the party platforms are identical for all voters, regardless of the number of immigrants that have lived in the different regions, provinces and municipalities.

By applying factor analysis to the types of measures/proposals written into each party platform (see Igartua *et al.*, 2005, and Muñiz *et al.*, 2008), we can understand the different electoral/ideological frameworks and compare them to each other. On the other hand, we can look at the interests of the immigrant population and determine how these measures affect them, classifying them as positive, negative or neutral. Positive measures are desirable and beneficial, since they facilitate the entrance and legalization of persons, they work against racism and xenophobia and encourage social integration; negative measures are those that may be judged to have undesirable or harmful consequences for the interests of immigrants, such as border control, deportation after having committed a crime, or requiring successful completion of an exam in order to gain legal status. We classify measures as neutral, or ambiguous, when there are no apparent, direct consequences to the development or interests of immigrants, as in the creation of an Integrated Plan or Migrations Agency.

2. Results: Treatment of immigrants in party platforms

Apart from the number of immigrants, political attention to the migratory phenomenon began in 1985, when the EEC required the State of Spain to establish a law that would limit and regulate the rights and duties of aliens: Organic Law 7/1985, 1st July. From this point forward, the different governments were obliged to delimit their obligations, focusing this effort in two large areas: first, to adjust the legislative framework to the new social reality, establishing influx control policies, specifying yearly quotas, deportation of illegal aliens, granting of visas, measures for family reunification, etc., within the supranational framework set by the Schengen agreements; second, to design social integration policies, principally at the state level and then delegated to the regional governments, including both ideology and action. We examine the ideological base, which is clearly discernible in detail in the measures outlined in the party platforms.

2.1. General Elections, 12th March 2000

The *Partido Popular* [People's Party, or *PP*] won the elections with an absolute majority, obtaining 10,321,178 votes (44.5%) and 183 seats in parliament – 27 more than in the 1996 elections, where their candidate, José María Aznar, won a simple majority, with 156 seats.

Partido Socialista Obrero Español (PSOE)

The *Partido Socialista Obrero Español* [Spanish Socialist Workers Party, or PSOE] presented their candidate Joaquín Almunia, recently named Party Chairman, under the slogan: "Vote Joaquín Almunia. Vote the Socialist Party. What's up next"[2]. The program focused around four themes: "A society with a future", "No one left behind", "A blueprint for Spain", "More democracy, better democracy". The said program has 95 pages and from now on the specific pages will be indicated in brackets.

Immigration falls within the second theme, where a two-pronged approach was taken, one having a global character and the other oriented geographically toward renewal of 400 neighborhoods around the country. The phenomenon was a "new dimension": "The new century will be the scene of large migratory movements, and the developed regions must prepare themselves to receive and integrate them" (p. 74). Immigrants are "The new social frontier". The socialists would carry out a strict border control policy, without forgetting that "integration is the primary border that immigrants are forced to cross" (p. 77). They proposed 8 measures: (1) promote tolerance and respect, creating specific plans in education; (2) develop bilateral agreement policies with the principal immigrant sending countries, such as those in North Africa and Latin America; (3) grant "all immigrants, regardless of legal residency, rights to health care and full coverage in terms of on-the-job accidents and occupational illnesses" (p. 77); (4) grant work permission automatically to those legally residing in Spain, and guarantee the right to family reunification; (5) recognize the Spanish nationality of children born in Spain if one of the parents was a legal resident in Spain at the time of birth; (6) reduce the required period of legal residency in Spain in order to acquire nationality by residency; (7) guarantee the right of immigrants to equal access to social rights and to basic, compulsory, free education; (8) finally, adopt specific policies to prevent and penalize illegal employment of aliens, as well as any racist or xenophobic behavior involved in justifying it (p. 78).

Partido Popular (PP)

The PP presented their candidate José María Aznar, incumbent president, under the slogan: "The commitment of the moderates. Let's take it further". Formerly they had run a campaign to publicize the achievements of their government, under the slogan: "Facts". The party platform revolved around five themes: "From the euro to full employment", "Investing in the future", "Caring for what's essential – the people", "The new, 21st century administration" and "Constitutional Spain, guaranteeing our common purpose". The said program has 207 pages and from now on the specific pages will be indicated in brackets.

Immigration and immigrants are addressed in the third theme, dedicated in broad terms to the "Family", "Women", "Seniors", "Health", "The Disabled", "Housing", "Consumers", "Youth", "Volunteers", "An Open Nation" (pp. 152-154), "Sports" and "Drugs". The PP understands immigration within the context of "A common, European-Union policy of asylum and migration", and recognizes that people are going to enter the country "because we need them" (p. 152). Toward this end they proposed: first, "Cooperation with sending countries", and second, "Integrating immigrants", where they refer to "Counteracting racism and xenophobia" and "Non-discrimination", and in terms of facilitating entry, "Spain will take into account not only its capacity for immigrants ..., but also its historical and cultural ties with the sending countries" (p. 153), a clear reference to Latin American countries. The third proposal, "Influx control", was to fight against human trafficking, and even to collaborate in voluntary repatriation and to work together with the sending countries to combat illegal migration. The final proposal referred to "a common European system of asylum".

Notwithstanding, despite the reference to social integration, no concrete measure was specified. In other words, all such intentions would fall within a common European policy of influx control, applying the Geneva Convention. This was to be made manifest two years later in the agreements on "Asylum and immigration", which Spain would push through in Seville in June of 2002, in its term of presidency in the Council of Europe.

2.2. General Elections, 14th March 2004

The PSOE, headed by José Luis Rodríguez-Zapatero, won the elections with a simple majority, obtaining 11,026,163 votes (42.6%) and 164 seats in parliament, regaining 39. Three days earlier, commuter trains in Madrid had been blown up in an act of Islamist terrorism.

Partido Socialista Obrero Español (PSOE)

Under the slogan, "We deserve a better Spain. Zapatero for President. Solutions Now", the party presented a platform revolving around six themes: "Spain in the world", "The democracy of men and women citizens", "A Plural Spain – A Constitutional Spain", "A fresh boost to the welfare society", "Towards a more productive economy", "Education, our basic priority" and "Culture with the people". The said program has 209 pages and from now on the specific pages will be indicated in brackets.

The immigration phenomenon is recognized throughout the platform, in such varied contexts as the "Introduction", immigration's importance to Spain as part of the EU, in Spain's relations with the Arab world, in social justice matters and in access to public services, recognition of the cultural diversity that results from immigrants' different ethnic origins – in the creation of a "Cultural Diversity Act" (p. 200), not to mention in the fishing sector (p. 150), in integration of immigrant groups through sports, and facilitating recruitment of workers from abroad.

Immigrants are understood as people with the same needs as the rest of the population: "we know that we are facing one of the greatest challenges of this century and we wish therefore to address it responsibly and in depth, as a matter of State. Immigration is an objective need of advanced societies: the challenge consists of meeting this need in a well-rounded, balanced manner, simultaneously addressing its economic, political and social dimensions" (p. 124).

Nevertheless, where the immigration phenomenon primarily appears is the section on the labor market, where they are included as manpower; as such, they form part of the third theme, Section IV: "Revitalizing society: including people and putting them to work", along with policies on employment, entrepreneurship, self-employment and the social economy, pensions and housing (pp. 117-130).

Proposals on "Immigration" are listed in 12 points on pages 124-125. The first and second are very significant, since they call for formulation of a "State Pact on Immigration", to be approved by all political forces, labor unions, employers and social organizations, and the creation of the "Spanish Agency on Migrations", which centralizes all authority for granting visas; coordinates with the Autonomous Region governments for social integration of immigrants; creates offices for hiring workers abroad; extends the period of a work search visa, making it significantly longer than a tourism visa; and setting a 45-day limit on answering residency and work permit applications; combating labor exploitation and the underground economy, promoting a legal specialization in prosecuting labor exploitation crimes, human trafficking and crimes against workers' rights. Reminiscent of the German *Gastarbeiter*, the figure of "guest worker" is created. A proposed Statute for integration of immigrants would respect preservation of customs and "the actual practice of religious freedom as recognized by the Constitution". Similarly, creation of an "Integrated Plan for Preferred Action" was proposed for areas with greater migratory pressure, both to encourage the immigrant's initial integration, as well as to strengthen security and border control. Finally, the PSOE wanted to avoid *squatters* and *household cramming* by making "necessary legislative changes in the area of rentals and housing standards, preventing households where the number of persons clearly surpasses the size and suitability of the dwelling" (p. 125).

Partido Popular (PP)

The PP presented a new candidate, Mariano Rajoy, who lost the elections. The elections slogan was: "Advancing together". The party platform was ordered around six themes: "Closer to full employment", "Toward greater welfare", "For a better future", "A Spain that counts", "Our commitment to the Constitution" and "Ten goals to keep moving forward". The said program has 426 pages and from now on the specific pages will be indicated in brackets.

Section 21, entitled "Ordered immigration in an open society" (pp. 199-206), expressed the principles of their policy on this matter, which falls under the second theme. Each section is structured and presented in three blocks: assessment of the situation, principles and objectives, and our proposals. The first aim was to show how 8 government actions had brought about progress in every area, most notably in passage of the Aliens Act (8/2000, 22nd December), the GRECO program, the *Foro* and the *OPI* [3], influx regulation through agreements with non-EU countries, and the fight against illegal immigration through the EU, pursued from Spain's presidency of the Council of Europe, with the Seville agreements in 2002.

Principles and objectives are summarized in seven points. Given that Spain is one of the most developed countries of the world, and as such will attract many immigrants, it must be kept in mind that "this phenomenon affects our country and will continue to do so" (p. 202); therefore, we must establish a border control policy, fight against illegal immigration and support the development of non-EU countries, always from within EU policies. Immigrants are considered to be manpower, and Spain's capacity to receive them is a function of the number of jobs that we can offer them. Integration in our society will be under equality of conditions, obligations and rights with Spaniards. This requires acceptance of the values and social norms on which our society is based, our legal and constitutional framework, and respect for the rights and obligations that uphold it (p. 202).

In a total of 27 proposals, the party focused on "legal immigration" (8), "true, effective integration of foreigners" (6), "illegal immigration" (4), "cooperation for development" (2), "driving a common European policy" (5) and "protection for the persecuted"[2]. It is a broad spectrum, intervening in influx control; hiring of laborers from their home country, through agreements with sending countries; seasonal permits; the hiring of highly qualified immigrants; programs to facilitate social and work placement, and to encourage an understanding of our customs, regulations and democratic values; specific treatment for minors deprived of parental care (MENA); collaboration with NGOs for carrying out integration; border control, especially sea surveillance, and immediate repatriation of illegal aliens; increased labor inspections to combat foreign worker exploitation; prosecution of human trafficking rings; cooperation for development, with national and international policies; working toward a common migratory policy, with a legislative framework and non-European border control; combating illegal immigration in the EU; creation of a statute for the long-term foreign resident; maintaining norms for asylum and refuge through cooperation among the different public administrations.

Section 22 is dedicated to Spanish emigrants around the world. Section 30, entitled "Spain, active in Europe and the world", within the theme of "A Spain that counts", insists further on integration of legal residents, the fight against illegal immigration and cooperation with non-EU countries.

2.3. General Elections, 9th March 2008

The PSOE and Rodríguez-Zapatero win the elections again, though still without an absolute majority. The party obtains 11,289,335 votes (43.9%) and 169 seats in parliament. The PP, led by Mariano Rajoy, wins 154 seats in parliament, with 10,280,010 votes (39.9% of the voters).

Partido Socialista Obrero Español (PSOE)

The incumbent president, José Luis Rodríguez-Zapatero, runs for reelection under the slogan: "Reasons to grow". The economic crisis that is emerging around the world will color all government action. The platform is built around three large themes, each of them further divided into different chapters. "Employment and social welfare" contained: "Towards full employment", "Strengthening the welfare system", "Energizing our social model" and "Financing public policies while maintaining budgetary stability". "Innovation, knowledge and sustainable progress" contained: "Driving modernization: capitalization of the economy, more competition and efficient markets" and "Sustainable progress: climate change, an opportunity for the future". Finally, "Freedom, peaceful coexistence and rights in a globalized world" contained: "more democracy, more citizen involvement" and "A stronger Spain in a more just world". The program has 317 pages and from now on the specific pages will be indicated in brackets.

Of the 45 total epigraphs in the platform, I.1.2 is dedicated to "Immigration linked to employment" (pp. 37-46). The title perfectly matched the present platform philosophy: "If last term's policy focused on ensuring legalized forms of entry and access to our society, the next term's policy will seek first of all to guarantee peaceful coexistence and development for all those living in Spain. New arrivals in Spain, always within the framework of our labor market's employment needs, must now be subject also to family reunification and the employment of immigrants already living among us" (p. 37).

Two principles were to guarantee peaceful coexistence: (1) ordered channeling of the immigrant influx and the fight against illegal immigration, along with cooperation and aid agreements with sending and transit countries; and (2), modern, effective administration of immigration, fully coordinated with the Autonomous Regions.

The program reviews the achievements of the prior administration, especially pointing out the improved efficiency of sea and land border controls, in procedures for deporting illegal immigrants, in improved conditions in detention centers, and in cooperation with immigrant-sending or transit countries. The 39 proposals are more declarations of intent than actions in themselves. The vast majority (29) are directed toward "stricter penalties, measures and economic sanctions against leaders and members of human trafficking networks and rings"; entry control, always linked to the needs of the labor market; detainment and deportation of illegal aliens; stricter rules and sanctions against employers who hire illegal aliens; more resources for police forces (through FRONTEX); promoting returns to the home country, and at the same time, facilitating family reunification with legalized aliens; promoting entry of qualified workers; and coordinating the different seasonal jobs across the country. Migration policy should be managed always through coordination with the different administrations, creating a State Migrations Agency. The agency would promote extension of powers to all the Autonomous Regions for granting initial work permits to foreigners. For the second principle, regarding integration and social cohesion, ten proposals address topics ranging from a "National Strategy" for strengthening public education and healthcare services; to prevention and intervention in overcrowded housing and residential segregation in problem neighborhoods; to promoting an integrated welcome model; development of plans for managing diversity and interculturality; the fight against racism and xenophobia; and help with the remittances that are sent to their home countries, as a means of driving development.

Partido Popular (PP)

Mariano Rajoy, party chairman, is again the PP candidate. The platform slogan is: "With Rajoy, a clear course is possible". The platform pivots on two large axes. The first, "A new consensus", contained five subcategories: "Stopping terrorism", "Working together to build Spain", "Improving the quality of our democracy", "Making Spain a safer country" and "Regaining our voice in the world". The second, "Protecting our social model", contained another ten subcategories: "Making Spain one of the top five world economies", "Reaching full employment", "Achieving one of the best educational systems", "A society with more equality", "Protecting the environment", "Full integration of immigrants", "Increased social welfare", "More economic proposals", "More social proposals" and "Conclusions". The program has 326 pages and from now on the specific pages will be indicated in brackets. Each of the total 45 epigraphs was presented using the model of principles, challenges, objectives and proposals.

Both in "The need to integrate immigration" (p.16) and in the corresponding epigraph, the idea is again that Spain is a country of immigrants, that they are a source of economic, social and cultural wealth; therefore, there should be two objectives: (1) legality and integration, "living together without discrimination" and ensuring equality, "without demagoguery or improvisations"; and, (2) counteract illegal entries and stays, through border control in conjunction with the EU. "The big challenge for Spanish society in the coming years is to find the right model for integrating the immigrant population" (p. 215), based on equality of rights, duties, obligations and opportunities.

The program contains 45 proposals for integration (from 1203 to 1248). Of these, 21 have a restrictive nature, focusing on the fight against illegal immigration, closing and controlling borders (SIVE improvement), deportation of persons, penalizing those who commit crimes, etc.; 11 may be considered neutral, such as the creation of an agency for immigration and employment; and 13 have a more positive role, truly focused on integration, as in adult training courses, support for housing acquisition and validation of academic degrees. The most novel proposals were: "We will prohibit by law mass legalization of aliens", "we will create a new permit system for legal entry in Spain, doing away with quotas", "creation of private hiring agencies that will be responsible for the immigrant's return to his/her home country, if after a certain time they are unable to enter the Spanish labor market", the number of visas that include work permission will be set each year in line with expectations for economic growth. Interested foreign applicants will be ranked according to a point system, where work permits will be granted as a function of the circumstances that favor their integration, such as knowledge of the language, professional experience and degrees, knowledge of the Spanish legal system, history and culture. "They will sign a letter promising to leave Spain if after one year they have been unable to successfully join the labor market", "We will lift the current prohibition that prevents the reunified family member from working", "any foreigner that commits a misdemeanor will be immediately expelled", "We will create an Integration Contract for those immigrants that wish to settle in our country. The contract is to be signed by any non-EU immigrant that requests their first renewal of residency and work permission. In the Integration Contract, the immigrant promises to abide by the laws and respect the principles, values and customs of Spaniards, to learn their language, to pay their taxes and contributions, to work actively toward integration, and to return to their country if during a certain time they lack employment and means", "the Spanish Administration promises to guarantee them the same rights and services as Spaniards, to assist them in their integration, to respect their beliefs and customs – inasmuch as these do not conflict with Spanish law. Evaluation mechanisms may be established in order to enforce contract fulfillment".

2.4. General elections, 20th November 2011

Elections are won by the PP, with Mariano Rajoy. The party obtained 10,866,566 votes (44.6%) and 186 seats in parliament. The PSOE obtained 7,003,511 votes (28.8%) and 110 seats in parliament, their worst result in Spain's democratic history.

Partido Socialista Obrero Español (PSOE)

The PSOE, with Alfredo Pérez-Rubalcaba, lost the elections. Campaign posters announced the slogan, "Fight for what you care about", and other slogans such as "We must defend what we've accomplished" and "Because it matters to you", but on the written party platform these do not appear. The document is labeled only: "PSOE. Party Platform. General Elections 2011". The platform is organized along five themes: "A platform for winning the future", "A healthier, more competitive economy", "What's urgent: employment", "21st century equality means equal opportunity" and "Democracy". The program has 181 pages and from now on the specific pages will be indicated in brackets.

The broadest theme by far is the fourth one, divided into a total of 24 chapters, each with epigraphs and sub-epigraphs. Each epigraph, after its introduction, is followed by many government proposals, for a grand total of 621. Immigration is covered in Chapter IV.7: "Coexistence and integration in 21st century society", IV.7.2: "The future of integration policies for socialists: new challenges, better solutions", IV.7.2.4: "Integration of what's different: immigration policies". At this same level we find the social security system, aging, persons with disabilities, poverty, volunteerism and NGOs, and consumer rights. The PSOE presents 17 platform proposals for improved integration of immigrants. Immigrants are referred to as "a group of new citizens, men and women, who have come to live among us" (p. 133) opting for a migratory model that allows for influx control. There is a commitment to full integration in key contexts, such as the school, business and the neighborhood, taking immigration as a crosscutting issue. Policies will be strengthened along these lines: prevention of social exclusion; recognition of foreign qualifications; family planning for women immigrants; combating residential segregation, shanty towns and makeshift settlements; and fostering interculturality, built on a basis of aliens' respect for the Spanish Constitution and laws. In coordination with the different administrations, emphasis also goes to border control, cooperation for development, return to home country, and ease of access to information about procedures, rights and duties of immigrants.

Partido Popular (PP)

Mariano Rajoy, party chairman, returns as the candidate. The platform slogan is: "What Spain needs". There are six pivotal themes: "Employment stability and reform", "Education, the road to opportunity", "Committed to welfare", "The administration, driving change", "An exemplary democracy", "European policy and international positioning". These chapters are divided into epigraphs, each presented with its diagnosis, objectives and measures. The program has 214 pages and from now on the specific pages will be indicated in brackets.

The platform contains a total of 43 epigraphs and 409 measures; 8 of these correspond to the immigration phenomenon, including epigraph "3.6. Integration: same rights, same obligations", and the remainder on family, health, the elderly, equality, recreation, culture and environment. Attention is drawn first to the "exceptional integration" of the more than five million foreigners in Spanish society, recognizing that they are the ones who most severely suffer from the crisis. Once again, Spain is seen as under the guidelines of the EU, in matters of border control and counteracting illegal immigration. The objectives again are "legal, ordered immigration", for a "plural society, and individual integration (…) with special attention to second generations" (p. 123). The aim is for a new immigration model, linked to quality employment, supporting second generations and developing a "circular immigration model". The measures proposed do not differ at all from those shown in 2008: immigration that is "legal, ordered and linked to employment, putting an end to mass legalizations", hiring through "a point system where qualifications take priority", "eliminating the geographic restriction that hinders mobility", legislation for the MENAs, integration for children in the school environment, with reinforcement and Spanish-language learning, recognition of foreign qualifications, a program to attract young foreign talent, and the requirement of "sufficient knowledge of the Spanish language, history and culture, in order to obtain Spanish nationality", etc. (p. 125).

2.5. Measures/proposals on immigration. Platform typology

We have reviewed all the references to immigration and to immigrants found in the platforms of the two major parties, PSOE and PP, from the last four general election races (2000-2011). The following tables group these together to show how the parties address the migratory phenomenon.

As shown in Table 7-1, all party platforms are structured along pivotal themes, with groups of proposals that revolve around each one. Although there is an average of 5 themes per platform, for the 2008 elections these pillars came down to three for the PSOE, and only two for the PP. The topic most often repeated refers to social welfare, or welfare of persons, whether understood as a "model" or linked to job market access. Immigration continues to fall within the ample sphere of "social services", although with time this is replaced by the "social welfare" concept.

The baseline, or perception, of immigration is quite similar for both groups: border control is necessary for orderly influx, along with support for development in non-EU (sending) countries, while working at the same time towards integration of legal immigrants on the home front. The *Partido Popular* placed more emphasis on acting from within a common European policy, and not without fruit; when Spain presided over the Council of Europe during the first half of 2002, nine new measures on asylum and immigration were passed in the "European Summit of Seville". These measures aimed particularly to reinforce borders, combat illegal immigration, create a new visa policy and take steps to penalize those countries that do not seek to stop illegal departures from their territory, and afterward must readmit those deported.

If we look at the total number of platform measures or proposals dealing with the migratory phenomenon during this period, the numbers are not dissimilar: 76 in the socialist party platforms, and 92 in the people's party. Moreover, this number rises and falls at the same time: the PSOE went from 8 to 12 to 39, dropping to 17 for the last elections; the PP increased from 12 to 27 to 45, dropping back to 8.

Whereas immigration drew little attention in the year 2000 (only 12 proposals), four years later both parties gave it a substantial boost. Not in vain had the Spaniards rated "immigration" among the problems that most affected them, along with unemployment, terrorism, public safety and housing. According to measures from the Center for Sociological Research (*CIS*), immigration occupied fifth place in 2000, sixth place in 2001, fourth place in 2002 and 2003, and third place in 2004. Even though no more than 18% of those surveyed stated that it affected them (higher ranking problems always exceeded 43%), it is still significant that immigration appears as a noteworthy problem.

Table 7-1. PSOE and PP platform references to immigration general elections (2000-2011).

	2000		2004		2008		2011	
	PSOE	**PP**	**PSOE**	**PP**	**PSOE**	**PP**	**PSOE**	**PP**
Platform themes	4 (2): "No one left behind"	5 (3): "Caring for what's essential – the people"	6 (3): "A fresh boost to the welfare society"	6 (2): "Toward greater welfare"	3 (1): "Employment and social welfare"	2 (2): "Protecting our social model"	5 (4): "21st century equality means equal opportun ity"	6 (3): "Committed to welfare"
Baseline for addressing the immigration phenomenon	The 21st century will be charac-terized by migrations. There must be influx control.	State policy within a common European policy (immigratio n and asylum)	Immigrants are people with the same needs.	Border control policy, since Spain is a developed country. Build on the govern-ment's accomplishments .	Influx control and managing diversity in social integra-tion	Immigra-tion based on legality (legal entries) and social integration	Integrati ng the differenc e	Continuing to combat illegal immigration. Legal immigrants are full-fledged citizens, integrating them through employ-ment
Measures / Proposals	8	12	12	27	39	45	17	8

Source: PSOE and PP party platforms. Compiled by the authors (the theme that includes immigration is shown in parenthesis).

The place of immigration reaches its peak in the 2008 elections, with a total of 84 proposals, with both parties starting from a common idea: there must be influx regulation and an effort towards social integration. At the moment when these elections were held, the immigration phenomenon began to show signs of becoming a true problem, as one gathers from constant news in the media and from statements by PP leaders, who presented it as a political battle against the PSOE around the whole country. By the end of 2005, the barometer showed that 40% of those surveyed were concerned about immigration, in second place after employment, for the first time rising above terrorism, housing and public safety. Of those surveyed, 60% responded that there were "too many" immigrants residing in the country. This perception continued to rise, so that by 2006, a total of 59.2% placed immigration as the "main problem that exists in Spain", surpassing unemployment (42.1%), housing (21%) and terrorism (18%)[4]. Moreover, the socialist government had just carried out a mass legalization process in 2005, bringing to visibility nearly one million illegal aliens. The mass legalization was portrayed by the PP as having a "pull effect", very harmful to the economy. One year later, just months before the elections, it remained among the top problems that concerned Spaniards, despite having dropped from nearly 60% to 26.9%, now below terrorism, the economy, unemployment and housing. This explains why the major parties included so many proposals in their political agendas and party platforms, most of them referring to border control (11 in the PSOE and 13 in the PP).

What happened with the onslaught of the financial-economic crisis in 2008? Immigration receded from the forefront of the PP political agenda or platform, dropping from 45 proposals to only 8, even lower than at the beginning of the decade. In the PSOE, the number of measures dropped by more than half, with these being included under the ideological intent of "integrating the difference". Other social problems took priority. The *CIS* barometer in February 2011 speaks for itself: unemployment was a concern for 83.9% (never had a single problem received such a high percentage), followed by "problems of an economic nature" (51.6%) and the political class (17.8%); immigration, though it falls in fourth place, does not reach 13%. The winning party adopted the fight against illegal immigration as its baseline for governing. Laws passed in the following months (on education, healthcare, labor reform, etc.) would show that immigrants were the first victims of the crisis, in every sense.

When we analyze these measures more in depth, factor analysis places the proposals into ten categories (see Table 7-2).

Table 7-2. Platform categorization and number of measures, general elections, PSOE and PP (2000-2011).

	2000			2004			2008			2011			Total
	PSOE	PP	Total	PSOE	PP	Total	PSOE	PP	Total	PSOE	PP	Total	
Influx Control		4	**4**	2		**2**	11	13	**24**	2	3	**3**	**33**
Cooperation for develop-ment	1	2	**3**		2	**2**	8	5	**13**	1		**1**	**19**
Social integration	2	4	**6**	1	6	**7**	8	8	**16**	9	3	**12**	**41**
Documenta-tion and legalizations	3	2	**5**	1		**1**	2	3	**5**	1	1	**2**	**13**
Racism, xenophobia and labor exploitation	2		**2**	1	2	**3**	1	3	**4**	2		**2**	**11**
Integral Plan				2		**2**	7	4	**11**	2		**2**	**15**
Legislative Changes				2		**2**	2	6	**8**		1	**1**	**9**
Asylum					5	**5**							**5**
(Il) legal immigration					12	**12**		1	**1**				**13**
Other				3		**3**		2	**2**				**5**
Totals	8	12	**20**	12	27	**39**	39	45	**84**	17	8	**25**	**168**

Source: PSOE and PP party platforms, general elections (2000-2011). Compiled by the authors.

Two aspects emerge above the rest: one, social integration of these groups (a total of 41 measures/proposals); two, influx control, closed borders or combating illegal immigration (33 proposals). The greatest emphasis on counteracting "the avalanche of immigrants" is seen in the 2008 party platforms, appearing in no less than 24 proposals. Ideas promulgated in earlier years prevail, namely the "pull effect", and how so many immigrants "wreak havoc" on the economy and on the native population, from whom they are "taking away jobs". Moreover, the third vector in terms of number of measures – cooperation for development in countries that export manpower – is expressed in a total of 13 measures from the two parties, for these same elections. This topic is repeatedly associated with border control, under the global idea that immigrants and future immigrants can stay in their native countries if the Western developed world collaborated in the generation of wealth within each country. These last two emphases, taken together, constitute a total of 37 measures, such that 44% of all measures are concerned more with potential immigrants that have not yet entered the country, than with those already living here. In other words, at a time when Spanish society had reached one of its highest levels of immigrant presence (more than 5,200,000, or 11% of the total population), the two parties together produced a large number of measures aimed at stemming the tide of immigrants, more than twice the number of measures for encouraging social integration (37 compared to 16). This was nothing new: in the 2000 elections as well there were more total proposals for influx control and cooperation for development than for social integration, even when the immigrant presence was still less than one million (2.28% of the total population).

Quite a large group of proposals fall under the umbrella of integration, as we have said, although only in the most recent elections of 2011 were these measures much more numerous than the rest (especially because of the emphasis given by the PSOE, 9 of the 12 proposals); in earlier terms there were only 6 proposals (2000) and 7 (2004). In order to achieve true integration of immigrants, the PSOE and PP believed it was necessary to create an Integral Plan. Though it was not in the 2000 party platforms, since then it has always been present. Each government in office has put something together, but in reality it has never had much social impact[5].

Aspects of documentation and legalization of immigrants occupy fifth place in the total number of platform proposals (13). All of these recognize that there are pockets of illegal immigration, and that they should be addressed as such. However, there is reluctance to do so, other than from the opposition, and during election seasons, when the present administration is blamed for its failure to control borders – precisely the area where the most effort and economic resources have been applied. In this line there are also measures to penalize illegal immigrants, once they have established themselves in Spanish territory (another 13 measures). We already saw that in 2008 the PP proposed the expulsion of any immigrant who committed a crime. In order to carry out many of these measures, the parties would be forced to implement legislative changes. The 2008 elections marked the highest incidence of this.

Do we find noticeable differences between the two parties? Numerical differences are small. We have already noted that the numbers rise and fall in unison, guided by socioeconomic circumstances. The most important theme for the PSOE, according to their proposals over the last four general elections, is social integration (20 proposals), followed by influx control (15) and cooperation for development (10). The PP follows a similar line: 21 measures are devoted to social intervention, 20 to influx control and another 10 to cooperation for development. The biggest spread is found in the treatment of illegal immigration (12 PP proposals in 2004, none from the PSOE) and the need to adapt the legislative framework (6 proposals compared to 2), especially in the sense of penalizing the presence of illegal aliens and abuses committed by them. Moreover, the People's Party platforms show greater rigidity regarding the presence of illegal aliens, going so far as to associate them with an increase in delinquency[6].

The above summary provides a global idea of the measures that the political parties would put into place after gaining power. Looking at their classifications, in most cases we have an idea of whether they fall into favorable or unfavorable spheres in terms of the interests of immigrants. But things are not always as they seem, and the grouping in Table 7-2 may lead to false expectations. In order to more accurately determine the classification, we analyzed each and every one of the 168 measures in detail, screening them according to the interests of immigrants, and grouping them into positive, neutral and harmful measures, according to the criteria discussed earlier. Here we meet our first obstacle: a large percentage of measures/proposals cannot be classified without risk of error, above all because they are not actual measures, no matter how much the political party would like to see them as such: they are imprecise, broad, vague, and are limited to the sphere of desires and intents, they state facts, but they are not true proposals that can be quantified, nor can concrete measures or actions be projected from them, further than the idea expressed. For example, the PP platform for 2000 reads thus: "We support a policy of integration that seeks to grant rights and obligations comparable to those of EU citizens, as well as promoting freedom from discrimination in economic, social and cultural life, and to develop measures against racism and xenophobia". Certainly this proposal cannot be considered negative or neutral, since it has a positive appearance, but, is it really positive? We feel that it is not, since it specifies no concrete measures to be put in place for "promoting freedom from discrimination in economic life", and several such measures could easily by specified. For this reason, we group such proposals under "unclassified or difficult-to-classify". In several cases where we detected that the same measure addresses several aspects, and even contradictory ones, we count it more than once.

In any case, nearly half the measures put forward by either party can be considered positive, that is, they really benefit immigrant integration, such as "We will establish simple, clear procedures that facilitate legal entry to our country and we will streamline processing of authorizations and permits" (PP, 2004, 203), and "We will grant all immigrants, whether or not they are considered legal residents of Spain, rights to health care and full worker benefits in terms of on-the-job accidents and occupational illnesses" (PSOE, 2000, 77).

On the other hand, 21% of the measures can be considered as negative. We concluded that putting these measures into practice would in no way benefit immigrants in Spain, regardless of their administrative status, as they refer to repatriation, deportations, border control, or modifying legislation to accommodate these circumstances: "We will prohibit mass legalization by law, thus delivering a clear, unmistakable message against illegal immigration" (PP, 2008, 216), "Streamline procedures to deport foreigners that have an illegal status, especially those who commit a crime, practice antisocial behavior, or disturb the peace or public safety" (PSOE, 2008, 40). Certainly Spain has quite ample experience with illegal immigration, and every government has strived to establish control of the southern border, something that still has not been achieved no matter how many technical or human controls have been put in place in recent years. Indeed, entry by crossing the Strait of Gibraltar has been drastically reduced, but other entry points have been created, such as the beaches of Portugal, and there is a rise in entries by air and land, from Eastern Europe. We recognize that illegal entry of persons, and their stay in the country, are very controversial topics, but it is contradictory to establish that in the era of globalization, all merchandise may cross borders freely, but not persons, who are relegated to their place of birth. For this reason the Western world speaks of aiding development in countries that export manpower.

Finally, 15% of the proposals were neutral in nature, including such measures on aid for development, but especially measures that aimed to create placement offices or plans for integration. These measures are comprehensible given the need for legislative adjustments and for a state-wide model to direct government action. "The immigration phenomenon requires a policy of State. We wish to develop this policy with as much agreement as possible among political forces in parliament" (PP, 2000, 152), "To develop a National Strategy to reinforce public health and education services, designed to ensure quality in the health and education systems of districts and towns that receive the greatest number of immigrants" (PSOE, 2008, 45).

Table 7-3. Typology of measures/proposals. PSOE and PP, general elections (2000-2011).

	2000		2004		2008		2011		Total
	PSOE	PP	PSOE	PP	PSOE	PP	PSOE	PP	
Positive	7	2	8	12	18	22	5	4	78
Negative		2	4	4	10	12	1	3	36
Neutral	1			5	8	8	3	1	26
Unclassifid		8		6	3	5	8		30

Source: PSOE and PP party platforms, for general elections (2000-2011). Compiled by the authors.

However, it is noteworthy that nearly 18% of the proposals do not qualify as measures, since they are so vague or broad that it is impossible to classify them, such as "We will move forward within the framework of the Area of Freedom, Security and Justice, in order to ensure free movement within the European Union", "We will improve and facilitate access to information about procedures, rights and duties of immigrants" (PSOE, 2011, 135), "The great challenge for Spanish society in the coming years is to adopt the right model for integrating the immigrant population. The correct choice of this model is key to the prosperity of Spanish society" (PP, 2008, 16). In these cases immigration is left merely with statements of intent, presented as measures, but at the same time unattainable, since their practical application is impossible to specify, or, even more difficult, to know whether such actions would favor social integration.

If we look at the distribution of platform proposals, the greatest difference between parties is precisely in this aspect, in difficult-to-classify proposals (19 from the PP compared to 11 from the PSOE) and in the negative group (21 from the PP compared to 15 from the socialists); in the former case, the PP errs on the side of vagueness, in the latter case, their party platforms weigh heavily in favor of closed borders, deportations and sanctions, as we have described earlier. The PP also produced a greater number of positive measures (42 compared to 38), especially in the 2008 elections; though at the start of the decade the PSOE had presented the most proposals, when immigration did not produce as much expectation or as much controversy.

3. Conclusions

We have collected all the references to immigration and immigrants in the party platforms of the two major parties, PP and PSOE, from the last four election periods (2000-2011). We were able to observe that the attention received by this group has varied over time, and, ultimately, the proposals are quite similar and common to both parties, despite their ideologies. We can draw the following general outline from our analysis.

First, the use of language is never harmless. When we speak of migrations and of immigrants in almost every sphere, a reductionist, sterile conception comes through, though we may not always be aware of it. Politicians confuse subject with object, creating stereotypes that often translate into scape goats. The "catch" in the term *immigration* lies in its etymological prefix in-. It defines a place of destination, indicating the direction of movement. But its popular, indiscriminate use is only for a group of persons who come from less developed countries, and not for the "tourist-foreigner" types, meaning that immigrants, at their destination, are pigeon-holed into a social image even before arriving – into a homogeneous, defined whole, with administrative and people categories. However, in the real world, homogeneity does not exist: "plurality is the condition of human action because we are all the same, that is, human, in such a way that nobody is ever the same as anyone else who ever lived, lives, or will live". (Arendt, 1988, 22).

Aside from this, the same concept of "immigrant" is used in the platforms to identify not only the entire group, but also those with legal status, the illegal aliens, the workers, the temporary workers, the qualified workers, or those that "turn to our country to escape from hunger and poverty" (PSOE, 2000, 74), etc. If the fundamental term is not clarified, neither is the rest of the terminology. Thus, the concepts used are never narrowed or defined; they are confusing, imprecise, abstract, even vague and useless. Among these we find: interculturality, multiculturality, social participation, aid to development, training and preparation, education and health, priority aid, social justice, etc.

In reality, to introduce concepts like interculturality and multiculturality, together with the concept of immigrant, is a de facto denial of the multiculturality, interculturality and migrations that existed among the inhabitants of any place before the "new immigrants" arrived. And what is more important, a large number of measures remain undefined, as we have seen, and are simply generalist intentions.

Second, starting from imprecise, abstract concepts, one can proceed to promises for action that have no specific commitments, generalities such as: cooperating with NGOs or sustaining dialogue with them, developing projects for social integration, fostering a sense of solidarity and multiculturality, counteracting discrimination and social exclusion, promoting participation and co-development programs with non-EU countries, etc. In some cases, it is possible to deduce possible measures to be adopted from the universal needs of all immigrants, though mainly the "legal ones"; however, their heterogeneity is so apparent that any action that sought to be entirely egalitarian would only produce even greater inequalities among them than those that already exist. Nonetheless, in the more recent elections of 2008 and 2011, certain proposals are indeed more concrete, as in expanding the *SIVE* (integrated system for border surveillance), facilitating voluntary repatriation, creation of the Immigration Agency, application for the integration contract (PP) or extending the maximum stay in a detention center from 40 to 60 days (PSOE); they also propose to work on streamlining the validation of foreign academic degrees, or in favor of women.

Third, in practically all platforms, immigration and the immigrant are relegated to what we call the broad spectrum of Social Services: for the chronically ill, disabled, ethnic minorities, seniors, youth, minors, women, etc. Some of these are what Sorman (1992) called "the barbarians". Groups that are only on the receiving end of aid policies or need some very specific treatment within these. Only in the latest elections was the immigrant recognized as generating economic benefit from his/her work, while at the same time needing housing, education, and good healthcare. For this reason, given that "immigrants cannot lose their right to be treated as human beings" (PSOE, 2000, 77), such concepts appear in many other different sections. In these recent platforms the classic concept of Social

Services disappears, replaced by Welfare, Equality and Citizenship, but the players are practically the same.

Fourth, there is a desire to show movement toward full social integration. This ambiguous concept appears as one key toward solving what has been socially construed as a problem. However, when this is not understood as assimilation, it becomes reduced to a strange or vague view where the immigrant is left alone to choose whether or not to be integrated. *Integration* always has positive connotations, but underneath this apparent agreement in terms there are very different meanings. *Integration* has come to represent every individual idea of what immigrant adaptation to the receiving society should look like. In other words, this ambiguous, undefined term, with multiple meanings, takes on any meaning convention that we want to give it and to be valid. The term integration ought to be reserved for legal, socioeconomic content that refers to equal opportunities and that forms part of human rights. This is the problem: when speaking of immigration, the parties tend to focus it almost entirely as the personal, exclusive responsibility of the legal immigrant. "Individual integration, where each person, without abandoning their roots, and by means of their own effort, feels a part of society and accomplishes the objectives they have set for themselves" (PP, 2011, 123). Pure assimilation. The clearest idea seems to be encouraging training and preparation of immigrants for integration into social life or at work or to collaborate in active integration policies.

Nonetheless, it is quite encouraging to read that both parties understand that immigration presents "new challenges" that require "better solutions", even if these are not clearly specified in the party platforms. In summary, the political parties show proposals and statements of intent in their party platforms that on occasion surpass even what can really be done. Such proposals and statements of intent do not take shape, but they still create ideas and influence public opinion, since they are publicized using well-targeted media. Society comes to adopt them as their own and uses them to explain the reality of national immigration.

This is what Zapata (2009) calls the governance hypothesis, such that if the government confronted integration of immigrants inclusively, offering them civic citizenship, instead of credentialist, or stopped transmitting to the population the efforts they are making to control flows, the negative sentiment toward the outgroup would be even higher.

Therefore, in increasingly multiethnic societies, efforts must be made to strengthen a pluralistic view, adding new frames which overcome the view of immigration as a threat and a problem.

Notes

1. This was the case in El Ejido (Almería) in racist demonstrations against North Africans, considered to be the most notable incident in Spain and one of the most notorious in all of Europe in recent years (see Checa (dir), 2000 and Checa *et al.*, 2010). But far from being an isolated case, this type of racial protest has been occurring little by little around Spain. While on a few occasions entire groups were attacked – such as the Chinese in Elche (Alicante), or the Moroccans in Tarrassa (Barcelona) – usually hostility is expressed toward particular individuals in the spheres of daily life.
2. The PSOE joined with the left-wing party (IU) in a pact involving three commitments: a program agreement on minimums, particularly on 59 principles of public policy, a vote-of-confidence pact whereby the IU committed its support to the socialist candidate for the Presidency, and an electoral alliance in 27 electoral districts of the Senate (see A. Sánchez-Sierra, 2005, for an in-depth analysis of the consequences of this pact).
3. *GRECO*, Global Program for Coordination and Regulation of Foreigners and Immigration (2001-2004), was launched with much stir in the media, but no budget allocation. *OPI*, the Permanent Observatory on Immigration, is the body responsible for the collection, analysis, study and dissemination of data related to migratory movements in Spain; and is coordinator of the National Point of Contact of the European Migrations Network. The *Foro*, Forum for Immigrant Integration, is the "organism for reference, information and advising on matters of immigrant integration (no executive capacity).
4. The country was benefiting at that time from a ceasefire announced by the terrorist group, ETA, thus explaining this decline.
5. The PP approved the GRECO Plan (2001-2004), and the PSOE launched the PECI (Strategic Plan for Citizenship and Integration) on two occasions, for terms 2007-2010 and 2011-2014.
6. In May of 2006, parliamentarian A. Acebes, PP party chairman and Minister of the Interior under the Aznar administration, in a congressional speech, linked the arrival of illegal aliens to delinquent gangs: "our borders have become totally permeable to the avalanche of immigrants" … and "the breaking and entering in our homes has to do with gangs that are trafficking in human beings".

Bibliography

Arendt, Hannad. 1988. *La condición humana*. Barcelona: Paidós.

Bauer, Tomas K., Magnus Lofstrom and K.L. Zimmermann. 2000. "Immigration policy, assimilation of immigrants and natives sentiments towards immigrants: evidence from 12 OECD countries". *Papers* 187. Institute for the study of Labor, Bonn.

Cea D'Ancona, Mª Ángeles. 2005. "La exteriorización de la xenofobia". *Revista Española de Investigaciones Sociológicas* 112: 197-230.

—. 2009. "La compleja detección del racismo y la xenofobia a través de encuesta. Un paso adelante en su medición". *Revista Española de Investigaciones Sociológicas* 125: 13-45.

Celaya, Carlos N. 1997. "La política en la frontera: inmigración y partidos políticos en España durante 1996". *Migraciones* 2: 27-57.

Checa, Francisco (dir.). 2000. *El Ejido, la ciudad-cortijo. Claves socioeconómicas para entender el conflicto étnico*. Barcelona: Icaria.

Checa, Francisco, Juan C. Checa Olmos and Ángeles Arjona. 2000. "Partidos políticos e inmigrantes. La representación de la alteridad en los programas electorales". In *Convivencia entre culturas. El fenómeno migratorio en España*, eds. Francisco Checa, Juan C. Checa and Ángeles Arjona, 187-243. Sevilla: Signatura Demos.

—. 2010. "El Ejido: la convivencia como desafío". *Scripta Nova. Revista electrónica de Geografía y ciencias sociales* Vol. XIV (315). http://www.ub.es/geocrit/sn/sn-315.htm Last accessed on 20 July 2012.

Dearing, James W. and Everett M. Rogers. 1996. *Agenda Setting*. Thousand Oaks: Sage.

Igartua, Juan José, Carlos Muñiz and Lifen Cheng. 2005. "La inmigración en la prensa española. Aportaciones empíricas y metodológicas desde la teoría del encuadre noticioso". *Migraciones* 17: 143-181.

Lahav, Gallya. 2004. *Immigration and politics in the new Europe: Reinventing borders*. Cambridge: Cambridge University Press.

La Palombra, Joseph and Myron Weiner. 1996. *Political parties and political development*. Princenton: Princenton University Press.

Muñiz, Carlos, Juan J. Igartua and José Otero. 2008. "Recepción e impacto socio-cognitivo de las noticias sobre inmigración. *Revista de Psicología social* 23 (1): 3-16.

Sánchez-Sierra, Ana. 2005. "El Pacto PSOE-IU en las elecciones generales de 2000: estrategia electoral, proceso negociador y efectos". Madrid: Universidad Autónoma de Madrid, Facultad de Derecho, Estudio/Working Paper, 44/2005.

Scheufele, Dietram A. 2000. "Agenda-setting, priming and framing revisited: another look at cognitive effects of political communication". *Mass Communication and Society* 3 (2-3): 297-316.

Simon, Rita J. and James P. Lynch. 1999. "A comparative assessment of public opinion toward immigrants and immigration policies". *International Migration Review* 33 (2): 455-467.

Sorman, Guy. 1992. *Esperando a los bárbaros*. Barcelona: Seix Barral.

Valkenburg, Patti M., Holli A. Semetko and Claes, H. De Vreese. 1999. "The effects of news frames on reader's thoughts and recall". *Communication Research* 26: 550-69.

Zapata-Barrero, Ricard. 2004. *Inmigración, innovación política y cultura de acomodación en España*. Barcelona: CIBOD.

—. 2009. "Policies and public opinion towards immigrants: the Spanish case". *Ethnic and Racial Studies* 32 (7): 1101-1120.

CHAPTER EIGHT

HOW COME YOU'RE NOT A CRIMINAL?: IMMIGRANT STEREOTYPING AND ETHNIC PROFILING IN THE PRESS

JAN CHOVANEC
MASARYK UNIVERSITY, BRNO

1. Introduction

The region of Central and Eastern Europe (CEE) has not yet experienced an influx of immigrants comparable to the countries of Western and Southern Europe. So far, CEE countries have been used as transit areas rather than actual destinations for large numbers of immigrants. This, however, does not mean that the public domain is free from the discourses of discrimination and intolerance that tend to be associated with the issues of migration. Rather, such discourses are oriented towards different targets: groups of people from within the country who come to be redefined in various ways as outsiders or, less specifically, as the out-group of "not Us".

In the Czech Republic, for instance, it is only rarely the case that people encounter true linguistic, ethnic and cultural "otherness", although they are aware of at least four distinct groups of foreigners and immigrants: Slovaks, Central and Eastern Europeans, Western Europeans, and others, typically coming from third world countries. With the end of the Balkans war in the 1990s and the accession to the Schengen area in 2008, the situation in the country with respect to immigration has even calmed down, which stands in a sharp contrast to what some western European countries, such as the UK, have experienced over the past few years. In recent years, however, discourses of intolerance and discrimination have been on the increase; arguably as a result of the worsening economic situation and the need to identify scapegoats for all kinds of social wrongs, whether genuine or perceived. Paradoxically, such discourses centre—

most likely because of the lack of a visible presence of immigrants and foreigners—on the search for various "internal outsiders", most notably the Roma.

2. Immigrants and other out-groups—a socio-historical background

As a prelude to the analysis of a series of newspaper articles that deal with the representation of social actors in crime reports involving Czech citizens of immigrant backgrounds, it will be helpful to provide a brief overview of immigration to the Czech Republic over the past couple of decades. Our discussion of foreigners living in contemporary Czech society must also be complemented by reference to the Roma, the country's largest domestic out-group and the one which has repeatedly been subject to the most vicious racist attacks.

2.1. Immigration in the Czech Republic

According to data from the Czech Statistical Office, there were 417,887 foreigners living in the country in 2010, i.e. 3.97 per cent of the total population.[1] While there was a steady increase in the number of foreigners from the early 1990s until 2008, the figure has remained relatively stable over the last three years, even going down a little in the last year (cf. 407,564 in 2008 and 425,758 in 2009). Clearly, the post-2008 economic crisis has not led to any increase at all in the number of foreigners in the country.[2] Neither has it affected the composition of foreigners—that has remained very stable over the years, with the four most numerous national groups being Ukrainians (29 per cent), Slovaks (17 per cent), the Vietnamese (14 per cent) and Russians (8 per cent).[3] This is not to say that some minor changes have not occurred; there have been reports, for instance, of a slight increase in immigration from some other EU countries, even from the traditionally more wealthy ones (e.g. Italy). This sort of reversed migration, marginal as it may be, concerns people who arrive in the Czech Republic, despite the country's comparatively lower salaries, in search of professional positions and experience and in order to escape high unemployment and related social problems in their home countries.

As regards the issue of illegal immigration, which tends to feature prominently in the media discourse in many countries, it has all but disappeared from the public attention: according to the official statistics, illegal migration has gone down from 53,116 people recorded in 2000 to just 2,987 in 2010.[4] While the 2000 figure includes over 30,000 persons who crossed the border illegally, the 2010 figure is made up of people with illegal residence only, i.e. typically those who overstay their visas. The official data does not register any illegal entrants after 2008, which is the result of the entry of the Czech Republic into the Schengen area in December 2007. Surrounded only by other EU states, the country ceased having any external Schengen borders and the chances of entering the country illegally are thus minimal. The country is no longer the point of entry for non-EU citizens, which has removed one of the crucial rhetorical moves through which foreigners are represented, i.e. their criminalization arising from the way they enter the country (cf. El Refaie, 2001).

The Czech Republic has traditionally been a transit country for various groups of migrants crossing its eastern borders on their way further to the west. That was particularly the case during the Balkans war of the 1990s, when people trafficking was prominent in border areas. The situation changed not only with the end of the military conflict but also after the entry of the country into the EU in 2004 and, particularly, when the borders were effectively dissolved after joining the Schengen area in 2007. The free movement of people within the EU and the lack of external borders mean that the issue of illegal immigration is not prominent in the society and is not perceived or presented by the media as a problem.

2.2. Foreigners and "internal outsiders"

As regards immigrants and foreign residents in the country, their presence is not very visible, at least beyond the capital city (11.5 per cent). The proportion of foreigners in the whole country (4 per cent) is relatively small—it is hardly comparable to the situation in some of the economically developed western European countries, both as regards real numbers of immigrants and their percentage in the population. In terms of the proportion of foreigners relative to the total number of inhabitants, the country ranks as the 21st in Europe, just after Portugal and before Slovenia, Hungary, the Netherlands, Finland, Latvia, Slovakia, Bulgaria, Romania and Poland.[5]

As mentioned above, the most numerous groups are Ukrainians, Slovaks, the Vietnamese and Russians. While Slovaks are not—for historical and linguistic reasons—considered as "real" foreigners, Ukrainians and Russians benefit from the similarity of their languages that belong to the same language family as Czech, and thus these speakers of Slavic tongues have the potential of merging with the majority population more easily. By contrast, the Vietnamese are the only immigrant community that is ethnically (and in the case of the first generation also linguistically) perceptibly different. They are likely to be easily identified and singled out as "others".

Together these facts indicate that immigrants and "external outsiders", groups readily construed as others and against whom the growing discontent of people at times of crises might be channelled, either are not there in sufficiently large numbers or are not ostensibly different to make them a genuine target.[6] Instead, the discourse of intolerance has become directed towards another major group of people who are ethnically, culturally and even linguistically perceived to be different from the majority: the Roma. In the Czech Republic, no official figures exist specifying the number of people who belong to this minority (unlike people of foreign origin) since such ethnic/racial profiling has become politically unacceptable. However, estimates place the number of Roma at 150,000-300,000, making them the single largest out-group within the country. Most of the Roma are Czech citizens, though some may have come from Slovakia. (The period of the break-up of Czechoslovakia in 1991 was marked by heated anti-Roma discourse arising from the fear of a possible influx of the Roma from Slovakia into what was to become the Czech Republic, possibly in anticipation of an (initially) better economic situation—cf. the analysis of the media discourse in Nekvapil and Leudar, 2002.)

The danger that, at a time of crisis, the majority population turns against not only foreigners but also against domestic out-groups is recognized in the report of the European Commission against Racism and Intolerance (ECRI):

> "The ongoing economic crisis has created a vicious cycle in which many of the groups of concern to ECRI (vulnerable groups) are trapped. Diminished economic opportunities and welfare cuts push them into poverty, which breeds negative feelings on both sides of the social divide. Immigrants and some historical minorities are perceived as a burden to society. Old myths about [...] influence in the financial world are revived. The "multiculturalism model" is questioned. Discrimination in employment is rife. Racism and intolerance are on the rise in Europe today and the resulting tension sometimes leads to racist violence". (ECRI, 2012, 7)

The emergence of intolerant, if not outright racist and xenophobic discourse is also mirrored in the rising acceptance of such discursive practices. Prominent public figures are increasingly vilifying others, particularly when verbal attacks on foreigners—as well as domestic minorities—serve as a tool for achieving their populist goals. In its Annual Report for 2011, ECRI also warns against the rise of xenophobic discourse and aggressive rhetoric which is progressively used by various parties to obtain support and gain seats in national Parliaments (ECRI, 2012, 8-9). Several examples of covert racist discourse in political advertising that skillfully plays with background knowledge and shared presuppositions concerning ethnically defined out-groups are discussed in Chovanec (2012), who observes that political discourse tends to be veiled and non-committal in order to preserve a semblance of public decency (cf. van Dijk, 1992), yet it often operates—in a hide-and-seek game of allusions, semantic indeterminacy and deniable meanings—with the same underlying racist stereotypes and assumptions as those that are openly advocated by the more extreme political groupings.

3. Methodology and theoretical assumptions

Operating within the critically-oriented tradition of discourse analysis, this study draws inspiration from the discourse-historical approach developed in the Vienna school of CDA by Ruth Wodak and her colleagues (Wodak *et al.*, 1999; Reisigl and Wodak, 2001; Wodak, 2009). When analysing particular texts, this approach considers (1) the content of the data, (2) the discursive strategies employed, and (3) the linguistic realizations of both the content and the strategies (cf. van Leeuwen and Wodak, 1999; Wodak, 2002). It aims to deconstruct, in a multi-dimensional way, the topoi and arguments encountered in political discourse and the ways in which they are recontextualized and reformulated. The "historical" dimension of the approach follows from the fact that discursive events are embedded within historical backgrounds and are subject to diachronic change (cf. van Leeuwen and Wodak, 1999).

Wodak (2002) schematizes the analysis of discourses, discourse topics, genres and texts as a complex combination of intertextual and interdiscursive relations. She operates with a notion of "context" that involves the immediate text; the intertextual and interdiscursive relationships; the extralinguistic social variables and institutional frames; as well as the sociopolitical and historical contexts within which discursive practices are embedded (Wodak, 2002, 67).

This perspective is close to van Dijk's multidisciplinary socio-cognitive approach that "tries to 'triangulate' social issues in terms of a combined study of discursive, cognitive and social dimensions of a problem" (van Dijk, 2005, 66). Van Dijk proposes that CDA should be open and multidisciplinary, drawing on eclectic tools rather than trapped in theoretical dogmas. In his view, the discipline should be critical, interested in "the role of discourse in the production and reproduction of power abuse and dominance" (van Dijk, 2002, 96).

In his earlier work on racist discourse (1992, 1993), van Dijk developed the idea of the "ideological square". This concept reflects the conviction that discourse is a socio-cognitive phenomenon and that discursive practices are governed by underlying ideologies. Racist and other discriminatory discourses are typically geared towards the discursive construction of two mutually opposed groups, the in-group (Us) and the out-group (Them), who are systematically presented and predicated in terms of a binary contrast: the positive self-presentation of the in-group and the negative other-presentation of the out-group. The recurrent affective representations of in-groups and out-groups in certain predictable ways result in the formation, strengthening and perpetuation of stereotypes. As a consequence, individuals are treated en bloc as typical representatives of their groups (cf. Fowler, 1991; Richardson, 2007).

Prejudiced public discourse about immigrants, asylum seekers and foreigners has been subject to numerous studies from a variety of critical perspectives (van Dijk, 1992; Santa Ana, 1999; El Refaie, 2001; Charteris-Black, 2006; Hart, 2011). By contrast, research on domestic minorities and other internal outcasts such as the Roma has been less frequent. Leudar and Nekvapil (2000) and Nekvapil and Leudar (2002) provided several early studies on categorization of the ethnic minority in the Czech media, as did Homoláč *et al.* (2003) with some data from the Slovak and Hungarian media as well. While Erjavec (2001) describes discriminatory anti-Roma discourse in Slovenia, Tileaga (2005) has dealt with extreme prejudice in conversations among Romanian speakers on the topic of the Roma. Arguably, there is a need to study prejudiced public discourse directed at domestic groups as well, since it can help us to understand how "the enemy within" is discursively constructed and treated. What is of interest here is how the Us group can be internally subdivided to allow for the exclusion of a particular segment of Us and its relegation into the Them group (cf. also Chovanec, 2010 for such group re-negotiation in political discourse).

Common prejudices against immigrants can be recycled to apply to other traditional out-groups in what has been called neo-racist discourse (Wodak and Matouschek, 1993). New racism is oriented towards cultural, rather than biological differences, viewing minority cultures in terms of deficiencies, dependence on welfare, and other negative characteristics (cf. van Dijk, 2000, 34). As Blackledge (2010, 145) observes, "common-sense public discourse identifies cultural practices which are different from those of the dominant group, and they become symbols of the 'Otherness' of the minority. That is, cultural practices become racialized, and come to represent a group." This is where stereotyping appears: after differences are identified, they are generalized into negative categories and assigned to whole groups. As Wodak writes:

> "It is not the existence of differences that produces discrimination or racism, but the generalization of such differences into negative categories and their attribution to whole groups, which constitutes stereotyping. Each individual experience with a foreigner, Jew, gay person etc. is viewed as explanatory for the whole group (while, interestingly, positive experiences with migrants, Jews, Others, are classified as exceptions.)" (Wodak, 2008, 295)

Even stronger kinds of prejudiced discourse can be directed against marginalized domestic groups such as the Roma. They are not only perceived as distinct from the dominant group and denied inclusion within the "Us" in-group but subject to an even stronger degree of alienation. They may be conceived of as beyond the human realm and represented in terms of animalistic metaphors. Tileaga (2005, 603), when writing about the Roma, notes that they are subject to discourse that is "more extreme than the anti-alien, anti-immigrant prejudiced talk" because they "are not merely portrayed as being different, but also as being beyond the moral order, beyond nationhood, difference and comparison". Blackledge (2010, 144), in reference to Schmidt (2002) makes a similar point about the general process of "racialization", which is the process of ascribing "to groups certain characteristics which render them so foreign or 'alien' that it is impossible to conceive of them as equal members of the same community as the dominant group".

To illustrate the stereotypical perception and representation of some domestic out-groups, the following section sets out to analyse two recent cases from the Czech media. I show how the media recontextualize news reports involving members of out-groups in terms of stereotypes present in the majority populations, while noting the emphasis they place on the ethnic background of the social actors, even when it is of no material relevance to the case.

4. The media in search of outsiders

This section discusses two cases that deal with minority groups in the media. Both revolve around the representation of victims and perpetrators of criminal offences—the first case describes how the media probed into family background to evoke the majority group's ethnic stereotypes, and the second case notes how proper names and category labels were used to cancel out negative stereotypes arising from foreign origin, as long as another out-group could be targeted through negative stereotyping.

4.1. Case 1: The Vietnamese and ethnic profiling

In March 2012, a Czech lobbyist—who had just been exposed in the media as being in a very close and friendly contact with the former Mayor of Prague in a scandal that amounted to one of the most serious allegations of clientelism and political corruption in the country—failed to brake at a red traffic signal and collided with the car in front of him. When the other driver, a Vietnamese woman, got out and approached his car, the lobbyist struck her down with his car and drove away. Shortly afterwards, the man was captured by the police who chased him down in a park some distance away. While the man, whose breath test revealed that he was under the influence of alcohol, was rather informally handled by the police, the woman driver was taken to hospital with serious injuries. In the days that followed, the incident filled the front pages of newspapers, particularly in connection with the non-standard treatment of the lobbyist by the police and the speculations of his possible political connections. Little was known about the victim other than the initially provided information that she was Vietnamese and drove a Volvo.

A few days after the event, the Czech online daily newspaper *Týden.cz* published a short interview with the woman driver's lawyer. The interview consisted of 13 brief questions, out of which 2 dealt with the woman's physical and mental condition, 4 addressed the way the police handled the lobbyist after the accident and the legal classification of his acts and 2 were general questions about the woman's police protection and the possibility of her comments for the media. What is significant, however, is that 5 of the 13 questions probed the woman's background, although such information was not relevant to the case at all. The questions in point are provided below, together with the lawyer's answers made on behalf of his female client.[7] The questions are analyzed and interpreted to illustrate the preoccupation of the media with ethnic stereotypes since they reveal implicit prejudices that are likely to have been at play in this case.

(1)

	English translation	Czech original
Q5	Has her family already had any bad experience of a similar kind during its stay in our republic?	Má její rodina již nějaké špatné zkušenosti podobného ražení z pobytu v naší republice?
A5	They have been here for a long time, I think since 1984. They have never encountered anything like that.	Jsou tady již dlouhou dobu, myslím, že od roku 1984. Nikdy se s ničím podobným nesetkali.
Q6	Has any family member been criminally prosecuted?	Byl někdo z nich trestně stíhán?
A6	No. They have never had any conflict with law.	Nikoli. Žádný konflikt se zákonem nikdy neměli.
Q7	Do they have any connection with the infamous Vietnamese SAPA Market Hall in Prague, which is considered as the hotbed of crime?	Mají něco společného s neblaze proslulou vietnamskou tržnicí SAPA v Praze, která je považována za semeniště zločinu?
A7	Certainly not. They work completely elsewhere.	Rozhodně ne. Pracují úplně jinde.
Q8	In what field?	V jakém oboru?
A8	I would not like to disclose that. The husband is an entrepreneur, my client works with him.	To bych nechtěl prozrazovat. Manžel je podnikatel, klientka pracuje s ním.
Q9	What do their children do?	Co dělají jejich děti?
A9	The son is studying at university and so is the daughter, I guess.	Syn studuje vysokou školu a dcera tuším již také.
		(Source: týden.cz, 26 March 2012)

Let's consider how the newspaper, which enjoys a good reputation in print and online, handles the issue of "otherness" and the related stereotypes. This part of the interview reveals a strong prejudice since the questions would not, in most likelihood, have been asked if the victim's minority ethnicity had not been known.

The section of the interview reproduced above is noteworthy for several phenomena underlying its interpretation of the text as a strong example of prejudiced and xenophobic discourse. The noteworthy elements include the presuppositions, the manipulation of the social roles of the discourse participants, the generalization of the issue from a single individual to her family, and the construction of dichotomizing group contrasts that draw on background assumptions and negative ethnic stereotypes. The phenomena are related. I discuss them turn by turn in the sections below.

After establishing general information about the case, the interview proceeds with Question 5: "*Has her family already had any bad experience of a similar kind during its stay in our republic?*". This opens the section that is focused on the "discourse of otherness". The actual formulation of Question 5 may appear as somewhat unclear. The interviewer uses the vague phrase "*of a similar kind*", which can hardly be taken literally: how could any prior involvement in a traffic accident (cf. "*bad experience of a similar kind*") be relevant in this particular case?[8]

An extensive interpretation of the question seems more likely: It aims to elicit any negative experience suffered by the family. The question could be interpreted as a sympathetic act on the part of the journalist, who—using the prompt "*of a similar kind*"—tries to obtain information about possible unlawful acts directed against the woman and her family. However, as the other questions in the interview reveal, it is a quasi-sympathy that launches a persistent probing into the family background. The question is insidious in that it concerns the woman's family rather than just herself. It appears to make sense only if it is read in connection with the stereotype that presupposes the likelihood of such an experience, while the generalization of the issue from a single individual to other family members is possibly the result of seeing the victim through the lens of her ethnicity. She is perceived as a foreigner rather than a victim of an offence. Should the interviewer's question be information-seeking only, rather than exploiting an underlying stereotype of otherness, it would have been formulated as **Has anything like that happened to her before?* An information-seeking question like that would lack the bias contained in Question 5 because it would not perform the metonymic generalization of the victim (of a *pars pro toto* type, i.e. one stands for all) that is common in cases of out-group members, and it would not represent the victim explicitly as an outsider.

Question 5 also has a discourse-organizing function: it provides an introductory frame for the questions that follow. Through Question 5, the journalist sets the agenda by introducing the negative concept of "bad experience" or "trouble" in connection with not only the victim but also her entire family. Such a generalization is related to the discursive strategy of collectivization, through which individuals are presented as representatives of larger groups (cf. van Leeuwen, 1996). The strategy is much less commonly applied in connection with the majority group, whose members are treated on an individual basis and whose individual acts are much less likely perceived as being representative of the larger group. In the data under analysis, the link between the family and the negative concept of "trouble" is sustained across several turns. That is so regardless of the fact that any shade of doubt is eventually expelled: the link is made nevertheless.

Interestingly, the negative context into which the victim and the family are placed is not static; it develops with the questions that follow. From the point of view of semantic role analysis (cf. Fowler, 1991; Richardson, 2007), Question 5 places the woman and her family into the role of victims, passive experiencers of negative actions. With the next question, however, the perspective not only shifts but it is reversed. While Question 5 represents the family as semantic patients of an impersonal process ("X happening to THEM"), Question 6 represents the family in the same semantic role through the passive structure (cf. *Has any family member been criminally prosecuted?*). The unexpressed agent is, of course, "the police" (omitted in the passive but retrievable on the basis of shared knowledge of the "criminal prosecution" script), yielding the passive syntactic structure of "THEY are criminally prosecuted [by the police]" that is being queried. However, this structure is merely a surface phenomenon, since—in terms of the representation of social actors—there is another underlying predication, namely "THEY have committed a crime". That predication is much more significant since it reveals the inference-based operation of the negative stereotype about the out-group: if someone is criminally prosecuted, it means that they have committed (or are suspected of having committed) unlawful acts. The victim and her family are predicated as having an underlying semantic agency, connecting them with the anticipated violation of law. The shift from Question 5 to Question 6 thus embodies a discursive shift in the rhetorical construction of others: the representation of THEM switches from victims to perpetrators. It does not matter that the proposition which the question addresses is eventually turned down: what is significant is the fact that the question is raised at all, with that particular stereotype-based proposition built into it.

In addition to introducing the negative frame, Question 5—as mentioned above—achieves an important discursive transformation by re-contextualizing the individual victim into the basic binary contrast present in discriminatory discourse, the "Us" vs. "Them" dichotomy. The way this contrast is worked into the interview is achieved by means of extending the current bad experience of a single individual to the possible bad experience of the entire family in the past. The victim is thus not treated as an individual person but becomes collectivized within her family. This pluralizes the victim, who does not need to be discursively handled as an individual anymore and becomes subsumed within a group instead. And, as part of a group, the victim can be more easily perceived or predicated in opposition to other groups than if she were to be presented as a single individual. Once the victim is collectivized into the group-denoting expression "family", she can be presented as an outsider—a member of the out-group—"Them"—that contrasts with "Us".

There are two lexical indications in the journalist's question that construct the group contrast between what might be (with reservations) described as "Foreigners" vs. "Us". The first is the phrase "*during its stay*", which indicates temporality rather than permanent presence within the country. The phrase implies outside origin and the existence of two distinct times "before arriving here" and "after arriving here". The second is the immediately following prepositional phrase "*in our republic*" that subtly co-constructs and enhances the contrast between the discursively established groups. In Czech, the phrase "*in our republic*" ("*v naší republice*") is used as a relatively common way of referring to the country. The use of the possessive pronoun *our*, however, is significant in that it implies a binary contrast of "Us" vs. "Them", even in the absence of any mention of an out-group. That is not the case, however, in Question 5: since the family has already been established as a group and predicated as an outside group (cf. "*during its stay*"), the pronoun *our* is explicitly involved in presenting the victim and her family as "others", foreigners or non-Czechs. The contrast indicates that the pronoun is used as a so-called exclusive we. This conclusion seems to be supported by the fact that the journalist certainly had other options to choose from—there is a whole paradigmatic set of expressions that code the concept of "here" in a more neutral and less dichotomizing way, such as "*in this country*" ("*v této zemi*"), "*in the Czech Republic*" ("*v České republice*") or "*in Czechia*" ("*v Česku*"). Although the choice of the phrase "*in our republic*" may have been unconscious, it articulates the underlying dichotomizing perspective which excludes Them from the majority group.

As regards Question 6 ("*Has any family member been criminally prosecuted?*"), it has been shown above to reverse the orientation of the semantic roles of the family members from the general context of "sufferers of bad experience" to "perpetrators of criminality". Significantly, the question not only realizes the switch of the role from passive recipients/experiencers to active doers, but also establishes a more specific, though certainly different situation. Namely, the vague and semantically indeterminate "*bad experience of a similar kind*" in Question 5 (possibly referring to the accident or other negative acts directed against the family) is turned into the highly specific process of "*being criminally prosecuted*" in Question 6. Although the lawyer could have objected to such an irrelevant—and offensive—question, he did provide an answer in the negative by extending the negative scope of the proposition to "*any conflict with law*", not just criminal matters.

By giving the answer to the highly problematic Question 6 ("*No. They have never had any conflict with law.*")—as well as answering the questions that follow—the lawyer helps to construct the client's family as respectable and counters the stereotypes and prejudices to which it could otherwise be subject to by the public or in media speculations. The point is that when confronted with a series of such biased questions, a speaker may not really have the option of objecting to the inappropriateness and irrelevance of the information that the questions seek to establish and the stereotypes that they presuppose. Any refusal to answer such questions could be interpreted as an admission of the validity of the stereotype which is being probed since by refusing to answer, the speaker could be seen as both unable to answer in the negative and not willing to answer in the affirmative, instead attacking the grounds on which such unjustifiable questions are asked. The doggedness with which such questions are asked might be defended by some as the journalist's committed dedication to discovering the facts, though it is, rather, a manifestation of the underlying discriminatory and racist ideologies that the journalist does not resist voicing.

Question 6, along with the remaining questions, would not, in all probability, be asked if the victim was a Czech citizen of local ethnic origin. Without a corresponding negative stereotype affecting the majority population, there would be no purpose in trying to establish the nature of the criminal history, economic livelihood and similar details of the victim of a criminal act, not to speak of establishing similar credentials for other family members. This particular question needs to be seen as the journalist's articulation of the culturally shared stereotype of associating the Vietnamese community with socially pathological phenomena by presuming their criminality. Owing to racist prejudice, the presumption of criminality remains until it is disclaimed.

In Question 7 ("*Do they have any connection to the infamous Vietnamese SAPA Market Hall in Prague, which is considered as the hotbed of crime?*"), the negative stereotype of crime is pursued by the journalist once again. Although all potential problems with law have been discounted in the lawyer's previous answer ("*No. They have never had any conflict with law.*"), this question builds on the same stereotype, yet somewhat differently—by trying to associate the family with the "foreigner crime" stereotype in a less direct way. The question is very general, seeking to verify any connection with a major market place that forms the centre of Vietnamese-run trade and that has suffered from a bad reputation (at least among non-Vietnamese citizens), partly on account of police raids in search of pirated trademark goods and the negative presentation in the media etc. However, the journalist not only mentions the negative evaluation of the place in his question ("*infamous*") but also adds a relative clause with a passive verb that communicates a "general truth" (cf. the unacknowledged source of the proposition in the passive construction "*is considered*") about the link of the place to crime ("*hotbed of crime*").

The question is interesting because of the degree of explicitness with which it is formulated. If the journalist had been trying to establish the facts (in this otherwise entirely irrelevant matter), he could have avoided the evaluative explication of the underlying prejudice, which not only reactivates but also strengthens the stereotype in the readers' minds. Should the answer to the question be in the positive, it would link the victim's family to crime again, despite the negative answer to Question 6, because of the possible but wrong inference that "if someone has anything to do with a place that is seen as a hotbed of crime, they are (most likely) associated with crime." The mere association of any family member with the place would associate the family, and thus the victim, with the negative stereotype of "criminality" based on the topos of justice (cf. Wodak, 2009). On the formal level of linguistic analysis, it also needs to be mentioned that the phrase "*hotbed of crime*" (the literal translation from Czech is "seeding-place", an expression that collocates with "disease") is a token of an underlying metaphor that could be stated as "ETHNIC CRIME IS A DISEASE": it points out that crime is not contained within a limited place but spreads, disease-style, to other areas from a central place. On a broader level, it is related to the relatively common metaphorical presentation of immigrants and other outsiders as a threat (cf. Lynn and Lea, 2003; Martín Rojo and van Dijk, 1997).

Finally, in Questions 8 and 9, the interviewer continues to pursue the stereotype-inspired agenda of establishing whether the family has any problematic background, first by asking in what area of business they are involved (Q8: "*In what field?*") and then establishing similar information about their children (Q9: "*What do their children do?*"). In the former case, the lawyer declines to specify, merely pointing out a general type of activity (A8: "*The husband is an entrepreneur...*") and in the latter he provides information that can actually counter the negative stereotype (A9: "*The son is studying at university and so is the daughter, I guess.*"). After such extensive questioning, the media—and the public—can rest assured that there is nothing in the victim's (and the family's) background that could potentially be objected to. It is as if it has finally been established that there is nothing that would justify why the victim should NOT be viewed as anything else than what she is: the victim of a criminal offence.

The extract in (1) above indicates that the media can have a prurient interest in irrelevant matters that are raised solely on account of a person's ethnic background. The interest originates in the stereotypes and prejudices that the majority group may hold about a particular ethnic/minority community.

My analysis of the extract also finds that while relatively little information is communicated explicitly in the interview, a number of other significant facts can be inferred from the shared cultural context in which the interview takes places. There are at least three inferences that can be drawn from the extract and the little information known about the victim at the time of the interview. Inevitably, the inferences contribute towards the characterization of the victim:

(1) Since the family came into the country in 1984 (28 years ago), their arrival has little connection with contemporary patterns of immigration. Prior to 1989, the then Czechoslovakia had a number of agreements with other socialist countries under which workers from "friendly" countries (such as Vietnam) were invited to receive training and professional skills in a wide range of fields. That also means that these visiting workers who stayed in the country represent a different form of immigration from the one that most European countries face today. This is a case not of immigrants coming into the country but of guest workers not returning to their country of origin.

(2) It can also be inferred that the children are likely to have been born in the Czech Republic and spent their entire lives there, i.e. constituting a second generation that tends to become—except for its ethnic origin—indistinguishable from the local population as regards its linguistic skills, lifestyle, etc. That, of course, raises further questions about the validity of predicating the family as "others" and, more generally, how and when people of foreign origin—immigrants and their descendants—eventually come to be perceived as "us", or whether such a perception is possible at all, since individuals of certain ethnic backgrounds may be automatically presupposed not to be local citizens but "outsiders".

(3) Finally, a significant socio-economic inference can be drawn from the type of car that the woman drove: since a Volvo is by no means a common choice among Czechs; this brand (mentioned in

countless media reports and visually shown in TV broadcasts) indicates that the Vietnamese family must have been very successful in its business and is probably economically better off than the average Czech household. That inference may, in fact, have partly motivated the journalist's questions about the family background, particularly when it becomes interpreted in connection with the commonly held stereotype of the economic success of out-group members being the result of underhand, if not downright criminal, activities. That might explain the vehemence with which the journalist tries to establish the source of the economic wealth of the family by mentioning the frame of "illegal activities (see questions 6, 7, and 8) that amounts to one quarter of the brief interview.

4.2. Case 2: The Roma "did it"

The ethnic profiling documented in the previous case will be briefly contrasted with the differential treatment of people of foreign origin who find themselves presented as victims of crime, as illustrated in the next case. It is argued that foreign origin is partly backgrounded when prejudicial discourse becomes refocused on a different out-group: the Roma.

In April 2012, the media broadcast news of violent attack committed by three youths against a 15-year-old boy of Ukrainian origin in a small Czech town for refusing to give a cigarette to them. According to the boy's testimony, at least one of the attackers was a Roma. While no offenders were apprehended, the major claim to the story's newsworthiness appeared to be the easily accessible stereotype of "the Roma committing violent crime for no reason" that was reactivated by the claims of the alleged attackers' ethnic origin. The story was readily taken up by the media and remained the focus of public interest for over a month because of its serious consequences (see below). The unsubstantiated speculation of the ethnic origin of the offenders came to be taken for a fact, cf. the following:

(2a)	It may happen to another person, pleads the mother of the boy brutally beaten up by the Roma	Může se to stát dalšímu, burcuje matka chlapce brutálně zbitého Romy (17 Apr 2012, idnes.cz)

(2b)	*It is not the first Roma attack* This is not the first attack of aggressive Roma in Břeclav, whose victim was an unsuspecting member of the majority community. Four Roma are, according to the court, responsible for an assault during which they first attacked a Vietnamese owner of a game-hall in September 2010. [...]	*Nejde o první útok Romů* V Břeclavi se nejedná o první útok agresivních Romů, jejichž obětí byl nic netušící příslušník majoritní komunity. Čtyři Romové podle soudu mají na svědomí útok, při němž v září roku 2010 nejprve napadli vietnamského majitele herny. [...] (Source: www.novinky.cz, 16 April 2012)

The headline in (2a) illustrates that the alleged ethnic origin is taken for granted: it is not hedged or mitigated in any way, e.g. by means of the customary scare quotes used in the press to indicate reservation or distance from coded content. The subheadline from a different story in (2b) is similar, though it also expands the factual assumption by pointing out other—unrelated—incidents. It is noteworthy that the text in (2b) mentions a game-hall operated by a Vietnamese owner—an individual who might otherwise find it difficult to be co-classified with the "majority community".

The "beaten boy" case went on to develop in several directions. First, outrage at the boy's injuries led to a large public demonstration, originally organized by an extremist group, formally as a rally against violence. It was, however, generally understood as an anti-Roma protest, as was also clear from the placards carried by some of the participants. Second, three weeks after the event, one media channel broadcast the speculation (allegedly leaked from the police investigation) that the attack was an act of revenge on a drug dealer for supplying low-quality marihuana, which was hotly denied by the boy. Finally, in the most scandalous twist, it was revealed that the whole case was actually a hoax: the boy suffered the injuries as a result of falling out of a balcony when showing off to his friends and was afraid tell the truth to his mother. Instead, he made up the story of a Roma attack—a story that was only too plausible given the negative ethnic stereotype associated with this particular minority group. The entire event was subsequently widely commented on as an example of racist thinking on the part of the majority population as well as the media. The case highlighted an increased tendency to ascribe blame to the Roma for various kinds of incidents, including events that are entirely made up.[9]

Let us now very briefly juxtapose Case 1 and Case 2 to point out the complexity with which out-groups are constructed in the media. In both cases, the victims were members of immigrant communities and the media focus was primarily on the real and alleged offenders. However, the first case did not allow for the easy construction of an ethnically-based dichotomy of Us vs. Them since the offender was a member of the majority society, despite being a lobbyist associated strongly with political corruption, e.g. white-collar crime. The first case—also owing to the silence of the victim and her family—generated only a minimum of victim-focused stories but when it did, the person's foreign origin featured prominently. In the second case, by contrast, the Roma origin of the alleged perpetrators allowed for the possibility of redefining the whole event in terms of the Us vs. Them dichotomy, and pointing at "the enemy within". The number of media reports was striking and there were several interviews with the boy's mother, as well as mediated comments from the boy. However, in none of the articles was the family's background analyzed and it was only from incidental descriptive information that the public could work out that the family had actually immigrated to the country some 12 years previously. The national origin of the family was never highlighted, nor was it worked by the media into descriptive phrases.

The foreigner stereotype was present in some media reports, but only obliquely. For instance, some of the reports proceeded with identifying the boy's mother with a descriptive category label ("*'Why are rascals protected here more than we who work honestly and pay taxes,' says the university educated court translator angrily.*"[10]). Arguably, such a description cues a positive context that goes counter to the traditional stereotype of an immigrant/foreigner. Moreover, the use of the descriptive label precedes the media's mention of the mother's proper name, which comes later on in the text and which is distinctly foreign in its transliteration and easily recognizable as Ukrainian. If used initially, i.e. before the positive category label, the mere occurrence of the name could trigger the available (negative) stereotype. Used as it is, however, it cancels the stereotype by pre-emptively blocking possible negative prejudices that do not, unlike the analyzed interview in Case 1, come into play at all.

5. Conclusion

As argued in the article, the media significantly contribute to the formation of public opinion by tapping into existing negative stereotypes of ethnic and other minorities and engaging in a discourse of intolerance, prejudice, racism and xenophobia. In the Czech Republic, which lacks visible immigrant minorities, such prejudicial discourse tends to be channeled towards internal out-groups which, despite their citizenship, are systematically constructed as “others”. Some minorities, such as the Roma, are seen in more negative light than others. The media are attracted by mere suggestions or hints of suspected Roma involvement in criminal cases. Irrelevant claims of possible ethnic background are commonly presented as a fact and other incidents are cited in support of the underlying negative stereotype. The analysis of the first case has documented that a family of foreign origin may become subject to extensive questioning of their background in the media as if to make sure that there is no reason for considering the victim and the victim’s family as the out-group. The second case has illustrated how proper names and category labels can be dynamically used to cancel out potential negative stereotypes arising from a person’s foreign origin, particularly when this assists the negative representation of another out-group and the compassionate perception of the victims. It seems that in the case of minority groups, the presumption of innocence does not apply—they are deemed criminal unless proven otherwise.

Notes

1. Source: http://www.czso.cz/csu/cizinci.nsf/t/90003B917F/$File/c01r01.pdf
2. Neither has immigration increased in consequence of the political changes in North Africa in 2011, as was the case in some EU countries (ECRI, 2012, 9).
3. Data from the Czech Statistical Office as of 31.12.2010, http://www.czso.cz/csu/cizinci.nsf/engtab/B900404628.
4. See the chart in section on Illegal Migration at http://www.czso.cz/csu/ cizinci.nsf/engkapitola/ciz_nelegalni_migrace.
5. Source: Czech Statistical Office, www.czso.cz/czu/cizinci (based on Eurostat data collected as of 1.1.2010).
6. Of course, the absence of a target does not mean that intolerant discourse will be absent as well. For instance, some countries may have a strong anti-Semitic discourse despite the minimal number of Jewish people living there (such as Poland). Similarly, a recent poll in March 2012 has indicated that 42 per cent of Czechs believe that employing foreigners is wrong. The commonly held false stereotype that “foreigners take our jobs” has been strengthened since 2008, when fewer than one third of respondents answered the question in the same way. (Cf. the press release of the Public Opinion Research Centre of the Institute of Sociology of the Academy of Sciences of the Czech Republic, available online at www.cvvm.cas.cz/upl/zpravy/101272s_ov 120416.pdf.) Given that the number of foreigners has not changed, the shift in public opinion may reflect growing anti-foreigner sentiment among the majority population, arguably in consequence of the worsening economic situation during the crisis.

7. All translations into English by JC. The full text of the interview is available (in Czech) at the web page http://www.tyden.cz/rubriky/domaci/pravnik-srazene-zeny-vyslychat-janouska-opileho-je-na-nic_229278.html
8. The translation does not exactly correspond to the Czech original since Czech tends not to use any determiners in such questions as 5 and 6, particularly where the English determiner "some" would grammatically indicate a positive bias while "any" would be comparatively neutral. Although "any" appears in the English translation, it cannot be established with certainty whether the Czech formulation in Q5 presupposes some bad experience or not (cf. particularly the adverb "už" in the original, which might point towards the former, though it shows less positive bias than its English counterpart "already").
9. Not only do crime reports involving the Roma tend to be selected by the media but there were also at least three other false accusations of alleged Roma criminality in the preceding months.
10. Source: www.novinky.cz, 16 April 2012

References

Blackledge, Adrian. 2010. "Lost in translation? Racialization of a debate about language in a BBC news item". In *Language Ideologies and Media Discourse*, eds. Sally Johnson and Tommaso M. Milani, 143–161. London: Continuum Books.

Charteris-Black, Jonathan 2006. "Britain as a container: Immigration metaphors in the 2005 election campaign". *Discourse & Society* 17 (6): 563–582.

Chovanec, Jan. 2010. "Legitimation through differentiation: Discursive construction of Jacques *Le Worm* Chirac as an opponent to military action". In *Perspectives in Politics and Discourse*, eds. Urszula Okulska and Piotr Cap, 61–81. Amsterdam and Philadelphia: John Benjamins.

—. 2012 "Implicit meanings and racism in political advertising". In *Discourse Interpretation: Approaches and Applications*, eds. Olga Dontcheva-Navratilova and Renata Povolná, 55–78. Newcastle upon Tyne: Cambridge Scholars Publishing.

ECRI. 2012. *Annual Report on ECRI's Activities covering the period from 1 January to 31 December 2011*. CRI (2012) 23. http://www.coe.int/t/dghl/monitoring/ecri/activities/Annual_Reports/Annual report 2011.pdf. Last accessed on 24 April 2012.

El Refaie, Elisabeth. 2001. "Metaphors we discriminate by: Naturalized themes in Austrian newspaper articles about asylum seekers". *Journal of Sociolinguistics* 5 (3): 352–371.

Erjavec, Karmen. 2001. "Media Representation of the Discrimination against the Roma in Eastern Europe: The Case of Slovenia". *Discourse & Society* 12: 699–727.

Fowler, Roger. 1991. *Language in the News. Language and Ideology in the Press*. London: Routledge.

Hart, Christopher. 2011. "Moving beyond metaphor in the Cognitive Linguistic approach to CDA". In *Critical Discourse Studies in Context and Cognition*, ed. Christopher Hart, 171–192. Amsterdam and Philadelphia: John Benjamins.

Homoláč, Jiří, Kamila Karhanová and Jiří Nekvapil (eds.). 2003. *Obraz Romů v středoevropských masmédiích po roce 1989. [Presentations of Roma/Gypsies in the Central European Media after 1989]*. http://ulug.ff.cuni.cz/projekty/romove/obraz_romu.pdf, Praha. Last accessed on 24 April 2012.

Leudar, Ivan and Jiří Nekvapil. 2000. "Presentations of Romanies in the Czech media: On category work in television debates". *Discourse & Society* 11: 487–513.

Lynn, Nick and Susan Lea. 2003. "'A phantom menace and the new Apartheid': the social construction of asylum-seekers in the United Kingdom". *Discourse & Society* 14 (4): 425–452.

Martín Rojo, Luisa and Teun A. van Dijk. 1997. "'There was a Problem and It Was Solved!': Legitimating the Expulsion of 'Illegal' Migrants in Spanish Parliamentary Discourse". *Discourse & Society* 8 (4): 523–66.

Nekvapil, Jiří and Ivan Leudar. 2002. "On dialogical networks: Arguments about the migration law in Czech mass media in 1993". In *Language, Interaction and National Identity. Studies in the Social Organization of National Identity in Talk-in-Interaction*, eds. Stephen Hester and William Housley, 60–101. Aldershot: Ashgate.

Reisigl, Martin and Ruth Wodak. 2001. *Discourse and Discrimination*. London: Routledge.

Richardson, John E. 2007. *Analysing Newspapers. An Approach from Critical Discourse Analysis*. Basingstoke: Palgrave Macmillan.

Santa Ana, Otto. 1999. "Like an animal I was treated': anti-immigrant metaphor in US public discourse". *Discourse & Society* 10 (2): 191–224.

Tileaga, Cristian. 2005. "Accounting for extreme prejudice and legitimating blame in talk about the Romanies". *Discourse & Society* 16 (5): 603–624.

van Dijk, Teun A. 1992. "Discourse and the denial of racism." *Discourse & Society* 3: 87–118.

—. 1993. *Elite Discourse and Racism.* London: Sage Publications.
—. 2000. "New(s) Racism: A discourse analytical approach". In *Ethnic Minorities and the Media*, ed. Simon Cottle, 33–49. Milton Keynes, UK: Open University Press.
—. 2002. "Discourse and racism". In *The Blackwell Companion to Racial and Ethnic Studies*, eds. David Goldberg and John Solomos, 145–159. Oxford: Blackwell.
—. 2005. "War rhetoric of a little ally: Political implicatures of Aznar's Legitimization of the War in Iraq." *Journal of Language and Politics* 4 (1): 65–92.
van Leeuwen, Theo. 1996. "The representation of social actors". In *Texts and Practices: Readings in Critical Discourse Analysis*, eds. Carmen Rosa Caldas-Coulthard and Malcolm Coulthard, 32–70. London: Routledge.
van Leeuwen, Theo and Ruth Wodak. 1999. "Legitimizing immigration control: A discourse-historical approach." *Discourse Studies* 1 (1): 83–118.
Wodak, Ruth. 2002. "The discourse-historical approach". In *Methods of Critical Discourse Analysis*, ed. Ruth Wodak, 63–94. London: Sage Publications.
—. 2008. "The contribution of critical linguistics to the analysis of discriminatory prejudices and stereotypes in the language of politics." In *Handbook of Communication in the Public Sphere*, eds. Ruth Wodak and Veronika Koller, 291–316. Berlin: Mouton de Gruyter.
—. 2009. 'The semiotics of racism. A Critical Discourse-Historical Analysis.' In *Discourse, of Course. An Overview of Research in Discourse Studies*, ed. Jan Renkema, 311–326. Amsterdam and Philadelphia: John Benjamins.
Wodak, Ruth and Bernd Matouschek. 1993. "'We are dealing with people whose origins one can clearly tell just by looking': Critical discourse analysis and the study of neo-racism in contemporary Austria". *Discourse & Society* 4 (2): 225–248.
Wodak, Ruth, Rudolf de Cillia, Martin Reisigl and Karin Liebhart. 1999. *The Discursive Construction of National Identity.* Edinburgh: Edinburgh University Press.

CHAPTER NINE

HOW THE MEDIA AFFECT INTERCULTURAL RELATIONSHIPS IN TIMES OF CHANGE

NICOLÁS LORITE GARCÍA
UNIVERSITAT AUTÒNOMA DE BARCELONA
MIGRACOM[1]

1. Introduction

The financial crisis has led to transformations in the media's treatment of certain social dynamics, especially since 2010. It is important to bear these in mind in order to better understand how the Spanish media address immigration, thereby stimulating intercultural encounters and ideologically positioning themselves to represent these new social collectives, which the media have referred to as "sin papeles" (undocumented), "residentes" (residents), "irregulares" (irregulars) and "ilegales" (illegals).

Demographic data, particularly migration flows (INE, 2012), help us to better understand the changing media treatment of social issues. The arrival of the crisis has brought immigration to Spain to a standstill, while the number of immigrants leaving the country has increased. Rising unemployment and the challenges of surviving in the "promised land" have led many immigrants who moved to Spain during years of economic prosperity to return to their countries of origin. At the same time, the country is witnessing a new cycle wherein Spaniards are immigrating to other European countries like Germany, harkening back to the migration of the sixties and seventies. However, there is a key difference between these two periods: the earlier cycle was quantitative, seeking large numbers of untrained workers (since manpower of any type was sufficient to fill lower-level positions), whereas the current cycle is qualitative, seeking specialized workers with a university education.

The constant changes in the media brought on by the crisis are also of key importance (FAPE, 2012). Media outlets are constantly restructuring, merging and tightening their budgets; some have even closed up shop for good. Press, radio, and television – both state-run and regional outlets (which capture the attention of the most important audiences and consequently have the greatest impact on public opinion) – have significantly reduced staff, endeavoring to squeeze the same content out of employees who are working longer hours for lower pay – a key thrust of modern capitalism. Although it is difficult to obtain reliable data, it is thought that in Spain approximately 6,000 journalism jobs have been lost and 60 media outlets have closed since 2006, including excellent channels like *CNN+*. In addition to affecting the quality of news reporting, these decisions have shut down initiatives launched in moments of economic growth (and the increases in immigration which came with them). For example, we have lost journalists specializing in migration, who helped to provide more precise, factual information, thereby fostering a fair treatment of sociocultural diversity and avoiding discrimination in the form of racism and xenophobia.

These changes in how the media treat social issues in this time of crisis also impact regional media, particularly those local media outlets which are supported by public administrations (e.g. municipal press offices, municipal radio stations, local television channels, etc.). These microcontextual media were formed in the late '70s alongside the democratic government in Spain and have focused on stimulating positive relationships between people from diverse geographic, cultural and religious origins. Yet due to local budget cuts, they can no longer live up to their full possibilities.

However, new media and communication models have emerged alongside the crisis. These include internet-based options in the form of social networks like Facebook and Twitter, personal blogs and forums. As various types of media converge and new technological options like tablets and advances in cellular phones (which are constantly connected to the internet and feature "free" messaging services like WhatsApp) find success, they give rise to bidirectional, instantaneous ways of interacting with news. These innovations are seen as more decentralized and "democratic" than the traditional unidirectional model, yet are bound by the limitations of any new type of technology, which include the financial limitations of users and the ability of individuals to interact with them. Young people and teenagers are said to find them much easier to use. In fact, a hypothesis currently being considered suggests that these new communicative systems increase segregation and give rise to more multiculturalism than interculturalism, creating ghettos and having a racist and/or xenophobic impact rather than fostering respect for diversity. While it is true that information spreads more quickly and users become content producers in modern media, this also leads to an exponential increase in clichés and stereotypes about "others" and their different social, cultural and religious identities.

In any case, general-interest media outlets – particularly those which are part of the largest multimedia corporations in Spain (*Prisa, Vocento, Recoletos, Godó* and *Mediapro*) – as well as the most important news agency in the country, EFE, continue to hold clear social power (which is linked to political and economic power). Indeed, this has always been the case with the classical one-way communication model, which sent news messages from producers to recipients without any form of feedback. Public opinion continues to be "guided" by the news and by specific cases which these large media corporations select and broadcast; content is chosen by their editorial departments and follows traditional news routines, aligning with their editorial policies and political and ideological approaches.

However, at the same time, the crisis continues to give rise to news stories featuring a two-fold (explicit and implicit) perspective on immigration and the intercultural relationships between immigrants and the local population. In other words, although each media outlet implicitly has its own way of portraying migration (which is related to its editorial policy, sometimes leading it to take an inclusive or marginalizing approach to migration), all media outlets explicitly seem to condemn violent, racist and xenophobic attitudes toward immigrants. The media also seem to coincide in adopting a pro-European or even Eurocentric approach (Lorite, 2010). In other words, the media explicitly condemn racist and xenophobic attitudes, but do so from a European viewpoint which defends the values of a European society (though this has recently been called into question as a somewhat muddled boundary of the common territory has been outlined), remaining fairly defensive about "us" versus the "other," particularly in times of crisis.

2. Media expectations around multiple ethnicities: The case of Salt

All media – whether local or general, public or private – are waiting to see how coexistence between the native Catalan population (composed of Catalan-speaking, predominantly Catholic individuals born in Catalonia who follow regional traditions) and recent immigrants (who come from a variety of continents, cultures, languages and religions) pans out. As an example, they look (perhaps unconsciously) to towns like Salt, a municipality in the traditional geographic center of Catalonia with a population of 30,000. Immigrants comprise 45% of the town's population; the majority of these individuals arrived over the course of only seven years, between 2000 and 2007. Nevertheless, media coverage there has clearly chosen to focus on conflict rather than on normalization and integration. This is again in line with the maxim that "good news is no news" (Rodrigo, 2005), and is reflected in news reports about the town.

One story of conflict which received both national and international attention took place in January 2011. Mohamed Reda, a 16-year old boy, died when he fell from a roof after hiding from the local police who, according to Montse Barrera's report in the Catalan newspaper *El Punt Avui* on January 15, 2011, "el perseguia pels carrers de Salt mentre conduïa un ciclomotor suposadament robat" (chased him through the streets of Salt while he was riding a moped alleged to be stolen). Before he died, "Una cinquantena de joves es van concentrar [...] davant de l'ajuntament i després es van dispersar pel municipi, on van cremar set contenidors" (some fifty young adults assembled [...] in front of the town hall and then scattered across the municipality, where they set fire to seven dumpsters). The article's title, "Aldarulls a Salt en un acte de suport al lladre malferit" (Riots in Salt in support of badly wounded thief), took for granted that the individual in question was a thief (rather than an alleged thief) but did not include the fact that he was a Moroccan immigrant. However, *minutodigital.com* directly connected immigration to the crime; its January 17, 2011 headline stated, "Los inmigrantes de Salt continúan quemando coches" (Immigrants in Salt continue to burn cars) while the kicker, written in capital letters, proclaimed "INMIGRACIÓN Y DELINCUENCIA" (IMMIGRATION AND CRIME).

Another paper, *El Periódico de Catalunya*, pointed out an important component of the story, noting that "els joves estaven dirigits per persones majors d'edat, que els anaven dient com havien d'actuar en els actes de vandalism [...]" (the young protesters were led by adults who told them how to conduct their acts of vandalism [...]). Through this chain of news, we can see that the conflict was started by xenophobic locals – some of whom were connected to the *Plataforma per Catalunya* political party (which the media regularly declares to be racist and xenophobic) – rather than the immigrants. The event grew in various ways and gained importance in politics, with Josep Antoni Duran i Lleida, the leader of *Unió Democràtica de Catalunya* (a center-right Catalan political party), stating that he "[...] culpa de los altercados de Salt al 'exceso de extranjeros'" (blames the disputes in Salt on an 'excess of foreigners', *El Periódico de Catalunya*, 1/20/2011, p. 24).

The newsworthiness of a case like this cuts across various stages of the news, from the first shocking report to the conclusion of the story. Additionally, the initial portrayal has the greatest impact on public opinion, pointing out the differences between social "fronts" and giving rise to negative stereotypes about immigrants. Later pieces lessen the initial negative impact and may even turn it around into something positive. Nevertheless, the new, more factual, better-quality news tends to have a much smaller impact on recipients. The initial negative story complicates matters between people of different origins; positive stories which come out later struggle to repair these relationships.

This kind of treatment appears in similar cases which also attracted significant attention in the media (Lorite, 2010 and 2011), such as the 2008 death of Ousmane Kote, a Senegalese immigrant from a neighborhood in Roquetas de Mar called "Las 200 viviendas".[2] First the conflict broke out, and the public learned of the events through a hostile lens (in print, images, and audio clips). In this case, the media viewed quarrels and regular disputes between neighbors as a pitched battle. After the spectacle of this superficial yet shocking coverage, the media had time to delve into what actually happened and realized that early coverage had mislabeled some of the players in the story. For example, initial stories claimed that the possible assassin was a gypsy, although this was later found to be incorrect. However, although the media outlet made an effort to correct this mistake, it is unsurprising that this fell far short of the initial negative impact in the court of public opinion.

These "hostile" stories usually move on to a more in-depth explanation of the facts and end with the two "sides" – the natives and the immigrants – burying the hatchet, almost resembling a TV series. Along these lines, *El Mundo*, one of the most-read general-interest newspapers in Spain, summarized the profound causes of the conflict: "La alcaldesa culpa de los problemas a la pobreza y la falta de educación" (Mayor blames problems on poverty and lack of education), "La alcaldesa enmarca estos incidentes en el ámbito de la delincuencia y una juventud que 'ha perdido sus expectativas de futuro'" (Mayor frames these incidents in light of delinquency and youth who 'have lost expectations for the future'), and "El centro histórico son edificios hacinados, sin zonas verdes y sobreocupados" (The historic center is crowded with building after overpacked building, with no green areas). At the end of the news cycle, the paper also summed up the reconciliation between the "sides" under the headline "Inmigrantes, regidores y otros vecinos marchan juntos hoy por la convivencia" (Today immigrants, councilmen, and other residents march together for coexistence; *El Mundo.es Barcelona*, Eva Belmonte, 1/22/2011).

Even after reaching a point of reconciliation in such battles, the media expectantly await new "hostile" conflicts. They cannot seem to understand that a conflict in these urban contexts, the sites of recent cultural and ethnic diversity, could end there. In the case of the death of Mohamed Reda, a few days after "brokering a peace" in Salt, *Minutodigital.com* used another crime to proclaim "Sigue la batalla en Salt: detienen a un colombiano que asesinó a un joven de un golpe en la cabeza" (Battle continues in Salt: Colombian who murdered a young man with a blow to the head arrested; *Minutodigital.com*, 1/31/2011), with "INMIGRACIÓN" (IMMIGRATION) as their generic sub-header. They continued using a hostile tone, employing the word "battle," when they learned that "Los Mossos d'Esquadra han detenido a Anderson Jair S. P., de 23 años y origen colombiano, acusado de matar a Óscar Cruz, de 22 [….]" (the *Mossos d'Esquadra* [Catalan regional police force] arrested a Colombian man, Anderson Jair S.P., 23, accused of murdering Óscar Cruz, 22 […]).

TotSalt.cat, a news outlet in the town, also used the word "battle" when discussing an incident which took place at a soccer game in Salt in June of that year: "Un partit de futbol acaba en batalla campal al Camp Municipal de les Guixeres" (Soccer game ends in pitched battle at the Camp Municipal de les Guixeres; *TotSalt.cat*, 6/21/2011). In this case, the news focused on a clash not between locals and immigrants but between immigrants themselves. The tournament is organized each year by a group referred to as "FIFA," the popular name:

> "[…] amb el que es coneix a l'associació senegalesa de Salt que organitza aquest torneig "Copa Àfrica" des de fa uns anys. Hi participen un total de 16 clubs de tota la demarcació de Girona. Segons un dels responsables de l'organització aquest torneig pretén fomentar l'esport i la convivència entre els diferents membres de les comunitats africanes, però ha reconegut que moltes vegades la situació se'ls escapa de les mans, ja que a mesura que els partits comencen a ser decisius les eliminatòries es van escalfant, la tensió augmenta i el nombre d'espectadors es desborda sense que ells hi pugin fer res."
>
> ("[…] used to refer to the Senegalese association of Salt, which has been organizing the "Africa's Cup" for several years. Sixteen teams from all across Girona participate in the tournament. According to one of the association's coordinators, this tournament aims to encourage sports and coexistence among members of the different African communities. However, the organizer noted that the situation often gets out of control during the eliminatory rounds of the tournament, as things heat up,

tensions increase, and the number of spectators gets out of hand to the point that FIFA cannot do anything about it").

In addition to neighborly conflicts and "battles" of one kind or another, Salt has also made the news due to topics which become newsworthy because of their conflictive nature. For example, consider the complicated story of mosques in Salt and the political decisions about them. As the editorial in *El Periódico de Catalunya* noted on August 25, 2011:

> "[…] Salt vuelve a ser protagonista por decisiones relacionadas con la inmigración. En este caso, la suspensión durante un año de la concesión de licencias para centros de culto en el polígono de Torremirona, lo que en la práctica equivale a prohibir la apertura de más mezquitas. La aprobación del veto, una iniciativa del alcalde Jaume Torramadé, fue posible por los votos de CiU, el PP y dos de los tres ediles elegidos en la lista de la Plataforma per Catalunya (PxC), que ya han abandonado la disciplina del grupo xenófobo tras el tardío descubrimiento del auténtico cariz de Josep Anglada, que les reconvino por aspectos de su vida privada: una concejala tiene un novio camerunés y otro edil no oculta su relación con un dominicano […]. La crisis ha aumentado los problemas en zonas de gran concentración de inmigración como Salt. Y los ayuntamientos, con la economía en precario, no disponen de los recursos necesarios para planes que mejoren objetivamente la situación. Pero a lo que no pueden renunciar es a actuar con inteligencia y serenidad en pro de la convivencia. Habrá que ver si la prohibición de nuevas mezquitas en Salt conduce a ese objetivo o, por el contrario, es fuente de nuevos conflictos." (*El Periódico de Catalunya*, 25/08/2011).

("[…] Salt again has taken center stage because of decisions related to immigration. In this case, they have put a one-year hold on granting licenses for places of worship in the Torremirona development, in effect blocking further mosques from opening. The prohibition, spearheaded by mayor Jaume Torramadé, was possible due to votes from CiU, PP, and two of the three *Plataforma per Catalunya's* council members, who left the xenophobic party after belatedly discovering the true nature of Josep Anglada, who chided them for aspects of their personal lives: one council member has a boyfriend from Cameroon, while another has not hidden his relationship with a Dominican […] The crisis has escalated problems in areas with highly concentrated numbers of immigrants like Salt. And given the precarious nature of the economy, town councils lack the resources they would need to create plans to improve the situation. But what they cannot do is stop acting intelligently and calmly in favor of coexistence. It remains to be seen if this prohibition on new mosques in Salt achieves its goals, or conversely, if it is the source of new conflicts).

The challenging cultural and ethnic relationships had already been labeled as "hostile" when the first major conflict broke out in Salt in 2009. At the time, the Catalan public station, *Televisió de Catalunya (TV3)*, used the following headline in its evening news: "Batalla campal entre comunitats a Salt" (Pitched battle between communities in Salt; *Telenoticies vespre*; 8/26/2009). The story argued that the "hostile" confrontation was due to the fact that the town could see "[…] petits furts d'un grup de menors magrebins a diversos comerços de Salt regentats per pakistanesos" ([…] small incidents of theft among a group of underage Moroccans in several shops run by Pakistanis in Salt).

That day, another station, *324*, used the word "baralla" (quarrel, fight) instead of "batalla" (battle), running a story about a "baralla multitudinària entre ciutadans pakistanesos i marroquins" (massive fight between Pakistani and Moroccan citizens). Like TV3, the channel – which aims to provide relevant news to the public 24 hours a day – is part of the *Corporació Catalana de Mitjans Audiovisuals* (Catalan Broadcasting Corporation). The story went on to note:

> "Una baralla multitudinària a Salt, al Gironès, entre un grup de ciutadans pakistanesos i un altre de marroquins va provocar dilluns dos ferits lleus i va haver d'intervenir-hi diverses dotacions dels Mossos d'Esquadra i de la policia local […]. L'incident va tenir l'origen en el robatori d'una bossa de patates que va fer un menor magrebí en una botiga regentada per ciutadans pakistanesos […]. Aquesta és la primera vegada que hi ha un conflicte entre comunitats a Salt i segons l'alcaldessa en funcions del municipi, no hi ha constància que hi hagi problemes habituals entre ciutadans pakistanesos i magrebins."
>
> ("On Monday, a massive fight between a group of Pakistani citizens and a group of Moroccans in Salt, a town in the county of Gironès, led to two minor injuries. Several teams from the *Mossos d'Esquadra* (Catalan regional police) and local police had to intervene in the fight […]. The incident started when a Moroccan boy stole a bag of potatoes from a store run by Pakistani citizens […]. This is the first time such a conflict has taken place between different ethnic communities in Salt. According to the municipality's acting mayor, there is no evidence of regular problems between Pakistani and Moroccan citizens in the town").

The language used to refer to the two groups is particularly interesting. The Pakistanis are referred to as citizens from the very start, whereas the Moroccans are not called citizens until the end of the piece, when both groups are described using this word. If these groups are viewed as citizens, is it appropriate to continue to use this label? Doing so is inclusive (considering a person to be a citizen), yet at the same time, it is discriminatory (creating distance and segregating these groups). From a production standpoint and given the restrictions of production routines, this can be explained in light of the need to provide the maximum amount of detail about the individuals featured in the story. Nevertheless, the bodies which oversee the quality of reporting on immigration often criticize the media for not using the same term when referring to Catalan or Spanish citizens.

Cordinach's (2012) analysis of the coverage of this 2009 "battle" on channels with differing content, audiences, and approaches – including *TV de Girona* (a local station), *TV3* (the regional, Catalan station), and *TVE* (a public, state-run station) – reveals that all three channels used a favorable tone in the first few days of their coverage of the confrontation between cultures. *TV Girona* spent more time on the story than the other two channels (11.2% of the news for *TV Girona* vs. 3.1% for *TV3* and 2.2% for *TVE*). With regard to their sources, all three channels included non-immigrants more than immigrants; immigrants spoke for only 30% of the total time that interviews lasted. It should be noted that *TV Girona* often does not identify its sources (47.1% of speakers were not identified), which probably is a result of the local channel's limited technical and human resources (a fact that was verified in our study of their production of the news). *TV3* identifies the majority of its sources, archive footage, and publications, which stems from the fact that *TV3* can put more resources to work in identifying these and respecting diversity.

3. Politics and sports

During the crisis of the year 2011, three elections occurred: municipal and regional elections took place on May 22 while national elections were held on November 20. These elections shed light on trends in the political discourse on immigration. Regardless of their editorial policy, all media outlets seemed to oppose the racist and xenophobic videos used by the *Partido Popular* (the right-leaning 'Popular Party') and *Plataforma per Catalunya* (PxC; the far-right, racist and xenophobic 'Platform for Catalonia,' which resembles Le Pen's 'National Front' in France).

The PxC video used in the municipal elections features three girls with European-looking traits that resemble those of the native Catalan population (at the very least, it is clear that they are not African, Latin American, or Asian). The girls are jumping rope in a street; the image is labeled "Igualada, 2011." Then the clip cuts to a similar scene many years later, in 2025, which features three jump-roping girls dressed in burkas (see Table 9-1).

Table 9-1. Igualada 2011

	AUDIO: Traditional song in Catalan: "Passant per la Font del Gat" (Walking in front of the Cat Fountain).

	Girl with European-looking traits which visibly resemble those of the native Catalan population
	Song in Arabic

	Josep Anglada (in Catalan): "Primer els de casa. Vota Plataforma per Catalunya" ("Take care of our own first", literally "First the people from here"). Vote for *Plataforma per Catalunya*".

Source: http://www.youtube.com/watch?v=w7xY7STPMXc

Moreover, in PxC's video for the general elections:

> "Se ve a dos mujeres en dos lados opuestos de una mesa, una de ellas con un hiyab. Poco a poco van entrando diferentes hombres que le van quitando a una de ellas, de forma metafórica, la sanidad, la educación, la comida y, finalmente, la ropa —se queda en ropa interior—, para dárselo todo a la chica que representa la inmigración. Todo ello acompañado de la banda sonora original de la película 'Lo que el viento se llevó'".
>
> ("We see two women, one of whom is wearing a hijab, sitting at opposite sides of a table. Slowly but surely, various men enter the scene, metaphorically taking away health, education, food, and finally clothing (the woman is left wearing only undergarments) from the first and giving all of these things to the girl who represents immigration. All of this is set to the tune of the original soundtrack from *Gone with the Wind*"). (*Público.es*, 11/18/2011).

The ad ends with the slogan "Primer els de casa" ("Take care of our own first", literally "First the people from here").

The conservative Catalan nationalist party, *Convergencia i Unió* ("Convergence and Union"; CiU) also uses linguistic wordplay with the media to hide its xenophobic tendencies. For example, the candidate heading up the list for Barcelona, Josep Antoni Duran, said to be a "brilliant" orator, constantly justifies the poster which features his photograph and the slogan "La gent no se'n va del seu país per ganes sinó per gana. Però a Catalunya no hi cap tothom" (People leave their country not because they want to [*per ganes*] but because they are hungry [*per gana*]. But Catalonia doesn't have space for everyone).

The media have also been keeping track of some of the phrases Duran has used at political rallies, including "En España hay más inmigración de la que debería haber" (Spain has more immigration than it should", "la presencia de inmigrantes en un barrio es la causa del descenso del valor de los pisos" (Immigrants in a neighborhood lead to decreases in home values) and "los niños extranjeros son los responsables del retraso del rendimiento escolar" (Foreign students slow down academic progress). These types of political opinions are broadcast by all of the media. Although they are relativized by some people on the right, they are quickly counteracted by the opinions of certain social bodies and organizations. However, these belated corrections of errors committed when reporting on the "battles" continue to reappear in xenophobic statements from the candidates. Duran's quotations, rather than the complaints of anti-racist organizations, are seared into our minds when later manifestoes are published. Along these lines, *Público*, a leftward-leaning paper that went under during the crisis, stated that:

> "El discurso racista y xenófobo [de Duran i Lleida] tiene nefastas consecuencias en la convivencia y nos pone en peligro de fractura social", afirmaron en un comunicado SOS Racisme-Catalunya, CCOO de Catalunya, UGT de Catalunya y la Confederación de Asociaciones de Vecinos y Vecinas de Catalunya. Estas entidades sociales, vecinales y sindicales denuncian en el documento, titulado Basta al discurso político xenófobo y racista, "la falta de responsabilidad política y social del señor Duran i Lleida, que se aprovecha de un contexto difícil para culpar a personas de origen inmigrante de problemas transversales de la sociedad, como son la falta de inversión pública en educación o la situación de crisis en el mercado inmobiliario".
>
> ("'The racist and xenophobic discourse [utilized by Duran i Lleida] has disastrous implications for coexistence and runs the risk of creating social divisions,' noted *SOS Racisme-Catalunya* [S.O.S. Racism – Catalonia], *UGT de Catalunya* [the General Workers' Union of Catalonia], and the *Confederación de Asociaciones de Vecinos y Vecinas de Catalunya* [Confederation of Residents' Associations of Catalonia] in a press release. In a document entitled *Basta al discurso político xenófobo y racista* [Enough xenophobic and racist political discourse], these social organizations, neighborhood groups, and unions denounced "Mr. Duran i Lleida's lack of political and social responsibility, which takes advantage of a difficult situation to blame people with foreign origins for cross-cutting societal problems such as the lack of government investment in education or the crisis in the housing market").(*Público*, 10/5/2011, http://medios.mugak.eu/noticias/noticia/292465)

Some of these organizations, like *SOS Racisme*, tried to get a jump start on this kind of xenophobic discourse; before the election, the group published its *Manifiesto contra el uso demagógico y populista de la inmigración ante las próximas elecciones municipales* (Manifesto against the demagogic and populist use of immigration leading into the upcoming municipal elections), which underscored the need to pay careful attention to the discourse of hatred towards immigration. Like always, however, proposals to write positive stories based on factual research weren't news. Although these organizations work to prevent negative stories, they impact society far less than Duran's political rhetoric does.

A noteworthy phenomenon in 2011 concerned racist behavior in the sport of soccer. Sports journalists play a key role in fighting this kind of behavior from fans and players alike. However, due to the sensationalist and rather unilateral nature of this kind of news, reporters sometimes end up promoting such conduct. This happens when they speak out against calling Brazilian or African players "monkeys" or protest players who have used this expression to mock others. (In April and May, the media focused heavily on how FC Barcelona's trainer, Carlos Busquets, had used this expression to refer to Real Madrid's Marcelo Vieira da Silva.) However, the papers in Madrid (*As* and *Marca*) will always take a different view of this issue than their Catalan counterparts (*Sport* and *Mundo Deportivo*). Although these sources give different readings to the issue, each of them is both for and against racism, encouraging integration and respect for diversity while simultaneously creating conditions which underscore differences.

4. Quantitative data

Quantitative data highlights the true impact of the media on intercultural relationships (Lorite, 2004, 2010 and 2011). A first crucial piece of quantitative data is the presence of migration in the news, namely the percentage of time that focuses on migration (especially the arrival, settling in, and integration of immigrants) in those news broadcasts which have the largest share of the TV audience and social impact in Spain (MIGRACOM, 2006, 2007, 2008 and 2009). State-run television programs saw a considerable increase in the share of news focused on immigration between 1996 and 2006, a period which corresponded to significant immigration to Spain. In the TV news programs we analyzed, *Antena 3* (A3), *Tele 5* (Tele5), and *Televisión Española: La1* (TVE), only 0.8%, 0.6%, and 0.5%, respectively, of programming focused on immigration in 1996. However, ten years later, in 2006, this rose to nearly 10% (8.8% for A3, 9.2% for Tele5, and 9.6% for RVE). In other words, almost one of every ten minutes of the TV news addressed issues of immigration. Starting in 2007, these percentages dropped considerably, stabilizing between 3% and 5%, as depicted in Figure 9-1.

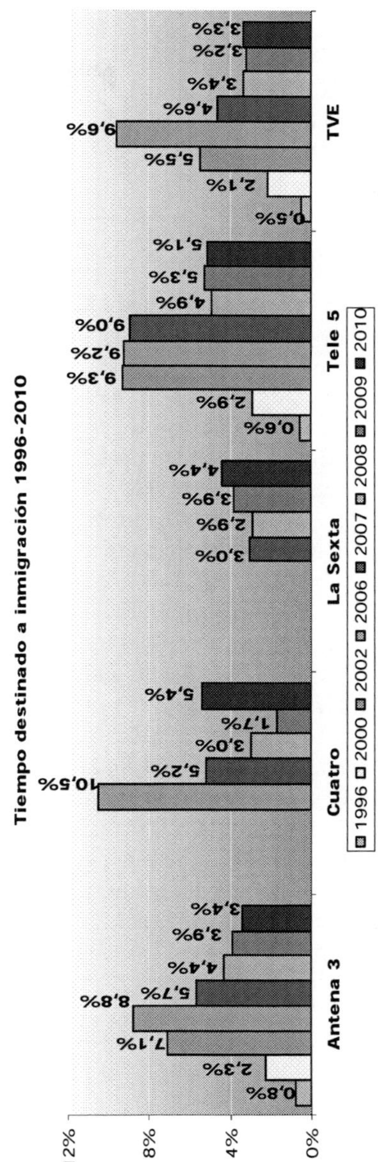

Figure 9-1. Time spent on immigration, 1996-2010.
Source: MIGRACOM: www.migracom.com

The same trend can be seen in the local TV news broadcasts in each of the autonomous regions of Spain – namely in Catalonia (TV3), Madrid (*Telemadrid*), Valencia (*Canal 9*), Andalusia (*Canal Sur*), the Basque Country (*ETB-2*) and Galicia (*TVG*) – although these spend somewhat less time on immigration. However, these channels do not all focus equally on the subject; a larger or smaller presence of reports on migration in the news is correlated to the percentage of immigrants living in each region in the given period. In addition to being regions where immigrants tend to settle, Madrid, Valencia, Andalusia and Catalonia gave particular weight to immigration in 2006 due to the "llegada masiva de cayucos" (widespread arrival of "cayucos," a kind of fishing boat from Senegal which can hold up to 50 passengers). However, the share of the news focused on migration almost completely evaporated in 2009 and 2010 with the growth of the financial crisis and halt in migration flows.

To shed light on the processes of intercultural encounters on TV news, a second important piece of data entails analyzing newsworthy topics in the field of migration. In this vein, a key year was 2008, when the crisis began and the first symptoms of this phenomenon could be seen. That year, TV focused on three macro-topics: politics, conflicts and arrivals (MIGRACOM, 2008).

However, as the crisis continued to develop in 2009 and 2010, programs spent less time on content relating immigration to criminal acts and social violence than in previous years. Furthermore, in a marked increase from the year before, 2010 saw the number of reports related to racism and xenophobia rise significantly, from 3.8% (the average value for evening news on *TVE*, *Tele5*, *A3*, *Cuatro* and *La Sexta*) in 2009 to 9.7% in 2010. The biggest increase was seen on the *Cuatro* channel, which went from not touching on these topics in 2007 to spending 15.9% of its programming on immigration in 2010. The most significant change was in content related to different aspects of integration. While the state-owned news channels spent almost no time on these topics beforehand, in 2010 this trend was reversed, with 15.6% of the evening news on the five state-run channels focused on immigration.

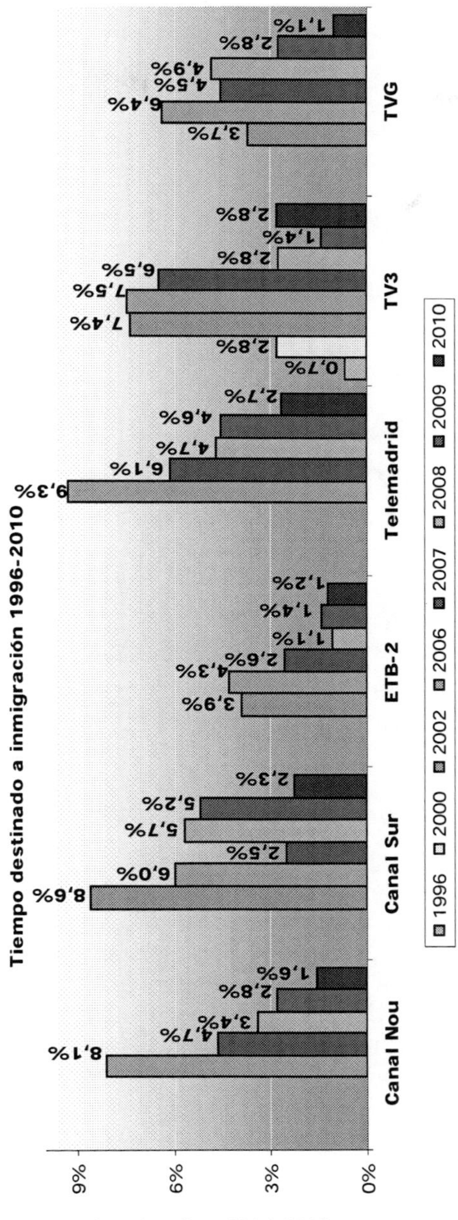

Figure 9-2. Time spent on immigration, 1996-2010.
Source: MIGRACOM: www.migracom.com

Another topic, the arrival of the *sin papeles* (undocumented) in boats called *pateras* or *cayucos* has played a key role since the 1990s. With the crisis, the media's interest in these kind of news stories (most of which were dramatic) logically fell as the number of immigrants who arrived decreased. Interestingly, this topic went from being the number one issue in 2007 to almost insignificant in 2010, as shown in Figure 9-3. However, interest in depicting the drama of arriving in the "promised land" is related to the type of news program and the channel's desire to capture audiences thirsty for morbid stories.

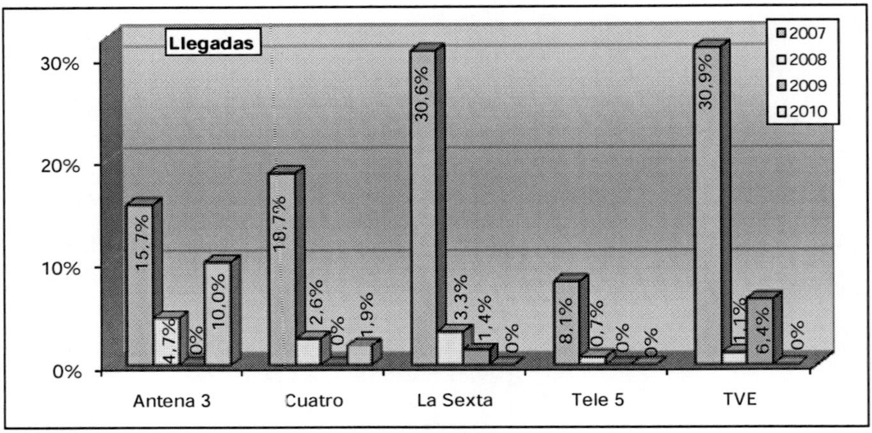

Figure 9-3. The arrivals of undocumented people.
Source: MIGRACOM: www.migracom.com

5. Conclusions

In order to objectively analyze the media's impact on intercultural relationships in times of crisis – particularly in countries which have recently seen large amounts of immigration from other regions, like Spain – four different types of data are necessary. First, demographic data provides key information on ongoing changes in migratory flows. Second, one must consider information on mergers and closures of media outlets – both general and local media, especially with regard to those groups which rely on the government for funding and aim to promote the integration of minority groups through media. Third, an up-to-date knowledge of emerging types of communication and social news channels like the internet (often accessed through mobile technology and tablets) demonstrates how news has become more interactive, simultaneously fostering both racism and anti-racism. Finally, one must analyze the media's two-pronged approach to immigration – which is explicitly anti-racist yet implicitly takes a Eurocentric view that tends to be xenophobic and reject "the other" – from multiple perspectives.

Case studies also provide objective data on the treatment of immigration. A relevant case study revolves around the ethnically diverse city of Salt, in Catalonia. The media are interested in the relationships between the native Catalan population (composed of Catalan-speaking, predominantly Catholic individuals born in Catalonia and following the traditions of this region) and recent immigrants (who come from a variety of continents, cultures, languages and religions). Media coverage of their interactions in 2011 frequently was slanted more towards social conflict (frequently referred to as "battles") than normal daily life. Interestingly, stories often portrayed conflicts ending in a peaceful resolution. Good news stemmed from bad news, yet the initial negative coverage had a much more significant social impact.

Third, it is important to pay special attention to how the media treat immigration during certain political activities (municipal elections) and sporting activities (soccer games). For example, in the municipal, regional, and general elections which took place in Spain in 2011, all media outlets, regardless of their editorial policies, opposed the racist and xenophobic videos used by the *Plataforma per Catalunya* (the far-right, racist and xenophobic 'Platform for Catalonia,' which resembles Le Pen's 'National Front' in France).

Fourth, this type of research must include quantitative, longitudinal data from observatories like MIGRACOM[1] on how state and regional television channels discuss immigration (and immigration-related topics). The data presented in this chapter demonstrate a significant increase in news coverage of immigration between 1996 and 2006. In fact, one of every ten minutes of the news focused on immigration in 2006. However, starting in 2007 this coverage decreased significantly, stabilizing between 3% and 5%. Consequently, the social impact of stories about migration and integration provided by these channels is but a small fraction of all news.

Finally, in times of crisis it is necessary to put a special emphasis on current recommendations for adequately treating diversity, such as those designed by the Catalan Broadcasting Council's (*Consell d'Audiovisual de Catalunya*, 2003) Round Table on Diversity and the Association of Journalists of Catalonia (*Col·legi de Periodistes de Catalunya*). We must continue to follow the lead of MIGRACOM, studying these processes using applied action research grounded in multi-modal methodology (which investigates the production, broadcasting and reception of messages) and adopting a qualitative and quantitative approach based on objective examples and case studies. This research aims to acquire unbiased, generalizable data and suggest the most appropriate discourses (in print, spoken, and audiovisual media) in order to encourage respect for cultural diversity and avoid racism and xenophobia in Spain.

The Government of Catalonia's first such study took place in 1996 and was conducted in collaboration with the professional association of Catalan journalists (the *Col·legi de Periodistes de Catalunya*) as well as other civil society organizations. Study results led to the *Manual de Estilo sobre Inmigración y Minorías Étnicas de España* (Style Guide on Immigration and Ethnic Minorities in Spain), a first in Spain and one of the earliest such manuals in Europe. In the 2000s, MIGRACOM carried out further studies on the *Tratamiento Informativo de la Inmigración en España* (Media Treatment of Immigration in Spain) for the Ministry of Labour and Immigration's General Directorate for the Integration of Immigrants and the Spanish Observatory on Racism and Xenophobia (OBERAXE). Such results have allowed us to push for quality treatment of diversity, supporting initiatives like the *Guía Práctica para los Profesionales de los Medios de Comunicación. Tratamiento Mediático de la Inmigración* (Practical Guide for Media Professionals: Media Treatment of Immigration; Sendín, 2008).

Notes

1. MIGRACOM is the Migration and Communication Observatory and Consolidated Research Group (2009 SGR675) at the Universitat Autònoma de Barcelona. www.migracom.com
2. In English, the name of the neighborhood "Las 200 viviendas" means "200 homes."

Bibliography

Barrera, Montse "Aldarulls a Salt en un acte de suport al lladre malferit". *El Punt Avui*, 15 January 2011. http://www.elpuntavui.cat/salt/mes/2-societat.html?start=400 Last accessed on 31 March 2012.

Belmonte, Eva. "Inmigrantes, regidores y otros vecinos marchan juntos hoy por la convivencia". *El Mundo.es Barcelona*, 22 January 2011. http://www.elmundo.es/elmundo/2011/01/21/barcelona/1295624795.html. Last accessed on 24 January 2012.

CAC. Mesa per la Diversitat a l'Audiovisual. 2002. *Manual sobre el Tratamiento de la inmigración en los medios de comunicación*, Barcelona: Consell de l'Audiovisual de Catalunya.

http://www.audiovisualcat.net/home/investigacion/inmigracion.pdf Last accessed on 31 March 2012.

Cogo, Denise and Nicolás Lorite García (coords.). 2005. *Mídia, migrações e interculturalidades*. Rio de Janeiro: Logos, UERJ.

Colegio de Periodistas de Cataluña. 1996. *Manual de Estilo sobre Minorías Étnicas*. http://www.aulaintercultural.org/IMG/pdf/manualdeestilo.pdf Last accessed on 31 March 2012.

Cordinach Fossas, Mariona. 2012. "El tractament informatiu de la immigració magrebí a les televisions catalanes". Paper presented at III Congreso Internacional de la Asociación Española de Investigación de la Comunicación- Tarragona, 18,19 and 20 January 2012.

Cardeñosa, Nicanor J. "Redes sociales: España a la cabeza mundial". *El Mundo,* 5 January 2012 . http://www.elmundo.es/yodona/blogs/yd_t/2012/01/05/redes-sociales-espana-a-la-cabeza.html Last accessed on 31 March 2012.

El Periódico de Catalunya. Salt, de nuevo". Editorial. 25 August 2011. http://www.elperiodico.com/es/noticias/opinion/salt-nuevo-1128611 Last accessed on 31 March 2012.

FAPE. 2012. Federación de Asociaciones de Periodistas de España.

Instituto Nacional de Estadística (INE). 2012. Flujos migratorios estimados. Migraciones exteriores. Serie 2010-2011. http://www.ine.es/jaxi/menu.do?type=pcaxis&path=%2Ft20%2Fp259 %2Fe01&file=pcaxis&L Last accessed on 31 March 2012.

Lorite García, Nicolás (dir). 2004. *Tratamiento informativo de la inmigración en España 2002*. Madrid: Instituto de Migraciones y Servicios Sociales.

—. 2010. "Televisión informativa y modelos de dinamización intercultural". In *Migraciones, discursos e ideologías en una sociedad globalizada. Claves para su mejor comprensión*, ed. María Martínez Lirola, 19-43. Alicante: Instituto Alicantino de Cultura Juan Gil-Albert.

—. 2011. "Informative Treatment of Immigration and Intercultural Dynamics of Spanish Mass Media". *Media, Migration and Public Opinion: Myths and Prejudices and the Challenge of Attaining Mutual Understending between Europe and North Africa*, ed. Ivan Ureta, 187-214. Bern, Berlin, Bruxelles, Frankfurt, New York, Oxford,Wien: Peter Lang.

MIGRACOM. 2006. *Tratamiento informativo de la inmigración en España. Año 2006*. Dir. Nicolás Lorite García. Barcelona: MIGRACOM, Madrid: OBERAXE.

http://www.migracom.com/publicaciones/fichero_52.pdf Last accessed on 31 March 2012.

—. 2007. *Tratamiento informativo de la inmigración en España. Año 2007.* Dir. Nicolás Lorite García. Barcelona: MIGRACOM, Madrid: OBERAXE. http://www.oberaxe.es/files/datos/499059da8ccc5/TratamInfesp2007.pdf Last accessed on 31 March 2012.

—. 2008. *Tratamiento informativo de la inmigración en España. Año 2008.* Dir. Nicolás Lorite García. Barcelona: MIGRACOM, Madrid: OBERAXE. http://www.migracom.com/publicaciones/fichero_56.pdf Last accessed on 31 March 2012.

—. 2009. *Tratamiento informativo de la inmigración en España. Año 2009.* Dir. Nicolás Lorite García. Barcelona: MIGRACOM, Madrid: OBERAXE. http://www.oberaxe.es/files/datos/4c404398ba627/MIGRACOM%202009%20110610.pdf Last accessed on 24 January 2012.

minutodigital.com "Los inmigrantes de Salt continúan quemando coches". 17 January 2011. http://www.minutodigital.com/2011/01/17/los-inmigrantes-de-salt-continuan-quemando-coches/ Last accessed on 31 March 2012.

—. "Sigue la batalla en Salt: detienen a un colombiano que asesinó a un joven de un golpe en la cabeza". 31 January 2011. http://www.minutodigital.com/2011/03/31/sigue-la-batalla-en-salt-detienen-a-un-colombiano-que-asesino-a-un-joven-de-un-golpe-en-la-cabeza/ Last accessed on 31 March 2012.

MUGAK Observatorio de la Diversidad. *Público,* 5 October 2011. http://medios.mugak.eu/noticias/noticia/292465 Last accessed on 31 March 2012.

Público. "El partido xenófobo PxC cierra la campaña con un vídeo racista". 18 November 2011. http://www.publico.es/espana/407708/el-partido-xenofobo-pxc-cierra-la-campana-con-un-video-racista-elecciones-generales-2011 Last accessed on 31 March 2012.

Rodrigo Alsina, Miquel. 2005. *La construcción de la noticia*. Barcelona: Paidós.

Roger, Maiol. "La crisis ahoga a los medios locales". *El País* 4 December 2011. http://elpais.com/diario/2011/12/04/catalunya/1322964447_850215.html Last accessed on 31 March 2012.

Sauri, Josep and Lluisa F. González "Durán culpa de los altercados de Salt al "exceso de extranjeros". *El Periodico de Catalunya*. 20 January 2011. http://es.scribd.com/doc/47245537/El-periodico-20-01-2011

Last accessed on 31 March 2012.

Sendín Gutiérrez, José Carlos (coord.). 2008. *Guía práctica para los profesionales de los medios de comunicación. Tratamiento informativo de la inmigración*. Madrid: Proyecto Promoequality, OBERAXE, Secretaria de Estado de Inmigración y Emigración. http://www.tt.mtas.es/periodico/inmigracion/200712/guia_medios.pdf Last accessed on 31 March 2012.

SOS Racisme. 2011. *Manifiesto contra el uso demagógico y populista de la inmigración ante las próximas elecciones municipales.* http://eapnmelilla.wordpress.com/2011/03/29/manifiesto-contra-el-uso-demagogico-y-populista-de-la-inmigracion-ante-las-proximas-elecciones/ Last accessed on 31 March 2012.

TV3. "Batalla campal entre comunitats a Salt" *Telenoticies vespre*, 26 August 2009. http://www.tv3.cat/videos/1457349 Last accessed on 31 March 2012.

Televisión de Catalunya, 324 "Baralla multitudinària a Salt entre ciutadans pakistanesos i marroquins" 26 August 2009. http://www.324.cat/noticia/401605/girones/Baralla-multitudinaria-a-Salt-entre-ciutadans-pakistanesos-i-marroquins Last accessed on 31 March 2012.

TotSalt.cat "Un partit de futbol acaba en batalla campal al Camp Municipal de les Guixeres", 21 June 2011. http://www.totsalt.cat/index.php?option=com_content&view=article&id=300:un-partit-de-futbol-acaba-en-batalla-campal-al-camp-municipal-de-les-guixeres&catid=1:esports&Itemid=19 Last accessed on 31 March 2012.

CHAPTER TEN

PARTICIPATION OF THE MEDIA ON COMBATING RACISM AND XENOPHOBIA[1]

ANTOLÍN GRANADOS MARTÍNEZ,
F. JAVIER GARCÍA CASTAÑO,
NINA KRESSOVA
LUCÍA CHOVANCOVA
AND JOSÉ FERNÁNDEZ ECHEVERRÍA
MIGRATIONS INSTITUTE, UNIVERSITY OF GRANADA

1. Introduction

The world that rose from the ashes after World War II faced great challenges to staunch the blood and suffering of millions of people. One of them was to lay the foundations for a new way of understanding relations between peoples in order to avoid what had happened twice already. Hand in hand with international organizations, some international agreements were reached and crystallised with the Charter of the United Nations in 1945, and the Universal Declaration of Human Rights in 1948, for instance. In some way, those documents constituted the germ of policies to fight discrimination, racism and xenophobia, which are the main focus of this article.

As a consequence of those policies, some mechanisms of control and supervision to put an end to violation of the rights of some specific groups of society have been developed in Europe, both by public and private institutions, such as companies, the media, etc. For example, the European Observatory for Racism and Xenophobia; and the European Commission against Racism and Intolerance were created to that end. In constitutional treaties and Community laws and Directives, the European Union (EU) stresses the struggle against all forms of discrimination of both European and non-European citizens within its institutions.

In fact, the European Union has made clear efforts to establish formal and judicial mechanisms against racism, xenophobia and discrimination based on gender, age or ethnic or cultural origin. One of the most efficient mechanisms is prevention. This means, basically, informing, educating and raising public awareness. School education of children and, therefore, their families, is the public sphere with the greatest responsibility for this task. Also, the mass media have a crucial role in implementing that triple task.

The concern for non-discrimination of minorities in the media can be also traced back to the post-World War II period. It was then when the western world realized the great power that the control of information provided. As we know, totalitarian regimes of all political wings used the media as a very effective tool to manipulate public opinion according to their interests. In order to strengthen the essence of participatory democracy and the contribution of the media to consolidate western democracies during the post-war period, the international community implemented measures with two main objectives. The first one was to design instruments to avoid the concentration of media groups. This could limit the pluralism in any society, especially the views and thoughts of minorities. The second measure, in parallel with the previous one, was to implement legal measures to guarantee both freedom of expression when exercising journalism and the right of all citizens to receive objective information, ethically committed to the basic principles of peaceful living and respect to the dignity of each person, group or culture.

We must remember that the media constitute the most important source of information for regular citizens to know about their social, economic, political and cultural realities. Therefore, they should be aware of their important role in shaping public opinion on different issues such as foreign immigration.

This article is intended to show that efforts made by public institutions (mainly, political ones) to eradicate racist, xenophobic or discriminatory attitudes and behaviours are not reflected as expected in the mass media regarding subjects such as migration, in spite of compulsory codes of professional ethics and style guides. In fact, the opinions expressed by citizens regarding this issue are very similar to the information given by the media.

2. International and national anti-discrimination legislations

As we mentioned, a series of documents aimed at combating racism and xenophobia were drafted after World War II. Said documents include the Charter of the United Nations of 1945 and the Universal Declaration of Human Rights of 1948[2]. Both documents influenced national regulations throughout the world, which gave them a truly universal meaning. Later, in 1965, the General Assembly of the United Nations adopted the International Convention on the Elimination of All Forms of Racial Discrimination[3]. This document expressed the signatories' commitment to condemn propaganda with ideas implying superiority of some groups over others based on differences such as skin colour or ethnic origin; and guarantee the respect and promotion of fundamental rights and tolerance.

Regarding anti-discrimination struggle in Europe, special mention must be made to the aforesaid European Observatory for Racism and Xenophobia[4] (which started to work in 1997 and integrated with the European Agency for Fundamental Rights in 2007) and the European Commission against Racism and Intolerance (ECRI) created in 1993 on agreement of all Member States of the European Council by the "Vienna Declaration"[5].

There are several Community Treaties and Directives that provided a legal background for these institutions. For example, the Tampere Council (1999), which mentions a common asylum and migration policy (defining possible scenarios of discrimination towards non-European population in Europe, especially those considered as immigrants, although it is well known that discrimination is not limited to such groups (see Colectivo IOÉ, 2009). Another product of this Council was the publication of Directive 2000/43/CE, which states the need for country to create an institution to ensure the promotion of equal treatment to all citizens; and which was reinforced by another Directive, published that year, which explores the subject (Directive 2000/78/CE).

Both Directives are crucial to combat racism and xenophobia; however, what may be considered as the most important measure implemented by European bodies is the promotion of this struggle in criminal law. The Framework Decision 2008/913/JAI, which is often referred to as "EU law on combating racism and xenophobia", is especially relevant in this context. Also, between Directives and Resolutions we find the Charter of Fundamental Rights of the European Union, which is a benchmark of reference when talking about issues related to equal treatment and non-discrimination and discrimination on the grounds of "racial origin" in the European Union.

Regarding the Spanish context, although those Directives must be considered as "minimum regulations" and "basis" for equality of treatment and non-discrimination, their transposition to Spanish legislation has been relatively slow. In the 1999 report of the European Commission on Racism and Intolerance published on Spain, this institution recommends the creation of some sort of "national" body to oversee those issues (ECRI, 1999, 10). Initially, the creation of the Spanish Observatory on Racism and Xenophobia could be considered as a response to European demands. Although the creation of this body is often attributed to the Organic Law 4/2000 on the Rights and Freedoms of Foreign Nationals Living in Spain and Their Social Integration[6], it was not until its second reform in 2003 when this body was founded—after a second request by the ECRI in its 2002 report (ECRI, 2003, 10).

Moreover, incorporating Community Directives into the Spanish legal system is not automatically translated as an effective implementation of activities aimed at reducing racism and xenophobia. According to Professor Francina Esteve García (2008, 198), "transposition, as legal mechanism, is open to criticism due to its lack of visibility and the fact that it did not cause any debate or political commitment during all these years". Lorenzo Cachón (2004, 13) also regrets that a "golden opportunity to educate the public in non-discrimination has been wasted". Anyway, we must say that Spain was ahead the EU in what constitutes one of the most important aspects in combating racism and xenophobia: criminal law. In fact, since 1996 the Spanish Penal Code covers racism as an offence, and "racist intentions" are considered as an aggravating factor, while this was not included in the "EU law on combating racism and xenophobia" until 2008.

Also, Royal Decree 1600/2004 of July 2 established a basic organic structure for the Ministry of Labour and Social Affairs where the Spanish Observatory for Racism and Xenophobia was created. It can be evidenced in the Royal Decree that reference to struggle against discrimination on the grounds of "ethnic origin" is limited to this secondment by the Observatory, although after restructuring the Ministry in 2008, as a consequence of the general elections of that year, more detailed references would be made on this matter. Therefore, when the Ministry became Ministry of Labour and Immigration, it included the aforementioned Immigration and Emigration State Office and the General Office for Integration of Immigrants was under the latter.

The Royal Decree that includes the basic structure of the new Ministry now considers the struggle against racial discrimination and xenophobia as one of the various functions of the General Office for Integration of Immigrants. This explains why the Spanish Observatory for Racism and Xenophobia, together with other bodies, is included within the structure of this General Office which now has the status of General Under-secretariat, contrary to the previous Ministry structure.

The most interesting aspect of this Observatory is its scope, especially, the study of all phenomena related to racism and discrimination, but, since this body is under the State Secretariat for Immigration and Emigration, it is highly probable that those studies are almost exclusively related to immigrant populations. As an example we can mention the report "Evolution of Racism and Xenophobia in Spain", entrusted by the Secretariat of State to the Observatory. It basically consists in analysing a survey to measure public opinion on immigration, which reduces the issue of racism and xenophobia to only one of the groups that may be affected by these phenomena. This does not mean, however, that the analysis or data production are of poor quality[7] as they are carried out by well-known professionals and the results are used to support plenty of researches, but there is a repeated coincidence between racism, xenophobia and immigrants.

Anyway, this inclination to associate migration and issues related to the struggle against racism and xenophobia, which we link to the fact that the Observatory is under an administrative body focused, precisely, on immigration and emigration issues, has been mitigated with the recent creation of the Council for the Promotion of Equality of Treatment and Non-Discrimination of Persons Based on Racial or Ethnic Origin by Law 62/2003, dated December 30, regarding Fiscal, Administrative and Social Measures, even if the composition of this body was not regulated until 2007 and even today it is not very active.

Apart from the aforesaid periodic report on the situation of racism and xenophobia in Spain —which is of core importance because, among other reasons, it is almost exclusive in the country and it fulfils one of the Observatory's crucial roles: "providing a regular diagnose of the situation of racism and xenophobia in Spain—, there are other critical functions the Observatory fulfils that we summarize below:

- The Observatory manages an Anti-Discrimination Resource Centre (known as CREADI).
- In relation to the previous Resource Centre, the Observatory also manages a Directory of Institutions interested in anti-racism and anti-xenophobia issues.

- The Observatory has supported for several years the RAXEN reports, published by the Movement against Intolerance.
- The Observatory directed the GESDI Project or "Gestión de la Diversidad en el mundo laboral" (Management of Diversity at Work). The "Guía para la gestión cultural en entornos profesionales" (Guide of cultural management in the professional environment) (2011) was one of the results of this project.
- Within the framework of the European PROGRESS Programme, the Observatory implemented a project called "Planes de Sensibilización: experiencias de éxito en el entorno local" (Awareness Plans: Success Stories on the Local Environment) (ESCI III).
- Within the framework of the EU Fundamental Rights and Citizenship programme (2007-2009) JLS/FRC/2007, the Observatory led the Trans-national Project: "Living Together: European Citizenship against Racism and Xenophobia". One of the final products of this project was the "Decalogue of European Citizenship against Racism and Xenophobia" published with a comprehensive comparative report made by each country.

These are some of the many important projects developed or led by the Spanish Observatory for Racism and Xenophobia. In fact, the list could be longer but the objective of this article is not presenting a detailed history of the activities carried out by the Observatory. However, such a list should include the intense work the Observatory conducts in all subjects related to training and promotion of codes and good practice regarding the Media. The Observatory promoted and edited a research on this issue by José Carlos Sendín Gutiérrez and Patricia Izquierdo Lázaro (2008). Moreover, it promoted annual reports on how information about immigration is addressed in Spain, written by Nicolás Lorite García and the research group that he leads, MIGRACOM.

For all the reasons stated above, linking this Observatory and our concern for the struggle against discrimination through the mass media is fully justified. Now we deem necessary to focus on those codes that are being created by professionals of the media with the aim of regulating everything related to this struggle.

3. What do Codes of Ethics[8] and Style Guides for journalists in Spain say?

After World War II, it became clear that the media were a powerful tool to shape public opinion. However, journalists were not the first to take the steps towards an ethical regulation of their work. It was mainly a consequence of the pressure exercised by international and European organisations mentioned in the previous section, and especially through their professional associations.

Following the already mentioned UN Charter of 1945, the Universal Declaration of Human Rights and the UN International Convention on the Elimination of all Forms of Racial Discrimination, UNESCO promoted in 1978 the adoption of the "Declaration on Fundamental Principles Concerning the Contribution of the Mass Media to Strengthening Peace and International Understanding, to the Promotion of Human Rights and to Countering Racialism, Apartheid and Incitement to War". All documents mentioned before are cited in the Preamble of this document, but it goes further than general considerations specifying the rights and obligations of the mass media.

Regarding documents drafted by and for journalists, we can mention the "Declaration of Principles on the Conduct of Journalists"[9]as one of the first adopted in 1954 in the Second International Federation of Journalists World Congress. Another one was that produced by the Consultative Club of International and Regional Organizations of Journalists in 1983, under the auspices of UNESCO, which is called "International Principles of Professional Ethics in Journalism"[10]. Nevertheless, if we compare those two documents written by journalists with the ethical nature of the Declaration of Fundamental Principles issued by UNESCO in 1978, the degree of awareness regarding discrimination seems clearly insufficient (Zalbidea and Pérez, 2008, 155-156).

Among European initiatives that had some impact in Spain, we find the recommendations made by the Parliamentary Assembly of the Council of Europe "on the cultural dimension of broadcasting in Europe"[11]. Back then, the Council of Europe expressed concern for the increase of private media and the lack of regulating mechanisms for their work. This document focused on education in values, representation of cultural diversity and equal treatment of linguistic and ethnic minorities within the European Community. Resolution 1003 on journalism ethics[12], adopted by the Parliamentary Assembly in 1993, persistently recommended all member states to exercise control on media productions and requested media groups to establish internal codes of ethics.

In the case of Spain, the progressive publication of codes of ethics by Spanish mass media has been conditioned, especially, by its development since Franco's dictatorship until today (see Bustamante, 1995; Retis, 2010). The adoption of ethical principles by Spanish journalists has gained importance since the nineties —and especially since the last decade— due to a combination of elements such as the proliferation of media, growth of private capital in the information field, but also economic prosperity and consequential labour immigration in Spain (attention towards treatment of national, ethnic and cultural diversity grew as immigration flows from third countries increased, see García *et al.*, 1998, 181). Finally, the spread of the Internet and digital journalism experienced since the beginning of the 21st century has made ethics one of the most pressing issues of communications today.

The Catalan Audiovisual Council took one of the first and strongest steps towards equality in Spanish mass media (Nuñez Encabo, 1997) with its "Declaration of Principles for Journalism in Catalonia"[13] published in 1992. The Spanish Federation of Press Associations (FAPE) adopted a code of ethics in 1993 that framed a fundamental criterion: to avoid mentioning characteristics referring to the affiliation of a person to a minority group provided this to be irrelevant to the information published[14]. The *Manual de estilo sobre minorías étnicas* (Style Guide on Ethnic Minorities), published by the Official Association of Journalists of Catalonia[15] in 1996, was the first to include specific instructions on how to tackle information related to foreign ethnic minorities with rigour and avoiding discriminatory prejudice. This guide became a relevant reference in times when Spain was becoming one of the countries of the European Union to receive most foreign immigrant population (this does not mean that all journalists know and use it in their routine work).

In the following lines we will briefly go through various internal codes of ethics used by the leading and most influential media in Spain[15]. The ethical principles are generally included in the Editorial Statutes[16] or Style Guides of each newspaper. Compliance with these documents is mandatory for the former and only suggested in the case of the latter. It is important to mention that in spite of what European Union Resolution 1003 establishes, few Spanish mass media have issued an Editorial Statute for their organisation.

El País published its Statutes in 1980, but the text does not make any reference to equal treatment of persons mentioned in the news covered by the newspaper[17]. On the contrary, the one published by *El Mundo* does include some reference: "*El Mundo* will pay special attention to the rights of minorities"[18]. *ABC,* the newspaper with the third highest circulation in Spain, has never published an Editorial Statute[19].

Regarding national broadcast media[20], only *RTVE*[21] and the network COPE[22] have issued a code of ethics. *Radio Televisión Española* (RTVE), a public media network, adopted a set of statutes in 2008 and added it to Section II "Rights and Obligations". However, only one of its nineteen ethical principles mentions non-discrimination on the grounds of race, religious belief or social and cultural origin.

The statutes issued by *EFE News Agency*—the world's largest news agency in Spanish[23]—is one of the most comprehensive ones. This document was adopted in 2006 and takes a clear stand on the commitment towards defending fundamental rights by adopting the "principles of professional ethics in journalism" issued by UNESCO, the Council of Europe and the International Federation of Journalists".

Style guides, on the other hand, are reference tools for journalists. Usually, the first part includes general considerations and then it is organized as a dictionary of common doubts, giving recommendations on preferential use for specific words and expressions.

El Mundo Style Guide, for example, presents the following remark, which is especially relevant:

> "Scornful expressions related to ethnic groups, religions or any given group are forbidden, and special attention must be paid to expressions that do not seem racist, but which can be considered as such depending on the context; for example, saying that some "gypsies" or "Moroccans" have been arrested in cases where the origin of those concerned is as irrelevant as if they were Aragonese, blond or Adventist."

Other style guides (such as the one published by Vocento Group, owner of *ABC,* but also those of *El País, La Vanguardia* and *El Periódico de Catalunya*) have few variations in comparison with the books described before (see Zalbidea and Pérez, 2008, 162-164).

After analysing codes of ethics and ethical principles developed and implemented in Spain, it becomes evident that in spite of the abundant and redundant recommendations for good practices in most news media, their real application in journalism is ineffective, especially regarding the private sector. In fact, many of the recommendations and/or explanations made are due to deficiencies journalists have had for a long time and continue to have in their professional practice; for example, we can still see news that refer to "Arabs" as if it were a race, or the "black race".

The results of many research works relating the mass media and immigration that blame the former for the public's perception regarding foreign immigrants are partly due to said deficiencies. In fact, many of said deficiencies are faithfully reflected in opinion polls, both questions and answers, carried out by the media.

4. What do opinion polls reveal about foreign immigration in Spain?

The role of the media in shaping public opinion, or the latter's role in shaping the former's agenda, is not easy to establish. It is therefore very difficult to determine and verify the media's degree of influence in shaping a state of mind about a particular social phenomenon. Certainly, one of the main issues regarding the role of the media in contemporary societies is their ability to influence, from a prevalent and privileged position, the public opinion of a country.

Avoiding the debate raised by Bourdieu (1973) back in his days on the way opinion polls are designed to gauge public opinion, and assuming his objections regarding their performance and functions, we believe it is a useful tool to learn what the citizens of a country think about a phenomenon such as immigration.

We know that opinion polls in Spain essentially reveal the relationship between what the public thinks and what the media publish about foreign immigration. We consider said relationship in terms of cause and effect in both directions: media-opinion and opinion-media.

We also recognize the importance of institutional and awareness policies in the European Union that support, protect and promote social and cultural diversity, represented by ethnic and national minorities present in its territory, as well as their rights. In line with these policies, ethical codes of conduct have been developed in Spain which set boundaries on those journalism practices that are disrespectful to social and cultural diversity. Their existence does not mean, however, that these actions have an influence on public opinion; that is, that the perception of the phenomenon has improved. This is what we gather from opinion poll results when these address issues related to foreign immigration.

The role of transmitter of certain knowledge about the migration phenomenon to the public opinion, usually ascribed to the media is, in light of the research produced, a shared attribution. That is, as part of their information production practices, the media create a certain view of the phenomenon. The resulting public opinion facilitates the reproduction of those practices by the media, simplifying and stereotyping the information model that is published. Thus, media consumers fit into a predetermined model or script ('immigrants', '*pateras*', 'Moroccan', 'Saharan', 'irregular', 'avalanche') that, in turn, enables the simplification of information units in the headlines.

Research carried out from a qualitative approach (in-depth interviews or focus groups) and from a quantitative approach (mainly through surveys) demonstrates the close relationship between the information published in newspapers, radio and television, and Spaniard's opinion regarding immigrants and immigration. The ground breaking reports conducted between 1995 and 2000[24] by the CIPIE Foundation and the most recent MIGRACOM[25] studies (Migration and Communication Observatory and Research Group) of the Universitat Autònoma de Barcelona, to name just two examples, establish conclusively the terms of said relationship.

The opinion generated about foreign immigration has proven to be subject to the flow of events and to its presence or absence in the media, which either amplify and magnify them, reduce them to almost nothing, or simply ignore them in favour of market-driven news that disregard their impact: disinformation and manipulation of reality. Research in Spain shows, for example, that one of the motives cited to explain why Spaniards consider immigration as a problematic and problematizing phenomenon lies in the way the media handle it (Granados, 1998; Cea D'Ancona, 2004, Colectivo IOÉ, 2005).

One of the pioneers of that research is the Centre for Sociological Research (CIS)[26], which has been conducting survey-based research focused on immigration[27] for years. Successive CIS Barometers have shown that the phenomenon of migration and foreign immigration, along with unemployment, ETA terrorism and socio-economic problems, is at the head of the country's problems. Some CIS Barometers' questions have been repeated periodically with a similar methodology, leading to the corresponding time series. As an example, and purely to illustrate the Spanish population's opinion of the migration phenomenon, we used the series published by the CIS in its barometers corresponding to the month of March of the last 12 years, with the exception of September 2000, when immigration was included as an option to the question shown in Figure 1.

As shown, only unemployment remains as the main problem, except during the first years of this period when it alternates with ETA terrorism. Primarily as a result of the economic crisis, in the last 5 years of the period unemployment and economic problems appear well above ETA terrorism —which goes from first to the least of the problems— and immigration, which, despite its decline during that period, remains one of the first problems perceived by the Spanish public.

In addition to the CIS, Spanish opinion on migration has been studied elsewhere.

At a regional level, Andalusia, through the Andalusian Permanent Observatory for Migration (OPAM), conducts the survey "Opinions and attitudes of the Andalusian population towards immigration", of which 4 editions have been published. The latest publication includes a chapter

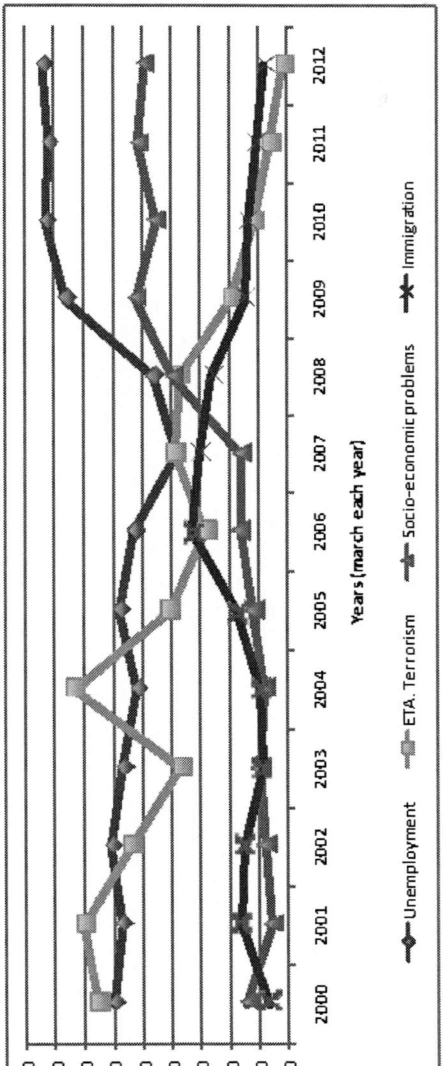

Figure 10-1. "What, in your opinion, are the three major problems that currently exist in Spain?' Source: prepared by the authors on the basis of CIS Barometers.

titled "Public opinion on immigration" (OPIA-IV, OPAM 2011, 93-131) which provides data relative to the whole of Spain and compares it to that available on Europe. Thus, the results of the OPIA-IV survey enable the contextualization of data concerning the whole of Spain with that of Europe.

In the Basque Country, the Basque Observatory of Immigration (*Ikuspegi*) conducts annual studies that gather the Basques' opinion on the migration phenomenon.

At a European level, the Eurobarometer[28] is a survey conducted biannually since 1973 in each of the 27 EU countries (Eurobarometer, 2011). Similarly to the CIS Barometers, the Eurobarometer regularly introduces questions about the two most important issues that must be faced as a country and individually. Immigration is one of the problems suggested out of a total of 16 (unemployment, housing, terrorism, etc.)

As previously noted, the Spanish Observatory for Racism and Xenophobia also publishes reports on the evolution of racism and xenophobia in Spain which include questions about immigration. In the 2010 report (Cea D'Ancona and Vallés, 2010) there is a section devoted to the role of the media in the views and imagery on immigration. That section recalls the old hypothesis—supported by specialized literature—that established a close relationship between the outcome of the first CIS surveys on immigration and racism and what is broadcasted by the media. "To try to demonstrate this relationship, one of the analytical resources was (and continues to be) the comparison between the so-called statistical or administrative reality and the reality of public opinion research" (Cea D'Ancona and Vallés, 2010, 301). The report's authors refer to the question that was first inserted into the 2009 CIS-OBERAXE survey to learn which is or are the sources that shape opinion on the migration phenomenon. A significant percentage (26%) of the answers to the question "In your view, the opinions people have about immigration are fundamentally influenced by…" point to "the news in the media" (Cea D'Ancona and Vallés, 2010, 302).

5. The difficult relationship between the media and public opinion in the task of representing and perceiving foreign immigration

In addition to the previously stated, our contribution to this line of work, at first from the Laboratory of Intercultural Studies (LdEI) and, secondly, from the Migration Institute of the University of Granada, goes back to

1998 when research was published as a Doctoral Thesis on immigration and media (Granados, 1998). The work analysed news about foreign immigrants (news with headline and/or subhead, subtitle and intro, and editorials, printed in *ABC*, *Diario 16*, *El Mundo* and *El País*) from a corpus of 10,164 copies published between 1985 and 1992. A pioneer in its way of approaching the image of foreign immigrants in the Spanish press, the research came to a series of conclusions from which —despite the 20 years passed off since the end of the period analysed in this study and the changes in Spanish society— in essence one could state that the today image continues to be designed, shaped, shown, narrated and interpreted in the same way by the press, and by extension by the rest of the media. The public's perception preserves a very marked bias towards a problematic and conflictive image that generates concern and reservations.

Since that first piece of work, others have come to light by different means and in different times (García, Granados and de la Fuente, 2008; Granados, 2001, 2004, 2006 and 2007; Kressova *et al.*, 2010; Granados, Olmos and Kressova, 2012) and, all of them show new data revealing the close dependence of the Spanish public opinion on the media regarding the way the migration phenomenon and foreign immigration are perceived.

To demonstrate this dependence with a specific example, we will go into detail about one of the works cited (García, Granados and de la Fuente, 2008) because it was based on a new source (compared to those previously used). We set out to analyse two versions of the migration phenomenon: the one gathered from official statistics on foreign residents in Spain, and the one presented in print media. We were trying to demonstrate how the press made a very particular reading of the statistics published by the National Institute of Statistics (INE, for its acronym in Spanish). To this end, using data from the Municipal Register sought to contrast the INE "Press Releases" with what was offered and published in some newspapers the following day. After each INE Press Release, the media usually echo the information provided and generate their own news analysing its content. The work takes into account, on the one hand, the Press Releases issued by the INE between 2003 and 2007 and, on the other hand, the news published in four newspapers that represent a wide, varied and heterogeneous ideological spectrum: *El País*, *El Mundo*, *La Vanguardia* and *ABC*.

Out of the various interpretations gathered from the analysis comparing INE Press Releases and information units published by the four newspapers, a very specific profile of the migration phenomenon can be obtained: (1) newspapers ascribe an evident leading role to the foreign minority; (2) the most striking fact, however, is the repeated use and indiscriminate exchange of the terms foreigner and immigrant without providing any explanation to justify this association; (3) a widespread conceptual abuse—even though the INE expressly clarifies that a considerable part of the foreign population was born in Spain—when citing different nationalities, instead of countries of origin; (4) the Press Releases that include the statistical use of the Register have a structure and argumentative rhetoric that exposes their intention: they encourage newspaper writers to use them, with minor stylistic touches, as part of their newspaper headlines.

One has but to compare the INE Releases to the news headlines—subhead, title, subtitle(s) and intro. Thus, the print media act as a transmission belt of information whose main components are provided by the INE. Especially the press cause the migration phenomenon to be perceived as the driving force behind the Spanish population growth, over any other data that can be obtained from the Register. They transform those data into valuation figures that highlight and magnify foreigners. Opinion polls show the weight that this media construct has on the perception of the phenomenon: the average citizen does not regularly look at INE statistics but does read, hear and see those shown by the mass media.

To evidence the different filters through which INE statistical data strain to the media producing very specific effects on receptors' perception, one can cite the example of the Press Release issued on March 1st, 2007, which provides the "Statistical Use of the Municipal Register of January 1st, 2006. Final Data". The two large headlines in bold at the beginning of the note read as follows: "The population residing in Spain reaches 44,708,964 people on January 1st, 2006" and "The number of foreigners is 4,144,166, which accounts for 9.3% of the total registered". The first thing that stands out is why, out of all the variables that appear in the Register and that provide statistical data about the population—such as age, sex, educational level, marital status, etc.—the Press Release highlights first and foremost the number of foreigners. In fact, over 90% of the six pages of information gathered in the Release refer exclusively to data on the foreign population (by autonomous communities, municipalities, by nationality, etc.).

To make matters worse, the second paragraph of the Release reads: "Between 1st January 2005 and 1st January 2006, the number of Spaniards registered increased by 186,878 (0.5%), while foreigners increased by 413,556 (11.1%)". This is to say that there are increasingly less of us Spaniards and increasingly more foreigners, but not just any foreigners. The "Most numerous nationalities" section includes the following entry:

"The most numerous foreigners are Moroccans (563,012), followed by Ecuadorians (461,310), Romanians (407,159), UK citizens (274,722) and Colombians (265,141) [...]."

It is worth calling attention to the term "UK citizens" as opposed to the mere nationality of the other foreigners mentioned. There are no stylistic reasons to "break" with the list of the nationalities and speak of "British" unless, for some reason, there is an intention to stress the idea that "UK citizens" are not immigrants. Proof of this, beyond naive considerations, is that the British do not appear on the survey answers. It should not come as a surprise, then, that most answers to the question of whom Spaniards think of when it comes to immigrants living in Spain are those identified as 'North African (Moroccan, Moorish, Maghrebi, Algerians)'. The percentage of answers that follows identifies them as 'African, sub-Saharan, black', whose countries are included among the most numerous in the Press Release. It is conceivable, then, that the persistent reports in the media about the arrival of people identified as 'black' (Africans and sub-Saharans) in *pateras* or *cayucos,* i.e., small boats often used for illegal immigration, are feeding those answers.

6. Conclusion

Following the policies to combat racism and discrimination in Europe and the measures aimed at raising awareness among European citizens, particularly from the media, it is difficult not to recognize the impact of the latter on their opinion regarding foreign immigration. While there has been significant progress, especially in the use of negative and/or discriminatory terms and expressions, as well as in the use of certain images on television, the fact remains that the most recent studies on the representation of immigration in the media do not offer very significant differences from the way in which such representations were made 20 years ago.

Different opinion polls in Spain and other EU countries are not especially encouraging in regards to the assessment they make of the diversity represented by citizens (foreigners or not; immigrants or not) whose image is drawn on the basis of generic traits that highlight their status as different and their otherness. Successive plans for raising local, national or supranational awareness and the integration policies that have been developed in recent years have failed to break the "glass ceiling" represented by the media as mediators between the immigration reality and public opinion.

Neither codes of ethics nor good professional practices or style guides have been able to overcome the information production customs. Consequently, despite their good intentions and the considerable number of recommendations they make to the daily practice of ethically committed journalism regarding the recognition of human dignity, they have failed to substantially change the format and rhetoric of news, be they about immigration, domestic violence or any other social phenomena. The supposed alliance between the first and the fourth power and its role in the service towards structural changes in society seem more a work of fiction (and wishful thinking) than reality.

Perhaps the realization of failure lies in having projected onto the media expectations regarding their role in reducing or eliminating racism and discrimination that are not justified, either because of its social function or its operating business logic. Either way, the feeling of frustration that stems from the alleged failure deserves at least some consideration, both from the media themselves and all political bodies that promote legislative initiatives or anti-racism. Perhaps the origin of the mistake lies in considering the media as promoters of discourses that reproduce behaviours, attitudes and opinions that exclude or denote the difference represented by a foreign immigrant. Thus, it is seen as fit, by political bodies that promote the struggle against racism, to involve the media in that struggle.

In any case, there is one verifiable fact: the development of internal codes of ethics remains an unfinished task for most of the Spanish media. Its absence in major private media groups, and especially in radio and television, is particularly alarming. According to data from AIMS[29] for 2011, 14.6% of media consumption in Spain corresponds to print media, 23.4% to radio, and 35% to television. This means that the most consumed media by Spaniards are, by far, radio and, especially, television. However, those types of media have fewer mechanisms to regulate and control their way of producing information. Furthermore, one must not forget the growing importance of information provided over the Internet. Its use affects 17% of Spaniards and the trend is clearly increasing. One must also take into account the digital media that often live on the fringes of professional associations and who are not interested in drafting their own codes of ethics.

The situation of crisis, particularly in Europe, pushes the issue of combating racism and xenophobia, discrimination against minorities and promoting equal treatment to peripheral positions from its very start, disappearing from politicians' speeches and media attention. However, ideological stances are strongly resurfacing in this context, in the shape of political forces associated with Europe's far right, which revive old racist and discriminatory discourses of times considered to be over. The focus of these discourses is the foreign immigrant population from countries outside Europe, as well as ethnic minorities, groups of people of a certain sexual orientation, etc. We therefore believe that now more than ever it is necessary to keep fighting for equal rights for all, because if we stand still, we might wake up one day in a world in which Breivik's ideas permeate our leader's speeches and guide their policies.

Notes

1. This text is aimed at providing some basis for the relation between the mass media and racist and xenophobe discourses that we have developed in the project "Discourses on Foreign Nationals in Andalusian Media: Discursive and Visual Construction of the New Andalusia" (Excellence Project of the Government of Andalusia – reference: TIC–6517– of 2010 call, head researcher is Professor Antolín Granados Martínez). The contribution of Lucia Chovancova has been possible thanks to Introduction to the Research Scholarship, given by the Vice-Rector's Office for Science and Research (University of Granada).
2. Our observations are based on a monograph written by Blázquez (2000) and an article by Begoña Zalbidea and Juan Carlos Pérez Fuentes (2008). Please, refer to them for more information on the history of ethics in Spanish mass media.
3. Available at:http://www2.ohchr.org/english/law/pdf/cerd.pdf .
4. Available at: http://europa.eu/legislation_summaries/other/c10411_es.htm.
5. The complete text of the Declaration can be accessed at:
http://www.eycb.coe.int/edupack/fr_68.html.
6. See, for example, the Observatory web site where it is stated that it was created "under the dispositions of Article 71 of 4/2000 Organic Law"
(http://www.oberaxe.es/quienes/).
7. Reports on the evolution of racism and xenophobia in Spain are drafted by M. Ángeles Cea and Miguel S. Valles who use a national survey conducted by the Centro de Investigaciones Sociológicas (CIS)—requested by the Ministry of Labour and Immigration—on the Spanish population about "Attitudes towards discrimination based on racial or ethnic origin" (2008 report was based on survey conducted in 2007) and "Attitudes towards immigration" (2009 and 2010 reports were based on surveys conducted in 2008 and 2009, respectively). Before that, in 2005 and 2006, the Observatory had requested a research on "Spaniards' opinions about racism and xenophobia" (See Manuel Pérez Yruela's work included in the References) to the *Instituto de Estudios Sociales Avanzados de Andalucía* (IESA) under the Consejo Superior de Investigaciones Científicas (CSIC). Apart from those reports, Prof. M. Ángeles Cea has issued several publications aimed at "measuring" racism and xenophobia; we have mentioned the most relevant in the references This topic will be further developed in the foregoing pages.
8. By 'codes of ethics in communications', we mean the group of specific principles, rules and precepts presented in a logical and systematic manner as

initiative from the information sector to correctly guide their work" (Niceto Blázquez, 2000, 72).

9. It can be seen at http://www.ifj.org/docs/ETHICS-E.DOC

10. Available at:
http://ethicnet.uta.fi/international/international_principles_of_professional_ethics_in_journalism

11. Recommendation 1067 (1987) on the cultural dimension of broadcast in Europe. Available in
http://assembly.coe.int//main.asp?link=http://assembly.coe.int/documents/adoptedtext/TA87/erec1067.htm

12. *Resolution 1003 (1993) on the ethics of journalism*. It can be seen at
http://assembly.coe.int/main.asp?link=http://assembly.coe.int/documents/adoptedtext/ta93/eres1003.htm#1

13. The "Declaració de principis de la professió periodística a Catalunya" can be seen at http://www.periodistes.org/documents_codi_deontologic

14. Available athttp://www.comisiondequejas.com/Codigo/Codigo.htm

15. The complete text of this Guide is published at:
http://www.cac.cat/pfw_files/cma/recerca/quaderns_cac/Q12manual_ES.pdf

15. See Nordenstreng (2000) to know more about the history and current situation of the issue of ethic principles and communication in Europe.

16. Editorial Statutes define internal regulation and participation mechanisms. They usually establish the framework within which professional relations are developed, including rights and obligations of information workers and participation bodies (editorial councils, professional committees).

17. The Editorial Statute published by *El País* can be accessed at
http://elpais.com/diario/1980/06/21/economia/330386406_850215.html

18. Data published by the Asociación para la Investigación de los Medios de Comunicación (http://www.aimc.es).

19. Other regional newspapers also have their Editorial Statute. In Catalonia *La Vanguardia*, *El Periódico de Catalunya* and *El Punt*; and in Galicia *La Voz de Galicia*.

20. Some broadcast media with Editorial Statute are TV3 (radio and TV network in Catalonia), Canal 9 and Radio Nou (Valencian Community), Canal Sur TV and Canal Sur Radio (Andalusia). Especially, the Canal Sur Style Guide since it contains wide comments and suggestions on the treatment of the image of immigrants. This document is available at:
http://www.canalsur.es/resources/archivos/2010/3/22/1269268079994LibrodeestiloCanalSur.pdf

21. Acronym in Spanish for public company Corporación Radio y Televisión Española. The document mentioned is called "*Estatuto de información de la Corporación RTVE*" (Information Statute of RTVE Corporation) and is available at: http://www.rtve.es/files/70-9843-FICHERO/ESTATUTO_DE_INFORMATIVOS_v1.pdf.

22. Available at: http://www.cope.es/ideario

23. Available at:http://efe.com/FicherosDocumentosEFE/estatuto.pdf

24. Available at: http://www.eurosur.org/CIPIE/prensa.htm

25. Information treatment of immigration in Spain: research conducted in 2002, 2006, 2007 and 2008 (http://www.migracom.com/migracom), which we refer to above.
26. Available at: http://www.cis.es/cis/opencms/ES/index.html
27. The studies we refer to are the following: Research 1882 September 1990, immigration and racism (I); Research 1964 April 1991, immigration and racism (II); Study 2051, March 1993, attitudes towards immigration (I); Research 2214, June 1996, Research attitudes towards immigration (II); Research 2131, January 1995, attitudes towards immigration (I); Research 2773, September 2008, attitudes towards immigration (II); Research 2817, October 2009, attitudes towards immigration (III); Research 2846, September 2010, attitudes towards immigration (IV) y Research 2731, September 2007 attitudes towards discrimination due to race or ethnicity.
28. Available at: http://ec.europa.eu/public_opinion/index_fr.htm
29. Data obtained from http://www.aimc.es/-Datos-EGM-Resumen-General-.html

Bibliography

Blázquez, Niceto. 2000. *El Desafío ético de la Información*. Salamanca: Editorial San Esteban.

Bourdieu, Pierre. 1973. "L'opinion publique n'existe pas." *Les temps moderns* 318: 1292-1309.

Bustamante, Enrique. 1995. "The Mass-Media: A Problematic Modernization." In *Spanish cultural studies: an introduction: the struggle for modernity*, ed. Helen Graham and Jo Labanyi, 356-380. New York: Oxford University Press.

Cachón Rodríguez, Lorenzo. 2004. "España y la Directiva 2000/43: de la 'ocasión perdida' a una legislación general sobre igualdad de trato." *Tiempo de Paz* 73: 13–22.

Cea D'Ancona, M. Ángeles and Miguel S. Valles Martínez. 2010. *Evolución del racismo y la xenofobia en España [Informe 2010]*. Madrid: OBERAXE. Ministerio de Trabajo e Inmigración.

Cea D'Ancona, M. Ángeles. 2004. *La activación de la xenofobia en España. ¿Qué miden las encuestas?* Madrid: CIS/Siglo XXI.

Colectivo IOÉ and Eliconia. 2009. *Motivos de discriminación en España. Estudio exploratorio*. http://www.colectivoioe.org/ Last accessed on 12 May 2012.

Colectivo IOÉ. 2005. "Ciudadanos o intrusos: la opinión pública española ante los inmigrantes." *Papeles de Economía Española* 104: 194-209.

ECRI (European Commission against Racism and Intolerance). 1999. *Report on Spain*. Strasbourg: ECRI. http://hudoc.ecri.coe.int/XMLEcri/ENGLISH/Cycle_01/01_CbC_eng/01-cbc-spain-eng.pdf. Last accessed on 10 May 2012.

ECRI (European Commission against Racism and Intolerance). 2003. *Second Report on Spain*. Strasbourg: ECRI. http://hudoc.ecri.coe.int/XMLEcri/ENGLISH/Cycle_02/02_CbC_eng/02-cbc-spain-eng.pdf. Last accessed on 10 May 2012.

Esteve García, Francina. 2008. "Las directivas europeas contra la discriminación racial y la creación de organismos especializados para promover la igualdad. Análisis comparativo de su transposición en España y en Francia." *Revista de Derecho Constitucional Europeo* 10: 189–230.

Eurobarometer = Dirección General de Comunicación de la Comisión Europea. 2011. *Eurobarómetro Standard 76. Opinión pública en la Unión Europea. Otoño 2011. Informe Nacional: España*. http://ec.europa.eu/public_opinion/archives/eb/eb76/eb76_es_es_nat.pdf. Last accessed on 10 May 2012.

García Castaño, F. Javier and Nina Kressova. Forthcoming. "El Observatorio Español del Racismo y la Xenofobia." In *Comentario a la ley y al reglamento de extranjería, inmigración e integración social*, ed. José Luís Monereo Pérez. Granada: Comares.

García Castaño, F. Javier, Antolín Granados Martínez and Begoña de la Fuente. 2008. "La población inmigrante extranjera, el padrón municipal y su reflejo en la prensa." In *Manual sobre comunicación e inmigración*, ed. Antonio M. Bañón Hernández and Javier Fornieles Alcaraz, 255-279. Donostia/San Sebastián: Gakoa.

García Castaño, F. Javier, Antolín Granados Martínez and María García Cano-Torrico. 1998. "Racialismo en el curriculum y en los libros de texto. La transmisión de discursos de la diferencia en el curriculum oficial de la Comunidad Autónoma andaluza y en los libros de texto de la educación primaria." In *La educación intercultural en Europa. Un enfoque curricular*, ed. Xavier Besalú, Giovanna Campani and Josep Miguel Palaudàrias, 181-209. Barcelona: Pomares-Corredor.

Granados, Antolín, Antonia Olmos and Nina Kressova. Forthcoming. "Medios de comunicación e inmigración extranjera en Andalucía. Breves apuntes sobre el estado de la cuestión." In *La inmigración en Andalucía. Instituciones, aspectos jurídico-sociales y culturales*, ed. José Luís Monereo Pérez. Granada: Comares.

Granados, Antolín. 1998. *La imagen del inmigrante extranjero en la prensa española: ABC, Diario 16, El Mundo y El País (1985-1992)*. Ph.D dissertation. Granada: Universidad de Granada.

—. 2001. "La construcción de la realidad de la inmigración: el inmigrante extranjero en la prensa de Andalucía." In *I Jornades per a la integració, la convivència i la ciutadania*, ed. Ajuntament de Terrassa, 135-168. Terrassa: Ajuntament de Terrassa.

—. 2004. "El tratamiento de la inmigración marroquí en la prensa española." In *Atlas de la inmigración marroquí en España*, ed. Bernabé López García and Mohamed Berriane, 438-439. Madrid: Universidad Autónoma de Madrid.

—. 2006. "Reflexiones en torno al fenómeno migratorio." In *Medios de comunicación, opinión y diversidad (social y cultural)*, ed. Manuel Lario Bastida, 59-84. Murcia: Caja de Ahorros del Mediterráneo.

—. 2007. "La realidad narrada y la realidad opinada de la inmigración extranjera en España." In *Medios de comunicación, inmigración y sociedad*, ed. Juan José Igartua and Carlos Muñiz, 35-59. Salamanca: Ediciones Universidad de Salamanca.

Kressova, Nina, Marta Granados, F. Javier García Castaño and Antolín Granados. 2010. "Poniendo adjetivos a la inmigración. Observaciones sobre la imagen del colectivo inmigrante proyectada desde la prensa andaluza." In *Mediterráneo migrante: tres décadas de flujos migratorios*, ed. Carlos de Castro, Elena Gadea, Natalia Moraes and Andrés Pedreño, 217-239. Murcia: Universidad de Murcia.

Nordenstreng, Kaarle. 2002. "Media ethics in Europe: in search of core values". In *Ethics and mass communication in Europe,* ed. Vincent Porter, 27-35. London: University of Westminster.

Nuñez Encabo, Manuel. 1997. "Código deontológico o Código Penal." *El País. Edición digital.* http://elpais.com/diario/1997/01/07/sociedad/852591609_850215.html Last accessed on 12 May 2012.

OPAM. 2011. *Informe Anual «Andalucía e Inmigración 2010»*. Sevilla: Dirección General de Coordinación de Políticas Migratorias, Consejería de Empleo, Junta de Andalucía.

Retis, Jéssica (ed). 2010. *Los informativos diarios en BBC y TVE*. Madrid: Ediciones de la Torre

Sendín Gutiérrez, José Carlos and Patricia Izquierdo Lázaro. 2008. *Guía práctica para los profesionales de los medios de comunicación: tratamiento mediático de la inmigración.* Madrid: Ministerio de Trabajo y Asuntos Sociales.

Zalbidea, Begoña and Juan Carlos Pérez Fuentes. 2008. "La ética y la deontología de los medios en el tratamiento de la inmigración." In *Manual sobre comunicación e inmigración*, ed. Antonio M. Bañón Hernández and Javier Fornieles Alcaraz, 153-180. Donostia/San Sebastián: Gakoa.

CHAPTER ELEVEN

SPANISH POLITICAL DISCOURSE ON IMMIGRATION IN TIMES OF CRISIS

GEMA RUBIO CARBONERO
GRITIM (GRUP DE RECERCA INTERDISCIPLINARI SOBRE IMMIGRACIÓ- INTERDISCIPLINARY RESEARCH GROUP ON IMMIGRATION)
POMPEU FABRA UNIVERSITY

1. Introduction

This chapter aims to analyze political discourse on immigration in the context of the economic crisis in Spain. The main objective of this analysis is to understand the social representation of immigration depicted by Spanish politicians. How a politician depicts a particular social reality directly affects the way society interprets and assesses this reality. Hence, it is essential to understand the political representation in order to understand some of the perceptions and stereotypes that are currently present in Spanish (and Western European) society. This chapter also aims to explore the ways in which different attitudes and opinions about immigration are legitimated and justified by Spanish politicians.

Our assumption is that the current context of economic crisis in Spain has shaped and conditioned political discourse, and in particular that the way immigrants are represented and referred to may have changed with respect to the political discourse before the crisis started.

Therefore, in this study we carry out a systematic Discourse Analysis from a critical perspective in order to understand how immigration is portrayed, specifically focusing on parliamentary debates on immigration during the years 2010 and 2011.

These two years correspond to the end of the Socialist (PSOE) administration, led by President José Luis Rodríguez Zapatero, which was in power from March, 2004 to November, 2011. The socialists were ousted in the presidential elections at the end of 2011, which saw the election of current president Mariano Rajoy, leader of the more conservative Popular Party (PP). As a result of these presidential elections, there were no parliamentary sessions from September to December of 2011.

In order to provide a comprehensive account of this complex reality, this chapter is organized as follows: in Section 2, we provide the theoretical background to the study, discussing the tenets of Critical Discourse Analysis and previous studies that have used this method to analyze parliamentary discourse on immigration; in Section 3, we present the methods of selecting our corpus, and the categories of analysis used to accomplish our research goals; Section 4 presents and discusses the results of our analysis, presenting specific examples that illustrate the social representation of immigrants in relation to different topics; finally, Section 5 summarizes our findings and presents some conclusions derived from this research.

2. Theoretical Framework

The present study evaluates Spanish political discourse on immigration using Discourse Analysis with a critical perspective. This perspective involves a multidisciplinary study of the relationships between discourse, power and social inequality, in which the researcher takes a critical attitude towards a particular social reality and analyzes this reality based on the general discipline of Discourse Analysis.

López and de Santiago (2000) point out that in political communication it is particularly important to produce emotive discourse that, through representations, can shape the opinions of the audience. Hence, political discourse is, by definition, persuasive. The element of persuasion is achieved not only by what is said, but also by the way it is said: what is stated explicitly and what remains implied; the choice of lexis, argumentation, rhetorical style, etc. A sophisticated, multidisciplinary and systematic method is required to explore these various strategies and to account not only for the political discourse about immigration, but also for the representation which emerges from this discourse and the consequences this might have on the audience's interpretation.

It has been well documented that the way politicians portray a particular reality has an impact on the way the audience (i.e. society) interprets and assesses this reality (Ribas, 2000). Thus, the systematic analysis of political discourse allows us to discover the social representation of a particular reality. Social representations (see Moscovici, 2001; Martín Serrano, 2004) emphasize a particular interpretation of reality to the detriment of other interpretations, which are obviated, as well as promote some evaluations instead of others. How politicians represent immigration is particularly relevant due to their privileged position, in that they have access to a large audience and can influence and shape their opinions and attitudes about immigration.

Immigration has been a frequent and controversial topic in Spanish political discourse over the last years, and the object of considerable research interest (Márquez, 2007; Ribas, 2009; Rubio-Carbonero, 2011a; Zapata-Barrero *et al.*, 2008). These studies have identified a tendency to homogenize immigrants through the use of generalizations and stereotypes, which depersonalize them and portray them as a collective, with a different culture, that does not want to integrate or adapt to Spanish norms and values. It has also shown a discourse based on fear, which depicts immigration as a threat to Spanish society.

Though informed by the observations of these previous studies, we assume that the current economic crisis in Spain has affected political discourse on immigration. We thus aim to analyze Spanish political discourse on immigration within this context, and then to consider whether any changes have occurred.

3. Methodology

In this section we present the methods of selecting our corpus and the categories of analysis applied.

3.1. Collection and selection of corpus

To obtain our corpus we explored all the parliamentary debates occurring in the Spanish Courts (*Pleno y diputación permanente*) during the years 2010 and 2011, and identified all the debates on the topic of immigration.

In 2010 there were 78 sessions of parliamentary debates; however only 14 of them dealt with the topic of immigration in any way.

Similarly, in 2011, there were 57 sessions but only 11 touched on immigration. These numbers are striking if we consider that during 2005, and 2006 there were 45 parliamentary debates on immigration (Rubio-Carbonero, 2011a)

From these data, it becomes apparent that during this period of economic crisis, the topic of immigration is not as prominent in the political agenda as it was in the years before the crisis started.

The following table shows the number of sessions and the number of interventions (made by different politicians) covering topics related to immigration, during the two years analyzed.

Table 11-1. General corpus. Source: own elaboration.

Year	Number of sessions	Number of interventions
2010	14	56
2011	11	42

After exploring all the debates and interventions in which immigration was mentioned in some way, we then identified those in which immigration was the central topic (reported in Table 11-2). The remainder of debates were discarded and this reduced set of debates, centered specifically on immigration, became the focus of our analysis.

Table 11-2. Selected corpus. Source: own elaboration.

Year	Number of sessions	Number of interventions
2010	7	19
2011	7	30

Our corpus thus consisted of a total of 49 interventions from politicians of different political parties. We made no attempt to differentiate between politicians from different political parties, which was outside the scope of this study, but undertook a systematic analysis of all 49 interventions, in order to explore the social representation of immigration established by politicians in their discourse. We analyzed these interventions by means of highly specific categories suited to our research goals, which are described in the next section.

3.2. Categories of analysis

In order to uncover the social representation of immigration in Spanish political discourse during the economic crisis, we set out to study the roles and attributes given to the different social actors and the most relevant pragmatic presuppositions and implications which can be inferred.

The study of roles and attributes (see Van Leeuwen, 1995, 1996) given to the different social actors (immigrants, politicians, Spaniards) helps us understand how immigrants are depicted (as active, passive, victims, aggressors, saviors, etc.).

Pragmatic presuppositions and implications (Simon-Vanderbengen, White and Aijmer, 2007) are propositions that the speaker thinks the hearer knows, and which are not explicitly stated in the discourse. However, while presuppositions are taken for granted, implications are implied. Both types of propositions are considered pragmatic because they can be inferred from the context and thus are context-related. The study of what is explicitly and implicitly said provides us with an important perspective on how immigrants are represented and what attitudes politicians have about immigration.

In order to understand what strategies politicians use to justify and legitimate their different opinions and attitudes towards immigration, we focus on argumentative and rhetorical structures.

Within argumentative strategies, we specifically focus on *topoi* (Reisigl and Wodak, 2000, 2001) and *fallacies* (Van Eemeren and Grootendorst, 1992). *Topoi* are social beliefs, shared by a cultural community, which rely on norms and values that are only valid in certain contexts, but are presented in a generalized way, as if they were irrefutable truths which, since they are supposedly shared, do not need to be explained.

In relation to immigration, the most common *topoi* are those of *advantage* and *burden* (Rubio-Carbonero, 2011a). As we will see in detail in the following section, the *topos* of *burden* relies on the logical premise that, since immigration is a *burden*, we must take measures to control it.

The *topos of advantage* follows the logic that if an action is useful, it must be taken (and accordingly, if an action is not useful, it does not have to be taken). Through this lens, we see that most decisions about immigration policies are made by arguing that they will benefit a particular sector of society (generally autochthonous Spaniards).

Fallacies, following Van Eemeren and Grootendorst (1992, 208-209), are violations of one or more of the rules for critical discussion. The observance of these rules is essential for the resolution of any dispute, and any violation will thwart the resolution and thus be considered a *fallacy*. Fallacies, then, are arguments that may seem to be logical, but actually rely less on logic than on sociological values (for example, arguments that put pressure on the audience by appealing to their feelings).

Finally, we study the most relevant rhetorical structures, which are conscious modifications of language. Rhetorical structures can help to emphasize and de-emphasize different meanings, depending on the speaker's interests, and may be used to influence how the audience will understand and evaluate these meanings. Therefore, the study of structures such as *metaphors*, *disclaimers*, *repetitions*, *number game* or *hyperbole*, helps us understand how persuasion is achieved.

Bold letters are added to the examples in order to emphasize the different structures that are mentioned in the analysis, so that the reader can pinpoint them easily.

4. Results and discussion

Much ideological discourse relies on the ideological strategy (see Van Dijk, 1998; Martínez Lirola, 2008) of creating a polarity between *Us* (the *ingroup*, which in this case might be Spain or the specific political party) and *Them* (the *outgroup*: immigrants). Within this polarization, the general strategy is to emphasize *Their* negative aspects and *Our* positive ones; and de-emphasize (or minimize) *Our* negative aspects and *Their* positive ones. Clearly, political discourse is highly ideological discourse and so it is unsurprising that these strategies were frequent in the political discourse on immigration during the period analyzed.

As mentioned above, in our analysis, we address the use of different discursive strategies in relation to a set of common thematic points, or topics associated with immigration. Our analysis is structured thematically so that we may observe not only how politicians speak about immigration, but also what kind of topics they associate with this reality. Together these help us understand the social representation of immigration established by politicians, and how different attitudes are justified. We detected seven main topics related to immigration: the law for immigrants under 18, the arrest of foreigners, unemployment, the arrival of immigrants, domestic violence, overcrowded flats, and forced marriages.

All these topics have one contextual factor in common: the economic crisis. All topics related to immigration are frequently accompanied by discussion of the budget cuts reducing governmental support for immigrants. These cuts are always presumed to negatively affect integration, which in turn negatively affects Spaniards. Therefore, the budget cuts serve to strengthen the presupposed negative effects of immigration on Spain. These effects are not described or explained, but simply mentioned and taken for granted. Hence, the context of the economic crisis serves to increase the negative effects of immigration in the domains of education, health, social security, unemployment, etc. References to the decreased investment in services promoting immigrants' integration are also used to attack the government's performance and are mentioned, by members of opposing political parties, in relation to all of the topics described.

Thus, as we will see below, even in examples that are not explicitly focused on economic issues, the context of the crisis is always referred to as a backdrop that makes the situation worse.

4.1 The law for immigrants under 18

At the end of 2009, a law for foreign non-accompanied minors was passed[1], which provided benefits to minors that were not extended to immigrants over the age of 18. For example, minors could be cared for by social services and given a permit to stay in Spain if their families could not be found. The law also declared their right to an education during their stay in the country. Obviously, this law generated plenty of debate in parliament during 2010.

In this context, there is a very negative representation of immigrants, who are represented as swindlers, as seen in the following example:

> Primero, que se está produciendo un **fraude masivo y continuado** por parte de **gran número de inmigrantes** ilegales que asumen la condición de menor de edad sin serlo, con el objetivo de acogerse a los beneficios que ello les depara. Segundo, que la situación es tan **escandalosamente generalizada** que alcanza en algunas ocasiones a más del 60 por ciento de los acogidos por los servicios competentes de las comunidades autónomas. Tercero, que es del dominio público la participación de mafias organizadas dedicadas a proveer a estos falsos menores de la oportuna documentación, falsificada por supuesto, con el objeto de **burlar** a las autoridades de nuestro país, algo que constituye además un grave delito. (Vicente Ferrer, PP. 16 de febrero de 2010)
> (Firstly, a **massive and continuous fraud** is being perpetrated by **a great number of illegal immigrants** who pretend to be under 18, aiming to take advantage of the benefits this brings. Secondly, the situation is **so scandalously generalized** that it often applies to more than 60% of those obtaining the relevant services of the autonomous regions. Thirdly, there is widely acknowledged participation of organized mafias that provide these minors with the necessary documentation, of course falsified, with the objective of **evading** the authorities of our country, which is, furthermore, a serious offense. (Vicente Ferrer, PP. 16th February, 2010))

As we can see, immigrants are represented as people who are taking advantage of the law in order to evade the Spanish authorities. The use of *hyperbole* increases the scope and generalizes this representation to "a great number of illegal immigrants". In the same way, the hyperbolic phrase "scandalously generalized" maximizes the scope, representing (the vast majority of) immigrants as swindlers who are committing "massive and continuous fraud".

Furthermore, by using the *fallacy ad metum* (see Van Eemeren and Grootendorst, 1992), the speaker puts pressure on the audience by means of playing on their fears and depicting immigrants as a threat to Spanish stability. In contrast, the government is positively represented as being worried about minors, as seen in the example below:

> El Gobierno ha mostrado en múltiples ocasiones su disposición para ofrecer la mejor atención y protección de los menores extranjeros y se ha mostrado abierto a estudiar las propuestas tendentes a perfeccionar el sistema en todo lo que redunde en un mejor tratamiento jurídico de la inmigración juvenil. (Óscar Seco, PSOE. 16 de febrero de 2010).
> (The government has shown on multiple occasions its willingness to offer the best attention and protection to foreign minors, and has demonstrated it is open to study proposals geared towards improving the system in all ways related to the better juridical treatment of juvenile immigration. (Óscar Seco, PSOE. 16th February, 2010))

Here the discourse is full of lexis with positive connotations (*willingness, attention, protection, open to study, improve, to a better juridical treatment*), which represents the government positively, as active, determined and having a positive attitude towards foreign minors.

In accordance with this, there is an effort to minimize *Our* negative aspects. Thus, it is admitted that in some regions there are negative attitudes towards immigrant children, but this is depicted in an abstract, nominal way, in order to minimize the negative representation of Spaniards:

> Mi grupo parlamentario les ha ofrecido ahondar en los motivos por los que hay comunidades autónomas que son hostiles a los menores y que **introducen factores de discriminación negativa** en niños **por tener la condición de extranjeros**, ofreciéndonos a establecer e impulsar mecanismos de solidaridad interterritorial que posibiliten lo que usted, señor Olabarría, llamaba el pasado miércoles *reubicación territorial.* (Óscar Seco, PSOE. 16 de febrero de 2010)
> (My parliamentary group has offered to study in depth the reasons why there are autonomous communities that are hostile to minors and **introduce factors of negative discrimination** towards children **because they have a foreign condition**, and we have offered to establish and improve mechanisms of inter-territorial solidarity which would allow what you, Mr. Olabarría, called last Wednesday *territorial resettling.* (Óscar Seco, PSOE. 16th February, 2010))

As we can see, even though it is explicitly admitted that some regions of Spain are hostile to immigrants, the way it is phrased is highly abstract. The use of obscure and not very natural language serves to minimize the negative effect that would be produced in the hearer's mind if the speaker declared Spain to be racist or prejudiced against immigrants. Instead, this politician chooses abstract and de-personalized terms, describing these prejudices as "factors of negative discrimination" against children "because they have a foreign condition" (as if being a foreigner were a condition somebody has).

Thus the use of abstraction and obscure language minimizes the negative effect of what is stated. This strategy is widely used by politicians and the media when speaking about Spaniards' negative attitudes about immigration (Rubio-Carbonero, 2011a).

4.2 The arrest of foreigners

In relation to this topic, we found frequent references to a group of "immigrants related to delinquency". The type of delinquency is not specified, nor is the way in which these immigrants are 'related to' it; the relationship is simply assumed and regularly presented as fact. As a consequence, deporting such immigrants from Spain is considered positive and presented as something to be proud of:

> Sí hay instrucciones del ministerio en materia de ilegales. Se las voy a repetir una vez más. Tenemos una preocupación y es que **en materia de ilegales, en materia de expulsiones**, la policía concentre su trabajo en aquellos irregulares que tienen **bien relaciones con la delincuencia, bien antecedentes penales o bien acaban de salir de la cárcel**. Entendemos que ese es el trabajo más eficaz y para eso hemos creado una brigada especial de expulsiones, que estoy seguro de que a usted le alegrará saber que está trabajando bien. **El año pasado expulsó a 7.591 de estos irregulares, relacionados, vamos a decirlo así, con el delito**. Creemos que es una forma primero de cumplir la ley y segundo de beneficiar a los ciudadanos, puesto que estos **irregulares en relación con el delito lo que hacen es aumentar la inseguridad ciudadana**. (Alfredo Pérez Rubalcaba, PSOE. 24 de febrero de 2010).
> (There are instructions from the ministry on the matter of illegal (people). I am going to repeat them once more. We have one concern and it is that, on the matter of **illegal (people), on the matter of deportation,** the police should focus on those irregulars **who are related to delinquency, or have criminal records, or have just come out of prison**. We understand this is the most effective work, and that is why we have created a special deportation squad which, I am sure you will be glad to know, is working

well. **Last year, it deported 7.591 of these irregulars who are related, we'll put it that way, to delinquency**. We think this is a way firstly to ensure that the law is upheld and secondly to benefit the citizens, since **these irregulars related to delinquency decrease public safety**. (Alfredo Pérez Rubalcaba, PSOE. 24th February, 2010))

On the one hand, the discourse used here is again highly abstract and depersonalized. Immigrants are referred to as "illegal" or "irregular". In this way, they are objectified and, the hearer is spared from feeling any kind of empathy towards deported immigrants (see Rubio-Carbonero, 2011). In the same way, using the term "matter" in order to speak about people and deportation is another way to depersonalize these people and the act of expelling them from Spain.

On the other hand, the deportation of immigrants is depicted as something positive that benefits (native) citizens. The *topos of advantage* and, in particular, the *topos* of *pro bono nobis* (Reisigl and Wodak, 2000, 2001) is used here to justify the need to deport immigrants related to delinquency. In other words, it is posited that since deporting immigrants is positive for Spanish citizens, we must deport them. By appealing to this *topos*, and due to the common sense it evokes, no other explanation is needed in order to justify why immigrants (related to delinquency) should be deported.

4.3 Unemployment

As might be expected, the unemployment rate, and its steady increase, is among the most common topics related to the economic crisis. Accordingly, when speaking about immigration, there are frequent references to unemployment and to the poor working conditions of immigrants:

Señor ministro, la combinación de una **política económica desastrosa** y una política de inmigración **disparatada** ha colocado en una **situación dramática** a cientos de miles de españoles y de extranjeros. El paro entre inmigrantes, **según la EPA**, está en el 30 por ciento y supera el millón de personas, además otros 900.000 **inmigrantes trabajan en la economía sumergida**, y la ilegalidad real y la sobrevenida acechan a **cientos de miles** de extranjeros inmigrantes. Hoy **hay en España más inmigrantes que nunca y en una situación más precaria que nunca**. (Hernando Fraile, PP. 14 de abril de 2010).
(Mr. Minister, the combination of a **disastrous economic policy** and an **absurd immigration policy** has placed hundreds of thousands of Spaniards and foreigners in a **dramatic situation**. The unemployment rate

> of immigrants, **according to the EPA**, is at 30 per cent, or more than one million people; in addition, another 900.000 **immigrants work in the black market economy**, and real or forthcoming illegality threatens **hundreds of thousands** of foreign immigrants. Today **in Spain there are more immigrants than ever and they are in a more precarious situation than ever**. (Hernando Fraile, PP. 14th April, 2010))

As we can see, in this example there is a liberal use of *hyperbole*, which increases the scope of the issue and also helps to dramatize the situation. The use of adjectives such as "disastrous", "dramatic" or "precarious", together with the use of the expression "hundreds of thousands of foreign immigrants" exploits the effect of victimization of immigrants while appealing to pity and empathy. This *fallacy ad Misericordiam* (Van Eemeren and Grootendorst, 1992) constructs immigrants as passive victims of the government, which is constructed negatively, as an active aggressor provoking this negative situation. The speaker aims to reach the audience by appealing to pity and empathy; thus he does not offer any logical argument to support his claims, but instead appeals to the emotions of the audience.

Furthermore, in order to reinforce his claim, he also uses the fallacy of *argumentum ad verecundiam* (ibid), when he makes reference to the "EPA", appealing to an authority. Here, the EPA is presented as a reliable source, the author of the presented data, while Hernando Fraile appears as a mere transmitter of the data. Thus, the claim seems to be backed by an authority, a strategy to make it more convincing and, at the same time, to hide the responsibility of the speaker about what has been said.

In this context of economic crisis, *number game* (Van Dijk, 2003) is a very common discursive strategy, used to enhance persuasiveness and to provide discourse with apparent objectivity. Accordingly, in the period analyzed we found constant references to numbers: unemployed immigrants, budget cuts on funds for integration, health and education of immigrants, etc. Again, through the strategy of *number game*, immigration is portrayed as a threat to Spanish society, since the lack of funds for immigrants' integration is posited as negatively affecting the stability and well-being of Spanish society. Therefore, it manages to both represent immigration negatively and also to attack the government's performance and budget cuts.

4.4 The arrival of immigrants

In line with the general political (and media) discourse, which tends to represent the arrival of immigrants as a threat to Spain, during the period of time analyzed, the arrival of immigrants is presented as negative and depicted as a crisis which must be stopped, as seen in the following example:

> En julio, cuando empezó la **crisis fronteriza** sencillamente auspiciada por **alborotadores marroquíes** con la complacencia de la policía de aquel país y que tuvo una grave repercusión en nuestra ciudad, creíamos que con su visita a Rabat—bien es verdad que sin pasar por Melilla— se **iba a cerrar** la **crisis**. Pero la **crisis** de inmigración, señor ministro del Interior, **no se ha cerrado** y usted lo sabe bien. **No se ha cerrado** porque desde entonces, desde ese 15 de julio, hay un **goteo permanente** de inmigrantes subsaharianos que no llegan en pateras, que no llegan por la frontera sino que llegan en pequeñas balsas neumáticas, todas iguales, todos provistos con los mismos chalecos salvavidas, que parece que se han comprado en el mismo comercio. **No se ha cerrado**, señor ministro, porque ayer mismo —y estoy seguro de que S.S., con la atención que dedica a todo lo referente a Melilla lo ha leído en la prensa— hubo dos subsaharianos más que, a nado, desde el cercano puerto de Beni Enzar, llegaron a Melilla. (Antonio Gutierrez, PP. 15 de septiembre de 2010).
> (In July, when the **border crisis** began, instigated by **Moroccan troublemakers,** with the indulgence of the police of that country, which had a very serious impact on our city, we thought that with your visit to Rabat—it is true without passing through Melilla- the **crisis was going to be over**. But the immigration **crisis**, Mr. Minister of Internal Affairs, **is not over** and you know it very well. **It is not over** because since then, since that 15th of July, there has been a **steady trickle** of Sub-Saharan immigrants, arriving not in open boats, not across the border, but in rubber rafts, all the same, all equipped with the same lifejackets, that all seem to have been bought in the same shop. **It is not over**, Mr. Minister, because yesterday—I'm sure that you, considering all the attention you pay to everything related to Melilla, have read about it in the press- there were two more Sub-Saharans who arrived, swimming, in Melilla from the nearby port of Beni Enzar. (Antonio Gutierrez, PP. 15th September, 2010))

The *repetition* of the word "crisis" three times in the same intervention reinforces the effort to dramatize the situation by presenting it as a crisis. The use of the *metaphor* of the 'steady trickle' to represent the continuous arrival of people provides a concrete image for something which might be quite abstract. By using this *metaphor*, the image of water continuously dripping helps to reinforce the conceptualization of the crisis and threat (see Charteris-Black, 2004, 2006). In the same way, the *repetition* of the expression "it is not over", four times, increases the sense of danger and, at the same time, implies a lack of action by the government to prevent this danger. Thus, the arrival of immigrants appears as a danger which generates a crisis in Spain and, hence, needs to be controlled and stopped.

Furthermore, the irony used to describe the people who arrive is highly dehumanizing, since it reduces these people to images which seem to be the same. By unifying them and depicting them as copies of one another, the reasons why these people are arriving disappear; the important message is that they are all the same, and no attention is given to the reasons why they are arriving and/or escaping from their countries. Similarly, the description of immigrants as 'Moroccan troublemakers' also reinforces this dehumanization and hides the causes and the consequences of these people's arrival in Spain. Consequently, immigrants are ridiculed and depicted as being disruptive and creating problems, while their motives for coming to Spain or leaving their own countries are ignored.

Another common *metaphor* used to speak about the arrival of immigrants, the "avalanche", is also used here:

> Le voy a dar algunos datos. Tuvimos **una avalancha** —esa sí que sí—, **una presión migratoria muy fuerte** cuando el asunto de la valla —¿se acuerda?— en 2005. Entonces tuvimos que tomar medidas excepcionales. Reparamos la valla y mejoramos su seguridad, y nos gastamos en eso, el conjunto de los españoles, 36 millones de euros. (Alfredo Pérez Rubalcaba, PSOE. 15 de septiembre de 2010).
> (I'm going to provide you with some data. We had **an avalanche-** yes, that we did- **a very strong migratory pressure,** when the issue of the fence- do you remember?—in 2005. Then, we had to take exceptional measures. We repaired the fence and improved its security, and we spent on that, all Spaniards did, 36 million euros. (Alfredo Pérez Rubalcaba, PSOE. 15th September, 2010))

Once again, immigration is represented as a threat, through the use of the *metaphor* of the "avalanche", depicting immigration as a natural disaster. The use of this *metaphor* activates the domain of danger in the hearer's mind. This is reinforced by the reference to "migratory pressure", which insists on the representation of immigration as negative and dangerous and, hence, as a phenomenon which should be controlled. For this reason, the investment of money to stop and control the arrival of immigrants serves to positively represent the government, as a savior who has prevented the danger that immigration means to Spain.

In times of austerity, when government spending needs to be justified and legitimized, the representation of the arrival of immigrants as a danger serves as a self-sufficient justification for spending public money in order to stop and control this phenomenon, this threat (once more, appealing to fear by means of the *fallacy ad metum*).

4.5 Domestic violence

The topic of domestic violence, in relation to immigrant women, was also quite frequent during this time. The claim made is that a large percentage of domestic violence is against immigrant women, who are especially vulnerable due to their irregular legal situation, as seen in the following extract:

> En segundo lugar, por lo que se refiere al artículo 31 bis, a la residencia temporal de trabajo de mujeres extranjeras víctimas de violencia de género, **resulta evidente**, señorías, que las mujeres inmigrantes en situación de ilegalidad constituyen un grupo de personas sobre las que la vulnerabilidad de la violencia se hace más intensa. Porque la propia situación de ilegalidad, y, por tanto, su imposibilidad de acceder a un permiso de trabajo, las hace aún más dependientes de sus parejas, exparejas o personas con las que conviven. En **2009**, cincuenta y cinco mujeres murieron asesinadas en España, fruto de la violencia de género. Solo el **21** por ciento había denunciado previamente a su agresor, y de ellas el **37** por ciento eran extranjeras. En **2010** han sido setenta y tres mujeres, un **32,7** por ciento más, el **30** por ciento había denunciado a su agresor y el **35** por ciento de las víctimas eran extranjeras, a pesar de que las mujeres extranjeras constituyen tan solo el **10** por ciento de la población femenina de nuestro país. [...] Porque, señorías, por increíble que pueda parecer, todavía existen entre nosotros individuos capaces de ejercitar las más brutales de las violencias contra otros seres humanos de forma continua y permanente. La invisibilidad social de su víctima lo único que hace es favorecer la violencia de esas personas, su lucro y sus vicios. Las mujeres o los menores en situación de ilegalidad son las víctimas más vulnerables ante sus actividades. (Rafael Hernando, PP. 8 de febrero de 2011)
> (Secondly, as per article 31bis in relation to temporary work permits for foreign women who are victims of domestic violence, **it is obvious**, Honorable members, that immigrant women who are in illegal situations constitute a group of people whose vulnerability to domestic violence is more intense. Because this illegal situation, and hence, their inability to obtain work, makes them even more dependent on their partners, ex-partners or the people they live with. In **2009**, fifty-five women were killed in Spain due to domestic violence. Only **21%** had previously filed complaints against their aggressors, and of these **37%** were foreigners. In **2010**, there have been seventy-three women, a **32.7%** increase. **30%** had filed complaints against their aggressors and **35%** of the victims were foreigners, in spite of the fact that foreign women make up only **10%** of the female population in our country. [...] because, Honorable members, though it seems unbelievable, there are individuals among us who are able to enact the most savage violence against other human beings on a

> continuous and permanent basis. The social invisibility of their victims simply feeds the violence of these people, and their vices. Women and minors in illegal situations are the most vulnerable victims of their activities (Rafael Hernando, PP. 8th February, 2011))

Here we find a highly persuasive discourse that aims to persuade the audience of the need to pay attention to immigrant women who are in illegal administrative situations, since they are more vulnerable as victims of domestic violence. This persuasion is achieved through the use of three discursive strategies: firstly, the use of many numbers (see *Number game*, Van Dijk, 2003), which provides the speech with an apparent objectivity, even though the source of these numbers is not given; secondly, the use of the expression "it is obvious", which involves the audience by claiming that what has been said is something that everybody knows; thirdly, by appealing to empathy while victimizing immigrant women. This third strategy, apart from being very persuasive, helps depict immigrants as passive victims and positions politicians as active saviors, while also presenting them as paternalist actors. Thus, we find a negative representation of immigrants as passive beings not able to lead their lives and a positive representation of politicians as the ones who must help immigrants. This representation is strengthened by the dramatization of the situation, which aims to appeal to pity and empathy, using the *fallacy ad misericordiam* (see Van Eemeren and Grootendorst, 1992), as in the following example:

> Por eso lo celebramos porque estamos hablando **del eslabón más frágil** de entre las mujeres que sufren **explotación, violencia de género, violencia machista, violación de los derechos humanos** en todo aquello que afecta **al tráfico y la trata**. Lo celebramos, porque **el eslabón más frágil** entre las mujeres oprimidas son las mujeres inmigrantes. (Joan Tardà, Esquerra Republicana. 8 de febrero de 2011)
> (That's why we are celebrating it, because we are talking about the **weakest link** among the women who suffer from **exploitation**, **domestic violence, sexist violence, the violation of human rights** in everything affecting **human traffic and trade**. We are celebrating it, because the **weakest link** among oppressed women are immigrant women. (Joan Tardà, Esquerra Republicana. 8th February, 2011))

The appeal to empathy is managed here by emphasizing the negative effects of domestic violence. By using different nouns to describe the situation ("exploitation", "violence", "violation") the speaker emphasizes the bad situation of immigrant women, which incites the audience to feel pity and empathy and the parliamentary members to react. In this way, persuasiveness is achieved through playing with the audience's feelings, rather than using logical and rational arguments.

4.6 Overcrowded flats

As previously mentioned, when speaking publicly about immigration, it is important not only how immigration is depicted but also which topics are most frequently associated with it. In this case, the negative description of over-crowded flats is directly associated with immigrants, as those who primarily provoke this situation:

> Por ejemplo, en Madrid, según la encuesta regional de inmigración, los pisos en los que viven más de seis extranjeros han crecido hasta alcanzar el 36,7 por ciento. Por tanto, este es un fenómeno creciente que se da en nuestras ciudades, que cada vez afecta a más ciudadanos, buena parte de los cuales, **por motivos obvios**, son extranjeros. (Pere Macias, CiU. 15 de febrero de 2011)
> (For example, in Madrid, according to the regional survey on immigration, the number of flats where more than six foreign people live has increased to 36.7%. Therefore, this is a growing phenomenon in our cities, which is affecting more and more citizens, most of them**, for obvious reasons**, foreigners. (Pere Macias, CiU. 15th February, 2011))

As we can see, it is presupposed that most of the people in overcrowded flats are immigrants, but the reasons for this are not mentioned. Instead, it is simply stated that the reasons are obvious. In this way, by appealing to the obviousness of his arguments, the speaker involves the audience and makes them part of his claims, without really providing logical reasons for them.

When speaking about this topic, immigrants are represented as active aggressors, who disrupt and create problems for autochthonous citizens, but, at the same time, they are represented as passive victims who have no choice:

> El primer párrafo es de **un tal** Ahmed, nacido en Bangladesh, y dice: Al principio, cuando llegué aquí, no tenía nada. Los primeros tiempos en Madrid fueron muy duros; no conocía a nadie, ni tenía amigos, no hablaba español. Quería un lugar para vivir; **la calle da miedo, miedo**, quería un techo. Encontró un techo, pero un techo con unas condiciones de hacinamiento realmente importantes, pero **para este señor** era más importante, era mucho más importante, poder conseguir un techo que estar en la calle. Frente a esta opinión está también la de otras personas que nos hablan de los problemas de los vecinos. Por ejemplo, dice Rosario: Nos han reventado la puerta en más de una ocasión, porque no

siempre todos tienen llaves. En un piso de 55 metros cuadrados en ocasiones duermen más de quince personas. Yo creo que unos y otros, Ahmed y Rosario, necesitan que tomemos decisiones. (Pere Macias, CiU. 15 de febrero de 2011).
(The first paragraph is by **some** Ahmed, born in Bangladesh, and he says: In the beginning, when I arrived here, I had nothing. The first moments in Madrid were really hard; I didn't know anyone, I didn't have friends, I didn't speak Spanish. I wanted a place to live; **the street is scary, very scary**, I wanted a house. He found a house, but a house with very serious overcrowding conditions, but **for this man** it was more important, much more important, to obtain a house, rather than staying on the street. In contrast to this opinion, we also have the opinions of others, who talk about problems with the neighbors. For example, Rosario says: They have kicked the door down more than once, because not all of them have keys. It is a 55 square meter flat where sometimes more than fifteen people live. I think both groups, both Ahmed and Rosario, need us to make decisions. (Pere Macia, CiU. 15th February, 2011))

It is particularly interesting how these two participants are referred to in the above intervention. While Ahmed is referred to as "some Ahmed" or "this man", Rosario is simply designated by her name. This may seem irrelevant but, in a way, "some Ahmed" sounds like one among many others, while "Rosario" sounds like a unique individual; this difference guides the attitude of the listeners, leading them towards sympathizing more with Rosario.

There are additional contrasts here as well. On the one hand, the immigrant Ahmed is depicted as a vulnerable, victimized person. Giving him a name reinforces his human side, and victimization is achieved by the description of his bad situation, feeling lost and lonely in Madrid, and strengthened by the *repetition* of the word "scary". On the other hand, we find the immigrant in the role of the aggressor, disrupting Rosario. The goal of this discourse is to exemplify typical situations and, by arguing through example, the discourse becomes more concrete (less abstract), more descriptive and has a greater impact. The strategy of using one example to exemplify many situations has a highly persuasive effect and unavoidably produces a generalization that tends to homogenize immigrants as a group.

4.7 Forced marriages

The assumption that the culture and customs of immigrants are worse than *Ours* is a constant in the Spanish and European political discourse on immigration (see, for example, Rubio-Carbonero, 2011a; Ribas, 2000,

2009; Bañón, 2002) and the political discourse analyzed here is no exception. When dealing with the topic of forced marriages, it is common to present *Their* (worse) customs and values in opposition to *Ours* (better), as can be seen in the example below:

> Los Mossos d'Esquadra **liberaron** durante el año 2010 a quince niñas de entre 10 y 21 años, la mitad de ellas menores de edad, de bodas que no deseaban; jóvenes nacidas en España en la mayoría de los casos, escolarizadas **entre nosotros**, que han crecido y han sido educadas de acuerdo con **nuestros valores y nuestras libertades**, que están integradas en nuestro sistema, pero que **tienen la desgracia de nacer** en familias **que no asumen ni respetan** las leyes y los derechos del país que las ha **acogido**. Sin duda hablamos de un tema delicado, donde la convivencia entre culturas distintas en un mismo territorio produce fricciones que es conveniente salvar a través de la **educación y la prevención**, algo que consideramos completamente compatible con actuar sin vacilaciones en el terreno legislativo. (Susana Camarero, PP. 3 de mayo de 2011).
> (During the year 2010, The Catalan Police **released** fifteen girls between 10 and 21 years old, half of them minors, from weddings that they didn't want; girls born in Spain, for the most part, educated **among us**, who have grown up and have been taught in line with **our values and freedoms**, who are integrated in **our system**, but who have **the misfortune of being born into families** that **neither follow nor respect** the laws and rights of the country that has **welcomed** them. No doubt we are speaking about a sensitive issue, where the coexistence of different cultures in the same territory produces friction that should be reduced through **education and prevention**, something that we consider completely compatible with acting without hesitation in the legislative domain. (Susana Camarero, PP. 3rd May, 2011))

The polarization between *Us* and *Them* is very clear in this extract. Firstly, *We* are represented as saviors who "release" immigrants from *Their* own customs. Secondly, it is explicitly said that *We* have values and freedoms and it is presupposed that these values and freedoms are better than the ones *They* have. Thirdly, it is stated that *We* have welcomed *Them,* which represents *Us* positively, as a welcoming country, as opposed to *Them*, who are depicted negatively, as intolerant people who neither follow nor respect *Our* laws.

Furthermore, *They* are represented as having worse culture and traditions than *Us,* and as being intolerant and unable to adapt to *Our* culture and norms. *They* appear as transgressors who impose *Their* customs in spite of being welcomed by *Us*. This depicts *Them* as a threat to Spain, which has to be stopped through "education and prevention".

This representation of immigrants as a threat to our society is also achieved by associating immigrants' customs with something that existed in the past in Spain, but has since been eradicated. In this way, there is a contrast between past and present, and immigrants' customs are presented as anachronistic, as we can see in the example below:

> Los matrimonios forzados, los que obligan a las mujeres a casarse por la fuerza con hombres que no conocen, es una costumbre milenaria que persiste en países como Pakistán, India o Marruecos, **países con un claro déficit de igualdad entre hombres y mujeres**. Sin embargo, la realidad nos muestra que ni **son cosas del pasado ni ocurre solo en tierras exóticas**. Con la llegada de la inmigración, **algunas prácticas agresivas impuestas por sus religiones** y que ya se consideraban **desterradas en España** vuelven a estar de actualidad. Desde el Grupo Popular consideramos importante **plantar cara** a esta realidad que viven muchas mujeres en nuestro país: matrimonios a la fuerza con menores, sin consentimiento de la víctima, que **esconden tras el velo de anacrónicas tradiciones evidentes malos tratos**. (Susana Camarero, PP. 3 de mayo de 2011)
> (Forced marriages, those where women are obliged to get married, by force, to men that they don't know, is a thousand-year-old custom which persists in countries such as Pakistan, India, or Morocco, countries **with a clear deficit of equality between men and women**. However, the reality is that these are **not things of the past, nor do they only happen in exotic lands**. With the arrival of immigration, **certain aggressive practices imposed by their religions,** and which were considered to have been **eradicated in Spain**, now occur again. In the Popular Group we consider it important to stand up to this reality which many women are living in our country: marriages of minors by force, without the victim's consent, which hide **obvious mistreatment behind the veil of anachronistic traditions**. (Susana Camarero, PP. 3rd May, 2011))

In this example we also find a clear association between forced marriages and religion, and find the use of the veil linked to mistreatment. The first association might have some logical basis, but the second one seems to fall back upon the stereotype in which the use of the veil is associated with women suffering mistreatment (which might or might not be the case). The use of the adjective "obvious" frames this association as something undeniable and indisputable without providing the reasons for this link.

Furthermore, together with the pragmatic presupposition (Simon-Vanderbengen, White and Aijmer, 2007) that *Their* culture is worse, there is also a pragmatic (contextually related) implication that *They* are a danger to Spain, since *They* are imposing old practices that are no longer allowed here. In this way, once more, we can see the representation of immigration as a threat and a danger to Spain. Hence, instead of offering logically-based arguments to persuade the audience, they are using fear to pressure and convince.

It can be concluded from what has already been said that the representation of immigration is globally negative in the political discourse during this period. There was only one positive representation found, which is presented in the following fragment:

> Hace diez años, en el año 1999, en España había 800.000 extranjeros; en el año 2009, hay 4.791.000. Si vemos los acontecimientos que han pasado en esta última década, sin duda este aparece como uno de los temas de mayor trascendencia e importancia. A la vez, ese fenómeno ha tenido una traslación en muchos órdenes de la vida y de la propia economía, **en positivo; el crecimiento económico en España no hubiese sido posible al ritmo que lo hizo en los pasados años**, que contribuyó de una manera decidida a la generación de empleo y a la generación de riqueza, sin la aportación de esa población activa que se incorporó a nuestras ciudades, a nuestros barrios, a nuestras escaleras. Eso modificó en parte nuestras propias realidades. (Celestino Corbacho, PSOE. 14 de abril de 2010).
> (Ten years ago, in 1999, there were 800.000 foreigners in Spain; in 2009, there are 4.791.000. If we consider the events of the last decade, without a doubt this becomes one of the most transcendent and important issues. At the same time, this phenomenon has changed many aspects of life and the economy, **in a positive way: the pace of economic growth in Spain over the last years**, which contributed in a decisive way to the creation of jobs and the creation of wealth, **wouldn't have been possible** without the contribution of this active population that joined our cities, our neighborhoods, our ladder. This modified our reality in a way. (Celestino Corbacho, PSOE. 14th April, 2010))

In the whole period analyzed, this was the only positive representation of immigration, as contributing to the Spanish economy and development. All of the other positive representations of immigration appeared in the form of *disclaimers* (Van Dijk, 2003), always followed by a "but". This strategy aims to minimize the negative effect of what it comes after the "but" (which is always a negative representation of immigration), as in the following example:

> Señorías, la inmigración nos ha traído **muchas cosas positivas, pero** también nos ha obligado en los últimos años a legislar sobre temas como la mutilación genital femenina o el uso del burka, y ha llegado el momento de **plantar cara** a una práctica que choca frontalmente con una

> sociedad democrática, libre e igualitaria como la nuestra. (Susana Camarero, PP. 3 de mayo de 2011).
> (Honorable members, immigration has brought **a lot of positive things, but** it has also obliged us in the last years to legislate about genital mutilation or the use of burka, and it is now the moment to **stand up to** these practices which clash dramatically with a democratic, free and egalitarian society like ours. (Susana Camarero, PP. 3rd May, 2011))

Thus, although the speech begins by saying something positive about immigration, the important message comes after the "but", where immigration is represented as a problem that Spaniards need to face, legislate, and "stand up to". Therefore, instead of describing immigration as a positive phenomenon, the main message here positions society in a defensive stance against it. In this way, the positive representation at the beginning of the sentence is just a strategy to minimize the negative effect that the second part of the sentence might have on the image of the speaker (See Brown and Levinson, 1987).

Furthermore, it is explicitly said that *Our* society is "democratic, free and egalitarian". This positive representation of Spain also carries the pragmatic implication that *Their* societies are not democratic, free or egalitarian. Hence, once more, *Their* societies are comparatively presented as worse than *Ours*.

5. Conclusions

From what has already been said, it can be concluded that Spanish political discourse on immigration during the period of time analyzed follows more or less the same pattern as in the previous years, before the crisis started (Rubio-Carbonero, 2011a, Rubio-Carbonero and Van Dijk, 2011). Immigration is still represented quite negatively, as a threat and a danger that disrupts Spanish society and thus has to be legislated and controlled in order to prevent further problems.

When not represented as a threat, immigrants appear as victims of their own reality: passive victims who cannot lead their own lives and need to be saved by the government, by *Our* laws, *Our* norms and *Our* values. Related to this, there is the general presupposition that *Their* culture and values are worse than *Ours* and they are anachronistic. That is, *Their* current values are intrinsically compared with values Spain used to have many years ago and which are no longer considered valid. In this way, *Their* culture and values are represented as out-of-date, undeveloped and non-egalitarian. In contrast, *Our* society is represented as democratic, modern, equal and, in the end, better. Accordingly, Spaniards, and particularly Spanish politicians, are represented as the saviors who have to free immigrants from the *unfair* values and customs *They* have.

It should have become apparent that there is a clear distinction between *Us* and *Them* and that both groups are homogenized and apparently irreconcilably separated. Intrinsically, the representation of immigrants as a threat positions Spaniards in a defensive stance towards immigrants, which will have unavoidable consequences on the way Spaniards interact with immigrants.

This representation of immigrants as a threat is the main argumentative strategy used in order to justify all kinds of political actions and measures. The *fallacy ad metum,* by instilling fear in the audience, is used to justify the need to control the arrival of immigrants and to invest money and effort to make sure *They* integrate in *Our* society following *Our* norms and values.

The other most common means of justifying these and other political measures regarding immigration is to fall back upon the *topoi of the burden* and the *topoi of the advantage*. Since immigration is represented as a burden to Spain, it becomes necessary (for the good of Spaniards) to control and legislate firmly, in order to minimize the burden's disruptive effects.

In addition, *repetition*, *metaphor* and *hyperbole* are used to dramatize and increase the scope of meanings, for example in depicting the arrival of immigrants as a global crisis. The well-known *metaphor* of the arrival of immigrants as a natural disaster appears several times, and the negative cognitive effects that these *metaphors* produce on the audience are clear. Hence, the representation of immigration as a threat is revisited and reinforced through these rhetorical strategies.

However, notwithstanding the similarities between the Spanish political discourse on immigration during this period and that before the onset of the crisis, there are also some noteworthy differences: firstly, there are far fewer parliamentary debates focusing on immigration than there were in previous years. Apparently, in a context of economic crisis, immigration is no longer such a prominent or recurrent topic.

Secondly, there is a constant use of numbers: the number of unemployed immigrants; the number of immigrants unable to integrate in school due to the budget cuts, etc. It might seem that these are used in defense of immigrant population, but a deeper look reveals that this victimization of immigrants is instead tied to a strategy used by opposing political parties to criticize the government's performance. Therefore, the critique of budget cuts that negatively impact immigrants does not belie a real concern for their well-being. This perspective is supported by the fact that even though immigrants are victimized, the ultimate victims, those who appear the most afflicted by the lack of money to invest in immigrants' integration, are Spaniards.

Finally, another main difference is that the arrival of immigrants is no longer such a frequent topic. While some years ago the arrival of immigrants was the most prominent topic, which almost monopolized political discourse on immigration (Martín Rojo, 2000; Rubio-Carbonero, 2011b), in this period of time it does not appear as often. Instead, the discourse on immigration now seems to be more focused on the problems that Spanish society has to face regarding integration.

That is, our analysis reveals that the political discourse on immigration largely focuses on actions that politicians should take to avoid problems which are associated with immigration, and on topics such as: forced marriages, the over-occupation of houses, domestic violence, unemployment, and delinquency.

Therefore, it should have become obvious that immigration is mostly represented as a problem for *Our* society, which politicians have the duty of solving. By contrast, positive representations of immigrants as participants in the economic and cultural growth of Spain are almost inexistent. This highly negative representation of immigration by politicians will have consequences on the negative interpretation of immigration by the audience, who eventually may develop negative attitudes and opinions against immigrants.

In order to avoid this, it would be desirable to develop a more balanced political discourse on immigration, paying heed to the many advantages that immigration brings to Spain in terms of economic, cultural and population growth and thus representing immigrants as people who enrich our society, as opposed to damaging it. It would also be useful to focus on empathy and develop political discourse that makes people aware of the terrible situations in some of the immigrants' countries of origin, and thus the reasons why many immigrants feel obliged to leave these countries in order to find a better life.

Notes

1 See http://www.maec.es/es/MenuPpal/Ministerio/EscuelaDiplomatica/MasterenDiplomaciayRelacionesInternacionales/Documents/LOEXRef%5B1%5D.pdf

Bibliography

Bañón, Antonio. 2002. *Discurso e inmigración. Propuestas para el análisis de un debate social.* Murcia: Universidad de Murcia.

Bañón, Antonio and Javier Fornieles (eds.). 2009. *Manual sobre comunicación e inmigración* San Sebastián/Donostia: Tercera Prensa/Gakoa.

Brown, Penelope and Stephen C. Levinson. 1987 [1978]. *Politeness. Some Universals in Language Usage.* Cambridge: Cambridge University Press.

Charteris-Black, Jonathan. 2004. *Corpus Approaches to Critical Metaphor Analysis.* Basingstoke: Palgrave Macmillan.

—. 2006. "Britain as a Container: Immigration Metaphors in the 2005 Election Campaign". *Discourse and Society* 17: 563-581.

Chilton, Paul and Christina Schäffner. 2002. *Politics as Text and Talk: Analytic Approaches to Political Discourse.* Amsterdam and Philadelphia: John Benjamins.

De la Fuente, Mario. 2002. "Análisis crítico del discurso y medios de comunicación". *Interlingüística,* 13: 129-142.

—. 2006. *La argumentación en el discurso periodístico sobre la inmigración.* Tesis doctoral Universidad de León. http://www.dissoc.org/recursos/tesis/Tesis_Garcia.pdf. Last accessed on 12 December 2011.

—. 2007. "Argumentación e Inmigración. Reflexiones sobre algunas estrategias empleadas en los medios de comunicación". In *Discurso periodístico y procesos migratorios,* ed. Antonio Bañón, 343-374. Donostia: Tercera Prensa.

Dios, Sofía. 2005. "Inmigración y extranjería en el debate parlamentario español". In *La condición inmigrante. Exploraciones e investigaciones desde la región de Murcia,* coords. Andrés Pedreño and Manuel Hernández, 175-180. Murcia: Universidad de Murcia.

Fetzer, Anita and Gerda Eva Lauerbach. 2007. *Political Discourse in the Media.* Amsterdam and Philadelphia: John Benjamins.

Giró, Xavier and José Manuel Jarque 2007. "El discurso editorial sobre inmigración de El País, La Vanguardia, El Periódico y El Avui, desde El Ejido hasta la cumbre europea de Sevilla (1999-2002)". In *Discursos sobre la inmigración en España: los Medios de Comunicación, los Parlamentos y las Administraciones* eds. Ricard Zapata-Barrero and Teun A. van Dijk, 45-67. Barcelona: Fundación CIDOB.

Lario, Manuel. 2009. "La representación de la inmigración y los inmigrantes en la prensa y en la radio. Estado de la cuestión". In *Manual de comunicación e inmigración,* eds. Antonio Bañón and Javier Fornieles, 195-214. San Sebastián: Gakoa.

López, Antonio and Javier De Santiago. 2000. *Retórica y comunicación política.* Madrid: Cátedra.

Márquez, Esther. 2007. "La gestión parlamentaria del discurso político sobre inmigración. In *Discursos sobre la inmigración en España: los Medios de Comunicación, los Parlamentos y las Administraciones* eds. Ricard Zapata-Barrero and Teun A. van Dijk, 93-128. Barcelona: Fundación CIDOB.

Martín Rojo, Luisa. 2000. "Spain, Outer wall of European Fortress. Analysis of the parliamentary debates on the immigration policy in Spain". In *Racism at the Top. Parliamentary Discourses on Ethnic Issues in Six European States,* eds. Ruth Wodak, Teun A. Van Dijk, 169-220. Klagenfurt: Drava.

Martín Serrano, Manuel. 2004. *La producción social de comunicación.* Madrid: Alianza Editorial.

Martínez Lirola, María (ed.). 2008. *Inmigración, discurso y medios de comunicación* . Alicante: Fundación Juan Gil Albert.

Moscovici, Serge. 2001. "Why a theory of social representation?" *Representations of the social. Bringing theoretical traditions*, eds. Kay Deaux and Gina Philogène, 8-35. Massachussetts: Blackwell.

Musolff, Andreas. 2000. "Political imagery of Europe: A house without exit doors?". *Journal of Multilingual and Multicultural Development,* 21 (3): 216-229.

O'Keeffe, Anne. 2006. *Investigating Media Discourse.* London: Routledge.

Reisigl, Martin and Ruth Wodak. 2000. *The Semiotics of Racism: Approaches in CDA.* Vienna: Passagen Verlag.

Reisigl, Martin and Ruth Wodak. 2001. *Discourse and Discrimination: Rhetoric of Racism and Anti-Semitism*. London: Routlege.

Ribas, Montserrat. 2000. *Discurs parlamentari i representacions socials: la representació de la immigració que emergeix de les preguntes d'una Comissió d'Estudi Parlamentària*. Unpublished Ph.D thesis Barcelona: Universidad de Barcelona.

—. 2009. "Discurso parlamentario e inmigración". In *Manual de comunicación e inmigración,* eds. Antonio Bañón and Javier Fornieles, 453-468. San Sebastián: Gakoa.

Rubio-Carbonero, Gema. 2011a. *Los discursos políticos del Partido Popular sobre inmigración.* Unpublished Ph.D thesis. Barcelona: Universidad Pompeu Fabra.

—. 2011b. Representación social de la inmigración en el discurso del Partido Popular. *Cultura, Lenguaje y Representación. Número especial sobre discurso político.* IX: 173-199.

Rubio-Carbonero, Gema and Teun A. Van Dijk. 2011. "Inmigrantes en el parlamento catalán y en la prensa española y catalana (2010)". *Articles per la reflexió*. Catalunya: Sos Racisme Catalunya.

Sachetti, Elena and Juan J. Trigo. 2009. *El discurso político español sobre inmigración. Análisis crítico*. Sevilla: Andalucía Acoge.

Sbisá, Marina. 1999b. Presupposition, implicature and context in text understanding. In *Context'99,* eds. Paolo Bouquet, Luciano Serafini, Patrick Brézillon, Massimo Benerecetti and Francesca Castellani, 324-338. Berlin: Springer-Verlag.

Semino, Elena. 2008. *Metaphors in Discourse.* Cambridge: Cambridge University Press.

Simon-Vanderbengen, Anne Marie, Peter R.R. White and Karin Aijmer. 2007. "Presupposition and 'taking for granted' in mass communicated political argument". In *Political Discourse in the Media,* eds. Anita Fetzer and Gerda Eva Lauerbach, 31-74. Amsterdam and Philadelphia: John Benjamins.

Van Dijk, Teun A. 1998. *Ideology: A Multidisciplinary Approach.* London, California, New Delhi: Sage Publications.

—. 2003. *Dominación étnica y racismo discursivo en España y Latino América*. Barcelona: Gedisa.

—. 2007. "Ideology and Discourse Analysis". In *The Meaning of Ideology. Cross-disciplinary Perspectives,* ed. Michael Freeden, 110-136. London: Routledge.

—. 2008. *Discourse and Context: A Sociocognitive Approach.* Cambridge: Cambridge University Press.

—. 2009. "Critical Discourse Studies: A Sociocognitive Approach". In *Methods of Critical Discourse Analysis,* eds. Ruth Wodak and Michael Meyer, 62-106. London: Sage Publications.

Van Eemeren, Frans H. and Rob Grootendorst. 1992. *Argumentation, Communication and Fallacies: A Pragma-Dialectical Perspective.* Hillsdale, New Jersey: Lawrence Erlbaum Associates, Inc., Publishers.

Van Leeuwen, Theo. 1995. "Representing Social Action." *Discourse & Society* 6 (81): 81-106.

—. 1996. "The Representation of Social Actors." In *Texts and Practices – Readings in Critical Discourse Analysis*. eds. Carmen Rosa Caldas-Coulthard and Malcom Coulthard, 32-79. USA/Canada: Routledge.

Walton, Douglas. 2007. *Media Argumentation: Dialectic, Persuasion and Rhetoric*. New York: Cambridge University Press.

Wodak Ruth and Michael Meyer. 2001. *Methods of Critical Discourse analysis.* London: Sage.

Wodak, Ruth and Teun A. van Dijk. 2000. *Racism at the Top. Parliamentary Discourses on Ethnic Issues in Six European States.* Klagenfurt: Drava.

Zapata-Barrero, Ricard, Elisabet González and Elena Sánchez. 2008. *El discurso político en torno a la inmigración en España y en la Unión Europea.* Ministerio de Trabajo e Inmigración: Subdirección General de Información.

CONTRIBUTORS

Isabel Alonso Belmonte is Associate Professor at the Universidad Autónoma de Madrid (Spain). Her areas of specialization are discourse analysis and applied linguistics to language teaching (both Spanish and English as a foreign language). Her more recent work on newspaper discourse has been published in prestigious journals such as *Text & Talk, Journal of Pragmatics,* and *Discourse & Communication*, to name a few. She has also led national and international research projects on foreign language learning and linguistic analysis.

Ángeles Arjona Garrido is Professor of Social Anthropology at the University of Almería. She is the director of the research group *Laboratory of Social Anthropology and Culture*. Her main area of research is ethnic economy. Dr. Arjona is the author of the monograph *Los colores del escaparate* (The Colors of the Window) (Icaria, Barcelona, 2008) and fifty international papers.

Antonio M. Bañón Hernández is Professor of the Department of Spanish Philology at the University of Almería, Spain. His main area of research is Critical Discourse Analysis. He has published numerous books such as *Racismo, discurso periodístico y didáctica de la lengua* (Servicio de Publicaciones de la Universidad de Almería, 1996), *Discurso e inmigración. Propuestas para el análisis de un debate social* (Servicio de publicaciones de la universidad de Murcia, 2002) and *Manual sobre comunicación e inmigración* (Tercera Prensa, 2008).

Francisco Checa Olmos is Professor of Social Anthropology at the University of Almería. He is the director of the *Center for the Study of Migration and Intercultural Relations* (CEMyRI). His main area of study is related to the cultural aspects covered by the social integration of immigrants and to the study of political discourse on immigration. He has authored hundreds of publications.

Juan Carlos Checa Olmos is Professor of Sociology at the University of Almería. He is the director of the *International Journal of Migration Studies*. Dr. Checa is a specialist on residential segregation and immigration. He is the author of the essay *Viviendo juntos aparte* (Living Together Apart) (Icaria, Barcelona, 2008) and thirty papers in international journals.

Daniel Chornet Roses has a PhD in Communication Studies from the University of Iowa, and currently works as Assistant Professor of intercultural communication, communication research methods and Communication Theory in the Department of Communication at Saint Louis University, Madrid Campus. His current research areas include culture and communication and intercultural communication.

Lucía Chovancova holds a Master's degree in Spanish Philology and a Master´s degree in Secondary Education and Language Schools Teaching, both by the University of Granada (Spain). Currently, she is finishing her studies in Social and Cultural Anthropology and works as a researcher in the Migrations Institute at the University of Granada. The main research areas she has worked in are the representation of immigrants and immigration in the mass-media and the relations between immigration and the educational system.

Jan Chovanec is Assistant Professor of English Linguistics at Masaryk University in Brno. Specializing in discourse analysis, stylistics and pragmatics, with a focus on media communication and legal discourse, he has dealt with such issues as multimodality, humour and the representation of "us" and "them" in the mass media. He has written 40 articles on discursive strategies in the British media that were published in journals and edited collections with John Benjamins, Peter Lang, Gunter Narr and Cambridge Scholars Publishing, and has co-written several book publications. He is the editor-in-chief of the journal *Brno Studies in English*.

Eliecer Crespo-Fernández is Associate Professor in the Department of Modern Philology at the University of Castilla-La Mancha. He has also taught at the University of Alicante and at Roehampton University (London) as visiting scholar. His research interests focus on the semantic and pragmatic dimensions of euphemism and dysphemism, particularly in the areas of immigration, politics, sex and death, which he has approached through Discourse Analysis and Cognitive Semantics. He has authored the book *El eufemismo y el disfemismo* (Universidad Alicante 2007) and has published articles in major international journals like *Spanish in Context* (2012), *Review of Cognitive Linguistics* (2011), *Bulletin of Hispanic Studies* (2010), *Atlantis* (2008) and *Estudios Filológicos* (2008), among others.

José Fernández Echeverría is Researcher at the Institute for Migration Studies of the University of Granada, Spain. Graduated in Pedagogy and Romance Languages, he is currently preparing his doctoral thesis on "Legislation regarding the presence of immigrants in the Andalusian educational system". He has participated in many national and European research projects and he is also author of several chapters and articles.

F. Javier García Castaño holds a Chair in Social Anthropology at the University of Granada. His research focuses in the anthropological analysis of the educational processes of cultural transmission and acquisition in the context of cultural diversity (Andalusia, Spain). Since 1984 he has taught at the University of Granada and other universities. He has been the coordinator of the Research Group Intercultural Studies Laboratory at the University of Granada. In 2009 he was appointed director "in office" of the Migration Institute at the University of Granada after its creation.

María Eugenia González Cortés has a PhD in Journalism, and has worked in the University of Málaga since 2002. She has published numerous articles about topics as varied as media consumption of immigrant communities and other social minorities, freedom of the press and media literacy. She has written many articles for specialized magazines and papers for many conferences, focused on research on communication and immigration. Among her titles are: *The construction of reality in the migration process. The mass media influence* (publication of her doctoral thesis), "The media attention to cultural diversity in Spain" (in the magazine *Tiempo de Paz*) and "The Spanish press associations, a consolidated model of professional organization".

Antolín Granados Martínez is Chair Professor of the Department of Sociology at the University of Granada and member of the Institute for Migration Studies of the same university. His interests lie at the intersection between sociology, anthropology, and human migration studies. He has published many book chapters and journal articles about communication, migration, mass-media, racism and nationalism. Among his major works are the following books: *Sociología de la educación. Viejas y nuevas cuestiones* (Málaga: Clave, 1994); *Educación: ¿integración o exclusión de* *la diversidad cultural?* (Granada: LdEI, 1997); *Lecturas para educación intercultural* (Madrid: Trotta, 1999), and *Interculturalidad y educación en la década de los noventa: una visión crític*a (Granada: Junta de Andalucía, 2001). He has also taught graduate courses at universities in Portugal, France, Italy and Mexico.

Nina Kressova graduated in Russian Philology from Saint Petersburg State University (1999) and obtained a PhD in Comparative Literature from the University of Granada, Spain (2007). Since 2007 she works as a postdoctoral researcher in the Institute for Migration Studies of the University of Granada. She has participated in several European and Spanish research projects. Recently she has awarded a two-year grant from the Estonian Science Foundation financed with a support of the FP7 Marie Curie COFUND the "People". Between her main research interests are storytelling and identity construction, and Mass-Media critical discourse analysis. She is author or editor of 4 books and about 20 chapters and journal articles.

Nicolás Lorite is Professor of Audiovisual Communication at the Faculty of Communication Sciences Universidad Autónoma de Barcelona, Spain. He has been responsible for projects on intercultural dinamization appointed by the Secretariat of State for Emigration and Immigration from the Spanish Government. He is the director of MIGRACOM (Observatory and Research Group of Migration and Communication). Dr. Lorite has published in many national and international journals.

María Martínez Lirola is Professor of the Department of English Studies at the University of Alicante, Spain and Research Fellow at the University of South Africa (UNISA). Her main areas of research are Critical Discourse Analysis, Systemic Functional Linguistics and Applied Linguistics. She has published more than 80 papers and seven books, such as *Main Processes of Thematization and Postponement in English* (Peter Lang, 2009). She has been a visiting scholar in different universities such as: UNISA (South Africa, Pretoria, 2012), the University of Anahuac Mayad (Mérida, Mexico, 2008), the University of Kwazulu-Natal (Pietermaritzburg, South Africa, 2006), and Macquarie University (Sydney, Australia, 2005). She has presented papers in international congresses all over the world.

Anne McCabe is Chair of the Languages and Literature Division at Saint Louis University, Madrid Campus. She holds a PhD in Language Studies, awarded in 2000 from Aston University, Birmingham, U.K. Her PhD dissertation analyzed textual patterns in a bilingual corpus of English and Spanish history text books. She has published on the construction of evaluation and authority in history and journalistic texts. Her current areas of interest are discourse analysis, systemic functional theory, and cross-linguistic studies of genre, among others.

Samantha Requena Romero is Assistant Lecturer of the Department of *Spanish Philology* at the University of Almería, Spain. She is working on her PhD Thesis which will offer a critical discourse analysis of a new topic: 'rare diseases' and their representation in mass media. Her main area of research is Critical Discourse Analysis applied to health contexts. She is co-editor of the recently published book *Lenguaje, Comunicación y Salud* (ArCiBel, 2011). She has also written several chapters in books such as *Notes on political discourse on Rare Diseases* (CIBERER, 2010) and *The discursive Treatment of Research and Researchers in the Field of Rare Diseases* (CIBERER, 2010).

Maria Rubio Gómez has a degree in Social Anthropology, Master in Migration Studies and is currently pursuing a PhD at the University of Granada. She is member of the Migrations Institute (*Instituto de Migraciones*) at the same university. Her research interests include the construction of diversity, identity and otherness, educational discourses on migration and intercultural education.

Antonia Olmos Alcaraz holds a PhD in Social Anthropology (Granada University, 2009). Since 2010 she has been lecturer in Anthropology in Granada University. She is a member of the Migrations Institute (*Instituto de Migraciones*) at the same university. Her research interests are Spanish migration policies, identity and otherness, politician discourse of migration, racism and intercultural education.

Jéssica Retis is Assistant Professor in the Journalism Department at the Mike Curb College of Arts, Media, and Communications in California State University Northridge (CSUN). Dr. Retis has conducted research and has taught in Mexico, Spain and USA. She specializes in the analysis of contemporary Diaspora and its media implications. Prior to teaching, Retis has more than 18 years of experience as a journalist. She has several academic publications. Her last work includes *Cultural Consumption of Latin American Immigrants in Spain: Transnational Context of Cultural Practices*" (Fundación Alternativas, 2011), *Daily news cast on BBC and TVE. Discourses of producers and audiences* (Ediciones La Torre, 2010),

Media spaces of immigration in Madrid: Genesis and Evolution (OMCI, 2008).

Gema Rubio Carbonero has a degree in English Studies by Complutense University of Madrid and a Master on Linguistics by Lancaster University. She has also got a PhD on Linguistic Communication and Multilingual Mediation. She specializes in Critical Analysis of political discourse and discourse on immigration. She has published studies on these topics and is currently involved in further research on these areas. She has also presented several papers in international congresses about her research. She currently belongs to Gritim (Interdisciplinary group on immigration) of Pompeu Fabra University where she coordinates a project which studies intercultural policies of different City Councils.